TO FLOURISH AMONG GIANTS

TO FLOURISH AMONG GIANTS

Creative Management for Mid-Sized Firms

ROBERT LAWRENCE KUHN

JOHN WILEY & SONS

New York · Chichester · Brisbane · Toronto · Singapore

Copyright © 1985 by Robert Lawrence Kuhn
Published by John Wiley & Sons, Inc.

All rights reserved. Published simultaneously in Canada.

Reproduction or translation of any part of this work
beyond that permitted by Section 107 or 108 of the
1976 United States Copyright Act without the permission
of the copyright owner is unlawful. Requests for
permission or further information should be addressed to
the Permissions Department, John Wiley & Sons, Inc.

This publication is designed to provide accurate and
authoritative information in regard to the subject
matter covered. It is sold with the understanding that
the publisher is not engaged in rendering legal, accounting,
or other professional service. If legal advice or other
expert assistance is required, the services of a competent
professional person should be sought. *From a Declaration
of Principles jointly adopted by a Committee of the
American Bar Association and a Committee of Publishers.*

Library of Congress Cataloging in Publication Data:

Kuhn, Robert Lawrence.
  To flourish among giants.

  Includes index.
  1. Management.   I. Title.
HD31.K73 1985   658.4   84-17233
ISBN 0-471-80911-X

Printed in the United States of America

10 9 8 7 6 5 4 3 2 1

PREFACE

"Medium size means dynamic potential." So states George Kozmetsky, Director of the IC^2 Institute of the University of Texas at Austin. Dr. Kozmetsky co-founded one large corporation (Teledyne) and advises many smaller ones. "You can't ignore company size. You can't confuse medium with large or small. Mid-sized firms offer great opportunity for innovative growth, but you must know how to manage them."

Size management is a new concept, a fresh perspective for viewing companies. Medium is not large and not small, and strategies and structures are not the same. The game is the same, but the rules differ. Medium-sized organizations radiate their own energy; they are volatile caldrons of products and people. Making mid-sized success requires a special kind of magic.

Managing medium-sized companies is both important and different, important for the national economy, different from general management. The objectives we seek are better businesses, stronger strategies, higher profits. The principles we present are practical, meaningful, applicable.

Why is managing medium-sized companies *important* for the national economy? Mid-sized firms not only represent a fundamental American tradition, they are also more innovative and productive, and they generate greater worker satisfaction. They assure the efficiency of the economic sector and secure the pluralism of the political sector.

Though they grow weaker as a class, mid-sized firms are a critical component of modern society.[1] A surprisingly high percentage of the gross national product is churned out by such enterprises, especially when one includes operating divisions of major corporations. Some of the best-managed, best-structured companies are stuck in the middle of their markets, and though neither entrepreneurial nor multinational, much of our industrial hopes are riding right on them. These paragons we meet and enjoy.

How is managing medium-sized companies *different* from general management? Strategy and tactics are "size specific," that is, contingent on absolute organizational dimensions and relative competitive strength. Size counts. What is proper and productive in large companies may be improper and counterproductive in smaller ones. What is apt and fit in the middle may be inept and awkward on either end.

We seek progress and prosperity, the causes and conditions. How can some medium-sized firms "flourish" in a hostile environment populated by "mammoths and gnats," the former with crushing strength, the latter with noisome sting? How to hide and how to swat?

How to function and flourish when surrounded? How can executives design and direct businesses based between large and small? How to position products, formulate ideas, evaluate options, structure organizations? How, in short, to build successful mid-sized firms?

We combine business administration and business scholarship, weaving practice with theory and bolstering managerial fighters at the competitive front. Content and thrust are founded on insight and analysis. Modern methods of management provide weapons and armor.

We highlight crack companies, the finest practitioners of the "middlepower" art. We build a "model" from the best, and apply it for the rest. Top performers are the input, the outstanding success stories from numerous industries. Creative strategies are the output, the tangible tools for businesspeople. We produce practical principles for on-line managers. What we learn we apply; and what applies succeeds.

Description and prescription are the things we do, the former portraying the brightest of the bunch, the latter providing options for all. The stories are fun, the cases live. We teach through example and personality. We pose problems demanding strategic sense and innovative solution. We use real companies and real people. The narratives entertain while the principles instruct.

There is wide bearing here. More may be subsumed in the middle than meets the eye. Though developed for medium-sized companies, the essence and elements, strategies and models, have broader appeal. Managers of small businesses will find, I trust, much material for stimulation and application. After all, they too live in "Giantland."

Nor do we discriminate against bigness. Since our concern is business function, not financial structure, smaller units embedded within larger organizations are covered by our managerial umbrella. The captive companies, for example, of a Teledyne, Textron, or IT&T operate much like independent mid-sized firms. Finally, going all the way up, heads of major corporations should know how they are perceived, who's coming after them, and how.

A bit of personal history. In 1979 I was a Sloan Fellow (for mid-career executives) at the Sloan School of Management at the Massachusetts Institute of Technology (where I was also a research affiliate in psychology). "Medium-sized firms" was the natural intersection of my business interests in several companies and my academic interests in strategy and creativity.[2] The literature in the area was sparse, virtually nonexistent—attention was paid to large enterprises and small proprietorships, not those in between. Reference to middle companies, if any, was more by omission than allusion, or if mentioned at all was tossed off as a mere aside.

Medium-sized companies, as beleaguered platoons on the economic battlefield, were losing ground. Theory predicted it; data confirmed it. Massive corporations just had too much market power, too many economies of scale. Their march seemed inexorable; the trend, troubling. Yet mid-sized firms were vital for the economy. What to do? When you start out so negative, you need all possible advantage.

So I searched. Scanning thousands of mid-sized companies, I uncovered hundreds of "top performers," middle-market firms that achieved higher returns than industry leaders. Consistently! How did they do it? What was going on within these theory-busting organizations? How in the same industry could certain medium-sized companies run faster uphill than their larger rivals could downhill? Were there "critical success strategies" causing superior profit performance? Were "creative strategies" quietly at work?

This work is founded on such Creative Strategies, *ten* to be precise, principles that emerged from examining dozens of superb businesses and hundreds of excellent ones, principles rich in substance and ready for application. These critical paths for mid-sized success form our framework; they are presented in Chapter 1 and employed in each company analysis thereafter.

In Part One, the bulk of the book, we examine the best of the breed—sensing winning spirits, engaging driving mechanisms, meeting chief executives, watching Creative Strategies. We define mid-sized firms; check the class collectively; isolate top performers individually; search for competitive advantage among all; discern outstanding characteristics among some; learn strategic and creative management; compare good and bad companies by matched pairs; and build a model for optimal mid-sized performance—all the while interweaving fiery examples of barn-burners in action.

In Part Two, we take a different tack. Each Creative Strategy, one through ten, has its own minichapter. We open each with a few problems, mid-sized companies in some trouble or facing some dilemmas, and we suggest some possible solutions. Then we develop the Creative Strategy through several real-life examples (shorter than those in Part One). The chapters in Part Two are not arranged linearly. It is possible, even desirable, to access them randomly, to tackle them in order of interest, not number. The reader is encouraged to select the Creative Strategies from Part Two while reading the expositions of Part One, and with many short bursts absorb them all.

This book, to my knowledge, is the first comprehensive work on medium-sized companies.[3] Why the subject has been neglected is less important than making sure it is no longer ignored. Too much is at stake. *To Flourish Among Giants* must be more than parochial prescriptions for profit performance. That is the part, not the whole; the means, not the end. If our short-term objective is to improve strategies for mid-sized firms, our long-term goal is to better the whole of society.

The focus throughout is on firms that *flourish*—finding them, watching them, matching them, emulating them. We bring benefit to business. We provoke management. What have these winners got, and how can you get some too? How can commercial concerns sandwiched in the middle exploit distinctive competency and develop competitive advantage? How can business organizations of intermediary size produce potent profits with confidence and consistency? This is our quest. Personal intensity and guts amplify corporate strategy and policy.

We go inside. We take a detailed, personalized look at several dozen top-performing medium-sized firms. We probe deeply. We examine the numbers; we talk to employees; we visit the boss; we analyze the strategies; we check the critics. The question before the house: What made these companies so successful in industries where competitors are so dominant? We seek action and results, not elegance and reflection. What's here is what works.

Robert Lawrence Kuhn

New York, New York
January 1985

CONTENTS

Part Two: Creative Strategies in Action   325

TO FLOURISH AMONG GIANTS

PART ONE

MID-SIZED FIRMS THAT FLOURISH

CHAPTER 1

FINDING FLOURISHERS

Seeing Strategies,
Discovering Secrets

"You shagging me?" asked Stephen J. Cannell, head of Hollywood's hottest studio, as he shot back a sharp glance. He caught a pair of eyes, panicked and reddened as they tracked him with aggressive intent. The studio was Steve's, and with four series on network television, including "The A-Team," it was scorching. The "tail" was a weary line producer, and with multiple deadlines screaming short, including one the next morning, he was determined to confront the boss.

Steve was moving fast, bounding through his elegant offices of rich woods and ancient emblems, but he couldn't shake those eyes. The producer was desperate, and he telegraphed his punch.

Cannell knew the script and read the cue. A preemptive strike was the plot mechanic. He stared at the man.

"I'm showing some friends around and we've got dinner. It can wait. Catch you later." The voice was assertive but the tone was not. Something about Steve's posture betrayed conditioned surrender. He slowed, reached for a chair. No contest here; the outcome was never in doubt. Steve's feeble effort at escape was almost a charade—he knew what was coming; he'd been here before.

"It *can't* wait. Catch me *now*," said the producer seizing the initiative and almost tackling the big fellow with beard and pipe and electric eyes. "One of my editors just quit and the print's gotta go in the morning."

It might have been a scene from a war flick, with the producer as battle-shocked commander returning from the front and Cannell as commander-in-chief hearing the sad status report.

"Pay him extra," Steve ventured gamely. He was now sitting, not bounding, listening, not talking. The tour was stopped, the dinner delayed. It was yet another problem that only the creative founder could solve.

"Stuff the money. No lump of dough'll get this kid into a reel tonight. He was my best. I've no backup, no alternative. *I'll* have to edit the film. *You'll* have to make the final cut. . . . Right now."

Steve spent time, but not too much, somehow negotiating a caucus early the next morning (Saturday). We eventually got to dinner, and not too late. We were chauffeured in a special limousine, one prepared for work, not show. Inside was an elaborate videotape setup, designed by his wife, on which Steve viewed his "dailies," the rough film shot for each series each day. No time to kill traveling. Though he was now running a substantial enterprise, with business and financial responsibilities in addition to artistic ones, he still watched those "dailies," just as he always had.

For every hour on television, they say, some six are left on the cutting room floor. Steve would know every minute of them, virtually every angle for every shot for every scene for every episode for every series. If this wasn't obsession, it gave good imitation. He never took notes; he simply "knew" what looked better and remembered where it could be found. He'd amaze associates by telling them to find a certain angle for a certain scene. Even if the shooting directors and film editors couldn't recall, Steve would. Nothing distracted his drive toward the end product. Making that final cut as perfect as possible was his compulsion.

Fifteen years in the business at just 43, Steve was producing on that night before Christmas Eve 1983, in addition to the muscular smash "A-Team" (always top ten, often top three), "Hardcastle and McCormick" (solid hit), "The Rousters" (cancelled), and

"Riptide" (steady climb, reaching top ten). Cannell had had a good run with "The Greatest American Hero," gave "The Quest" a quick burial, had a pilot in the can, and several more in secret scripts ("Hunter" premiered in fall 1984). He was negotiating constantly with network heads and cable moguls, and allocated three or so hours a week for media interviews. He had a staff of hundreds, a prominent building on Hollywood Boulevard, several sound stages around town, and an annual budget over $100 million. With four hour-long series on the air, Steve's studio was the third largest supplier of television in America. In less than four years, Stephen J. Cannell Productions, a medium-sized outfit in an industry dominated by "The Majors," was flourishing.

CRITICAL SUCCESS STRATEGIES

Steve Cannell never took a management course in his life. Probably a good thing. "If it ain't broke," goes the old adage, "don't fix it." He and his studio personify, as do many of our medium-sized companies, what it takes to survive in an industrial jungle ruled by ravenous rivals—what it takes, in short, to flourish among giants.

How can some mid-sized firms achieve superb financial returns year after year, even though they lack the market power and economies of scale enjoyed by their more massive opponents? How can certain smaller companies best industry leaders in every area of financial performance short of sheer size? Hundreds of companies do exactly that. And many don't stop.

In numerous industries smaller businesses simply outrun larger businesses. More profits. Better ratios. Greater efficiency. *Consistently*. In fact, there are hundreds of medium-sized firms, and thousands of small ones, that year-in and year-out achieve higher returns on sales and equities than do their larger-sized competitors. Why do they? How do they? What goals do these magical companies have? What strategies do they use? Surely, for these successful businesses, self-determined strategy is more precious than government-imposed regulation. The former is hard and sure, the latter laced with whim and caprice.

What are these "critical success strategies," the key moves and thrusts of company policy responsible for outstanding and consistent performance?

The quest for "critical success strategies" is what this book is all about. We search selectively among America's leading mid-sized firms. What do they have that others do not? What's their secret, their card in the hole? We tell the stories of successful firms, what they do and how they do it; and we watch for emerging business principles, the practical procedures for managers.

We start with the story of Stephen Cannell, a tale as compelling as any of his shows. More is here than mere entertainment; more can be learned than inner workings of television production. Note what Steve did and does: how he runs his business; how he positions his products; how he treats his people. What are the underlying motivations, his basic goals and ambitions? Why did he start his own studio? What attitudes and ideas generate prosperity and triumph? Stephen J. Cannell Productions is our first mid-sized case. See if you can spot "critical success strategies" in action. Try discerning these first; then check the list that follows.

SCRIPTING FOR SUCCESS

Pretty nice, all those kudos, all that glory. "A-Team" on top; picture in *People*; fees in the stratosphere. Cannell is courted by network execs and pursued by media mags. It wasn't always that way.

To set up his own production company, Steve had to bear substantial personal risk, well masked by star-spangled glamour. He had turned down a huge guarantee from Universal, his former employer, for whom he had created such shows as "The Rockford Files," "Baretta," "Tenspeed and Brownshoe," and "Baa Baa Black Sheep" in addition to having written over 150 hours of series episodes. (In this business the numbers following dollar signs are staggering. "We're all overpaid," says Steve candidly.)

Cannell began as a writer, and though he creates and produces and directs and sells and owns, a writer is what he will always be. That's his self-image; like a scientist-entrepreneur in the R&D lab, it's where he's happiest. It took years for Steve to sell his first script, and the second one didn't come soon or easy. Yet after churning out some 20,000 pages of dialogue, the great joy still energizes. (He wrote *eighteen* episodes in 1984 alone, triple the average writer.) Stephen Cannell is never more expansive or expressive than when he's telling some story. And if that story happens to be his latest show, though the theme be adolescent, you would just about swear it was the greatest ever told.

Starting his own studio—now that took some doing. Don't be fooled by the glitter. Problem number one, no capital—no financial resources to compete with industry megaliths. Problem number two, it wasn't even a corporation—no balance sheet; no corporate shields; no personal protections. "It's just *me*," Steve explains. "I don't have to give personal guarantees for bank loans, since my entire net worth is *always* on the line." (There are some tax benefits that balance—but do not attenuate—the increased risk.)

No matter, you think, not with all those shows? Think again. The economics of television production is fascinating, its own universe regulated by its own rules. It's a tough, tight business where more shirts are lost than fortunes made. In this world network brass holds ultimate power; by their word series live and die, by their decisions big bucks are made and lost.

On every show his studio produces, hit or miss, Steve *loses* money, often piles of it. An "A-Team" episode costs about a million to make. (Actors, extras, writers, directors, producers, cameramen, locations, travel, action when shooting, time when editing—these add up quickly, especially at union rates.) Steve pays that bundle himself, literally out of his own pocket. The networks pay Steve *less* than cost, say about $800,000. The difference, 200 grand per episode, Steve loses. That's real cash, and it's out the door, if not down the drain. Actually, it's an investment—but if the series doesn't make major hit, the cash swirls downward someplace between cesspool and sewer.

The common assumption that any show on any channel is packing a fat wad for its producer-owners is often false. On a new series the actors, extras, writers, directors, assistants are all making good money, but the studio itself is losing money, betting wholly on the come.

"In A-Team's first year," Steve reflects, "even though the show was Number One a half dozen times, I tanked a couple mill. Next year, I'll have to get more. I have no choice. I can't bankroll losses for three to five years until syndication. Otherwise I take action out of the show—and NBC can't jeopardize its biggest hit."

Don't feel too sorry for him. Steve made a good part back through his own fees for writing and producing and creating—his personal output is enormous—but the cash flow was still negative and red ink cannot continue flowing forever. Yet Steve refuses to cheapen a show by stripping the action to leach out expense. ("I could break even on A-Team by doing some 'closet-shows'; that's where we spend 53 minutes trying to get Hannibal out of jail, prison or some other inexpensive enclosure.")

Cash flow management, seemingly out of place among fantasy and fun, is vital here. "If I can get enough up front, I can have the money working before I need to spend it. The interest makes up some of the losses. So do foreign sales. We now try to sell international rights early, to ease the shortfall."

The kicker in the business—"when we get fat"—is after a series becomes a hit. When the networks buy a show, they are purchasing only "two run deals" for their money, the first run and one summer rerun. The actors and staff are paid and paid well for their work; but what they get up front is what they get in toto. The studio owns the original print—the "negative" as they say—and if and when the series has a long enough run, with enough "negatives" available to "syndicate" nationally, the returns are astounding. ("Syndication" is the process of selling the show to dozens or even hundreds of independent stations across the country, potentially one in every area. Major independents, like Channels 5, 9, and 11 in New York or Los Angeles, will pay handsomely to rerun popular shows. A large segment of the population prefers old favorites and will watch them over new network offerings—and high program ratings are directly convertible into high advertising rates.)

If the "A-Team" runs, say, five years, each episode might bring in a staggering $1–2 million for syndication rights. And in five years, Steve would personally own more than 100 shows. (You do the multiplying; it's merely a matter of shifting some "zeros!") Remember, there are hardly any new costs here. Almost nothing more than opening old cans and paying minor commissions. Of course, and this is the gamble, only one show in fifteen lasts a season, and only one in fifty becomes a smash.

Before "A-Team," though he had many series, the very existence of Stephen J. Cannell Productions was never assured. (If you lose money on each show, you can't catch up by increased volume.) His capital resources were tenuously thin compared to the financial foundation of The Majors.

"I can't afford to invest in dozens of ideas and have 90% of them sit on the shelf," Steve asserts. "Efficiency for me isn't 'a good idea,' it's survival. If I make a pilot, it *must* be bought. I can't play the game of making 'one of these and one of those,' hoping for a random hit. Necessity makes me boil down proposals, keep tight reign on production, and maintain continuous contact with the public and the networks. I've got to be ready to shift and strike whenever ideas click."

Why did Steve go it alone? Why risk bankrolling an independent studio? Why assume the personal pressure? Why chance disaster? What motivation drives such gamble? Though Steve points to the tremendous financial leverage of owning a long-running show, one is not convinced by comic claims of avarice. Sure, monetary astuteness is part of the story, but it's not the whole story, and probably not the best part. There's no way that commercial killing was the prime driver. Stephen Cannell plunged for different reasons.

He did it, I believe, just to do it. Playing ball in the Big Leagues was his ambition, and Steve bought his franchise with brilliance and guts and not a little chutzpah. Going up against The Majors (Universal, 20th Century, MGM, etc.) carries special reward. When Steve says that he has more hours on television than all but one major studio, or that his batting average for turning pilots into series is 1.000 ("eight for eight"), those words mean more to him than the megabucks queuing up for his account. ("Take away the money and I'll still be at my typewriter 6:30 tomorrow morning.")

Steve's shows are as well crafted as they are received. His artistic "signature" is stamped on each creation; and just as any music lover can identify Bach, Beethoven, or Brahms, any reasonably aware television watcher can spot a Cannell production. He's in a class by himself, and that's not meant figuratively as a patronizing cliché but literally as a descriptive judgment. His shows have a certain rhythm, a special beat, a particular cadence. Not profound but magnetic. Not enduring but entertaining. (Steve has no illusions of grandeur: "Nothing I write has lasting value." But he stops, ponders what he just said, then continues; "All the people I know who think they're doing 'important work' aren't. Shakespeare wrote to pay the rent.")

The "Cannell style" connotes action with humor—and it marks all of his shows. He receives criticism for violence ("A-Team" scores high in violent acts per hour), but critics may miss the point. Cannell's "violence" is more whimsy than gore, with escapism, not exploitation, the objective. (Try to catch anyone actually *dying* in "A-Team." Sure, people brawl, buildings explode, and machine guns rattle—but no bullets bursting flesh and little blood being spilled.)

At its best, the Cannell style is witty and light, effervescent and intoxicating, earthy in action yet sophisticated in spirit—a brief respite from a truly violent world. It is resonant with the tastes of contemporary audiences and, in the opinion of many, is the top of its class.

Cannell knows what he knows and knows what he doesn't know. He understands his niche and he pounds it to pieces. But to venture beyond? "Can you believe," he asks with incredulity, "that some studio jock offered me an outrageous advance to write a musical-dance movie? I can choreograph car chases, but soft shoe?"

Yet Cannell is constantly on search; he seeks new vistas for his special talents. Though he has never made feature films for theatrical distribution, it is a market he is eying. Cannell claims competitive advantage: "We know the audience; we know the appetite. And the dollars? A television producer is cost-conscious by definition. Compare our A-Team pilot—for $3.2 million—with major studio motion pictures for three times as much. We put more on the screen."

At the final edit of an early "Riptide" episode, a dozen or so writers and producers grouped themselves around Cannell in the screening room. When it was over, some seconds of silence. Tension. The wait was for Steve. What did the boss think?

A question about the music. A hesitant answer. Steve cuts through the diplomacy. Who's responsible and how to get it right? Everyone snaps to action. "Fault" is not the issue, perfection is.

So he hires the staff and writes the checks, but that's not why they listen to him. "The King and His Court" was not what was playing here. Steve was the *content* leader, not just the process controller. He created the ideas, devised the themes, casted the characters, supervised the scripts, directed the directors, and sold the shows. He wrote as many episodes as did full-time writers. If ever a chief executive had command of his organization, Steve had it. The company was the extension of the man, and both prospered in the dynamic relationship.

One gets the measure of a manager by observing office design. Where does the chief executive put his people? Who's near the boss? Surrounding Steve's suite are creative types, his producers and writers for each of his shows. No administrative, financial, or investment people in sight, certainly not on the top floor. And he takes pride in giving his creatives tremendous opportunity. ("Four years ago one of my writers was driving a truck; today he makes a half million a year.")

No empire builder this guy, but no ascetic either. Steve Cannell's goal is to pack his bundle full, no denying it, but that's part form and part fun. Steve loves the game, and financial worth is how you keep score.

There's no neglecting either end of the "fame and fortune" rainbow. Just check credits at the close of a Cannell Production. Sure can't miss the The Boss. ("We're all hams," smiles Steve.) Excessive humility is not one of his faults. (Note what he's doing—*writing*—not producing, bossing, or sunning.)

His serious substance, without doubt, is sculpting words on paper. He harbors no ambition to build his studio into a self-perpetuating Major, swelling, as have some, into a communications conglomerate. He does what he does best, and he allows growth to fluctuate and size to find its own level. "The next season is always up for grabs," says Steve, "I could double my production, or I could be sliced in half."

Cannell crackles with energy when describing his dream: A new-age studio is his ultimate goal, the sparking electricity of individual creativity without bureaucratic inertia. He wants to be on the sets, near the actors, connected to content. He hates to be the "big man upstairs."

Negatives can reveal more than positives. According to rumor, Steve has turned down several offers to run major studios. The corporate types assigned to entice Steve used "power" as bait; it was their only ploy—money wouldn't work; it was impossible to match the outright ownership of shows (impossible, that is, short of throwing in an oil field or West Los Angeles acreage—though the former was really tried by a famous financier).

Boy, did those three-piece suits have the wrong approach! Nirvana to Steve is freedom to write, not power to boss. Minions fawning over him mean nothing. His dream is to craft novels— perhaps, giving luxury some due, on a yacht in the Mediterranean. Yet Stephen Cannell has flair and vision and commitment and honest self-assessment of a kind not common in Hollywood. Come to think of it, it might do Tinseltown some good if those electric eyes could be cajoled into watching over a Major. . . .

TEN CREATIVE STRATEGIES

The cause of Steve's success is not magic and not random. Cannell Productions is a winner for the same reasons that other top-performing medium-sized enterprises are winners. The entertainment business is granted no protection from jungle competition.

Several years ago, I began an extensive investigation of mid-sized firms in America; I checked thousands, studied hundreds. All sources of information were examined, five-year financial statements, annual reports, press reports, investment analyses, informed opinions. My objective was to identify the finest firms. My goal was to find out what made them so fine. The results comprise this work, and they are designed to enlighten business managers and entertain general readers.

What factors were causative of success? Would I discover "critical success strategies?" Over 100 ideas were categorized and analyzed across hundreds of companies. Many emerged significant. The best we call "Creative Strategies," since we intend active intervention, not passive reflection.[1]

Each Creative Strategy will be discussed, dissected, exemplified, and applied. Each will be used in live situations, to discern reasons for mid-sized success; each will be used in sample problems, to guide strategic direction and structural repair. As the first example, following a quick cut of the Creative Strategies, we view Cannell

Productions in their light. What is the real-world relevance of these principles, and how can they be put into place? This question we answer throughout the book.

In subsequent chapters we deal in depth with strategy and structure, creativity and innovation, analyzing the elements and compounds building successful mid-sized firms. Here we list the conclusions, up front, for orientation and emphasis. By doing so, we do not give away our story. The excitement comes in living with real companies and playing with active applications. Exploration and simulation give the kicks. We learn in Part One and test in Part Two. (Readers may want to take early shots at solving the problems and experiencing the examples of Part Two.)

We watch winners and losers. We track trends and observe patterns. What does it take for mid-sized firms to triumph in the marketplace, to outfox voracious competitors?

Following are ten Creative Strategies. Listed in order of importance, some are universal, applicable any time any place; some are contingent, requiring certain conditions. All are useful; all can be employed by managers. (We again note that these Creative Strategies are not restricted to medium-sized companies. Though derived from such businesses, they are, we suspect, helpful for

---

1. **Dominance:** Dominate your corporate niche

2. **Product Emphasis:** Be product-oriented

3. **Distinctiveness/Uniqueness:** Be different

4. **Focus/Coherence:** Strive for strategic tightness

5. **High-Profile Chief Executive:** Have a committed boss

6. **Employee Opportunity:** Satisfy/fulfill personnel

7. **Efficient Innovation:** Optimize new products, services, methods

8. **External Perception:** Know the industrial/market environment

9. **Growth–Profits Tradeoff:** Weigh top line with bottom line

10. **Flexibility/Opportunism:** Change direction and move quickly

---

FIGURE 1.1. Creative strategies.

smaller companies and even for smaller divisions of large companies.)

The ten Creative Strategies are *leit motifs*, composed in Part One and comprising Part Two (Figure 1.1). They sound their theme continuously, unifying the diverse corporate cases. What follows make melodies; all else are harmony and timbre, orchestration, and overtone.

1. *Dominance:* *Dominate Your Corporate Niche.* Segment markets. Narrowcast products. Achieve and sustain maximum share within minimum markets. Tailor products tightly; define domains toughly. Segment by specific item, customer, price, quality, brand, distribution, geography, service, and so on—do anything to segment. Seek control through perceived superiority. Be a big fish in a little pond. Remember, small can still dominate.

2. *Product Emphasis:* *Be Product-Oriented.* Give primary importance to company output. Stress product focus, essence, name, reliability, service. Visualize products from customers' viewpoint. Never make products subservient, not to executive desire, not to financial comfort. See each product in its broadest sense; understand the needs it fills and the desires it satisfies. Be service-oriented.

3. *Distinctiveness/Uniqueness:* *Be Different.* Make the firm overtly dissimilar to competitors. Strive for originality; find something to set the company apart in customer perception. Impact the end user. Seek differentiation in each functional area impacting buyers. Cater to customers. Service them well. Be noticed. Be remembered.

4. *Focus/Coherence:* *Strive for Strategic Tightness.* Establish goals/ objectives/strategies with clarity of thought and coherence of content. Build new businesses on the central skills, resources, facilities, or competencies of old businesses. Structure on managerial strengths. Set corporate coherence and business focus as means, not ends. Relatedness is contingent on business/industry environment: A mid-sized firm in a declining or dying industry/market should not fear diversification, yet should always develop new opportunities on past competencies.

5. *High-Profile Chief Executive:* *Have a Committed Boss.* The CEO should be more than a CEO. Personal charisma, profound dedication, pulsating presence—these are what counts. The CEO should project high levels of commitment and radiate intense auras of energy. There should be desire, even compulsion, to involve oneself all-pervasively in every aspect of the business. Contingent on industry and company traditions.

   6. *Employee Opportunity: Satisfy/Fulfill Personnel.* Exploit the comparative advantage of smaller firms to attract entrepreneurial people; offer executives and managers greater job content and individual satisfaction. Be people-oriented. Give employees a real sense of self-worth and personal participation, both emotionally and financially. Develop meaningful stock ownership programs. Get the right executives, then give them what they want—on the job and in the bank.

   7. *Efficient Innovation: Optimize New Products, Services, Methods.* Develop and commercialize new technologies. Exploit the comparative advantage of smaller firms to introduce new products sooner and swifter. Encourage creative types to weave their wonders. Attack market leaders if they protect current positions by withholding innovation (as often happens). Emphasize efficiency in research; optimize development for rapid, cost-conscious results. Never attack broadside; focus R&D for maximum effectiveness. Use rifles, not shotguns.

   8. *External Perception: Know the Industrial/Market Environment.* Monitor all opportunities and threats, current and potential. Stay attuned to market conditions and customer needs. Know your customers; develop personal relationships. Have a keen sense of competitors. Appreciate issues of industrial organization: market share,[2] concentration ratios,[3] growth patterns and trends,[4] powers of suppliers and buyers,[5] threats of new entrants and substitute products.[6] Observe long-term forecasts, and watch them change. Be prepared for sudden discontinuities and be ready to exploit them.

   9. *Growth–Profits Tradeoff: Weigh Top Line with Bottom Line.* Eschew growth for growth's sake, but seek growth for business's sake. Market products forcefully. Visualize longer time horizons for profit return. The bottom line, not the top one, is what counts. Billion-dollar corporations have gone bankrupt, while many

very small firms have made their owners and executives very rich. Highly contingent on firm's comparative position within its market. Weaker mid-sized companies should prize profits far more than growth. Stronger mid-sized firms should not fear sacrificing short-term profits for long-term growth. When top performers establish strong market position, ultimate profits become much greater and more secure.

10. *Flexibility/Opportunism: Change Direction and Move Quickly.* Develop dynamic decision making. Be prepared to react rapidly to changes in products or markets. Be ready to turn on a dime and beat larger competitors to new opportunities. Retreat when the enemy attacks. Attack when the enemy retreats. Contingent on industry/market position. Weaker mid-sized firms should emphasize flexibility and opportunity more so than stronger firms.

A word of warning for the eager mid-sized manager. These Creative Strategies may seem obvious and easy; do not allow the former to discourage you or the latter to fool you. The points are powerful and pragmatic; they are derived from hundreds of contemporary companies and we see their stuff in fast action. On the other hand, any simplistic advice—of which the above can be considered classic—should not be used as a magic wand. Smooth aphorisms are no panacea for confused executives. (Such platitudes often appear when management consultants, who usually haven't run real businesses, spout traditional wisdom.) Generalized prescription, never forget, is one thing; realistic recommendation quite another.

One can question the direction of causation. It can be argued that being successful generates Creative Strategies, not the reverse. Which came first, the success or the Dominance; the success or the Product Emphasis; the success or the Distinctiveness? Which is the "chicken" and which is the "egg"? Causation is admittedly an issue, but the Creative Strategies are nonetheless real.

Observing management principles in current combat is vital. The struggle of company units on industrial battlefields is the ultimate touchstone. Each Creative Strategy must be field tested in hard fighting. Before jumping to hasty conclusions, wait for these practical examples. Then get set to solve some problems.

MAPPING CANNELL PRODUCTIONS

Where does Stephen J. Cannell (SJC) Productions fit on the above model? How does this top-performing medium-sized studio stack up against the ten Creative Strategies? (Process here is as important as content; the approach pervades every case, the attitude affects every application.)

1. *Dominance.* SJC is a leader in producing action-drama series for network television; it can be said to dominate the more whimsical segment of the escapist scene.

2. *Product Emphasis.* SJC stresses programming above all else; Cannell himself is obsessed with the content of his productions, every facet of every show.

3. *Distinctiveness.* SJC gives networks and audiences programs in its own special style, which, if not unique, is certainly refreshing.

4. *Focus/Coherence.* SJC targets heavy action-drama with a humorous touch; no attempt is made to provide diverse kinds of programming.

5. *High-Profile Chief Executive.* SJC has an extremely dominant CEO, almost to a fault; Steve pervades the whole company, he virtually is the company.

6. *Employee Opportunity.* SJC gives creative personnel substantial occasion for artistic expression, financial reward, and external recognition.

7. *Efficient Innovation.* SJC must be cost-conscious since capital is limited and well below competitors'. Ideas must be narrowed, and pilots restricted. All R&D, that is, new programming, must be bought before produced. No room here for speculation.

8. *External Perception.* SJC tries to keep ahead of public tastes, catching some trends and creating others.

9. *Growth–Profits Tradeoff.* SJC is not afraid to grow but doesn't seek expansion for size alone. Maximizing value of current competencies and properties is stressed.

10. *Flexibility/Opportunism.* SJC is always ready to tackle a new opportunity whenever inspiration hits. The flexibility to collapse overheads if series are canceled is critical.

SOME TOP PERFORMERS

We now sweep the landscape. We scan across top-performing mid-sized companies. We ask why each outguns industry leaders. Answers, though the companies are complex, can come simple; the categories, rather often, conform to the Ten. To get started, we give examples.

Note that we choose only one Creative Strategy for each company—quite the opposite from SJC Productions where we analyzed the one company in each category. Both procedures are appropriate, just as both are artificial. Strategic success is generated by a diverse mixture of method and approach. (The numbers in parentheses are annual gross sales for fiscal 1983, each only a fraction of industry giants. We discuss many of these companies in some depth.)

1.   *Dominance.* *Tokheim* ($118 million) is the leader in control mechanisms for retail gasoline pumps. *Russell* ($319 million) is the largest manufacturer of athletic apparel. *Omark* ($257 million) is the world's leading producer of cutting chain for electric saws. *Great Lakes Chemical* ($228 million) is the world's foremost producer of bromine. *Hillenbrand* ($433 million) is the largest manufacturer of metal and hardwood burial caskets, and electrically operated hospital beds, and is the second largest manufacturer of luggage.

2.   *Product Emphasis.* *Binney & Smith* ($125 million) stresses products supporting its Crayola crayons. *Tampax* ($346 million), *Maytag* ($597 million), *Noxell* ($304 million) and *Bacardi Rum* ($175 million) each have established brand names connoting strong product identification and high quality reputation.

3.   *Distinctiveness/Uniqueness.* *Neutrogena* ($46 million) makes a soft soap with characteristic transparency and mild feel for sensitive skin. *A.T. Cross* ($118 million) sets the class standard in pens and pencils. *La-Z-Boy* ($197 million) promotes its famous reclining chair and associated furniture. *Trus Joist* ($96 million) manufactures special structural components used in building.

4. *Focus/Coherence.* *Tennant* ($107 million) concentrates on industrial floor maintenance equipment. *Loctite* ($216 million) stresses industrial adhesives. *Deluxe Check Printers* ($620 million) targets printing for financial institutions and their depositors. *Commerce Clearing House* ($378 million) produces updated reference material for attorneys and accountants. *Applied Magnetics* ($102 million) manufactures magnetic heads for tape and computer disk drives. *Goulds Pumps* ($275 million) manufactures centrifugal pumps.

5. *High-Profile Chief Executive.* *Tyco* ($586 million) was built from a small R&D shop ($216 million in 1979) by the dynamic Joseph Gaziano (recently deceased). *MCO Holdings* ($166 million), in real estate and energy, was turned around completely by Charles Hurwitz. *Wang* ($1538 million), a mid-sized firm alumnus ($97 million in 1976), is totally controlled by An Wang. *Jorgensen Steel* ($229 million) is run by Earle M. and his family.

6. *Employee Opportunity.* *MacDermid* ($61 million) encourages its employees to risk and develop; they combine a healthy bonus and stock option plan with the motto, "Have the Guts to Fail." *Molex* ($176 million) creates an entrepreneurial spirit by strong decentralization and divisional autonomy. *Shaklee* ($314 million) grew on the strength of its part-time, multilevel sales force. *Ametek* ($424 million) highlights decentralized managerial control.

7. *Efficient Innovation.* *Marion Laboratories* ($181 million) allocates no R&D to basic chemistry; all expenditures "search and develop" new drugs created by other drug companies in foreign countries. *Worthington Industries* ($450 million) targets close-tolerance steel. *Guilford Mills* ($255 million) uses automation to become a low-cost producer and achieve high sales per employee.

8. *External Perception.* *La Quinta Motor Inns* ($113 million) combines Sun Belt expansion with low-rental rooms. *Palm Beach* ($492 million) has moved with the rapidly changing apparel market, including designer labels and retail stores. *PharmaControl* ($1 million) has drug delivery systems and a soluble aspirin that may create huge markets. *Plantronics* ($114 million) senses changing markets and exploits technological conditions.

9. *Growth–Profits Tradeoff.* *Versa Technologies* ($25 million) keeps size small and balance sheet strong. *J. L. Clark* ($159 million) concentrates on a small segment of the metal can industry, stressing consistency and customer support. *Dr. Pepper* ($560 million) is a classic case of what mid-sized firms should and should not do; having prospered with profits, it now struggles with growth.

10. *Flexibility/Opportunism.* *Dynatech* ($99 million) uses its R&D technological strength to attack multiple markets, each too small for big companies to fool with. *Carlisle* ($412 million) uses diversity as a base for rapid reaction to new businesses.

One factor pervades all, a certain spark, an electric excitement. You sense momentum, action, forward movement. One is taken by tension, caught by the current. Nothing "stuck" about these top-performing mid-sized firms.

WHEN COMMODITIES ARE NOT COMMODITIES

Premier Industries is in the very boring business of distributing electrical and industrial parts for maintenance and repairs. (It's hardly Hollywood.) What are some of these very boring products? Try nuts and bolts, batteries, circuit breakers, and lubricating oils. Pity Premier? Not to fret. Check the profit performance of this Cleveland-based company. It's anything but boring: 1983 revenues, $317 million; profits, $31 million; 1980–1983 return on sales, 10 percent; current ratio, 5.3 to 1; 1977–1982 return on equity, 25 percent; 1977–1982 compound growth in earnings per share, 24 percent.[7]

The distribution business, as a general rule, operates on very thin margins. How to make money on very thin margins? Traditional wisdom recommends the obvious—very high volume. Premier snickers at traditional wisdom and shatters the general rule—the company generates 18 percent pretax profits with high margin and low volume.

"We make uncommon profits on a common line of products," says Mort Mandel, Chairman and CEO, one of three founding brothers who still own 62 percent of the company. (The brothers are close family; though two are no longer active, one is Chairman of the Executive Committee and the other of the Finance Com-

mittee.) Collectively the three Mandels share a market value os-
cillating between $200 and $400 million. In an industry where
discounting is the norm, Premier does not cut price. The key to
their success? They have converted commodities into value-added
products. How? That's the neat trick. First a general answer—
through perception of market demand and sensitivity to customer
needs, by serving a segment and serving it best. "What we offer
is more value," states the senior vice-president. "We've picked a
niche that gives us the appropriate returns and our customers the
appropriate value."

Premier has three basic businesses: electrical and electronics
distribution (generating 55 percent of sales and 63 percent of profits,
considered the area of future growth); industrial maintenance distribution (products made to order by outside suppliers, 37 percent
of revenues, 29 percent of profits); fire-fighting equipment (8 percent
of revenues and profits).

In the distribution business, what is value added? In a word,
availability. This is the specific answer. Premier maintains a comprehensive inventory of virtually every conceivable product and
fulfills customer orders in incredibly short periods of time. (Of 102
items ordered by Zenith Radio, for example, 98 were delivered
within hours. Now that's service!) "Superior service is a key factor
in our marketing strategy, and we are constantly seeking ways to
improve it." A recent example was the purchase of 300,000 square
feet of additional warehousing capability.

Most of Premier's business—indeed its market specialty—comes
from small accounts, those maintenance and repair shops that
competitors (such as Avnet and Arrow) find too small to fuss over.
What the competition finds unprofitable is Premier's bread and
butter. (Premier's average order is $100, compared to $400 at Arrow.)
In fact, it is not unusual for rival companies to refer "too-small"
business to Premier. Of its 100,000 customers, none account for
more than 1 percent of sales.

In Premier's industrial products division, the strategy shifts.
Here, high margins reflect high quality. Its products are simply
better; its custom-made items are tougher, stronger, and especially
easy to use. Fasteners break less often (rather critical, we would
think, for fasteners); since 1960, every car raced in the Indianapolis

500 has been held together with Premier Supertanium fasteners, said to be the strongest commercially available. Fire-fighting equipment weighs less—important for cities where females are being recruited. Supertreated diesel oil, formulated by company experts, is markedly superior: though costing twice as much per gallon, $5 vs. $2.50, it extends distance between overhauls for heavy vehicles from 350,000 miles to 500,000; furthermore, Premier will test customer samples to determine current conditions of oil and engine.

Even though Premier handles a wide range of products, it is still a coherent company. Claiming "market leadership in industrial maintenance and repair . . . a vast and growing market," Premier believes that its success is derived from a "unique marketing approach" of finding and filling buyer need, backed up by an ability to develop "problem-solving products." Its large selling organization is buttressed by specialists providing customers with full support. Thus Premier defines a basic corporate strength as its "customer service capability" and everything the company does and plans to do augments this fundamental thrust.

The three Mandel brothers bought their uncle's auto parts operation in 1940 for $900. What to do with the shop? "We didn't want to run a small business," recalls Mort. So they conducted some early surveys: They talked to customers. They learned there were a huge number of parts—"thingamajigs" is Mort's "technical" name for them—that were hard to describe and harder to find. So the brothers put "thingamajigs" on display; stacked in cigar boxes, these chunks and hunks, gizmos and gadgets, encouraged buyer browsing. When seekers found what they needed the first time, they came back the second time—and told their friends the third time.

The concept proved so successful the brothers soon outgrew the store. They couldn't lug those leaded cigar boxes around, of course, so they created a catalog. The book was felt-lined and had the actual sample parts included inside. Clever. But as business continued to expand, the catalog became too heavy. Sheer weight soon forced a change from samples to pictures. Premier's catalog is now the most comprehensive in the industry; some 800 pages long, it is referred to as "the Bible." "We're like Sears, except that we're selling to industrial accounts," said the head of the electronics operations. The new catalog has already been sent to over 500,000 purchasers and specifiers of electronic components; over its two-year life, about 1,000,000 copies will be distributed

Strategy remained consistent. Throughout the years, Premier stuck by its firm policy: It steadfastly refused to discount. It was solving difficult problems for customers who were only too happy to pay full value. Mort beams: "We discovered that by finding a niche and doing well in it, we could compete with anyone." Areas devoid of clear competitive advantage—such as brand-name spark plugs—they shunned. "We didn't get involved in things where we were amateurs."

Premier's products may not be high-tech, but its marketing is certainly state-of-the-art. Telephone sales from almost 200 branch offices are connected to a central computer that keeps a complete list of inventory and pricing information available instantly. The company's 200 product lines and tens of thousands of products allow "one-stop shopping." A prime strategy is penetrating new markets and building sales with existing customers. "Superior service" is called "a key factor in our marketing strategy," and management is "constantly seeking ways to improve it." (Never underestimate the importance of convenience. Time is money, and customers will pay full price for the luxury of not having to jump from vendor to vendor scouring for parts and pieces.)

No single items dominate Premier's product lines, just as no individual buyers dominate Premier's customers—and that's just the way the company likes it; it keeps power relationships all one-sided and senior management all full smiles. Premier turns its inventory five to six times a year, compared to an industry average of three to four.

As for the future, change is expected. Planned. Mandel does not stand still. He foresees a different mix in ten years—30 to 40 percent of products to be carried then are not being carried now. Electronics is targeted for expansion: At the present time only 25 percent of electronic products is sold through distributors (75 percent moves directly from manufacturers to industrial users); but proportions are shifting, products flowing through distributors are increasing, especially as high-tech manufacturers concentrate on what they do best—development and production—and forsake what others do best—marketing and distribution.

Premier is staking out a dominant position. It is on search for acquisitions to round out capabilities. (Recent purchases include small companies in electrical connectors, switches, and sockets.)

Premier likes to consider itself "one big happy family." The company's top 18 executives average over 23 years working there. It is common for senior managers to wander among employees and discover what's happening (the "random walk" technique). The company is committed to promotion from within. How such a corporate culture survives growth is tricky. "In the past we've looked at ourselves as a pretty big small company," Mort muses. "Now we see ourselves as a pretty small big company."

Creative Strategies at Premier? Check out the list.

Dominance.   They own the small-store, small-order market; this is the place for one-stop shopping and quick turnaround.

Product Emphasis.   Comprehensive selection; easy accessibility; current availability; superior quality.

Distinctiveness.   Products (everything in one place, even the impossible-to-find); marketing (on-line telephone system and comprehensive catalog); response time (complete inventory and rapid shipment).

Focus/Coherence.   Clear company image—distribution of every conceivable item for target markets; customer requirements are prime concern.

High-Profile Chief Executive.   Mort Mandel's philosophy perfuses the company (original objectives have hardly changed).

Employee Opportunity.   High satisfaction, internal promotions and loyalty; why else would senior executives stay so long?

Efficient Innovation.   All new products are market driven, all supply direct demand.

External Perception.   Customer needs are primary—buyer desire is the company touchstone. (Star this one.)

Growth–Profits Tradeoff.   Margins maintained at all costs—high volume through low pricing is eschewed; bottom line is always more important than top line.

Flexibility/Opportunism. Planning for a 30–40 percent change in products over the next decade; ready to make acquisitions to enhance product lines.

Executive succession is usually an issue in family dominated companies. Will the next generation have the requisite skills to manage? At Premier the question is moot. A strict rule forbids the hiring of relatives, especially if their names are Mandel.

WHEN HIGH TECH IS NOT HIGH TECH

Tandon Corp. is the world's largest independent manufacturer of floppy disk drives, the electromechanical devices that provide peripheral memory for microcomputers.[8] In October 1975 the company was started from scratch by a U.S.-educated mechanical engineer from India named Sirjang Lal ("Jugi") Tandon. Total capital, all he had: $7000. In three years Tandon was the largest independent supplier of recording heads for disk drives. A few years later, he grabbed leadership in making the drives themselves. You'd have thought a hundred companies would've had him for lunch.

A classic rags-to-riches saga, Jugi worked as a busboy while going to school. After taking his degree from Howard University, he returned to India as was his original intent; but when he couldn't find opportunity there, he was forced back to the United States. It was one of those chance occurrences that put Jugi Tandon into Memorex, and onto a team developing a small floppy disk drive. Later, after a stint at Pertec, when Jugi couldn't raise any money to form a company—"I was asking for $50,000 and would have probably given up 90 percent"—he simply started his own and kept it all himself.

In eight years Tandon skyrocketed from a standing start with zero revenues to explosive growth with $303 million in 1983. (The first half of fiscal 1984 was up 62 percent.) Profits hit $24 million, and the stock market has valued the company at well over $1 billion—more than many famous firms such as American Can, American Motors, and so on. In 1983 Tandon shipped 2.8 million disk drives, a market share better than 60 percent—incredibly high for a rapidly changing industry. (Most IBM Personal Computers, one of history's most successful new products, have Tandon disk drives tucked neatly inside.)

Tandon is headquartered in Chatsworth, California, in the San Fernando Valley just north of Los Angeles. The company was profitable from its first month in operation. A remarkable feat by itself. But then again, Jugi didn't have any choice. There were no deep pockets around—and his were about empty. But why was he so successful so quickly? For the same reason he continues to be successful today.

To hear Jugi Tandon talk, his strategy is more manufacturing than research. A critical concept, this—the heart of the matter. Spreading overheads over a larger base is far more important than creating new bells and whistles. Tandon doesn't get dreamy over technological innovation.

Surprised? Don't be. Reliability and low cost, not esoterica and high specs, are what sells equipment to consumers—and computers, now as consumer items, are no exception. Tandon makes disk drives that work and work well, with well-tested components and sure-fitting parts. Add price and you've heard most of the story.

Tandon is compulsive about manufacturing costs, and he is a habitual price cutter. "The computer industry," the master begins, "has historically been extremely good at research and development, but it didn't focus on manufacturing sophisticated electronic devices in large volumes. The basic technology in disk drives is the same as ten years ago. The difference is then that drives were produced for specialized customers. Now we are making a consumer product."

Since demand in microcomputers is directly related to cost, by slashing prices of its disk drives (which comprise 35–40 percent of a system's cost), Tandon not only increases its market share but also increases the total market—that is, the company gets a bigger slice of a bigger pie, the best of all worlds. Tandon, however, is not a predatory pricer—selling below cost to drive competitors out and then raising prices to fleece the public is not his style. Tandon always starts with lowest possible costs, sure, but the company always makes money on all its pricing structures. Always. But whenever volume production warrants another slide down the experience curve,[9] you can make book prices will be cut still further. "In this technology you have to keep bringing prices down. You can't afford to get sloppy."

Tandon is perhaps the most vertically integrated company in its segment of the computer industry. Tandon now produces its own printed circuit boards—20,000 a day—at plants in Singapore and California. The company of late has been shifting more manufacturing to India; labor costs for Tandon are a prime reason, giving something back for Jugi is probably another.

There is, of course, the perennial threat that some customer manufacturers will decide to bring disk drive production in-house. Tandon is not worried. Apple Computer, for example, has just gone the other way, halting its in-house manufacturing and starting to source externally.

Jugi smiles, "Three years ago I offered Apple my license [to build disk drives] free of charge. I knew they could not produce them as cheaply as I can. Now they have proved me right."

Tandon produces what its customers want. "We don't invent things for the sake of inventing things," says the founder. Engineers work directly with customers. "We say, 'How would you like it if we did this?' They say, 'Great,' or 'It makes no sense.'"

Such efficiency holds down R&D costs to a modest 4 percent of sales. Marketing expenses, as well, are not high, since prime customers are the large computer manufacturers, not consumers. In weighing future options, though he may consider making a host of products including entire personal computers, Jugi never thinks marketing. He will always sell to original equipment manufacturers (OEMs) for resale under their names.

Jugi Tandon knows what he is, and he knows what he isn't. What he built was a manufacturing company, and that is what it will remain. Marketing is not his game, and never will be. The point is fundamental—what energizes a company defines its essence. The difference is enormous. Though various companies may appear to produce similar products, there are vast gulfs among organizations driven by manufacturing, marketing, or R&D.

Regarding the future, don't kid yourself, Jugi worries. "I am always looking over my shoulder." What he's looking for are competitors. Most he knows are "sloppy," at least in manufacturing. But still he sleeps lightly. The industry is changing almost weekly, and a new company or a new technology could ambush him overnight.

Bottom line, quality and cost are where Tandon makes his stand. He is obsessed with squeezing out all unnecessary steps in production. Waste is his sworn enemy. No more pushing drives into hasty assembly and throwing them out the door, like the wild early days when too many substandard products were the price Tandon had to pay to secure new orders. "We are in our second phase now. We have the volume, we have the workhorse products. We can take a longer time to test products and see if we can cut costs."

Tandon has made some sixty of its employees millionaires, including an early production-line worker with $6 million worth of stock. Jugi himself? Have no concern. With 11 percent of the company, he's worth over $100 million—enough to keep him in multiple Lamborghinis for decades to come.

Creative Strategies at Tandon? Many and in abundance.

Dominance.   Yes sir, of floppy disk drives for microcomputers.

Product Emphasis.   That's Jugi's wholehearted commitment.

Distinctiveness.   Clear, in the hardball manufacturing strategy.

Focus/Coherence.   Unequivocally, on the one product and on making it reliable and cheap.

High-Profile CEO.   What more can one say about Jugi?

Employee Opportunity.   Look at those stock options.

Efficient Innovation.   A prime point (4 percent on R&D)—and no inventing things just for the sake of inventing things.

External Perception.   Giving customers what *they* want, and maintaining constant vigilance of competitors.

Growth–Profits Tradeoff.   Never buying market share with losses.

Flexibility.   Moving manufacturing to keep costs at lowest level.

Now that we have introduced the ten Creative Strategies, and given a few examples of each, we encourage early reading of the corporate cases in Part Two. There is no required order here, no critical path to follow. Just move through the stories as interest dictates. Part Two is organized by Creative Strategies, one mini-chapter each, and it contains numerous examples and problems of real companies in real situations. Part Two should be read in parallel with Part One—please don't wait until you've finished the first part before beginning the second part. In approaching Part Two, you can enter any Creative Strategy at any place in any way. Be inquisitive. Indulge curiosity. Get the flavor. Seek, feel, muse. We recommend "random access'—as on Jugi's disk drives. Appreciating the Creative Strategies is vital. Understanding how they work is what this book is all about.

CHAPTER 2

BETWEEN MAMMOTHS AND GNATS

Are You Caught?
Can You Escape?

Picture Gulliver beset by both Brobdingnagians and Lilliputians, not sequentially on separate islands but simultaneously on the same island. It is a land of monsters and midgets, and our traveling hero is trapped. Without respite he is pursued by mighty giants and badgered by crafty dwarfs; desperately he avoids the lumbering ferocity of the former and eludes the darting torments of the latter. The giants step with pulverizing weight; the dwarfs revel in piercing arrows. How to survive and how to escape? The task is tiring, the outlook grim.

Now switch mental gears from nineteenth-century literary fantasy to twentieth-century economic reality and you cut an image of the modern mid-size firm—a company class, experts say, that cannot survive.

CHECK OUT THIS MIDDLE

Experts? Look here. Right in the center of one tough industry. Read the case and watch the strategies.

Plenum Publishing is a medium-sized company, "caught in the middle," you might say, of the book publishing industry, "trapped" between corporate mammoths such as Simon & Schuster and Harper & Row on one side, and garage-shop gnats, numerous and nettlesome, on the other. Revenues of the giants overwhelm Plenum's by five to fifteen times. But shed no tears, every company should be so "trapped:" Plenum's incredible 17 + percent after tax return on sales—better than 20 percent! in 1983—puts them all to shame.

Sales revenues have grown steadily if not spectacularly, climbing at a compound rate of about 9 percent for five years, reaching $30 million in 1982 and $34 million in 1983. But profits are what counts; if revenues are a team's "hits," earnings are its "runs." Plenum's net profits were a sizzling $5.1 million in 1982 and $6.2 million in 1983. Average return on stockholders' equity approaches 40 percent. (International sales contribute over 40 percent of consolidated sales and profits.)

Who's choosing such an unbroken series of best-sellers? Even James Michener's sagas and Steven King's scares couldn't keep up with Plenum's picks. After all, how many different *Joys of . . .* can be published?

Let's add to the mystery. How many copies is a Plenum best-seller likely to sell? A million? A hundred thousand? Forget it! Maybe a few will hit 5000 copies in their lifetimes, barely a week's worth for an ordinary top book. What about a leading Plenum periodical—how many subscribers? Perhaps a couple will wring out a bare 4000, not a tenth of a percent of *Time's* circulation.

How much are those 5000 book buyers or 4000 magazine subscribers willing to pay? Now we're getting closer to pay dirt.

Here's another hint. In certain parts of the world, Plenum publications are required reading, *de rigueur* as they say, especially if you happen to work for either the Soviet KGB or the American CIA. What's going on here?

Plenum is in the business of "scientific publishing." Its more than 150 journals, published an average of eight times a year, carry such foreboding titles as *International Journal of Thermophysics, Hyperbaric Oxygen Review, Folia Morphologia.* Journals contribute about $14 million in annual revenues, almost 50 percent of sales—and all very profitable, thank you. Needless to say, if you want to keep current with *Optimization Theory and Applications, Chemical Ecology* or *Mathematical Geology,* you had better ante up the outrageous annual subscription price and not miss a single jam-packed issue.

In 1982 Plenum published 301 new scientific books, covering subjects from modifying human behavior to modifying molecular behavior, from collisions among family elements to collisions among atomic elements. (Don't look for any bargains here either; bring along at least a fifty if you want to bring back at least a book.) Just over 35 percent of Plenum's revenues come from books, up in volume but down in percentage from five years ago.

There is an important slant to almost two-thirds of Plenum's journals and about one-third of revenues derived from magazines and books. This is the real key. The material comes from the East, where Red is the color, Communism the system, and secrecy the god. Plenum owns ten-year rights to some ninety-five Soviet technical journals and has many leading Russian scientists under exclusive book contract.

No overtly defense-related research is published, of course, just the "pure" scientific stuff. (Some of the content, it is said, impacts military technologies, hence the sensitivity and the interest.) President Martin Tash says that the Soviet government is happy to assist Plenum make the right contacts. "They are eager to brag about their achievements," says Frank Columbus, who spends two months a year scouring Soviet science on its home turf. Agreement reached with the All-Union Institute of Scientific and Technical Information of the Soviet Union grants Plenum exclusive rights to translate into English and publish abstracts of Soviet articles on various scientific subjects. (Some sample journals are *Soviet Journal of Nondestructive Testing, Fibre Chemistry, Metal Science and Heat Treatment,* and *Strength of Materials.*)

How has Plenum achieved record sales and profits while the purchasing capacity of its primary market—institutional libraries and scientific research organizations—has been diminished by economic recession? It is a tribute to the strategy of the business and the importance of their products. But the company must look forward; the nature of the industry is changing.

As the technology of information transfer undergoes revolutionary shift, Plenum's basic philosophy, as articulated by its president, is "to seek out markets in need of the special expertise developed by Plenum. . . . and to develop unique services and products for these markets." Plenum sees its future growth in developing information data bases, made available to end users via computer-based telecommunications. (Three new data bases introduced during 1983 are abstracts in mental health, information science, and political science.)

Plenum is also exploring new industries, each of which builds on current competencies. One example is "Career Placement Registry," a personnel data base combined with a computerized job search program. Another example is video programming in scientific fields where Plenum is publishing actively. Exclusive programming from the Soviet Union in the areas of nature and wildlife, cultural affairs, sporting events, and travel are expected to attract interest from public and cable networks.

This company knows what it knows and does what it does best. (It recalls the story of the Armenian fiddler who was heard intoning a single repetitive sound. "Why are you playing just one note?" asked a friend frustrated by the grating sound. "Everyone else is looking for their note," answered the fiddler, "I've found mine.")

President Tash, an accountant by training, hardly fiddles with company cash. A self-confessed tightwad, he deserted the rarefied world of uptown New York publishing with its $50 a square foot rents to take up residence in lower Manhattan at $4 a square foot. When professional movers asked $200,000 to make the transition, Tash hired some workmen, bought a truck and did the job for $30,000. "I even helped pack the boxes myself," boasts the president.

Matching Plenum with the Creative Strategy categories makes easy fittings. The company certainly *Dominates* the Soviet scientific niche in publishing. *Product Emphasis, Distinctiveness,* and *Focus/Coherence* are all strong and self-evident. Employees enjoy the special character of the company. *External Perception* of new scientific fields, new areas of Eastern Bloc activity, and new technologies of information transfer are all critical for success. And finally, the low growth rates and extraordinarily high profit margins are testimony that Plenum has made the *Growth–Profits Tradeoff* well to the right.

TWO-FRONT WAR

Caught in the middle, goes conventional wisdom, is no place to be. The business of modest dimensions is just too small to confront the market power of huge enterprises and too large to match the organizational flexibility of tiny ventures. Medium-sized companies, it is said, mashed by multinational mammoths and nipped by entrepreneurial gnats, are an imperiled breed. Indeed, what amounts to an inexorable squeeze between the massive economies of scale of the titans and the opportunistic dexterity of the pygmies threatens the existence of many medium-sized companies. In an age of increasing inflationary pressures and decreasing profit margins, without media interest or political wallop, the mid-sized firm seems destined for disaster.

Medium-sized businesses are becoming an endangered species; in some industries they are almost extinct. Year after year, their percentages of assets, sales, and profits have been eroded steadily by the voracious growth of corporate colossi, the industrial behemoths that gobble and expand like "outer space blobs" time warped from a 1950s science fiction flick. While such economic concern (amplified often by political expediency) can trigger outcries from trust-busting bureaucrats, the orientation is almost always on the negative: Thwart the giants; limit mergers and acquisitions; break apart the megaliths—with an occasional bone for small business, especially in an election year.

Yet hardly a word about the companies lodged in the trough in the middle, companies, we shall see, vital to the American economy. And while some observers lament the shifting patterns, others acknowledge the "omnipresent laws of the marketplace"—reflecting the rage of "sociobiology" where Darwin's "survival of the fittest" mechanism oversteps its traditional boundaries.

Learned economists and fierce lobby groups line up on both sides of the political fence, arguing vigorously for their often self-serving positions. The pro-giant contingent, exemplifying Darwinian toughness, claims that if smaller companies can't hack it in the marketplace, they should be driven from the scene. If our large, highly efficient businesses are artificially restrained by government regulation, these corporate mouthpieces maintain, then the United States will be pushed progressively out of world markets, with ever-increasing balance of payments problems the inevitable results. Laissez-faire, leave us alone, the big boys inform Washington, and whatever will be, should be.

The pro-dwarf advocates, appealing to American tradition and human emotion, voice lugubrious concerns of megabuck greed and executive-suite corruption. Ever mindful of the vast numbers of small-business voters, they insist that governmental favoritism must give what small companies cannot get. Give us a break, give us a handout, the little guys beseech Congress, because although we're tiny on the balance sheet, we're huge on election day.

The little lobby has massive clout. They come to Washington with a long shopping list in one hand and a ballot-box club in the other. Tax benefits. Less paperwork. More contracts. Special biddings. Earmarked funds. Set-aside programs. Not unreasonable, but really necessary? Perhaps, but perhaps counterproductive—and that's where we confront authority and challenge the prevailing order.

PUBLIC POLICY ISSUES

While the above characterizations are a bit hyperbolic, they are also accurate. Industrial protection and company subsidies are hot topics of national debate. What should the government do for small businesses? It's one subject within an encyclopedia of economic conundrums. Should we subsidize American steel? Increase tariffs on textiles? Establish quotas for electronic chips? Bail out new Lockheeds and Chryslers? Break up AT&T? Leave IBM alone? Deregulate telecommunications, trucking, the airwaves, the airlines? Encourage research consortiums edging close to the antitrust precipice? The issues are endless—but none more important nor more volatile than the government's role in helping small business.

Small and medium-sized companies are a critical component of modern capitalism. They assure the efficiency of the economic sector by thwarting monopolies and secure the pluralism of the political sector by disrupting the hegemony between big business and big government. But neither fine tradition nor social value builds a healthy bottom line, an objective, consultants warn, hard to achieve and harder to sustain.

However vital for the country, small and medium-sized businesses must not be kept alive by artificial means; for not unlike brain-damaged humans maintained by machines, they would become living vegetables, objects of dole and pity, relics of the past, wards of the state, drained of vigor and energy, losing resolve and life-force, slowly degenerating, devoid of merit and bereft of worth. The only thing more tragic than the failure of small and medium-sized firms in the marketplace would be their counterfeit survival in the iron lung of bureaucracy.

Mid-sized companies must survive and prosper within the free-market system, not outside of it—facing its force directly, not protected by artificial barriers. Smaller firms must compete effectively and efficiently against the mammoths and the megaliths, guarding and guaranteeing their own existence. Anything less is self-defeating for the firm and counterproductive for society. Life dependent on largesse is life dependent on wind.

Can't do it, intones the well-schooled (and better paid) consultant; you can't compete against giants!

STRATEGIES OF DESTRUCTION

When a firm starts out on top and winds up on the bottom, there are lessons to be learned. When another firm in the same industry maintains a consistently high rate of return, in the face of much larger competitors, it too is worth a good look.

We investigate the mechanical instrument writing industry, *A.T. Cross* near the top, *Scripto* near the bottom. Our analysis builds to a comparison between the two firms in each Creative Strategy category.

Founded in 1923, Scripto was well positioned to dominate the writing instrument market in the United States. Why it didn't, and why it floundered, exemplifies the problems of mid-sized firms.[1]

Scripto's singular mission was to mass produce high-quality, low-price mechanical pencils. It was structured initially to be a one-product company stressing high-precision manufacturing and high-volume merchandizing. The formula was a good one, and Scripto earned rapid market acceptance, brand name identity, and industry dominance.

After World War II, Scripto's new president, seeing grander visions, broadened the strategic reach of the company. He articulated two objectives: (1) Scripto would become a "full-line" mechanical writing instrument firm (pens and pencils at all price points); and (2) Scripto would become the largest such manufacturer in the world. Some years later, in addition to full-line development and multinational expansion, Scripto introduced a cigarette lighter, the first of a series of diversified products. (Cigarette lighters per se are not as much diversification as they first appear. Similarities with writing instruments include materials, assembly techniques, and channels of distribution.)

By the early 1960s two new competitors began taking market leadership in specific segments of the low-price writing instrument market—Bic with the "stick" and Papermate with the "flair." The strategy of both companies emulated Scripto's original success— concentrate on a single product, produce it with high volume and high quality, and sell it at low price and to mass markets.

Scripto's strategy, on the other hand, broke and wandered. The company dropped its inexpensive ball-points and fountain pens as "low-margin products . . . uneconomical to produce and sell." It moved into new arenas, such as higher-priced writing instruments, and made wider, then wilder diversification moves through acquisitions and internal R&D—thermo-fax copier machines, wide-angle lens cameras, special butane lighters, tufted carpets, and imprinted ceramic products such as ashtrays. The theory was to increase profit margins with the higher-priced products, and reduce dependency on a single industry with the diversification. The theory was poor; the implementation worse.

Acquisitions were financed by debt, and sales revenues fell from a high of $36 million in 1965 to $31 million in 1973 (compared to Bic's steady increase from $6 million in 1964 to $58 million in 1973 to $179 million in 1979). Profit margins fell from 6.5 percent of sales in 1958 to 5.8 percent in 1963 to losses of 3.8 percent and 3.4 percent in 1969 and 1970 with bare profitability achieved in 1971–1973.

By the late sixties, Scripto, based in Atlanta, Georgia, was forced to cut back. The international program was curtailed and lighters were stressed. In the early seventies, another shift. Back to the low-price segment of the market; elimination of all products except writing instruments and lighters. Sights were still set on a full line of writing products, and markets across the board were attacked, from mass retail and chain stores to advertising and specialty sales. Scripto's retail market share in 1973 was 2 percent in all ball-point pens (priced $0.19–$0.98), compared with Bic's 66 percent and Papermate's 15 percent. (Scripto's market share had been 10 percent in the early sixties, and almost 20 percent in the fifties.) Only in mechanical pencils did Scripto preserve a decent position (13 percent in 1973).

Strategic confusion is underscored by Scripto's erratic advertising expenditures. Consumer advertising for writing instruments fell from $1.4 million in 1966 to a scant $56,000 in 1969, then shot back up to a healthy $1.8 million in 1971, only to drop back down again to $545,000 in 1973. (Advertising at Papermate and Bic, in contrast, rose steadily: from about $150,000 in 1963 to $2–$3 million in 1967 to $7–$9 million in 1973.) Scripto's fragmented, disrupted strategy is also reflected by its complementary advertising expenditures on cigarette lighters ($8600 in 1963; $533,000 in 1964; $312,000 in 1965; $1,006,000 in 1970; $175,000 in 1971; and a fat $"0" in 1973).

SIZE AND PROFITS

Perhaps the most widely repeated strategic axiom—and it is a mournful one for smaller companies—concerns the relationship between profitability and market share. A difference of ten percentage points in market share has been shown to be accompanied by a corresponding difference of about five percentage points in pretax profit (see Figure 2.1).

On both sides of the production–marketing coin, big companies wield more power: economies of scale in procurement, manufac-

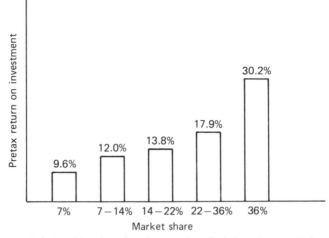

FIGURE 2.1. Relationship of market share and profitability. (*Source:* Sidney Schoeffler, Robert Bussell, and Donald Heany, "Impact of Strategic Planning on Profit Performance," *Harvard Business Review*, March–April 1974, p. 141.)

turing, and other cost components; and greater market power in bargaining, administering prices, and selling more units. The combination is potent, the results inevitable. For any given product, the dollars received go up and the expenses incurred go down; individual units are made for less and then sold for less, further increasing market share and accelerating market control. The feedback is positive, literally and figuratively, for firms that have dominant market positions; and negative, exceedingly negative, for firms that do not. Large-sized firms, in the end, simply obtain higher profits for any particular product. A success formula to be sure, and a powerful pathway to oblivion for firms at the other end of the stick.

A visual representation of this profitability–market share relationship was popularized by the Boston Consulting Group's (BCG) matrix of "star, cow, dog, question mark" (see Figure 2.2). Industry growth, high and low, is matched up with company market position, again high and low. We start in the lower left square. If the firm is in a low-growth industry but has a high share, then we can "milk" it for cash (since the high share means high profit generation and the low growth means low investment requirements)—hence the name "cow." If the firm is in a low-growth market and has a poor position, there is, according to the BCG, little hope for the sucker—hence the "dog" description. If the industry is growing rapidly and the firm's position is shooting skyward, that's ideal—hence the "star" accolade. If the firm has a poor position in an excellent industry, we are uncertain what to do—hence the "question mark" appellation.

Yet the hand may not be that pat, the script not that tight; for although the data on profitability and market share may be accurate, the conclusions may not. A contrarian *Harvard Business Review* article cautions that "One of the most dangerous inferences drawn from this generality [that profitability is proportional to market share, exemplified by the BCG's simplistic model] is that a low market share business faces only two strategic options: fight to increase its share, or withdraw from the industry. These prescriptions completely overlook the fact that, in many industries, companies having a low market share consistently outperform their large rivals and show very little inclination to either expand their share or withdraw from the fight."[2]

STRATEGIES OF CONSTRUCTION

A.T. Cross lives in the mechanical writing instrument industry along with Scripto, but it might as well be inhabiting the other

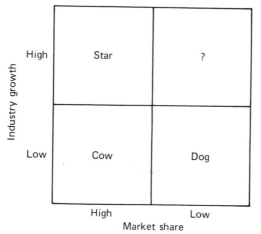

FIGURE 2.2. Strategic matrix. (The Boston Consulting Group Model.)

end of the universe. This is a company characterized by the high perceived worth of its products. The firm manufactures and markets fine precision instruments, gold and silver writing sets which are sold through selected stores of high repute (jewelry, department, stationery, gift, book, and other quality outlets). A.T. Cross's elegant, easily recognized pens and pencils set the standard of the industry. Indeed the company's claim that "a Cross writing instrument possesses an intrinsic value" is no idle boast.

In 1983 A.T. Cross earned $15.6 million on $118 million in revenues. Sales increased every year from 1973 ($32 million) to 1981 ($121 million), with net profits after taxes averaging a potent 15 + percent. Even in a down year, 1982 (revenues, $109 million), net profits were 13 percent of sales and dividends were increased for the fifteenth year in a row. Returns on stockholders' equity often approached or exceeded 30 percent. At the end of 1983, the financial position was extremely strong. The current ratio was 4.8–1, there was no long-term debt, and stockholders' equity was an almost incredible 80 percent of total assets (85 percent in 1982). Financial objectives call for returning 40–50 percent of annual earnings to shareholders.

A.T. Cross puts tremendous emphasis on its product. *Every* single fountain pen is hand-tested at the factory to assure that it meets design performance—not every ten-thousandth, according to some statistical formula, as is customary in large-scale manufacturing. Cross claims that they design, engineer, craft, and produce better writing instruments than anyone else in the world. Their standard operating procedure is that every employee is "a quality control inspector—from machine operator to assembler to packer. Anyone can reject an imperfect part handled in the course of a day's work, no matter what the reason."

New products and markets are carefully developed. "New product introductions," says the company, "are deliberate, thoroughly researched, and responsive to the changing marketplace." An example is the "Classic Black" line, which, following the adverse impact of the rising costs of gold and silver, now accounts for a considerable proportion of total sales.

All Cross writing instruments are guaranteed against mechanical defect for a lifetime, and, as the company is proud to point out, the service department has remained "remarkably small." They assert that "less than 2 percent of all units ever sold throughout the world has ever been returned, allowing Cross to maintain a 72-hour maximum turnaround policy on repairs." When *Fortune* magazine featured the nine best-made products in the world, Cross writing instruments were included in the select group.

Channels of distribution are matched to desired image. Retail stores are chosen and maintained at high levels. Another important market are those organizations that give Cross writing instruments and desk sets, with customized corporate emblems, as gifts and incentives to customers and employees. Over 400 "advertising specialty counselors" work this unique market.

Cross has a clear public image, and they work hard at building it. The primary goal of their marketing and advertising strategy? To create "greater awareness and recognition of the intrinsic value, the quality, and the image of Cross writing instruments around the world."

Since Walter Boss purchased the company in 1916, the Boss family has maintained control. (Three "Bosses" currently occupy the positions of president, chairman, and vice-chairman.) They continue to foster an internal environment where every employee is a craftsman and feels part of the company family.

Recently, A.T. Cross (based in Lincoln, Rhode Island) made its first acquisition: *Mark* Cross, the fine quality gift and leather goods company (based in New York), which markets through seventeen specialty stores and a well-known catalog. (The oddity of name similarity combined with high-quality product similarity has caused some confusion over the years. Also the closeness of founding dates, 1845 for Mark, 1846 for A.T.)

Although revenues ($10 million) and income are small in comparison, Messrs. Boss stress that Mark Cross's "reputation and respect in their field offer mutual benefits for our combined future." Maintaining accustomed caution, A.T. Cross does not contemplate any changes at Mark Cross, "but some time within the next two years, after proper planning, additional quality gift items may be introduced by A.T. Cross."

The president of Mark Cross, Edward Wasserberger, is pleased with his new Cross parent. He likes to tell the story of what can happen when big companies acquire small companies with elegant names. "It can become an ego trip for the new owners, and worse, a plaything for their wives. Nothing like a window design to encourage non-existent artistic talent."

MODELING STRATEGY FOR TOP AND BOTTOM

Good strategy can be learned by inverting poor performers as well as by emulating top performers. We again apply the ten Creative Strategies, the critical success categories for mid-sized firms. In each we compare and contrast Scripto and A.T. Cross. (Such a *"matched pair"* comparison is an important and recurring technique. See Chapter 9.)

1. *Dominance.* Cross controls the high-price, high-quality segment of the writing instrument market; Scripto controls nothing and is far outdistanced by major competitors in most areas (its full line claim should be more a moan than a boast).

2. *Product Emphasis.* Cross puts tremendous emphasis on products per se; Scripto stresses full-line capabilities.

3. *Distinctiveness.* Cross's writing instruments have clear identity, style, and cachet; Scripto's are unrecognizable.

4. *Focus.* Cross concentrates at the high end; Scripto goes full line. A.T. Cross's acquisition of Mark Cross, a concentric diversification bringing synergies of product and distribution, was its first. Scripto had gone on many adventures far outside its areas of expertise.

5. *High-Profile CEO.* The Boss family controls A.T. Cross, and has for almost seventy years; Scripto went through *five* presidents in less than ten years—each with contradictory strategies and opposing tactics.

6. *Employee Opportunity.* Cross gives employees intrinsic worth and a sense of participation in the company; Scripto faced "vocalism and absenteeism" among its labor force—manufacturing areas were noisy, dirty, and hot.

7. *Efficient Innovation.* Cross innovates with extreme caution and preparation; Scripto jumped widely and wildly, with large allocations to questionable projects (e.g., $1.5 million in R&D for that wide-angle lens camera).

8.   *External Perception.* Cross brought out its Classic Black line just as precious metal prices were making its traditional line too expensive; Scripto oscillated between high- and low-priced writing instruments, scattergunning products and misreading public tastes.

9.   *Growth–Profits Tradeoff.* Cross has maintained extremely high profit levels while enjoying good but not spectacular growth rates; Scripto desired to grow and become the "largest in the world," but wound up neither profitable nor large.

10.   *Flexibility.* Since Cross has maintained a steady product line, its powerful balance sheet would facilitate quick moves; Scripto, financed by debt, had become burdened and restricted.

THE EMERGENT REVOLUTION

There has been deep concern that medium-sized firms are no longer viable; that they have lost their competitive position; that they cannot keep up with technology, marketing needs, production capacities, distributional systems. Mid-sized firms, it is said, are languishing. The whipsawing violence of a decade's inflation and recession, we are told, has drained financial strength and assaulted psychic vitality, pinning them to the economic mat. Mid-sized firms, proclaim MBA types with terminals flickering and statistics flowing, are a relic of the past.

Yet there is a different tale to tell. Computer projection can blow dynamic perspective. The numbers are vague but the vision is clear. Some see medium-sized firms as hardy and resilient, as poised for great surges in technological development and business breakthroughs, as resonant with forecasted trends—as the new leaders of a new age. It is nothing less, goes the rumor, than industrial *transformation*—there is no mere "transition" here.

Mid-sized firms, say some futurists, have a competitive edge. Their new advantage is catalyzed by an ability to commercialize original ideas more quickly and to build novel structures more easily. It is a fertile climate that now exists for smaller companies;

for entrepreneurs with courage and executives with foresight; for a whole new wave of creative and innovative managers. Mid-sized firms can expect, if they recognize the challenge and position themselves properly, to share the revolution. Indeed they may trigger it. Mid-sized firms, we proffer, can forge the future.

Several forces are shaping this economic eruption:

☐ First, the sheer abundance of the American environment. Historically, the United States had it all—unlimited resources, unrestricted labor, unbounded imagination. Despite a variety of recent shortages, we still possess that abundance, and our populace is bursting to enjoy it once more. The result is greatly enhanced demand for new products and services, and the resultant opportunity for responsive firms to provide them.

☐ Second, the role of innovation. Scientific discovery and technology development are inextricably tied to the ingenuity of the American character, to what Alexander de Tocqueville called the greatest American trait, the willingness to innovate. Innovation, by all accounts, opens unparalleled occasion for widening markets, the expansion fed by fulfilling current needs and stimulating future ones.

☐ Third, the rapidity of change. In certain areas of high technology, generations are often measured in months, turnaround time in weeks. The capacity to respond with speed and intensity is vital. The ability to shift company resources and focus on new areas can create instant competitive advantage no larger organization can match.

☐ Fourth, the narrowcasting of demand. A world weaned on cable television and personal computers will not be satisfied by generalized products and services. Individual preference has increasing visibility in mass media and consumer outlets. Our populace is requiring more personalized items and options, each crafted specially for small segments of the market with particular wants and interests. The burgeoning demand for different products and services means that each must be manufactured or provided in smaller quantities. Such a diminished size of product run or reduced rate of similar service skews the market toward firms that can produce fewer numbers more efficiently; these are companies that do not have massive plant facilities or large personnel overheads.

☐ Fifth, the role of government as stimulator. Increasingly, both state and federal government are finding ways to encourage smaller firms to compete in the marketplace. Mechanisms include investment incentives, tax breaks, and the allocation of various resources.

☐ Sixth, and perhaps most important, the modern manager. Here is the raw energy to fire the engine of economic resurgence. These are the risk takers, the gutsy types who built this country, those with fire in their bellies as well as brains in their heads. The last decade nurtured men and women with fresh ideas—active, independent people eager to break ranks and give chase. Business school graduates, for example, are more inclined to work in smaller firms, where they sense opportunity to implement individual vision. Young people today want to exercise leadership, to be closer to decision-making, to be part of the control process.

THEORY BUSTERS

Market share low? Surrounded by giants? Consultants insulting? The market share matrix bugging you? Sitting in its worst sector? If your company has a small share of a flat industry, it is a "dog." What to do with dogs? Put them, say the experts, to sleep.

But what about small-share companies making good money in flat industries? Sorry if they confuse the overeducated, but what to do with them? We examine three such beauties—apostates from conventional wisdom, living fossils expected long dead—Unifi, in the yarn business; Republic Gypsum, in plaster; and AFG, in glass. What makes them tick?[3]

Commodities businesses all, these three companies compete in arenas where small should be fried and swallowed whole. Or so theory dictates. How in mature industries to thwart economies of scale? How to defy curve cost advantages? Watch.

Nobody calls the business of texturizing polyester filaments (adding bulk and stretch) high growth. Nor was Unifi's 2 percent share ten years ago anything to brag about. A case for the ASPCA? Not Unifi, which earned in 1983 $8.3 million on $176 million of fiber sales.

In wallboards, U.S. Gypsum (USG) and National Gypsum are billion-dollar steamrollers. But look who got flattened when Republic Gypsum's operating margin of 13.5 percent tripled USG's and quadrupled National's. Republic's sales? About $30 million in fiscal 1983, mostly in one plant. (In the first nine months of fiscal 1984 Republic earned $5 million on $32 million in volume.)

When AFG was formed in 1978 by consolidating two long-losing glassmakers with a combined share of 7 percent, management consultants must have shaken their heads with pity. Pity whom? In 1983 AFG increased profits 50 percent, to $14 million (on sales of $217 million), while glass giants PPG Industries and Libbey-Owens-Ford reported earnings declines and much smaller margins.

Unifi

They install the most modern machines while competitors still depreciate older ones. It's a high-tech push for productivity at Unifi's plant in Yadkinville, North Carolina. "In the last five years I've junked 62 texturizing machines," boasts CEO G. Allen Mebane, not a Harvard MBA.

Count them. Over 100 new mechanical marvels, made mostly in Germany, spinning yarn onto Unifi's 22,000 spindles at 28 miles per hour. Since Mebane cofounded Unifi in 1971, he has increased output per production worker fivefold.

The cost of modernizing has been high—depreciation as a percentage of original plant and equipment is double the industry average—but the cost of *not* modernizing would have been higher. Check the numbers: labor cost per pound of output has been halved, down to 6 cents; return on equity has averaged 27 percent; debt, once forebodingly high, has been thinned down to 38 percent of capitalization.

Curiously, once one of the smallest polyester texturizers, Unifi, headquartered in Greensboro, is now one of the largest. Since it is also one of the lowest-cost producers as well, some consultants might believe that its large size is the *cause* of its low cost—validating textbook theory of "riding down the experience curve."[4] Historical reality, however, proves the reverse. Unifi *became* the largest in size *because* it was *already* the lowest in cost—not the reverse. Quite a difference, that.

What happened to the giants? Celanese quit texturizing in 1982. Most of the rest are long gone. All that remains are one privately held firm and the captive production of the fabric houses.

"Monsanto, Celanese, Hoechst, Phillips, Rohm & Haas, they all stubbed their toes," notes Mebane. "It's the chemical company mentality. Monsanto had a plant that made 280 million pounds of fiber and texturized probably 30 million pounds a year. They had 225 salaried people just on the factory floor." Unifi churns out 220 million pounds a year—with only 185 salaries plus 826 production workers.

Cash is being thrown off as fast as that yarn, but Unifi is investing much of it in advanced R&D. Automatic yarn testers are being developed with MIT. Mebane is considering $22 million of industrial robots. Robots in low tech? This boy doesn't stop. Unifi is on a roll, with new applications for its yarn seen on the horizon.

So the "dog" became dominant. That's not supposed to happen, ever. How did it? Which Creative Strategies were working their magic? *Focus* and *coherence* all the way, amplified by *efficient innovation* and fueled by a *gutsy CEO*.

Republic Gypsum

"We're not big enough to affect the price," states O. Max Montgomery, chief executive of Republic Gypsum located in Garland, Texas, near Dallas. No kidding, pardner; 2 percent of the U.S. plasterboard market isn't going to nick U.S. Gypsum's 37 percent or National Gypsum's 27 percent.

Plant capacity is the issue in the industry, more to the point, keeping plants filled. Republic can produce 315 million square feet a year, double its 1964 output with the same manpower. But market reach, as much as plant efficiency, is the key. The Republic plant can serve both Dallas and Oklahoma City quite profitably. But when construction slackens and demand drops, the company must expand its selling radius—going south to San Antonio and Houston. They must meet the local prices, absorbing the extra freight and taking reduced margins. Can't the big boys do the same thing? No—they would just be trading dollars, taking from one plant and giving to another. Thus Republic's 94 percent capacity in 1982 was well above the industry average of 70 percent.

No sloughing off that freight expense, though. Compare the cost of gypsum, $3 a ton all quarried and crushed, with the cost of shipping from the plant to Houston, a whopping $34 a ton. Republic's solution is to operate a fleet of trucks, in conjunction with—and here's the clever part—a building supplies company in Dallas. So the trucks head south with plasterboard, and when they return back north, they're backhauling shingles and steel. This wholesaling business about breaks even, but absorbed in the costs is a good bite of those shipping charges. *Flexibility and opportunism* make a nice combination (Creative Strategy number ten).

Montgomery believes that Republic's own trucks augment customer confidence, and he pounds the point in selling. Competitors such as U.S. Gypsum use common carriers. "They lose control of it once it's on the truck." A late delivery delays a whole project, with hourly rates for machines and workers piling up.

A bit of encouragement to our consultant/theorist friends. Don't be too upset with Republic's low-share success. They certainly corroborate another classic maxim—stick to company competencies. They didn't and it hurt. Republic's numerous adventures into diverse areas—from mobile home construction to sawmills to oil and gas exploration—all failed. Now Montgomery is content to play his basic game plan and wait out the recession. Leaning to the profits side of the growth–profits tradeoff really makes sense.

AFG Industries

When Dee Hubbard took charge, the predecessor company was losing $1 million a month. "They had 28 different bank accounts. Sales would enter an order, manufacturing would decide not to run it, and never tell sales."

Hubbard went to work. He closed down outmoded plants, laid off 600 workers, and fired two-thirds of the salesmen and half the administrative staff. He brought in a brainy glass engineer from Ford and ran production faster. (He demanded and received concessions from creditors as a prior condition. No fool, this fellow.) "Even the people we laid off told me they didn't like it but they knew it had to be done."

In six months the company was breaking even, and in another ten had earned a whopping $6.8 million in profits. With that fresh kitty Hubbard bought AFG—no winner itself, having lost money in thirteen of its twenty years.

Again the Hubbard treatment—close, lay off, fire, hire, run faster. One more acquisition later, AFG was number five in flat glass—the classic trough for mid-sized firms. So wherefore all the profits for this Kingsport, Tennessee company?

Not from a specialized niche, and that's the interesting part. Hubbard dropped his two largest customers precisely because they were *too* specialized. When other glass manufacturers pushed into these high-margin arenas (such as with metallic-coated glass), he got out. Fat margins sound great, theoretically; but who needs all the competition? (And in price wars, what happens to the margins?)

Home window glass was a different story. A commodity, sure, it cost one-tenth of the special stuff. To make matters worse, lots of factories were turning out home windows, including The Majors. Why then Hubbard's interest? In a word, *quality*. AFG simply stressed the pure product, and turned out a better one (Creative Strategy number two). Credit that brainy engineer, and Hubbard for bringing him in.

The engineer, by the way, was given some stock for his efforts. That's nice. It's worth about $20 million. "I'm a strong believer in incentives," says Hubbard. Salesmen, too, have profited by this philosophy, earning twice as much as before. They drive Mercedes but they still produce. Here's one CEO that gives employees real opportunity.

Hubbard himself? Not to worry. He's got $42 million in stock, and reports say, 100 racehorses and flashy jewelry. "It was a lot of fun," he reflects. High-profile CEOs, flashy jewelry or not, are what mid-size companies need—especially to resuscitate basic industry.

ORIENTATION AND APPROACH

Must firms be industry leaders to be perennially successful? Of course, sniff consultants as they fold up their portable computers. We disagree.

Our search spans over 150 top-performing medium-sized companies, and indeed one criterion for selection is that each top-performing firm must be in an industry dominated by one or more giants many times its size. Yet our smaller firms regularly outperform their massive rivals. The underlying reasons are crucial. More important than governmental legislation, far beyond a firm's control, are the emergent "critical success strategies," the ten Creative Strategies, well within a firm's control.

We explore by example and principle—case and construct, practice and theory, world and model—with each mode articulating with the other. We seek general principles arising out of specific situations. We induce first, then deduce—strategic management is no game of logic; there are no "given" absolute axioms; there are no strict rules easily dissectible and readily discernible.

Relative performance is our touchstone. We compare relatively good mid-sized performance with relatively poor mid-sized performance, matching by pairs companies similar in size and product markets (e.g., A.T. Cross and Scripto in the sixties).

We compare and contrast the two companies comprising each pair. Why does one firm perform consistently better than the other? What factors are relevant? What factors are irrelevant? What elements are present? What elements are absent? What happens when the "matched-pair" data are averaged across a large data base? What signals emerge from noise? What operational concepts come blazing to light? And finally, how can other companies apply these Creative Strategies in similar situations?

We employ various techniques of observation and inquiry, each supported by content analysis of corporate documents. We look for company clues—strategies, structures, styles, fingerprints— whatever factors and figures correlate with success. Quiet nuances of corporate culture often supersede stated positions of business strategy. Such delicacies we treasure.

CHAPTER 3

TAGGING MID-SIZED FIRMS

What Are They?
How Do They Look?

"Let's get a piece of that deal. We share the downside; we should share the upside."

Take equity ownership along with asset security? The suggestion challenged tradition for the large savings and loan. But challenging tradition was commonplace for Charles E. Hurwitz, the brilliant Texas financier who remains a mystery in his home state though he is a legend across the country.[1]

Hurwitz is running many companies; a fascinating mix, they're all mid-sized of sorts, and all successful to be sure. The stories are not simple, but each business success can be traced to the same singular source—the man sees value and gain when others flee trouble and loss.

When Charles Hurwitz acquires a little part, everyone listens a whole lot. What type of man sports such a stellar track record for turning around fledgling firms and managing medium-sized companies? He'll get the Creative Strategy treatment.

We start with that savings and loan. A condominium developer, it seems, was requesting some $5 million in project construction loans from a subsidiary of Houston's United Financial Group, now Texas' second largest savings and loan after a Hurwitz-inspired merger with First American Financial, also of Houston. The builder had a good reputation, and the project seemed reasonable; but the man had little of his own cash in the deal and the area was known for quick swings in the market. Yet United needed to place money at good interest rates. The key question—should they spring for this deal?

It was the first board meeting for the soft-spoken Texan whose business impact ricochets daily from Wilshire Boulevard in Los Angeles through vast real estate and energy holdings to Wall Street in New York. His companies had recently become the S & L's largest shareholder, and the board meeting was a necessary part of his increasing participation. Reputation enhances influence, of course, and though he had expected to remain discreetly quiet, his opinion was solicited. After all, when Hurwitz invests, value increases—that's the man's record. His companies now owned almost 25 percent of United, with options for more.

"Look, our rates are barely over prime," observed Hurwitz in his deliberate tone, "we're bearing much risk and not getting much reward. We'll have to be doing some work tracking the project. Suppose we put the money out in bonds? We'd do almost as well with virtually no risk and no work. Risks can be taken, but rewards must be matched." Charles paused, made contact with twenty or so attentive faces, then made his point, "Let's tell them we'll provide the loan, but we want half that upside."

It was a good deal all around. The developer got his loan granted and his project started. United placed the funds and received 50 percent of the equity. It was the kind of deal he likes—everyone wins with big potential. Charles Hurwitz was starting to work his magic at United.

The United-American investment was vintage Hurwitz. Savings and loans nationally, whipsawed by long-term low-interest loans and short-term high-interest deposits, and hamstrung by restrictive regulations, were apparently crippled. United had lost $18.6 million in 1982 after losing $12.4 million in 1981; American's respective losses were $17.8 million and $3 million. The net worths of both companies had been eroded and were now dangerously thin. Their stock prices reflected disaster.

But when others see disaster, Hurwitz finds opportunity. Here was "fundamental value," a favorite phrase, and a large financial base, a favorite asset. Here, also, was real "leverage," a favorite technique—the opportunity to convert an investment of several million into control of several *billion*.

Merging the two companies seemed a natural. Combining United Savings's fifty-eight branches (across Texas) with First American's thirty-five branches (Houston area) enables the new entity to compete more effectively in attracting a larger depositor and borrower base in Texas—especially important considering recent trends toward deregulation and the looming competition of national financial powers (such as Merrill Lynch, Citibank, Shearson Lehman/ American Express, Sears Financial, and the major regional banks). Furthermore, the efficiencies of eliminating double overheads would help turn bottom-line ink back to black.

The move seems a good one, and after the usual litigation and minor protestations, apparently successful. United is being revitalized with energy and confidence; profitability is being restored, and stock prices are going up.

But Hurwitz is just beginning. A recent United acquisition of a large minority position in Weingarten Realty—which owns major shopping centers—beat out a well-known Texas family who, it was rumored, was willing to pay a pretty premium. He has also devised a fascinating plan to sell off up to forty-eight bank branches including their deposit liabilities and all real and personal property attributable to those branches. If he pulls it off, United will get a healthy premium—very healthy. A couple of Wall Street powerhouses are considering the transaction; if consummated, it would augment United's net worth by about $150 million, more than doubling what they've got in one shot. And with the higher net worth, don't forget, would come greater leveraging power. This is Charles Hurwitz at his best.

What's the current extent of Hurwitz's domain? United has an asset base of $3.5 billion, and combined with the billion or so of assets from his other companies (see below), Charles now influences or controls one of the largest financial–industrial empires in Texas. Some may call it "lucky timing," but Hurwitz is a master of "lucky timing."

Sheer size is no turn-on for this publicity-shy financial sleuth. Maximizing value is the name of his game. Options for aggressive financial development are being considered at United, innovative ideas for building company wealth. Nothing less than strong regional presence is projected, with merchant banking strengths on the national level a possibility. Asset valuation and investment creativity are his forte, and never, I can assure you, has he been called "timid."

Take a recent investment by a United subsidiary in an undervalued New York Stock Exchange listed company called Castle & Cook, the makers of Dole Pineapple and Bumble Bee Tuna. (Castle & Cook also has vast acreage in Hawaii—some say that's the "value" Charles saw.) Hurwitz's companies took the position in Castle & Cook stock when the latter was making its unsuccessful bid for Dr. Pepper. (A complex jungle, the takeover scene.) After a brief but acrimonious battle, Castle & Cook bought back United's stock, producing a $9 million capital gain in less than three months—an annualized rate of return of about 90 percent. (Sure beats those 25-year 8½ percent mortgages.) Another Hurwitz company (MCO, see below) made about $4 million on the deal—but a quick score, it appears, was not what Charles was seeking here. Augmenting long-term value is his usual objective.

Charles E. was born in Kilgore—an "East Texas farm boy," he calls himself with a disarming smile—the son of Mr. and Mrs. Hyman Hurwitz, well-established clothing merchants in the area. Just six years after graduating from the University of Oklahoma, with only a few years of army and investment experience behind him, the 27-year-old wunderkind began the "Hedge Fund of America" with $54 million. The event was a milestone. It was said to have been the first publicly underwritten hedge fund, the largest public offering ever in Texas, and the third largest in the United States. Hurwitz did, according to *Forbes*, what a dozen top New York money managers had been talking about for a year. ("Hedging" is the practice of selling stocks "short," so that if the price drops, you make money. Hurwitz's fund invested as a garden-variety mutual fund, but ventured into more speculative areas as well.)

Charles remembers an incident at the time: "I was flying from San Antonio, where I had my brokerage firm, to New York, where I was negotiating the fund. I had my head buried in stock charts when I noticed more than casual interest from the elderly gentlemen sitting next to me. I nodded, and he asked what I was doing. I proceeded to give him an education in hedge funds, explaining that I was putting together the first one to be offered publicly. Now you have to remember that I was all of 25 or 26 at the time. 'Impossible,' the gentlemen said, 'it can't be done.' Who, I wondered, was this spoilsport? I asked for his card and turned white. It was Joe King, the Chairman of the Board of Eastman, Dillon, one of the most powerful investment banks at the time. Well, now comes the best part. When the deal was done, I went up to Eastman, Dillon and asked to see Mr. King. I couldn't get past the secretaries. Suddenly Mr. King appeared. He recognized me and asked whatever became of my hedge fund. I told him it was done, and that his firm was the single largest investor, taking $17 million. How did he react? He was just thrilled. He took me into their vaunted partner's room and told everyone how he was getting too old, how young people are the life's blood of new ideas. . . ."

Hurwitz assembled on the fund's blue-ribbon board of directors a constellation of public stars including Dr. Willard Libby, Nobel Laureate; General Thomas Powers, former head of the Strategic Air Command; Dr. Paul McCracken, head of President Eisenhower's Council of Economic Advisers; and Dr. George Kozmetsky, the cofounder of Teledyne, a true visionary who had recently come to Texas to become dean of the School of Business at the University of Texas at Austin. The latter would come to have profound influence on the young financier extraordinaire.

Two years later, at 29, Charles was managing over $150 million of investors' funds and had gained notice in a popular book, *New Breed on Wall Street*. His simple secret? Asked at the time, he responded in characteristic modesty, "I guess we just work harder . . . we think we're good." (Although Hurwitz makes easy use of the plural pronoun "we"—and indeed works with many first-rate associates—one gets closer and quicker to the truth by substituting the singular pronoun "I." As a close friend commented, "It used to be that virtually all ideas came from Charles. But now that he's building a first-rate team, he's changing things. Charles is a good listener; he encourages his executives. But can he ever cut to the heart of a deal! He's seen them all, and goes right for the make-or-break issues—that bottom line.")

Several years and one run-in with the SEC later, Charles made his first move on a major corporation. This "investment" did not turn out, as the cliché goes, "just for investment purposes." Managerial control was not his objective, but that's exactly what he got. ("I try to remain uninvolved with the companies I invest in, but sometimes it doesn't work out that way.") The move would change his life.

When Hurwitz acquired 13 percent of McCulloch Oil Corporation in 1978, it seemed a most unlikely takeover target. In two years the company had lost $63 million. Its sprawling real estate properties (such as Lake Havasu City and Fountain Hills in Arizona) were poorly managed and hemorrhaging barrels of red ink; its oil and gas production was in decline; worse still, the company was entwined with a tangle of private lawsuits and public investigations by the Securities & Exchange Commission and the Federal Trade Commission. Yet where others saw bankruptcy and sought escape, Hurwitz detected "value" and sought gain.

Hurwitz began by acquiring options to purchase 2.2 million shares from Black & Decker at between $3.50 and $3.625 per share. He paid a nominal sum for the option (ten big bucks), and had a few weeks to study the company. His first investigations uncovered some serious problems, and he was undecided whether to proceed. Then a bombshell from McCulloch. The company made a formal announcement that they would fight Hurwitz. Well, that decided it. Hurwitz promptly exercised the options. Coincidentally, the annual meeting of the board was coming up, and within weeks Hurwitz had representation. Let no one misconstrue Charles' genteel southern manner.

Those shares? Oh yes, quite a bargain—"We made a nice buy," says Charles in his usual understatement. The stock headed skyward as Hurwitz made maximum use of McCulloch's assets, sheltered by a tax-loss carryforward of $85 million. Why did he want such a sick company? Hurwitz deadpanned: "To make it well."

And "make it well" he did indeed. The turnaround was remarkable, and dozens of corporate moguls must have kicked themselves for not having seen what Hurwitz had. But more than vision was required. Add tenacity and guts to the formula. Moving into McCulloch's sumptuous offices near UCLA in West Los Angeles (which, by the way, still embarrasses Charles—he would like to sublease), Hurwitz took charge. He sold off certain properties, restructured faulty contracts, made a whopping settlement on a coal property assumed worthless, and spun off most of the energy businesses into a separate public company.

McCulloch now boasts a robust net worth approaching $100 million and assets exceeding $500 million. Business interests have expanded dramatically with new acquisitions of land and equities. The stock market took note; McCulloch's price quadrupled in three years. Accolades galore. Just don't forget persistence and commitment.

The style of the MCO transaction, as much as its substance, gives insight into the man and his methods. At first, the entrenched MCO management vowed to fight their unwanted suitor with "all the legal means at our disposal." But when Charles was appointed chairman and chief executive officer less than two years later, these same people called him "imaginative and hard working." An ill-conceived lawsuit against the newcomer was dropped voluntarily. Hurwitz hadn't, according to insiders, pushed his weight around, but won over company managers with his "analytical mind, unshakable tenacity and low-key but affable nature."

Indeed, one high-ranking executive with much of his net worth tied up in McCulloch stock confessed, in submitting his resignation, that he was getting out of the way. Though invited to stay on, he declined. Why? As he said at the time, "Charles can make my stock a helluva lot more valuable than I can."

One thing that turned the skeptics around was Hurwitz's penetrating analysis of a strange transaction. McCulloch, it seems, had tried to solve some legal difficulties by optioning off its vast properties. But, as Hurwitz pointed out, the deal left the company holding the bag for residual liabilities. If the property appreciated, the options would be exercised and McCulloch's participation would be minuscule. "It was a classic case," recalls Hurwitz, "of giving up 100 percent of the upside and getting stuck with 100 percent of the downside." Hurwitz used all his resources to undo the mess. He brought in a new Big Eight firm to audit the old Big

Eight firm. Ultimately, he negotiated a recision of the transaction, which, one might add, appears to have been made at a length less than arms'.

The recoupment to McCulloch stockholders? The land holdings are immense—thousands of acres in Arizona and Colorado. "Very material," is all Hurwitz will say. Try nine figures, Charles.

Hurwitz made the McCulloch acquisition, whose name he changed to MCO Holdings, through Federated Development Company, a real estate and reinsurance firm that he acquired through a tender offer in 1973. Federated itself is a developer. The most interesting property is in Rancho Mirage, California, where the Hurwitz team (led by Dr. Barry Munitz, see below) lined up former President Gerald Ford and Ambassador Leonard Firestone to support rezoning petitions and referendums regarding the development of a virginal 600-acre plot on a majestic mountain site. The dispute made the national press, since Barbara Sinatra and husband Frank were standing in the opposite corner. At last check, Federated had cleared all but the final hurdles and was negotiating with some of the world's most luxurious hotels for anchoring the new resort.

With the Federated investment in MCO, Hurwitz began the leveraging of corporate control—leveraging, that's Hurwitz's long suit. Today, for example, Hurwitz controls Federated; Federated controls MCO; MCO controls the Simplicity Pattern Company (which, along with its high-share sewing pattern business, discussed later in this chapter, has almost $100 million available in cash and securities for discretionary investments). To continue, Simplicity bought Twin-Fair, an American Stock Exchange real estate company with interests in New York and Florida (and a nice $27 million tax-loss carryforward available for sheltering future profits); and Twin-Fair in turn purchased Maxxus, a highly liquid, former real estate investment trust also active in the southeast. Recently, Simplicity announced the sale of its original pattern business, retaining its cash, real estate, and a hefty $150+ million in net worth. (Following the long tale/tail?)

Hurwitz has used Simplicity as an active investment vehicle. He purchased 12.4 percent of Amstar, the world's largest sugar company in mid-1983. When Hurwitz declined an invitation from management to bid for the entire company, Simplicity was able to realize a huge capital gain of some $18 million in a matter of months when Amstar was sold in a leveraged buyout—an annualized rate of return of close to 100 percent before taxes. (In commenting on Hurwitz's leadership of Simplicity, the respected Value-Line investment service stated, "The new management is accomplishing its goals . . . the best may be yet to come. . . . We have no doubt management will increase Simplicity's worth dramatically.")

Though he still lives in Houston, Hurwitz is in either Los Angeles or New York almost every week. "Whatever time is necessary" is what he devotes. At home or on weekends, it doesn't matter, he's always accessible. Does his daily absence hurt his companies? Hurwitz is on the phone constantly, then muses, "I know some people who show up every other week whose presence is felt more than others who show up every day."

"We are proud of the way we manage companies" is his one boast. "We've been able to turn some around and make them successful." The effective management of his numerous businesses is Hurwitz's prime objective; the building of corporate value and stockholder wealth is where his sight is always set.

He is also involved with several smaller companies, a couple of which are start-ups—the one in hardware retailing, Home Centers of America (based in San Antonio), is an astonishing success. Hurwitz led the initial risk capital for Home Centers, and then engineered a public offering in May 1983—both before the company had generated a dollar's worth of sales. Within less than one year annualized volume was running at about $120 million, and the company was starting to spurt black ink on the bottom line. A new unit in Houston is projected to do about $20 million alone, and chain-wide volume is expected to approach $250 million next year. Home Centers recently sold to K-Mart, which paid $11/share; Hurwitz and his group had paid $.20 little more than one year before. The venture is being called one of the most successful in start-up retailing. The key to success here, as it is in almost every business, is management. The Home Center team is as good as they come, and it was on them that Charles placed his bet.

What's the worst accusation you can cast at Charles Hurwitz? Claim he is running his companies for his personal benefit at the expense of stockholders—an innuendo popping up now and again.

Those closest to him aver that the opposite is true, and the reason, they say, is the basic character of the man as well as the self-serving motivation.

"We are investing our own money," Hurwitz states, pointing out that the great majority of his own net worth is tied up in his companies. "My personal interests are right on the line with all the shareholders."

Hurwitz runs his companies more like an "owner" than a "professional manager," more like a proprietor than the proverbial "hired gun." Executive perks are severely attentuated, even his own salary level is below comparative salaries at other companies. Executive aircraft, for example, are sold off in Hurwitz companies, not bought. (The McCulloch "air force" had half a dozen planes until Hurwitz grounded and dismantled it.) Dividends are canceled when they are not supported by operating profits (as happened with Simplicity). The proof is the results, increasing value for all stockholders. Even his critics grant him that.

Not everything works, of course. An innovative scheme to exchange equity in a new company for real estate was terminated at a cost of $9 million. The venture was almost "too successful," with properties exceeding $1 billion being offered. Before the deal could be closed, the market changed, and Hurwitz wouldn't risk the potential stock price drop for investors and reputation drop for himself.

If you ask around, you might hear that Hurwitz is "a young man in too much of a hurry." A recent lawsuit claimed that he was trying to "squeeze out" shareholders of Federated by only offering current market prices (when the real value is supposedly much higher) and by forcing small shareholders to "round up" in a large reverse split (paying more money in to avoid being bought out). Hurwitz counters that "We were just responding to people who, having made 10, 20, 30 times their money, wanted to cash out." (In fact the price being offered was the highest at which the shares had ever sold, and although Hurwitz dropped the plan, Federated's chief financial officer and second largest stockholder took advantage of the opportunity and sold back his shares to the company at that precise price.)

Controversy is nothing new to this Kilgore favorite son. The 1971 SEC charge that he and forty-three others had engaged in improper securities trading is denied with remorse, not bitterness. "It was the worst experience of my business career. Because I was in the middle of a financing, I had to settle immediately. Unfortunately the connotation of a consent to settle belies the facts." Reputation, you can tell, is exceedingly important to the man. (As a footnote to the incident, the person most associated with Hurwitz in the contested transaction was not in the middle of a financing and so chose to fight. The battle took ten years, and in 1981 the SEC withdrew all charges.)

Several years ago, one New York investment banker made reference to Hurwitz's past skirmishes with regulatory bodies; the connotation was that the Texan was not "blue-chip" enough for his firm. Some checking around turned up the fact that the banker's firm had lost a bygone corporate confrontation with Charles. Today, the story is different. Entranced by Hurwitz's sparkling success record, the "Blue-Chippers" on the Street now compete for his favors—including the above investment banking firm.

As for the future? "There's a lot of value out there," says Charles. "We like to invest in companies where we think there's opportunity, where we can put up our own money and use our expertise to build equity."

What about Charles Hurwitz the person? Note the people with whom he's closest—it's a shortcut to real insight. The group is remarkable, hardly a one framed in the traditional corporate image. All have superb academic backgrounds. Some say they build the mystique.

Dr. George Kozmetsky has been a partner for fifteen years; he's on all the corporate boards and is chairman of MCO Resources, the oil, gas, and geothermal company (also in Houston). A Renaissance man for modern times, with significant interests in academic frontiers and public policy, he is Hurwitz's mentor and confidante. (He is currently Economic Associate to the University of Texas Board of Regents as well as president of the IC^2 Institute, a business think tank.) It is sheer joy to watch Dr. Kozmetsky, who is expert in both finance and technology, analyze a business problem and prepare it for solution.

Dr. Barry Munitz, an academic wunderkind, never managed a company in his life before Hurwitz offered him the presidency of Federated Development (and more recently, chairmanship of

United's Executive Committee). His background? Not a Wharton MBA in finance, but a Princeton Ph.D. in comparative literature! Though he had advised major corporations on governance and board representation for ten years, Dr. Munitz was known for academic administration, not Wall Street deal making. He had been offered several presidencies of well-known universities, but never a corporation. He had been academic vice-president of the University of Illinois at the astounding age of 29, and enjoyed a much praised tenure as chancellor of the University of Houston. Managing major academic institutions is increasingly akin to running major business organizations,[2] but nonetheless it takes vision, foresight, and even daring to bring such an individual into an exploding entrepreneurial environment. Give Charles the credit: Dr. Munitz is a superb business administrator, a creative and resourceful executive—and, interestingly enough, close to Hurwitz in age. He has brought great human skills to the combined group. "Charles makes the deals," says Barry. "Then I go to work." "Barry runs the store," says Charles. "So I can look for new locations."

Dr. William Leone, with a Ph.D. in nuclear engineering and a fine executive record in major corporations, runs MCO Holdings. A longtime associate of Dr. Kozmetsky, Leone had been president of Rheem Manufacturing and City Investing International and is now a key member of the Hurwitz team. Praised for his motivation of managers, Dr. Leone is a patient, practical man with a good, steady hand. He excels in managing complex situations.

Mr. Ezra Levin, practitioner and professor of corporate law and SEC regulations, is outside general counsel and sits on the boards of most Hurwitz corporations. (Hurwitz met Levin on opposite sides of a long-ago financing deal. "Next time," said Hurwitz, "I want that fellow sitting next to me.") Cut from the same mold as the other Hurwitz confidantes, Levin was an adjunct professor at Columbia University where he created an undergraduate course on the sociology of law and legal institutions. He is also vice-chairman of the New York Conference on Soviet Jewry, and is active in community affairs.

Charles Hurwitz is a private person. He prefers hard work to superficial publicity, and allows the "increased value" of his companies to make its own statement. His energy is boundless, his enthusiasm infectious. "Every day is too short, every night too long; I can't wait to get up in the morning, I don't like to quit in the evening."

He is not, however, a workaholic. The family is important His wife, Barbara, whom he met in college, shares his life, and time is spent with their two teenage sons. He also takes substantial interest in community activities. He is involved actively with M. D. Anderson Hospital in Houston and is a close friend of its president, Dr. Charles LeMaistre. No traditional fund raiser, Charles is aiding the commercial development of biotechnology—a fresh source of potential funding for medical research institutes.

His intimacy with M. D. Anderson is not random. Several years ago, Charles's mother was dying of cancer there. His father would make the long drive from Kilgore frequently, spending endless days with her in the hospital. Then, inexplicably, in one of those bitter quirks of human existence, his father too became afflicted. The cancer was virulent and growing fast. Both parents, tragically and ironically, were in the same hospital at the same time. "They were wheeled to the operating rooms together," Charles recalls with voice quavering, "holding hands."

A short time after, both were dead. Some five years later, a nurse remembered their names and rooms; she said they were her finest patients. That meant much to Charles. He credits his upbringing for much of his success, and he takes comfort that his parents could share his accomplishments.

"Personal, friendly, outgoing" was the way one old friend described Hurwitz. Explosive prosperity hasn't changed him a bit. The warmth he projects is genuine. Just don't mismanage one of his companies—or confront him in a takeover fight.

DOES HURWITZ RUN MID-SIZED COMPANIES?

In this chapter we explore the boundaries of mid-sized firms. What *is* a medium-sized company? A good place to start is with some specifics. Check out the following companies.

United Financial Groups. $3.5 billion in assets hardly sounds "medium-sized"; yet there is more to consider than pure assets. Net worth of about $100 million is certainly mid-sized, as are revenues of about $400 million. United is concentrated in Texas, true; but since the financial service industry is expanding and The Majors are becoming aggressive, United has many of the problems—and the opportunities—of classic mid-sized firms.

MCO Holdings.   Assets about $500 million and revenues about $175 million. Properties include several major parcels of development (thousands of acres each, e.g., 12,000 acres near Scottsdale, Arizona, 29,000 acres near Pueblo, Colorado) and a gas transmission company in Wyoming that functions like a monopoly.

MCO Resources.   Assets about $200 million and net worth about $75 million. Revenues about $80 million in oil, gas, and geothermal properties, concentrated in Texas, Oklahoma, and California. A mere tyke in the oil–energy business, but aggressive and tough. Actively seeking new reserves through acquisitions for stock.

Simplicity Pattern.   Revenues about $80 million; net worth about $150 million. The largest sewing pattern company in the world with a market share exceeding 40 percent. Considering other products for current customers, such as home products and specialty publishing. Using cash resources to diversify into other areas (real estate). In organizational characteristics, Simplicity is medium-sized; likewise in the general "fashion industry"—but in patterns per se, Simplicity is a giant. How to classify it?

Charles Hurwitz's companies are winners. Several threads unify all. Charles himself is surely a High-Profile Chief Executive (Creative Strategy 5). Though he delegates authority to his operating executives, his presence is always felt—he is always reachable and no one ever forgets who's boss.

Other Creative Strategies are at work. Hurwitz's executives earn good salaries and have excellent options; most important, they have the confidence to do their jobs (Employee Opportunity). Each company stresses what it does best (Focus/Coherence); and new deals can be closed quickly with a fast call to Houston (Flexibility/ Opportunism). Financial return on investment is the clear goal, with mere size being a means, not an end (Growth-Profits Tradeoff).

DEFINITIONS AND BOUNDARIES

What exactly is a mid-sized firm? A company whose vital signs fall between "small" and "large"? Reasoning in a circle rarely helps.[3]

The question is real; government economists have been trying for years to define "small business," still without consensus. Every survey or study of "mid" or "medium" or "intermediate" size firms have struggled for an appropriate measure of boundary or index of inclusion. General acceptance remains beyond reach and great variation is apparent.

Some would classify any company with over $5 million in gross revenues as medium-sized. At the other extreme, a respected *Harvard Business Review* article on profitability and market share established a "middle" range between $750 million and $1.5 billion — and this was counted in pre-1974 dollars.

The problem has many facets. How do you classify oil companies with total annual revenues under $200 million—like MCO Resources? Are they medium-sized? In the petroleum-producing industry, with sixteen companies each doing more than $10 billion per year, under $300 million is downright minuscule! Conversely, in book publishing, should industry-leading companies like Random House, Simon & Schuster and Harper & Row be considered large-sized companies, even though they do less than $300 million?

Note that we are differentiating "mid-sized" firms from "low-market-share" firms since it is possible to be either one and not be the other. (Plenum Publishing at $34 million in revenues is a medium-sized firm with a dominant position in English translations of Russian scientific books. Burroughs Computer at $4.1 billion of sales in mainframes, Crown Cork & Seal at $1.4 billion in packaging/canning, and Union Camp at $1.5 billion in forestry/paper are all low-market-share companies, but hardly medium-sized.)

Low-market-share firms, by definition, have only the one constraint—a minor percentage of industry sales. Mid-sized firms, on the other hand, require a more complex definition since firms with a relatively high market share may be included (pending definitions of market boundaries). We are concerned more with organizational issues than market forces. Thus companies with over $1 billion in revenues are not included.

Let's examine the problem logically. First, there are two modes of categorizing medium-sized businesses: *static* and *dynamic*. In the static mode we take a snapshot picture of the company at one instant in time. We assess the firm's characteristics at that precise moment and offer a categorizing scheme based on the numerical data. In the static mode we have no concern for changes over time, for rates of growth, for past position, or future forecast.

In establishing static boundaries for medium size, which company characteristics should we use as markers? Revenues, assets, number of employees, number of products, number of facilities, organizational structure, size of profits, geographical diversity? A long list can be made.

The first three are traditional choices:

1. Total *revenues*, the incoming annual volume on the profit-and-loss statement, is a good reflection of market share.

2. Total *assets*, the accounting valuation on the balance sheet, is a decent mirror of everything owned and hence company size.

3. Total *employees*, the physical number of personnel working, is a direct description of organizational scope.

In the dynamic mode the criterion is rates of change. The picture taken is moving, not still; effect is given to the laws of motion, the inertia of corporate history, and the trends of projected progress.

For dynamic classification, we pose three general categories of mid-sized firms:

1. Firms that are fundamentally small-sized, making a sudden spurt in growth—a level not likely to be sustained.

2. Firms that are intrinsically mid-sized with respect to external market and internal organization.

3. Firms that will become large sized quickly, and are just passing through this intermediate stage without pause or fuss.

One hot item will catapult even minuscule proprietorships into the first category; this is especially true in consumer products such as apparel and textiles, household wares and furnishings, even toys and books. Some years ago, for example, the Tenzor Light Company made a brief run at the corporate glories of mid-sized life with its high-intensity reading light, only to fall back to small status when the one product tailed off.

Companies that rocket to large size, leaping from entrepreneurial curiosity to major corporation, are usually acquisitive conglomerates or new technologies. An example of the former is Tyco Laboratories whose aggressive president parlayed a small research and development foundation into a substantial diversified company. An example of the latter is Apple Computer; it is hard to capture an instant when Apple was ever mid-sized, having virtually jumped from Steve Job's garage to the Big Board. (Of course we could, by hardening definitions, choose a moment when Apple had the requisite revenues, assets, and/or number of employees to be considered a mid-sized firm; this, however, would beg the question and miss the point.)

We are getting close, but not yet there. The above definitions have missed one essential element. Mid-sized firms, to be truly locked in the middle, cannot be classified in industrial isolation. Comparative data cannot be ignored. Assessing competitive position must be considered. (Neither, we note, is normally done.) Is a company really "medium sized," if, although meeting all revenue, asset, and employee criteria for mid-sized classification, it is the largest and most powerful firm in its industry?

For example, a small utility in a small Montana town would operate more like a monopoly (if not regulated) than a true mid-sized firm. Similarly, a firm with a very small asset base may turn those assets over many times and/or may operate with such labor intensiveness (low capital investment per employee) that the total sales or sheer number of employees would be indicative of a true mid-sized firm.

The Simplicity Pattern Company, as a manufacturing example, with its $80 million in sales and $175 million in assets, is bullseye on the mid-sized target. Yet Simplicity boasts the largest market share in the sewing pattern business, some 43 (formerly 60) percent, about double its nearest competitor. Is Simplicity a mid-sized firm? By financial and organizational characteristics, sure; by strict intra-industry comparison, no way. Yet what, really, is Simplicity's industry? If one argues that the company's patterns compete with finished clothing in the general fashion industry, then it is of course mid-sized in comparison with companies doing hundreds of millions of dollars per year (such as Warnaco, Kellwood, Leslie Fay, and Jones New York).

In categorizing a firm as mid-sized, we give high weight to relative standing within its own industry, if possible within its own product–market areas. In fact we go even further. We will require, in most cases, that each of our medium-sized firms be located within industries in which one or more rival firms are many times its size. (Simplicity, therefore, only qualifies in the broader industry definition.) In this manner the competitive point is made sharply: Mid-sized firms, to be "true" mid-sized firms, must compete against giants.

Other than the required presence of "mammoths and monsters," we establish some rather loose boundary conditions to stamp the mid-sized label on a firm. The chief guideline is realism: What is needed to make the firms "real-world relevant." Each company, therefore, is judged by both independent and comparative criteria.

The comparative criteria are clear. No mid-sized firm could be the leader in its general industry. In addition, that industry must include at least one very large company with dominating market strength.

The independent criteria are bounded by three dimensions: *Assets* represent capital size; *revenues* represent market size; number of *employees* represents organizational size. Numerical ranges chosen are broad, since industry-specific criteria will narrow them: assets, $10–$500 million; revenues, $10–$500 million; employees, 100–10,000.[4]

These ranges may seem excessively wide. The reason is the wide variability of mid-sized criteria between different industries, between, say, original airframe manufacturing and wholesale jewelry distribution. What's "small" in the former would be "large" in the latter.

Another problem is correlations among companies. How to compare and contrast different firms in different businesses? How to control strategic management assessment? How to limit variability in examining complex organizations? The key is to conduct all corporate analyses within similar industries. Since different industries embed different characteristics, this basic principle of keeping the industry constant goes far in shrinking large discrepancies among diverse businesses. Furthermore, the "matching" of mid-sized companies in "pairs" (such as A.T. Cross and Scripto in Chapter 2) is a powerful comparative technique, especially when summed across a large data base (see Chapter 9).

Industries are chosen to maximize internal consistency and minimize external fluctuation. Each industry should be a "national market," with all companies able to sell their products everywhere with little penalty for transportation or local domination. Most firms discussed will be publicly owned, thus assuring standardized reporting.

QUICK COMPARISONS

Some sense of these mid-sized firms? How do they compare with their larger, more famous rivals? We give examples. The dollar amounts are fiscal 1983 revenues.

In beverages Bacardi Rum's revenues ($175 million) are but a small fraction of the billion-dollar revenues of Seagram, Heublein, and Schenley, but its returns on sales and equity are tops.

In textiles the fine performances of Guilford ($255 million) and Bassett-Walker ($222 million) occur in an industry dominated by Burlington ($3 billion), J. P. Stevens ($2 billion), and more than ten others each grossing over $500 million.

In apparel Russell ($319 million) outearns Levi Strauss ($2.6 billion) and Blue Bell ($1.3 billion).

In forest products Pacific Lumber ($240 million) outperforms the billion-dollar giants (Boise Cascade, $2.9; Evans Products, $1.2; Champion International, $3.7; Georgia-Pacific, $5.4).

In paper Fort Howard ($786 million) has consistently achieved higher returns than International Paper ($4 billion), Crown Zellerbach ($2.9 billion), and St. Regis Paper ($2.6 billion).

In chemicals Loctite ($216 million), Great Lakes Chemical ($228 million), and International Flavor and Fragrances ($461 million) best the multibillion-dollar giants (Union Carbide, $9 billion; Monsanto, $6 billion; and Celanese, $3 billion.)

In soaps little Neutrogena ($46 million) beats Colgate-Palmolive, $4.9 billion; and American Cyanamid, $3.5 billion. Noxell ($304 million) also does well.

In tires the relatively unknown Bandag ($304 million) well surpasses the giants in bottom-line performance in a tough-times industry (Goodyear, $8.7 billion; Firestone, $3.9 billion; Uniroyal, $3 billion).

In iron and steel, where showing any positive profits automatically outshines the "leaders" (U.S. Steel, $18 billion; Bethlehem, $5 billion), Worthington Industries ($450 million), Nucor ($543 million), and Jorgensen ($229 million) maintain fine performance.

In metal cans J. L. Clark ($159 million) outperforms Continental ($3.5 billion), American Can ($4 billion), and Crown Cork ($1.4 billion).

In household appliances Maytag ($597 million) bests Whirlpool ($2.3 billion).

In motor vehicle equipment Echlin ($565 million) is superior to Eaton ($2.5 billion) and Dana ($2.4 billion).

In electrical products Molex ($176 million) outearns Square D ($1.1 billion) and McGraw Edison ($2.3 billion).

In measuring and control equipment Keystone ($110 million) outclasses Johnson Controls ($1.3 billion).

In medical instruments and supplies Dynatech ($99 million) outperforms industry leaders (American Hospital Supply, $3 billion; and Becton, Dickinson, $1.1 billion).

Among diversified companies, comparisons are more difficult and conclusions more tenuous. Nonetheless, several medium-sized conglomerates outclass their well-known rivals (IT&T, $22 billion; LTV, $5 billion; Textron, $2.9 billion; Kidde, $2.7 billion). Some top-performing examples: Carlisle ($412 million), Premier Industries ($317 million), Tyco ($586 million).

DON'T LET THE NAME FOOL YOU

As a mid-sized company, Simplicity Pattern has been a paradox. For ten years it stressed certain strategies—Dominant in its industry segment; good emphasis on Product; clear Focus on patterns—

and dismissed other strategies—not Distinctive; little Innovation; minimal External Perception; no Flexibility or Opportunism. The company, make no mistake, had a remarkable run. Today, under Charles Hurwitz and team, it's preparing a new attack. What's coming is more than comeback.

Simplicity, headquartered in New York, is the world's largest manufacturer and marketer of patterns for home sewing, the paper designs sewers use to make items of cloth. Simplicity's collection includes over 900 designs and thousands of variations, reflecting the broad range of consumer interest in sewing and related craft activities. Patterns are inexpensive ($1.25–$5.00), and one can save up to two-thirds of the cost of clothing by making it oneself rather than purchasing it ready-made.

The eight years between 1973 and 1981 highlight a dramatic flip in corporate fortunes. Income from operations declined while income from investments increased. In 1973 Simplicity earned (pretax) $29 million from operations on a volume of $108 million, and $1.9 million from unrelated investments. In 1981 Simplicity earned (pretax) $3.8 million from operations on a volume of $82 million, and $11.5 million from unrelated investments. Operational income dropped 87 percent and investment income increased 600 percent—that says it all. (In 1983 the first full year of Hurwitz's control, Simplicity earned $9.6 million after tax on revenues of $71.7 million—not including the $18 million pretax profit from the Amstar stock investment and sale.)

The pattern business trended downward for two reasons: (1) the industry declined by one-third, from about 33 million sewers to about 22 million and (2) Simplicity's market share decreased from almost two-thirds to barely two-fifths.

Explanations for the declining sewing market? There are several. The increasing number of women working seems a primary factor, though some dispute its strength. Recent penchants toward later marriages and deferred childbirth are drivers. The falloff in the teaching of sewing in schools seems critical. Certainly the dropping of sewing centers by department stores and major chains has had impact (the inventory turn was too slow and volume per square foot too low), though the vacuum is being filled by specialty fabric stores with full commitment to the sewing customer. Industry analysts now feel that the 22 million will not decline further; these folk, they hope, are the "loyal core" sewers.

The reasons for Simplicity's declining market share is less easy to explain. The company took its leadership position for granted. It relied on power over retailers rather than creativity with products. "They sat on their reputation," commented one industry insider, "bullying stores to take patterns they didn't need at times they didn't want." Simplicity had a great name with consumers, but lost its position as the leader in style and design. Emphasis was shifted to manufacturing, distribution, and facilities, not marketing, sales, and promotion. McCall's and Vogue had their opening and, stressing fashion and high quality, became serious competitors.

Simplicity's enormous profits generated in the 1970s built into a huge bundle of cash, almost $100 million, well in excess of what the company needed for operations, indeed greater than the company's annual sales! (When a firm's current ratio is over 8–1, the financial condition is no longer prudent—it's inefficient.) Simplicity should have done more, perhaps made a complementary acquisition. When it didn't become the hunter, it became the hunted. The potential pistol had become the sitting target.

Beginning in 1981, several investors made a pass at Simplicity— control of the cash was the prize, surely not the declining pattern business. Corporate raiders Victor Posner and Carl Icahn took their shots, before an English and Australian group took over. After spending some $18 million of Simplicity's cash on interrelated projects, largely in energy and mining, one of the investors went into receivership, That's when Hurwitz came in. His vehicle was MCO.

With Hurwitz as CEO of Simplicity, things have changed. Cash is being conserved, and all investments are designed to increase shareholder wealth. No more using Simplicity resources to bolster outside interests of certain parties. The recent acquisition of a real estate company (Twin-Fair) adds properties with underappraised values and a tax-loss carryforward.

The President of Simplicity is Lilyan Affinito, a remarkable woman, the only female president of a New York Stock Exchange company. Affinito sits on numerous corporate boards including Chrysler and International Harvester. She runs the pattern business.

To manage the investment side of the company, Hurwitz brought in Robert Rosen, formerly executive vice-president of Shearson/American Express and president of Shearson Realty Group. Although given the mandate to diversify along with the title of vice-chairman, Rosen is fascinated with the potential of expanding the basic business. "The 'Simplicity' name is a major asset," asserts Rosen, "with high consumer identification for quality and integrity. We will capitalize on it. . . . You're looking at Simplicity with blinders if all you see are patterns and sewing. Our magazine has over 500,000 subscribers, with terrific demographics. A specialty publishing business could be developed here."

One must, according to Rosen, analyze Simplicity within the corporate group controlled by Hurwitz. "MCO Holdings," he says, "is a long-term, fixed asset play. We are short-term, liquid assets. We have cash resources, stable earnings, generate net free operating cash, and are listed on the New York Stock Exchange. We seek value opportunities through economic leverage of our financial structure and the substance of our underlying businesses."

Rosen describes three basic strategies for diversification: (1) *De novo* expansion into new areas; (2) medium-sized acquisitions—divestitures from larger companies—where management can be "incentified" as in leveraged buyouts but without the financial risks associated with crippled balance sheets; and (3) larger acquisitions—many times Simplicity's annual sales (divisions of large public companies)—where Simplicity's current debt capacity combined with management expertise can create outstanding appreciation. "What we look for," confides Rosen, "is *value*, discounts from true worth due to disequilibriums in the market or unrecognized assets. We are 'net free cash buyers,' paying cents on dollars." Very much, to be sure, in the Hurwitz tradition.

Also on the Hurwitz team is Dr. David Learner, president of the Market Research Corporation of America. Dr. Learner, a recognized business scholar, has been providing sophisticated marketing analyses and catalyzing imaginative product planning. The objective is to explore new areas of profitable activity, building on Simplicity's current competencies but not limited to current boundaries. "The pattern buyer," says Learner, "is a well-educated, upscale woman with substantial buying power. Our current customer base is a marketer's dream." In an industry flat and archaic and considered mundane, the Rosen–Learner team is something radical.

The Hurwitz group is not content to accept industry trends as inevitable. They plan active intervention to shift patterns (pardon the pun). New emphasis is being placed on *fashion*. Designers such as Adolfo, Mary McFadden, and John Weitz are now displayed strongly in the Simplicity Catalog, and celebrities such as Diana Ross and soap opera stars are featured prominently in the *Simplicity Today* magazine. Major in-store promotions and exposure in leading women's magazines typify the new aggressiveness.

"We should recover lost volume by encouraging current sewers to sew more often," asserts Dick Gyde, recently installed general manager of Simplicity's domestic operations. "The industry must do a better job of reinforcing gratification. We must give sewers the positive strokes they deserve." Gyde represents the new market-driven leadership replacing the previous production-driven managers.

Since Simplicity's fortunes are coupled closely to the industry, and since Learner's research has highlighted sewing programs in schools, the company's marketing thrust in the country's classrooms is being intensified. Not only is the program expected to increase current sales, but more important, alter future trends.

Simplicity actively supports in-school sewing programs. It distributes to home economics teachers a wide variety of educational material designed to stimulate an interest in fashion and to help students acquire basic sewing skills. Such materials include instructional leaflets, posters, fashion guidance booklets, and so on. These teaching aids are sent to almost 55,000 schools at the beginning of fall and spring semesters. Selected designs are offered to teachers at discount prices, and a toll-free telephone number is set aside for teachers to place orders. New avenues of communications using electronic media are being explored—including satellite seminars, video discs, and cassettes.

Motivating new adults to start sewing is important, especially if instruction can be given at convenient times and places. The innovative Corporate Sewing Program, consisting of lunch-hour or after-work sewing classes, continues to expand, as does the series of how-to sewing books being published (more than twenty).

Great consumer value—the traditional Simplicity strength—is being reemphasized, along with the fresh emphasis on fashion, "investment dressing," and personal satisfaction. Simplicity's new objective, under its new management, is not only to reinforce its position as the world leader in the pattern industry, but to expand that industry and reverse historical trends through altering sewing behavior.

Analyzing Simplicity in transformation by Creative Strategies, we observe several key additions.

☐ Product Emphasis is now a major priority, with marketing, not manufacturing, the driving factor.

☐ Distinctiveness (if not uniqueness) is achieved through sharp publishing, advertising, and educational programs.

☐ Efficient Innovation (in the planning) is the development of new products based on the distinctive strengths and comparative advantages of old products.

☐ External Perception is achieved by thorough research, which, when combined with ingenuity, can modify customer behavior and sewing trends.

☐ Opportunism is clearly the case, with independent investments, finding "value," and buying assets at discounts from true worth all Hurwitz trademarks.

What's interesting is that although Wall Street had largely written off the pattern business, and has been judging Simplicity based on its mound of cash, the real sleeper here may be the innovative opportunities emerging from the pattern business, as fashioned in the fertile minds of Hurwitz, Rosen, Affinito, Learner, et al. This team, let no one doubt, is cut from different cloth [Note: Simplicity's announced sale of its pattern business is very much in the Hurwitz style of maximizing value and optimizing resources. The premium purchase price (reflecting pattern business upswing) frees substantial net worth for innovative, opportunistic investments. Stay tuned.]

STREET FIGHTS IN MEDICAL LABS

International Clinical Laboratories (ICL) is one of the more profitable companies in the fiercely competitive world of medical laboratory testing (1983 revenues, $72 million; profits, $4.8 million). How does ICL, in *Forbes'* words, run rings around its rivals, most of whom are bigger and stronger?[5]

Strategic management is a good part of the answer (see Chapter 7), and it is almost an obsession for chief executive Bill O'Neil. "Ten years ago there were 15,000 medical test laboratories in the country," notes O'Neil from his Nashville, Tennessee office. "Today there are only 6,000 or 7,000. They're all going out of business or being acquired."

Entry barriers were low in the early days of this industry where customers are doctors (mostly in private practice)—anybody could get in on the cheap. Today with technology more sophisticated and computerized testing a necessity, substantial capital requirements have raised those barriers. And competition has become furious, so furious that most of the independents have sold out to giant companies (such as Hoffmann–La Roche, Revlon, American Hospital Supply, etc.). Bristol-Meyers and Upjohn, no pipsqueaks, have called it quits, and even SmithKline Beckmann, the industry leader, may be operating below breakeven (though the company vigorously affirms profitability for its lab testing division).

So how does ICL do it? "You have to spend the time to understand your business really well," says O'Neil, and his words come across as more than cliché.

This boss has thorough grasp of his company. When first called to take over the top spot, O'Neil went back to "square one." He defined the business "as having both a wholesale and a retail side. That, in turn, suggested that there ought to be two different pricing structures, which turned out to be very helpful." Next he broke the business down "into two basic elements of expense to compare one regional office with another." Then he "blueprinted the business" so ICL could "cookie-cut the offices . . . make them as similar as possible."

Dig deeper and you find that ICL's structure is designed to give the economies of scale that every lab owner needs—and this,

O'Neil believes, is his personal, entrepreneurial contribution to the industry. Other companies, he feels, maintain organizational concepts that conflict with real-world markets.

Giant SmithKline, called the industry cutthroater on price, is a favorite ICL target. ICL zeros in on its rival's alleged personality mismatches and market share nonsense. Says ICL's financial vice-president, "SmithKline seems to be adopting the pharmaceutical philosophy, which many did in the beginning. If a detail man is out there selling pills to the doctor, why can't he sell lab work too? What they don't realize is that those are two entirely different kinds of selling. In peddling pills you don't have to get the doctor to sign on the dotted line while you're sitting there. If you get him interested, he writes prescriptions for you later, and you find out you were successful. But in the lab business you're asking the doctor to make the unpleasant decision of agreeing right then and there to take his business from one lab and give it to yours. Those two sales require two different kinds of personalities."

"SmithKline went to the Boston Consulting Group several years ago and got some terribly bad advice," O'Neil continues, and you can tell he likes this subject. "It was the market share thing—you know, get market share at any price and everybody will die off and then you can raise your prices later. So they chopped their published pricing on some high-volume tests by something like 60 percent. And what did it get them? Nothing. I'm sure they're losing money in their lab business. I mean, we weren't going to let them take a dime's worth of business, no matter what we had to sell it at. Now, three years later, they've backed off that approach. But they screwed up the entire market in the interim." (SmithKline calls those comments gross exaggerations, asserting that they always set prices based on customers' location and volume.)

Looking at industry competition from the viewpoint of a medium-sized company, O'Neil takes a reflective tack, "You just don't tackle these big guys head-on. You fight them in a different way. It's kind of a buzzword, but I call it traveling the access road. All the big guys are out here on the superhighway, but there are plenty of access roads on which you can travel just as fast."

How does O'Neil's philosophical strategy translate into operational tactics? He is diversifying, from lab testing for individual doctors to lab management for entire hospitals. ICL was managing twelve hospitals at the end of 1983, accounting for one-quarter of its business. "It's a contract business," states O'Neil. "So you don't have to worry about someone else coming in and taking it away for a nickel like you do on the doctor side."

O'Neil confesses two prime threats amidst the overt optimism: massive price war among the giants and cutting back of governmental reimbursements. A good strategic thinker—"we spend a lot of time thinking about strategy"—he worries about his environment.

Creative Strategies at ICL? *External perception*—understanding the market, knowing how to sell and serve doctors and hospitals. *Distinctiveness*—finding and controlling the right "access road." *Coherence*—making all parts of the company fit together. *High-profile CEO*—O'Neil is all over that business.

CEO SLEUTHING

Want to learn a lot about medium-sized companies with little effort? Check out the chief executives.

When in short order the new president of Apple was brought in from Pepsi, and the new president of Atari arrived from Phillip Morris (since displaced), the meaning was clear. The entire industry, barely five years old, was being transformed. The home computer was no longer high tech; it was now a consumer item.

Pivotal issues were changing with remarkable speed. The dramatic drop in price accelerated rapid public acceptance; selling computers was suddenly a marketing game, and it was no different from selling diet drinks or cigarettes. RAM and disc memory was of minor matter, and even the availability of software was not really critical. Buying decisions were being controlled by buying behavior, and company strategy had a new thrust: advertising appeal to end users, shelf space in major retailers, perceived product differentiation, price point positioning, and the like. For Apple and Atari, new priorities required new skills, and new skills demanded new leaders.

Imagine giving a Rorshach test to a medium-sized company. "This is your next CEO," we would say while showing a neutral picture, "describe for me, please, his background and personality."

The description evoked would give good feel for that company. Is the person progressive or conservative in outlook? Authoritarian or participatory in style? From inside or outside the company? With what educational background? With what operational background—R&D, manufacturing, finance, marketing? The answers would be a quick read of present potential and corporate culture.

Another bellwether question: How long has the present CEO been at the helm? The shorter the time period, the more volatile the situation. Science-based companies are usually founded by scientists. If one of the founders is not CEO, it's worth finding out why.

Try a target company. Examine the chief executive. From what functional area did he come? If a technology firm is being run by a marketing or finance man, you learn something quickly. Current priorities suggest current concerns.

When the consortium of high-tech companies chose Admiral Bobby Inman as the organizing president of their innovative Microelectronics and Computer Technology Corporation, they made a strong statement. Inman was one of America's most respected officials in the intelligence community, with three decades of experience getting competing agencies to work together. He was articulate and had excellent rapport in Washington (where, it was reasoned, help would be needed to surmount antitrust and other legal problems).

When Harry Gray chose General Alexander Haig to be president of United Technologies, he had specific objectives in mind. International marketing, especially of its Pratt & Whitney jet engines and other industrial products, was a high priority. Haig had been commander of the NATO forces and was highly regarded in Europe.

What makes a good mid-sized CEO? A "high profile" is a recurrent theme. Look for these traits. He should converse fluently—almost at the state of the art—in each content area of his purview. He must visualize long-term implications. He must make independent judgments regarding the firm's distinctive competencies and should have the self-reliant capacity to devise innovative strategies and implement optimum structures. Similarly, to generate competitive advantage, the CEO must have broad conceptual reach and sense novel business relationships well before they hit the mass media. Yet, in order to make far-sighted decisions, to set priorities and plan products, the CEO must be distanced from accepted ideas and divorced from group thinking. What will the market require in ten years, and how can the firm provide it? That's the strategic trick.

In the flux and flow of contemporary business, needs flip without warning; what was valuable yesterday may be worthless tomorrow. The solution? Strategic management: socioeconomic scanning, alternative policy generation, rigorous policy evaluations accented by insight—the constant testing of company mission. Long-range planning is not a gimmick; it is life. Programmatic positioning—the matching of organizational resources to environmental interests—is vital. Corporations must develop particular strengths so that their distinctive competencies can generate competitive advantage. If they do not, whatever their market valuation, it will fall.

Intellectual output is as much the raw material for the Information Age as energy output was for the Industrial Age, and executive leadership here is both vital and delicate. Directing creativity and innovation is no textbook task. Great feeling and empathy—not sympathy or apathy—are required. One must have a special sense of the priorities of an academic, the concerns of a scientist, the intensity of an inventor, the rage of an artist. Managing mental types demands content knowledge and process sensitivity. People who produce intellectual output have little concern for anything else, not managerial issues, not organizational problems. Their work is their world, and upon it alone does the sun rise and set. Creativity is impossible to coerce. It must be coaxed, stroked, massaged, shaped. A chief executive must get his people to *internalize* whatever they do, or it just won't be done. Though management is becoming a science, it will never cease being an art.

We need executives with insight and guts; the former to discern what to do, the latter to determine how to do it. CEOs of mid-sized firms must be versed in the substance of their charge, visionary

in forecasting opportunities and threats, and inventive in formulating strategic response. They must be tough-minded enough to
assess internal strengths and weaknesses, establish unpopular
priorities, unify diverse constituencies, and lead the organization
with coherent policies. Society calls our best and brightest. If ever
America needed "The Right Stuff," it's for running medium-sized
companies.[6]

CHAPTER 4

TRACKING MID-SIZED FIRMS

Where Are They?
How Are They Doing?

Want to track three extraordinary medium-sized companies? Check out Tultex, Bassett-Walker, and Pannill Knitting. Who? Why are they so extraordinary? Seven reasons and counting.[1]

☐ First, they are nicely profitable in a tough industry, competing against a dozen companies bigger and stronger than all of them put together.

☐ Second, they are nicely profitable in textiles, a domestic industry assumed wasted by foreign imports.

☐ Third, they are all located in the same area—Martinsville, Virginia, the little city in the Blue Ridge Mountains called "the sweat shirt capital of the world."

☐ Fourth, all compete for private-label contracts through sales offices in similar locations, such as New York's Empire State Building.

☐ Fifth, all manufacture products largely using "fleeced" fabrics (e.g., sweat shirts), which have a furry fuzz on the inside— the result of tearing one side in a "napper."

☐   Sixth, all are industry low-cost producers.

☐   Seventh, all owe their existence to one man's decision, some eighty years ago, that the South should get into the knitted-underwear business, previously the domain of Northern mills.[2]

Regarding performance? Feast your eyes. Tultex: 1983 revenues, $288 million; profits, $14.6 million. Bassett-Walker: 1983 revenues, $222 million; profits, $27 million, a return on sales three times the industry average. Pannill Knitting: 1982 revenues, $145 million; profits, $19.6 million; return on equity, 36 percent.

All three companies are integrated vertically, a real advantage in mature industries. This means that they start with yarn—two even make their own yarn from raw fiber—and turn out finished garments fully packed and ready to be shipped to retail accounts. Now that's focus and coherence.

Sweat shirts, of course, have hit it big in health-conscious America, what with our new-found passion for fitness, jogging, and athletics. (Don't overlook sweat *pants* as well.) But these Martinsville Maulers went one step better, turning fitness into fashion. The athletic look is now in, and lots of people now wear active sportswear whether exercising or not, and that includes nonfitness freaks and even confirmed nonparticipants.

Though wages are low, $5–$7 per hour, so are prices. Living standards are reasonable, especially since many families have two salaries coming in. Workers are happy and vote down unions.

But what about the future, and the looming spectre of cheap imports—there are countries, such as China, that must earn hard dollars by keeping their factories open at any price. Though our three Martinsville companies keep alert constantly, there is no real anxiety. The relatively high weight of the fabric plays nicely with the relatively low labor content of the garments—both of which translate into smaller advantages for Far Eastern competitors. (High fabric weight means that transoceanic shipping costs become a higher percentage of total costs. Lower labor content means that the pricing advantages of lower labor rates are diluted.) Importers would rather take quota allocations in more labor-intensive, higher-margin items such as blouses.

Technology helps too; there's no way for China to take advantage of computer-controlled dye matching and pattern making. Tultex goes still further, installing spinning machines with rotors that whirl at 80,000 revolutions per minute and with robots that remove the cones automatically when filled with yarn. Plant capacity will be increased 60 percent, while the work force will be reduced 60 percent (250 to 100). That's efficient innovation.

Service is important in this business, and let no one forget it. Though imports are often cheaper, customers can't afford uncertainties of delivery and unevenness of quality. (Tultex, for example, is constructing a 500,000-square-foot distribution center.)

Marketing and fashion also heighten entry barriers. Branding is the key here. It creates uniqueness. No one can outprice you on your own brand. Tultex is developing its own proprietary sportswear line, such as "Nautilus" sweat shirts, under royalty arrangement. (Who says the best medium-sized firms don't "fleece" the public?)[3]

INDUSTRIAL ECONOMICS

How many medium-sized companies operate in the United States? What's happening to them? What slice do they cut of total assets and revenues? What are the trends—is that slice expanding or shrinking? Let's look at the numbers.

32,400 corporations with assets between $10 million and $250 million filed tax returns with the Internal Revenue Service in 1980 (1.2 percent of all 2,710,500 corporations). These medium-sized companies accounted for $1,397 billion in assets (18 percent). In comparison, the 2,900 corporations with assets greater than $250 million accounted for $5,358 billion in assets (70 percent).[4]

If we focus on manufacturing corporations, 5,890 with assets between $10 million and $250 million filed income tax returns in 1980 (2.4 percent of all 242,550 manufacturing corporations). These medium-sized companies accounted for $242 billion in assets (14 percent) and $384 billion in revenues (16 percent). In comparison, the 629 large-sized companies with assets greater than $250 million accounted for $1,317 billion in assets (77 percent) and $1,665 billion in revenues (69 percent).

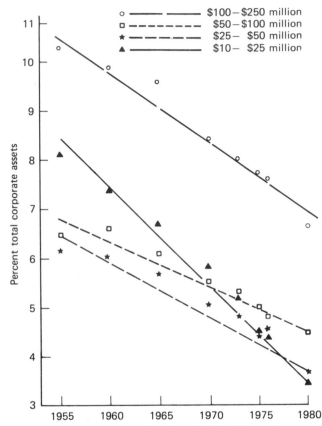

FIGURE 4.1. Asset size over time: less than $250 million. (*Source:* U.S. Internal Revenue Service, "Statistics of Income, Corporate Income Tax Returns," annual.)

In 1982, manufacturing corporations with assets between $10 million and $250 million generated $7.5 billion in profits (10.6 percent) while those with assets greater than $250 million generated $58 billion in profits (82.1 percent). (Note that mid-sized firms are weaker in earning power than they are in assets or revenues.)

The relative power of medium-sized companies as a class has been in long decline. Their control over total assets within all industries has been trending steadily downward. (Inflation, of course, is part of the reason, but not the whole reason. Firms are indeed elevated in bracket by the nonproductive force of increasing price levels, but the power of size well surmounts the effect of inflation.)

Figure 4.1 shows this erosion for four asset classes ($10–$25 million; $25–$50 million; $50–$100 million; $100–$250 million) from 1955 through 1980, the drop being between 2.0 and 4.7 percent. Figure 4.2 shows the corresponding total corporate assets controlled by companies with over $250 million in assets increasing from 43.4 percent in 1955 to 70.3 percent in 1980. (Note that these first figures represent all U.S. corporations, not just manufacturing, and are not adjusted for inflation.)

Figure 4.3 compares the relative control of corporate assets for manufacturing firms only. Here mid-sized companies are bounded broadly between $10 million and $1 billion in assets, and the same, almost mirror image is maintained. Between 1970 and 1982, manufacturing companies with over $1 billion in assets increased their control from 48.8 to 66.4 percent, while companies between $10 million and $1 billion slipped from 39.3 to 24.8 percent.

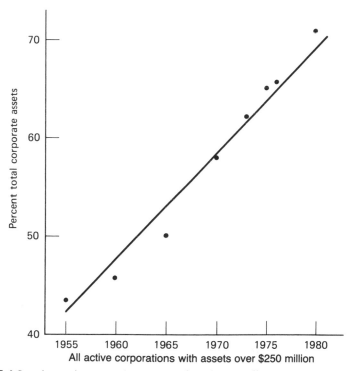

FIGURE 4.2. Asset size over time: more than $250 million. (*Source:* U.S. Internal Revenue Service, "Statistics of Income, Corporate Income Tax Returns," annual.)

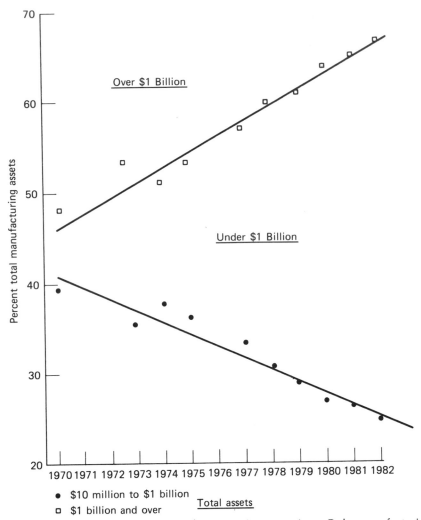

FIGURE 4.3. Manufacturing assets by asset size over time. Only manufacturing corporations are included. (*Source:* U.S. Internal Revenue Service, "Statistics of Income, Corporate Income Tax Returns," annual.)

The profit picture is virtually identical (Figure 4.4). The percentage of total profits from all manufacturing firms made by companies with over $1 billion in assets increased from 51.9 percent (1970) to 72.4 percent (1982), with a corresponding drop in the $10 million to $1 billion mid-sized group from 38.4 to 20.3 percent over the same time period.[5]

The rates of return on equity (Figure 4.5) and assets (Figure 4.6) of mid-sized manufacturing corporations, as reported by the Federal Trade Commission, show persistent depression in comparison with both larger and smaller companies (Table 4.1; Figures 4.5 and 4.6). The profit depression for mid-sized firms with assets between $10 and $250 million seems robust, occurring in almost every year.

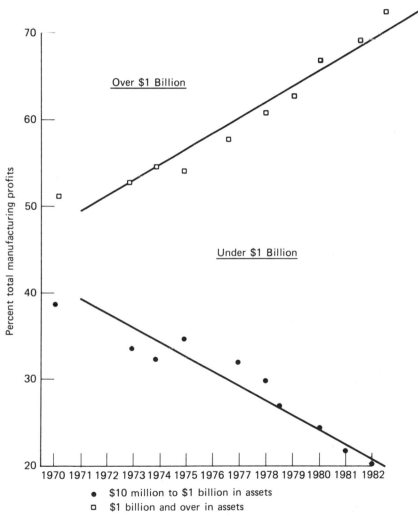

FIGURE 4.4. Manufacturing profits by asset size over time. Only manufacturing corporations are included. (*Source:* U.S. Internal Revenue Service, "Statistics of Income, Corporate Income Tax Returns," annual.)

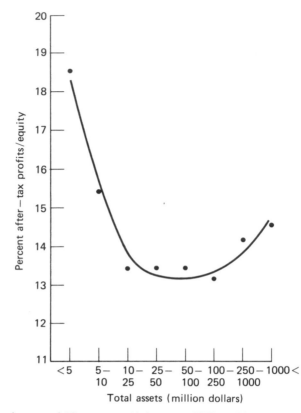

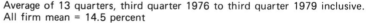

Average of 13 quarters, third quarter 1976 to third quarter 1979 inclusive.
All firm mean = 14.5 percent

FIGURE 4.5. Rates of after-tax profits on stockholder equity (manufacturing corporations by asset size). (*Source:* Federal Trade Commission, *Quarterly Financial
Report for Manufacturing, Mining and Trade Corporations.*)

Checking different phases of the business cycle, though shapes of
the curves shift, larger firms always achieve better returns than
mid-sized firms (Figure 4.7).[6]

Returns on sales evince a simpler relationship, more logical theoretically but more disturbing socially. From the smallest firm class
through the largest, there is an increasing positive relationship
between size and profitability as measured by returns on sales
(Figure 4.8).

Are economies of scale destroying the profits of mid-size firms?
The so-called survivor test gives some insight. "The logic is simple:

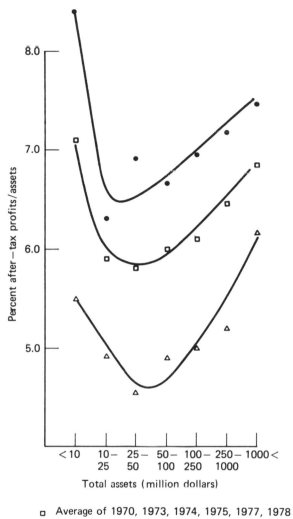

○ Average of 1970, 1973, 1974, 1975, 1977, 1978

● Average of 1977, 1978

△ Average of 1980, 1981, 1982

FIGURE 4.6. Rates of after-tax return on corporate assets (manufacturing corporations by asset size). (*Source:* Federal Trade Commission, *Quarterly Financial Report for Manufacturing, Mining and Trade Corporations.*)

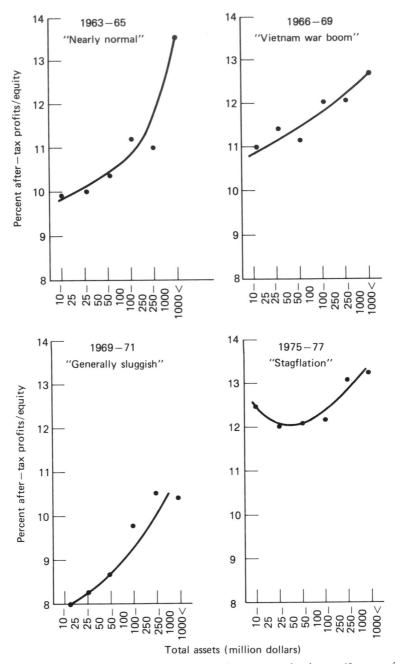

FIGURE 4.7. Profitability by firm size during business cycle phases. [Source of data and analysis: Scherer (1980, p. 92.) Data derived from FTC *Quarterly Financial Report for Manufacturing, Mining and Trade Corporations*.]

Firm or plant sizes that survive and contribute increasing proportions of an industry's output are assumed to be optimal; those that
supply a declining share of output are deemed too large or too
small. This test of optimality clearly covers a much broader range
of variables than mere production scale economies. As [Professor
George] Stigler states, under the survivor test an efficient firm size
'is one that meets any and all problems the entrepreneur actually
faces: strained labor relations, rapid innovation, government regulation, unstable foreign markets, and what not.'"[7]

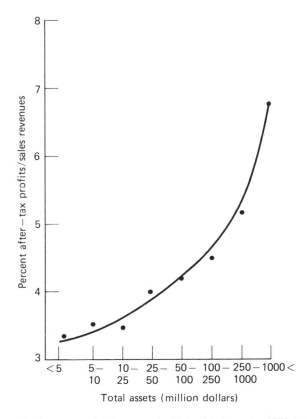

Average of 13 quarters, third quarter 1976 to third quarter 1979 inclusive.
All firm mean = 4.4 percent

FIGURE 4.8.   Rates of after-tax profits to sales revenues (manufacturing corporations
by asset size). (*Source*: Federal Trade Commission, *Quarterly Financial Report for
Manufacturing, Mining and Trade Corporations.*)

TABLE 4.1. Rates of Return by Asset Class (U.S. manufacturing corporations, third quarter 1976 to third quarter 1979 inclusive, in percents)

	Less Than $10 Million	$10–$250 Million	More Than $250 Million
Return on equity	16.88%	13.39%	14.36%
Standard deviation	3.74%	1.86%	1.66%

Note: Data are derived directly from the Federal Trade Commission's (FTC) *Quarterly Financial Report for Manufacturing, Mining and Trade Corporations.* Seventeen individual quarters were averaged together, third quarter 1976 to third quarter 1979 inclusive. For each quarter the data were aggregated into the three groups listed above (from the eight groups in the FTC data). Profits reflect after-tax profits. Returns are mean returns on equity.

A real-world application of the survivor test is interesting. In over 100 different industries "the minimum optimal plant or firm size is small relative to market size."[7] In one study 64 out of 91 industries had a minimum optimal plant size requiring the production of 1 percent or less of industry value added (1947–1954 time period).[8]

Thus a paradox is constructed by the two sets of data. On the one hand, mid-sized firms maintain a level of aggregate profit performance substantially below larger firms; and on the other hand, many mid-sized firms are apparently *above* the minimal size for optimal operations.

The solution to the paradox? The prevalent use of *sub*optimal strategies by mid-sized firms. What is needed? Creative Strategies! Indeed it is our underlying assumption that such strategies are both needed and able to maximize the comparative advantages of medium-sized companies.[9]

INNOVATING EFFICIENTLY

The pharmaceutical game, it is said, is one of the toughest for small fry. No sense playing the hand if you can't scrape up the ante. New drug development is both absolutely essential and wildly expensive. Marketing is cutthroat competitive. With more than a dozen or so fat cats sitting around the table, each slapping down a billion or more in revenues, what's left for the little guy?

What's left for Marion Laboratories, with not even $200 million in sales? One of the better performances in the industry, that's what!

Today's hot drug can be tomorrow's dud. New technologies can overturn a market overnight. It can take some $50 million invested with high risk for more than a decade to bring a new molecule from laboratory discovery to regulatory approval. The cost of product launch is measured in millions of dollars and timed in handfuls of days. It takes a substantial marketing organization to reach and support physicians and hospitals.

The rewards, of course, can be enormous. New drugs can generate annual revenues in the hundreds of millions of dollars, with gross profit margins above 75 percent. Patents protect companies for seventeen years, though few drugs have such a long practical lifetime. (SmithKline's Tagamet, the market leader in the antiulcer field with 1983 U.S. sales of $485 million, is the largest selling Rx product in the world.)

Marion Laboratories manufactures and markets ethical (prescription) and over-the-counter pharmaceutical products, generating 70–75 percent of volume from the former and 10–15 percent from the latter. Another 10–15 percent, according to senior management, will come from new procedures in clinical diagnoses and the sale of hospital products. The remaining 5–10 percent of the product mix is reserved for new technologies.

Marion was founded as a one-man company in 1950 by Ewing M. Kauffman, formerly a wholesale drug salesman and Marion's current chairman and chief executive. For most of its almost thirty-five years, sales volume and stockholder value increased steadily. (To capitalize the company, Kauffman invited seven men to invest $1000 each; when redeemed after five years, their investment had appreciated to $750,000.)

The first million dollars of sales were achieved in 1959; national distribution and $5 million of sales came in 1965; $100 million in 1977; and $180 million in 1983. Analysts estimate $300 million for fiscal 1985 and over $500 million by fiscal 1987. This top-performing mid-sized firm will, for better or worse, soon no longer be "mid-sized."

Marion is an efficient performer. After-tax profits at 8.2 percent of sales in fiscal 1983 were running at better than 10 percent of sales in fiscal 1984. In 1983 sales were up 19 percent and earnings 67 percent while inventories were down 3 percent. A receivable turnover of 5.9 indicates quick payment from customers. The balance sheet is exceptionally strong, with equity almost three-quarters of its $160+ million in assets. Marion's chief financial officer stated that "we are willing to take an R&D risk, a market risk and a product risk. We do not want to take a financial risk." Since compressed launches of new products generate significant risks, "we will take the risk out of the financial picture. We will not be a heavily leveraged company."

Energizing Marion are two powerful new products: Carafate ($28 million), an antiulcer agent nicking some sales from Tagamet; and Cardizem ($45 million), used for treating angina (the chest pain associated with heart disease)—the drug works by blocking the calcium channel causing spasms. From 20 percent of Marion's sales in 1983, these two products may provide some 34 percent in fiscal 1985 (over $100 million), a compound annual growth of 70 percent.

The key to Marion's success, indeed the reason it competes so effectively with industry giants, is that the company does *not* perform primary research. Carafate and Cardizem are both *licensed* from Japanese companies.

Without the resources to confront The Majors, Marion chose a different tack. The firm stresses its "interrelationships with outside professionals," combined with a corporate strategy that is simple yet brilliant in its tailored efficiency: "Whatever the causes, one fact stands out loud and clear . . . the time and money involved in discovering a new drug, testing it, and then getting it to market is increasing rapidly. . . . Add to this the high degree of uncertainty that any one new compound will ever make it to the market, and the enormous financial risks of basic research and development become apparent. . . . Marion employs a unique and effective strategy within the regulatory environment. We call it 'Search and Development.'"

Marion does not wildcat R&D. They do not initiate discovery of new molecular structures or breakthrough chemicals, the most expensive and speculative part of the R&D process. Rather, the company employs a system of "search Research and Development," conducting an aggressive, ongoing worldwide quest for compounds, products, or technologies that have identifiable pharmacological action and have demonstrated safety and effectiveness in their country of origin. The corporate research and development staff assists in evaluating such acquisition candidates. The search function is of prime importance; indeed, it commands top-management commitment and priority. Marion reviews some 5000 new products annually.

Why is little Marion an attractive choice for foreign manufacturers? First, it offers full attention to the U.S. and Canadian market without the internal competition of homegrown drugs. Second, it maneuvers advantage over larger rivals by negotiating simple royalty contracts as opposed to complex joint ventures.

Marion's president, Fred Lyons, Jr., stated that "when we negotiate, we strive for a mutually beneficial arrangement with our licensors." In one example, Marion sweetened the deal with stock options (exercisable when the New Drug Application is approved). Commented the president, a marketing man, "I think the company [licensor] feels good about the fact that it has the opportunity to ride with Marion's success, to which they will be contributing."

Once a product is obtained under license, the Marion R&D staff develops it for the U.S. market and guides it through the regulatory process. The objective is to bring products to market as rapidly as possible. Using this approach, entering at the applications end after the drug has been proven successful, Marion obtains unusual leverage. R&D is targeted to be results oriented and have high impact.

"Through this strategy, the tremendous capital investment and expenditure associated with basic research and development is avoided. Marion's R&D expertise is applied [focused] on laboratory and clinical research and regulatory approval. While its $25 million R&D budget is small by industry standards . . . the focused approach multiplies it into an effective productivity several times greater per dollar than traditional approaches."

"We do not have any Nobel prize winners at Marion," said Mr. Lyons, "but in our R&D effort, a New Drug Application is the equivalent of a Nobel Prize. . . . We have demonstrated the ability to compete in getting products to market without a $250 million a year budget." In addition, Marion estimates that it saves three to five years on each R&D project.

Search procedures for new compounds are focused on certain "organ systems," thereby concentrating "our activity on specific systems of the body, rather than diverting effort over a broad range of therapeutic agents. . . . we will be focused in those areas in which we can obtain a position of market leadership by building upon our knowledge base in both technological experience and credibility in the marketplace." Current organ systems are the cardiovascular (heart and circulatory) system; the gastrointestinal (digestive) system; wound healing products, and clinical diagnosis.

Organ system specialization benefits Marion in two primary ways:

1. Understanding a given organ system "greatly enhances our ability to recognize and evaluate compounds with potential differentiation." Then, in the research and clinical trial phase, "we can proceed in an environment of expertise" where a "relationship of confidence, trust and credibility" has been established with previous products.

2. Sales force training is aided by specialization. Representatives are taught (through modules) what an organ system does and how it operates when healthy; what happens when the system is not healthy; and what company products do and do *not* do. New offerings in similar organ systems facilitate the ability of reps to come up to speed quickly.

The search system applies to Marion's new Scientific Products Division. A recent example is *artificial skin*, licensed from the Massachusetts Institute of Technology, which is designed to be a temporary replacement for human skin in burn therapy. The two-layered membrane closes the wound immediately, protecting the body from life-threatening infections and fluid loss, and provides a matrix for the ingrowth of blood vessels and other cells. The product is currently in the FDA regulatory process and analysts estimate $10 million of sales by 1987.

Marion had compiled a sparkling compound yearly sales increase of 34 percent for twenty years, but sales and earnings became sporadic in the mid-to-late seventies. The cause was twofold: over-dependence on one product (35 percent of sales), which was adversely affected by regulatory issues, and the mediocre record of ten acquisitions.

Adversity promotes change and Marion began strategic planning at this time. It redefined its mission away from reliance on nondescript medications. Subsidiaries not fitting these plans were divested as Marion narrowed the scope and increased the depth of its basic businesses.

There are other factors founding success, some perhaps more causative from a strategic point of view. The company has excellent perception of the pharmaceutical and health care industry—and as a relatively small firm, its place in it. A growth strategy is clearly needed to achieve the minimal size necessary for survival in this increasingly difficult arena for smaller companies (especially with federal drug regulations).

Marion states that "marketing to professional specialists" is the cutting edge of their company, their sharp sword of competitive advantage. They employ a "multidiscipline" approach, that is, many types of marketing activities aimed at a common goal. Market preparation begins three to four years before the introduction of a new product and involves the integration and dissemination of medical information through media, symposia, and special programs.

A product launch is a main event. It is well coordinated. Marion sponsored, for example, a multicity teleconference on calcium channel blockers on the eve of the annual meeting of the American Heart Association. Remarkably, the event was held just nine days after the company received approval to begin marketing Cardizem in the United States. This major conference was sponsored jointly by eight medical schools and featured a distinguished international faculty of cardiologists and clinical investigators.

Technology diffusion is a prime concern, and Marion employs a "stepped" approach. The first wave is directed at the specialist who is better able to understand the technical aspects of the new product and its differentiation from older products. Credibility is also enhanced by marketing first to organ system experts and then to general practitioners. In this manner the specialists become a resource and a reference for the broader-based physicians.

Marion won the coveted 1982 award from the National Wholesale Druggists Association for "Best New Product Introduction" for the launch of Carafate. The distribution to all Marion's wholesale distributors in the United States was achieved within *three days* following approval to market by the FDA, and 90 percent of the retail trade had initial stocking within two weeks.

Marion is a market-driven company, specializing in providing unique chronic disease prescription drugs to a specific universe of family practitioners and internists. The company's most effective marketing resource is its highly touted sales organization which employs a "consultative approach" to physicians. This approach requires reps to have extensive education and training in order to be able to exchange information with doctors. Company salespeople are well paid and well motivated.

Marion enumerates three corporate missions: (1) people orientation; (2) market leadership through perceived differentiation in selected segments of health care; and (3) long-term returns for shareholders through the management of high risk relative to the external environment. This first is particularly interesting.

Marion states that no competitive strength is more significant than its people. They claim an "uncommon spirit" which, they say, "differentiates us from the industry." They call this undefined attitude the "Marion Spirit." This spirit, of which they speak with pride, generates a feeling of partnership among personnel and is supported by management's providing *clear* answers to the following questions:

☐   Where is the company trying to go? (Clarity of direction.)
☐   Who is responsible for getting each job done? (Clarity of structure.)
☐   How will we evaluate our program? (Clarity of measurement.)

Many companies mouth similar words, but here you believe them. The company, for example, has extensive stock-option plans and profit-sharing systems for executives and employees. Founder Kauffman started the company with the concept that "those who produce shall share in the results."

The majority of Marion's employees (1275 of 1700) work at corporate headquarters in Kansas City, Missouri; the balance represents the nationwide sales force. Marion has developed its own corporate culture—all employees from janitors to executives are called "associates." The company seeks to "achieve a performance and people-oriented working environment that stimulates integrity, entrepreneurial spirit, productivity and a sense of responsibility to all Marion associates and society."

When productivity exceeds plan, Marion declares what they call an "Uncommon Summer," which means Friday afternoons off. Really strong productivity means an "Uncommon Winter," which is time off between Christmas and New Year's. (These "productivity holidays" have been earned. Sales per "associate" increased 87 percent over the past four years, from $57,000 per associate to $107,000—accompanied by a profit increase of 118 percent.)

Even during the difficult retrenching days of the middle and late seventies, Marion preserved its *esprit de corps*. All employees continued to participate in the multiple incentive and bonus plans based on performance. Salespeople continued to be compensated at the top of industry scales.

On the first page of Marion's 1983 annual report, positioned prominently above the year's financial highlights, is a statement exemplifying the firm: "The financial statements in this report quantify all but one of Marion's assets. *People* are, and always have been, Marion's most important financial asset. An exaggeration? Hardly. Sales per associate have increased significantly during the most dynamic growth phase in the company's history." Another indication of the accent on people is Marion's "Office of the President" which consists of its *five* top executives—a near record, I'm sure.

Modeling Marion is easy. Though most Creative Strategies apply, several stand out.

1. *Efficient Innovation.* This, clearly, is its prime builder of success. No competing with giants in original research. No seeking corporate glory in scientific breakthroughs. Find the best drugs overseas and concentrate expertise in preparing them for the U.S. markets. (The strategy is compatible with foreign manufacturers who, having spent the basic R&D dollars, need access to the

American market but lack the regulatory knowledge and marketing access.)

2. *Focus/Coherence.* By concentrating on certain organ systems, Marion has built a corporate reputation for expertise in target areas.

3. *Flexibility/Opportunism.* This is the essence of "search." If there is something out there that fits, Marion will find it.

4. *Employee Opportunity.* Marion emphasizes people relationships, paying top dollar and offering ample psychic income. Treating people as balance sheet "assets" to be maximized instead of income statement "expenses" to be minimized is the basic principle of "human resource accounting."[10]

5. *External Perception.* The company is market driven; satisfying the end user—physicians—is the primary objective. Marketing stresses customer needs, providing constant information and service.

Some words of advice from Marion's president to a meeting of stock analysts: "If you ever see Marion losing that 'Marion Spirit,' sell fast."

INDUSTRIES FOR THE MIDDLE

We now close in on our quarry. Having scanned mid-sized companies in the economy as a whole, aggregating all industries together, we now dissect out certain industries for close inspection. The purpose of the excision? To determine potential preferences for medium-sized companies. Are there specific industries in which mid-sized companies fare better than in others?

A study of thirty industries for the year 1966, a time of relatively high economic activity, showed that in six of the industries "increasing size was accompanied by increasing profitability. . . . there were eight where the reverse was true [that is, profitability tended to *fall* with increasing size]. . . . [and] sixteen industries in which no clear relationship, either direct or inverse, between size and profitability was discernible."[11]

Industries exhibiting a direct relationship between size and profitability, where increasing size was accompanied by increasing profits, were motor vehicles and parts, woven and knit textiles, business machines, paperboard boxes, malt liquor, and iron and steel foundries.

Industries exhibiting an inverse relationship between size and profitability, where increasing size was accompanied by decreasing profits, were blast furnaces and steel mills, distilled liquors, primary aluminum, meat packing, non-ferrous metals (except aluminum), plumbing fixtures, pulp, paper, and paperboard, and ball and roller bearings.

A study of "leaders" and "followers" in thirty-eight industries (based on IRS data for 1963–65) found the average return on equity to be modestly higher among the leaders (11.68 percent) than the followers (10.84%).[12] In twenty-three industries leaders had superior returns; in fifteen industries followers came out on top. The investigator (Michael Porter of Harvard) comments that "the industries in which follower rates of return are higher appear generally to be those where economies of scale are either absent or not great (clothing, footwear, pottery, meat products, carpets) and/or where the industry is highly segmented into numerous distinct product lines or varieties (optical, medical, opthalmic, liquor, periodicals, carpets, toys, and sporting goods) and firms can potentially achieve high product differentiation by specializing in a particular niche [a persistent and critical strategy for smaller firms]. The industries where the leader group's rates of return are greatly higher seem to be generally those with heavy advertising (soap, perfumes, soft drinks, grain mill products, cutlery), and/or research outlays (radio and television, drugs, photographic equipment)."

Table 4.2 stratifies sixteen industries into large and medium-sized companies (1972–73 data)—total industrywide assets controlled by the top four large companies averaged 76 percent. In only one of the sixteen industries was the rate of return of the medium-sized companies greater than that of the large-sized companies (tires); in fourteen industries the rate of return of the large-sized companies was greater than the mid-sized companies; and in one they were about even. The mean rate of return for the large companies was 11.68 percent; for mid-sized companies across the

TABLE 4.2. Rate of Return within Industries: Mid-Sized versus Large-Sized Firms, 1972–73 Average

SIC	Industry	Number of Large-Sized Firms	Mean Percent	Standard Deviation Percent	Number of Mid-Sized Firms	Mean Percent	Standard Deviation Percent
201	Meat Products	4	10.0	4.6	8	9.2	13.6
202	Dairy Products	4	13.5	2.8	4	8.9	2.7
205	Bakery Products	4	9.6	5.5	4	−4.3	16.8
206	Sugar	4	10.0	5.6	4	4.6	7.1
2082	Malt Beverages	4	11.9	8.0	4	4.8	12.1
2085	Distilled Liquor	4	11.1	5.4	4	5.9	5.3
21	Tobacco	4	14.9	4.6	4	11.1	5.3
22	Textiles	4	6.8	2.0	4	6.0	1.9
261	Paper Mill	4	11.1	3.1	4	9.9	4.1
265	Paper Boxes	4	12.1	3.9	4	11.1	7.9
283	Drugs	4	20.8	5.6	8	20.9	5.1
301	Tires	4	10.1	2.1	4	10.5	3.2
314	Footwear	4	15.3	4.3	4	12.8	3.2
331	Iron & Steel	4	7.8	1.9	8	6.6	3.9
354	Machinery	4	7.6	3.3	4	5.6	8.6
3714	Motor Vehicle Parts	4	14.2	2.5	8	12.7	8.4

Source: Data derived from *Report of the Federal Trade Commission on Rates of Return in Selected Manufacturing Industries 1964-1973.* Rates of return are after-tax profits over stockholders' equity expressed as a percentage. Data for each company in the sample were included for two years, 1972 and 1973.

same sample, the mean was 8.52 percent. The standard deviation—a measure of the variance or dispersion around the mean—was larger for mid-sized firms than for large-sized firms in eleven of the sixteen industries.

Table 4.3 compiles 412 companies in twelve industries for the year 1974. (Revenues were used as the criteria for dividing large from medium-sized firms, the break being discerned by clear "gaps" or "jumps." In the diversified/conglomerate industry, the same number of firms was deliberately chosen for both large and medium groups; the large-sized firms ranged from ITT's $11.1 billion to Olin's $1.3 billion, the medium-sized firms from AMF's $1 billion to Chris-Craft's $64.5 million.)

In four of the twelve industries, the mid-sized firms exhibited a higher rate of return on stockholders' equity (women's apparel, chemicals, tires, electronics); in four of the industries, the large-sized firms evinced a higher return; and in the final four, the means were almost identical. For whatever reason, there are some industries in which mid-sized firms seem to outperform their larger rivals, at least during certain years.[13]

Summed across all 421 companies, the mean rate of return was higher for large companies (11.53 percent versus 10.84 percent), but not significant. The difference in standard deviation, however, was quite significant. In all twelve industries of the sample, the standard deviation of the mid-sized firm group (13.6 percent) was much larger than the standard deviation of the large-sized firm group (4.6 percent).[14]

This standard deviation brings with it some interesting ideas, especially *stability* and *risk*. Large-sized firms, apparently, are better able to maintain stability and spread risks; they support earnings through pricing policies and smooth earnings through accounting methods. Mid-sized firms, on average, are just less stable and more risky. This is clear. But there may be something more lurking here.

The high variance among medium-sized companies, combined with rates of return near their large rivals, forces the following conclusion: Some mid-sized firms must outperform large-sized firms within the same industry in any given year. Now, whether these better-performing mid-sized firms shift and vary from year

TABLE 4.3. Rate of Return within Industries: Mid-Sized versus Large-Sized Firms, 1974

SIC	Industry	Number of Large-Sized Firms	Mean Percent	Standard Deviation Percent	Number of Mid-Sized Firms	Mean Percent	Standard Deviation Percent
201	Meat Products	7	13.7	4.7	28	6.8	14.9
22	Textiles	3	10.4	0.7	45	7.3	12.0
232	Apparel-Men's	5	9.9	5.1	30	9.6	10.5
233	Apparel-Women's	3	8.3	5.7	34	11.1	11.4
262	Paper Mills	11	16.0	4.0	12	15.3	9.1
281	Chemicals	12	14.9	3.2	14	22.6	16.5
301	Tires	4	8.4	1.5	6	10.1	10.1
354	Machinery	6	9.9	4.9	21	9.4	8.5
357	Office Equipment	5	12.4	7.4	31	5.4	25.0
367	Electronics	6	9.8	5.2	37	10.5	23.9
384	Medical	4	13.0	2.3	26	12.7	10.0
398	Diversified	31	11.7	10.3	31	9.3	11.8

Source: Data derived from *30,000 Leading U.S. Corporations*, by the editors of *News Front*. Rates of return are after-tax profits over stockholders' equity expressed as a percentage.

to year in some random-walk process, or whether there are mid-sized firms that consistently outperform their industries' leaders, is the key question we address.

GOOD THINGS COME IN SMALL PACKAGES

In 1982, not an easy year, the Continental Group barely made 3 percent on over $5.5 billion in sales supported by almost $6 billion in assets. Crown, Cork & Seal also earned about 3 percent on its sales of $1.35 billion. The American Can Company, with a host of problems, *lost* $133 million on $4 billion revenues.

The metal can industry would seem to favor economies of scale, what with its huge volumes of products and long runs of production. How then to explain the profit performance of J. L. Clark, with a 1982 return of *8.4* percent on $156 million in sales. (However good that 8+ percent looks, it was the company's poorest in almost a decade. For each of the six years from 1976 through 1981, Clark exceeded a 10 percent return on sales, and well into the 20s on equity. In 1983, Clark earned $14 million on $159 million in volume; in the first nine months of 1984, sales and profits were up 14 percent and 23 percent respectively.)

The packaging/container industry is large and loaded with intense rivalry. The market share wars are fought between conflicting materials—plastic versus glass versus metal versus cardboard—as well as between competing manufacturers. Differentiation is difficult and proprietary products do not play a major role. Most can and bottle producers work with voluminous production runs and thin gross margins.

Clark bucks the trend and forges its own path. It attains profit leadership by cutting a tight niche in *customized packaging*, a segment deemed too small and too specialized for the above-mentioned giants. Clark's reputation for quality and reliability validates its premium pricing, thus delivering its considerably higher profit performance—almost three times industry averages in returns on sales and equity (without high leverage).

J. L. Clark, based in Rockford, Illinois, calls itself a leading manufacturer of customated packaging. "Customation," they say, "is the full spectrum of specialized skills, techniques and services blended to produce the highest quality product in the market-place. . . . [We] take an innovative package, or component, from concept to quality volume production as expeditiously as possible." The business has two principal product groups:

1. *Packaging.* Over 1000 different types and sizes of containers and metal packaging specialties are manufactured for customers. Products include finely lithographed metal and metal plastic containers, spiral- and convolutely wound composite containers, and collapsible metal tubes. Major brand manufacturers use these containers for spices, tea, snack items, cleaning and polishing compounds, drugs, toiletries, tobacco, toys, and other consumer products. (Customers include Band-Aid, Crayola crayons, McCormick spices, Brylcream; and Hills Bros. coffee.) Decorative metal specialty items such as battery shells, razor blade dispensers, wastepaper baskets, and so on are also manufactured. Today, packaging provides about 50 percent of the revenues (down from about 75 percent following the 1981 acquisition of the J. A. Baldwin Company)— and about 60 percent of the profits. Packaging products are sold through company salespeople who are trained to consult with customers on technical details of their particular requirements.

2. *Industrial.* Products include filters, paper and plastic tubes, and related products. The major portion of the group is the result of the acquisition of Baldwin, one of the leading manufacturers of premium-quality heavy-duty filters. The complete product line fields over 1700 types of oil, fuel, air, coolant, hydraulic, and transmission filters—used in almost every engine-related application. Spiral-wound tubes of paper or plastic are used as insulating components. The company also converts roll paper into pads, business machine forms, and tapes. Industrial products are sold through representatives.

Containers and metal packaging specialties are manufactured only upon orders received from customers, thus minimizing market exposure and inventory risk. Containers are designed and produced, usually with distinctive decoration (such as canisters with prints or pictures), to meet each customer's unique marketing and packaging requirements. Producing intricate embossing, using multiple colors, and applying special coatings are company competencies.

Take an example of Clark's highly efficient operation. What happens when Johnson & Johnson orders a new batch of their familiar Band-Aid metal boxes? Clark just pulls out its printing plate, packed with some fifty images of the can, and runs it through a high-speed printing press. The sheets are dried and the images cut into strips. The strips are then fed into stamping machines that mold the metal into individual containers to be packed and shipped to Johnson & Johnson.

Clark stresses product quality and customer service externally, and efficiency and consistency internally. The company is clearly not the low-cost producer, but thrives on its reputation for translating fine workmanship into large-scale production. They claim the highest quality in the industry.

The company puts high emphasis on manufacturing and productivity gains. Flexibility and cost-effectiveness are foremost concerns. Better control of materials and inventory and the installation of new production lines got top billing in the president's 1982 letter to stockholders. The purchase of two new automated lines of equipment was one of the year's highlights.

Efficient use of facilities is a primary concern of top management. There is virtual obsession with maintaining equipment in top condition. "Repairs," hardly polite talk for traditional corporate publicity, is an important theme. Recent retooling, for example, permitted the use of lighter-weight steel. "Upgrading and modernizing of the tool room" at a certain plant was deemed important enough to include in the president's 1981 letter. Not many a CEO will use his limited space to talk about "tool rooms."

Clark had enjoyed years of steady, solid growth, until changed by a sales spurt resulting from the Baldwin purchase. The company has a strong balance sheet, but the $46 million cash purchase price caused some stretch. The president claims that "while filters might seem quite different from containers," the companies have much in common, "founded on the principles of quality and service" and capitalizing on "innovation to maintain those principles." Clark, he says, is pleased to add a proprietary line of products to its traditional custom business, giving "new dimensions" and "good balance." Whether that balance will be kept is the question.

The Creative Strategies that predominate at J. L. Clark are evident: Product Emphasis. Efficient Innovation. Distinctiveness. Flexibility.

CHAPTER 5

MIDDLEPOWER

Pushing Pluses, Hiding Minuses

Strategy, in essence, is the search for competitive advantage, for areas of company competence that surmount rivals. Competitive advantage can assume various forms, most of which are firm specific. What we seek here are comparative strengths for medium-sized companies as a class. Are there elements of organizational structure by which enterprises in the middle can gain an edge? Can mid-sized firms ever *start out* at the head of the pack?

We have seen how mid-sized firms are thrown for initial loss, how they begin badly. Now we seek the opposite. Recent research has shown at least three corporate characteristics where medium-sized companies display initial advantage, three new constructs entering on the side of the underdogs. In the cutthroat business arena, where small-fry firms are locked in mortal battle with leviathan corporations, any leverage must be exploited.

The industrial economist William Shepherd states that "size does permit a slightly higher rate of return, thanks to pecuniary economies and a moderate market power effect. But this is more than offset by X-inefficiencies and related diseconomies of pure size."[1]

X-inefficiency is a technical term defined as "the excess of *unnecessary* cost as a percentage of actual cost"—and it seems to increase with increasing size. Why is this so? What mechanisms are involved? Some ideas offered include executive luxury nurtured by substantial profits (two corporate jets when one is questionable); managerial flabbiness spawned by hefty margins (swollen staffs); the bureaucratic burden of large organizations (massive personnel departments); the sluggishness of pure size (interminable "coordinating" committees).[2]

So the economy suffers at both ends of the large-firm stick: The public pays higher prices into the giant companies' coffers, and then some of these excess profits are frittered away through executive perks, bloated bureaucracies, and status quo softness. Thus the smaller firm is inherently more efficient. Is this the beginning of competitive advantage? (If, on the other hand, large-sized firms are more efficient as well as more effective, then any argument for mid-sized survival could be based on little more than the dubious notion of nostalgia.)

There are other *dis*economies of pure size. "Worker satisfaction"—the nature of work and social relationships inside the firm—is reduced by size of the company. Employees in larger companies have, in general, higher degrees of personal alienation and depressed levels of job satisfaction—both of which are tied to the rigid, unilateral type of power structure characteristic of increasing firm size.[3]

Employees in smaller companies have, in general, greater task variety, more individual responsibility, higher personal satisfaction, and an enhanced sense of local identity. Aggregating these elements together, psychologists who study organizations use the term *content*, and this content is said to be inversely proportional to firm size—that is, content decreases as firm size increases. Other things being equal, therefore, workers in smaller companies will produce more abundantly, do it more efficiently, and be happier in the process. Is this also competitive advantage?

Innovation too, while often used to justify large companies' garnering greater control of corporate assets, might be more compromised than enhanced in a business environment populated only by behemoths. The argument that increasing size is necessary to focus high R&D expenditures on complex problems is answered by statistical analysis of the past. Innovations in the steel, automobile, petroleum, drug, and other industries show consistent (but not uniform) patterns of small-share firms leading, and dominant firms following.[4]

Such research, albeit preliminary, suggests that innovation emerges most often from medium-sized firms, those companies with roughly a 5–20 percent share of the market.[5] Revolutionary ideas, on the other hand, germinate with high frequency from small firms, sociological structures with neither mental constraint nor prior predilection. Is this again competitive advantage?

In many industries (pending market definition), the "5–20 percent" share range includes at its lower end, several mid-sized firms at their upper end. Innovation, these data indicate, becomes a potential ally of small and medium-sized firms in their epic struggle "to flourish among giants."

Other sized firms, for diverse reasons (whether financial and numerical or organizational and psychological), do not appear to produce as well. Firms with lower market shares are often too small to apply adequate resources, human and technical as well as capital and financial. Large firms, those with shares greater than 20 percent, while not necessarily laggards in innovation because of size per se, may tend to delay the introduction of new ideas until forced to by market pressures. It is common knowledge that many of the largest companies—such as IBM, AT&T, Xerox, General Motors—will withhold announcing new computer families, communication technologies, copier lines, and automotive models long after they have been developed. Sounds implausible? Consider the motivation: to maintain the value of their present asset base and product offerings, thus minimizing internal competition and maximizing financial return.

SELF-DETERMINATION

What begins to emerge, then, is the social superiority of medium-size firms. X-efficiency, content, and innovation—they all contribute.

But general public benefit does not *ipso facto* become transformed into firm-specific financial success. Nor does the initial development of innovative products *ipso facto* guarantee jungle survival (much less prosperity) for the venturesome mid-sized firm. Indeed, a larger competitor may well take advantage of the new product or technology by its vastly more powerful procuring, producing, marketing, and distributional capacities. What's left for the original innovative firm? Only the dregs with which to cover its much higher costs of initial research and development. (The jungle analogy seems uncomfortably appropriate: The larger predator waits lazily until its smaller rival does all the work of seeking, finding, capturing, and gathering food—only then to steal it by brute strength.)

Mid-sized firms must know their environment; what their larger competitors will do; how their smaller competitors will react. It's a tight, tough game, with the results carrying meaning to society as well as the firm. Medium-sized firms are important—economically, politically, socially, technologically. Their self-determined survival and prosperity must be assured by the force of internal strength. The only way this will happen is with effective strategies. These we discover, describe, distill, and develop.

Small and medium-sized businesses are what made this country great. Their survival and prosperity is a national necessity, a collective resource. But prosperity cannot be provided by external directives. Survival, maybe; prosperity, never. Real success must come from inside, from managerial savvy and entrepreneurial guts. The government can help; but please, not too much.

LEVERAGING ENTREPRENEURS[7]

The formal meeting had just concluded, though something serious was still hanging. You could sense it. Negotiations were going well, but an unspoken problem had to be broached.

Marvin Blumenfeld, president of Eagle Clothes, had summarized the proposed joint venture following the detailed presentation from his senior staff. The executive vice-president of the prospective partner, a large public company, expressed satisfaction; but as the two groups began ambling out of the conference room he gave a body hint to Blumenfeld. The man wanted to talk privately.

"Look, Marvin," began the exec VP with some hesitation, "the vision was exciting, the plan realistic, and the team superb."

"But you have a problem," said Blumenfeld with his usual candor.

"A few of us are concerned about the fellow you've chosen as project director for the new venture. He's made a first-rate analysis; he has the experience, drive, and all requisite attributes, but, well, I guess we're concerned because he once went bankrupt."

Blumenfeld smiled, drew closer to his counterpart and pointed to pictures of top management and principal clients, "*Most* of us have gone bankrupt. That's why we're so good."

In October 1981 Eagle Clothes was doing some $6 million in annual revenues on which it had just *lost* $2.8 million; its net worth was a *negative* $4 million.

In October 1983, two years later, Eagle Clothes was doing some $100 million in annual revenues on which it had just *made* $5.3 million; its net worth was a *positive* $20 million.

Eagle Clothes is a fascinating case study for several reasons. Its long history as a premier American suit manufacturer; its uncontrolled growth in retailing; its precipitous decline into bankruptcy and subsequent reemergence; its acquisition of a company several times its size through an innovative financial structure—all are part of its story, but not ours.

We focus on the business that Eagle purchased. It's called "April-Marcus," and in the worst decade ever for menswear retailing it grew 20–40 percent per year.

Marvin Blumenfeld met Morty April in the liquidation of Marvin's clothing store. "I grew up in retailing," Blumenfeld recalls, "my family owned B & B Clothes in Jamaica, New York, ironically the old Eagle's first retail acquisition. I wanted to make it big. So I saved up $25,000 and opened my own store. I did great, and made the classic mistake. I took money out on the upswing. I thought business would continue forever. But the area was a resort community, and when a recession evaporated tourists and a new shopping center drew off locals, I hit trouble. From expecting to go ahead 25 percent, I fell behind 25 percent. I couldn't meet my obligations and that's when Morty came in.

"He did such a successful job that he 'liquidated' me right back into business. Then he asked me to work for him part-time. So

Monday through Thursday I was in New York; Friday through
Sunday at my upstate store. I remember what Morty told me when
I first came to work, 'Just follow me around for three months, and
don't say a word. I'll gamble $300 a week you'll learn some-
thing.'"

April-Marcus has the buying clout, merchandising savvy, and
financial strength to capture an important share of the burgeoning
off-price business. The company is, in essence, a service organization
with a guaranteed long-term commission on the retail volume of
each of its more than 200 client stores—without the liabilities and
commitments of retail ownership.

Though men's suits was a declining industry populated by giants,
this small consulting company prospered while many traditional
retailers, such as department stores, gave up men's clothing altogether. April-Marcus spurted when others contracted. (The reason
for industry shrinkage? With the whipsaw of recession and inflation
eroding buying power, many men were unwilling to pay higher
and higher prices for their clothing. After all, wife and children
came first; daddy last.)

As traditional retailers fell on hard times, and as department
store clothing sales languished and were dropped (due to slow
inventory turn and low volume per square foot), a void was created.
The number of places a man could buy suits diminished.

"We created a business," says Blumenfeld, "when others said
there was no business. When everyone did a 'Chicken Little' act
and said the sky was falling, we went out and built our city. We
found a vacuum and filled a need. We caught the flavor of the
times."

April-Marcus has a unique formula: The vast majority of its
client retail stores are not owned by the company. The stores are
owned independently by on-site entrepreneur-managers, men with
a twenty-four-hour-day, seven-day-week commitment to their
businesses. The mentality is different; and it's not just reward
potential. To these fellows, running stores is not a job; it is life.

April-Marcus supplies everything but the local management—
merchandising, buying, pricing, advertising, accounting, budg-
eting, site location, store setups, retail strategy. Says Blumenfeld,
"Our business is one entrepreneur selling one sport coat and one

tie to one customer, and then getting that customer to come back again and bring his friend."

One of the company's most valuable services is its buying power. Eagle, through its April-Marcus subsidiary, is one of the largest purchasers of men's clothing in the United States. Because it buys such large quantities of men's suits, slacks, sport coats, and accessories, the company is able to effect significant savings that are passed through to client stores. Much buying is done "in season," when manufacturers are forced to turn remaining inventories into cash. This merchandise, though a few months old and broken in sizes and colors, is first-rate in quality and very low in price.

April-Marcus's client stores are positioned solidly in their cities and communities as leaders in "off-price," one of the fastest-growing segments of retailing. (Off-price means that the stores sell the same merchandise for about 20–40 percent less than traditional stores. Many are famous brand names. The motto of Anders, a client chain of 30+ stores, is "We Name Names.")

Off-price is perennially profitable because, regardless of good times or bad, clothing shoppers demand value, quality, and fashion at the lowest possible price. That is precisely what Eagle clients offer the public with their "no-frills" service. (Additional price reductions are accomplished by reducing overhead and generating higher turnover.)

April-Marcus stores are clean and neat and loaded with merchandise. A typical 5000-square-foot store might carry 2500 suits and 1500 sport coats in addition to furnishings (shirts, ties, etc.). Consumers have the largest selections from which to choose.

Stores are usually located in low-to-medium rent areas, relying on heavy, hard-sell advertising to pull in consumers. These less-than-prestigious surroundings are often better known by route numbers than street names, although more recent stores are springing up in "strip centers" adjacent to major malls. Advertising expenses are high, reaching 10 percent of sales in some cases. (The basic formula is 15 percent of sales for both rent and advertising.)

The bottom line, of course, is what counts, and April-Marcus clients, even with their low prices, maintain better margins than many traditional retailers saddled with high rents for fancy addresses and splendiferous trappings. The reason is largely the buying power and expertise of April-Marcus. Concern for client success is the touchstone of every April-Marcus decision.

Demographics of customers reveal a broad and varied lot, including many businessmen and professionals. "I must wear a different suit every day," commented a bank vice-president shuffling through several dozen sized for his rather ample girth, "and I can pick up three fine suits here for what I might pay for one expensive suit at a high-price store."

Concentration and then dominance of market areas is the April-Marcus approach. Effective use of advertising media is stressed, and optimum saturation of an area generates maximum efficiency (the eighth store in Dallas, for example, takes advantage of the blanket advertising coverage already committed). Clients are encouraged to add more stores in their areas, as long as profitability is maintained, and usually only one client is accepted in any given area—though market segmentation by quality, price, and size ("big and tall") can enable more than one client to coexist in the same city.

Clients are clustered in metropolitan areas and have recognizable names of regional importance (such as Bond's in New York, Kuppenheimer in Texas, Clothing Clearance Centers in Chicago and San Francisco, Morville's in Philadelphia, Peck's in the midwest, and Anders in Baltimore and central Pennsylvania.)

A key to April-Marcus's ability to move merchandise to repeat customers is its private-label program. Some of these private brands began as national brands and still appear that way to shoppers. Others were created and supported by strong promotions. Exclusive to April-Marcus clients are men's suits carrying the well-known Eagle label, which since the acquisition of April-Marcus has been strengthened. (Blumenfeld resisted the natural inclination to reduce price by reducing quality. "The Eagle name is very important to us. We've improved the Eagle make. We give the customer real value. That secures our future.") A pilot program of "Eagle" stores, building on the national name, is in planning.

April-Marcus is compensated by a percentage of each client's annual sales, with contracts lasting a minimum of five to ten years. By not owning its own stores, the company has little exposure to the downside of retailing with its large fixed costs and overheads. The percentage arrangement allows upside participation. (April-Marcus makes no markup on merchandise. It passes through the exact cost of goods to its clients. Thus all clients gain the full advantage of mass buying power. April-Marcus makes its money strictly on commissions of gross sales.)

April-Marcus was founded forty years ago by Mortimer April, chairman of the board, an astute businessman whose specialty is liquidations and going-out-of-business sales for troubled retailers. April is expert at working with prospective clients, showing besieged retailers how to generate quick cash, and helping shaky retailers maintain good profits.

"Mr. April was so successful in running promotional sales," says Blumenfeld, "that we recognized that a marginal store could become successful. Just a few minor changes in retail strategy— merchandise mix, advertising slant, and the like—is sometimes all it takes."

Ask Blumenfeld the key to April-Marcus's success and you get a quick answer, "Finding the right people for the right job." He likes talking about his very successful group of entrepreneur-managers. "Several had been bankrupt; but we don't worry about the past, we learn from the past. We like to back hungry people, men with intensity and dedication, men who want to make money and maybe prove a thing or two."

Blumenfeld runs an open organization. He and April share a modest office that doubles as a conference room and triples as a lunch room. The door is always open and clients pop in every few moments. "I've developed a group of 'No-Men,'" says Blumenfeld. "Our executives fight for what they believe. Ideas are great, but implementation is key. We give people a sense of pride. We give freedom to employees until they prove they can't do the job. Our structure is informal. That's been an asset, though with rapid growth we must upgrade controls."

Blumenfeld's biggest problem? He'll tell it to you straight: "Not spending enough time running my business. For about two years, I was enmeshed in the legalities of making the original Eagle deal and the subsequent public offering. Wall Street is greedy; it can monopolize your time."

Blumenfeld's favorite story epitomizes April-Marcus. "One of my friends was in the toy business and got into trouble. He asked for our advice, but didn't take it and wound up bankrupt. He had the right spirit, though, the 'hunger' we look for, and we decided to back him in menswear. Well, the first year he listened to us *too much*, and didn't do well. He was not being forceful enough, not giving us the tough feedback from the 'front.' Finally he broke his fear and became very successful. Today he is probably the largest merchandiser of men's clothing in San Francisco. We must have our local entrepreneurs fight for what they need. They are the experts in their areas. We are here to support them."

Analyzing Eagle/April-Marcus is simplified by using Creative Strategies:

Dominance.   Client stores are concentrated in chosen geographic areas; maximum market share is sought (amortizing large advertising costs).

Distinctiveness.   Client stores are packed with merchandise. Brand names at discounts. Hard sell, unmistakable advertising. Heavy stress on "value," fine quality at low prices. No-frills atmosphere. (National chain of Eagle stores?)

Focus.   Heavy stress on men's clothing, suits, and sport coats. (April-Marcus resists temptations to develop women's apparel or even men's sportswear.)

High-Profile CEO.   Both April and Blumenfeld are well known in the menswear industry. Blumenfeld is directly involved with every client.

Employee Opportunity.   Many entrepreneurs backed by April-Marcus have done marvelously well and have fierce loyalty to the firm.

External Perception.   Building a business in a declining industry takes doing; filling the vacuum with a new approach works.

Opportunism.   Working with retailers in trouble generates mutual benefits. Buying end-of-season lots from manufacturers produces excellent prices.

ORGANIZATIONAL TYPES

Theorists have developed three distinct types of organizational structure. Each is well suited to its time, and the general chronological flow is Type I to Type II to Type III as the company grows (see Figure 5.1).[8]

TYPE I: The Entrepreneurial Model.   The company is the personification of the chief executive, who is usually the founder and owner. Its business activities are the extension of his personal interests, and they are enhanced by his strengths and limited by

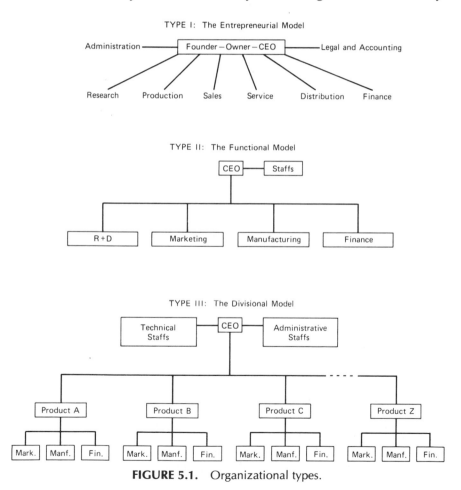

FIGURE 5.1.   Organizational types.

his weaknesses. Often the firm emphasizes the founder's own area of expertise, for example, research (like Polaroid under Land).[9]

TYPE II: The Functional Model. The firm is organized vertically by functional areas, such as marketing, production, finance, and so on. This means that all manufacturing, no matter how diverse the products, reports through the vice-president of manufacturing. Stressing efficient use of resources and the coordination of functional departments, this model works best with a few product lines (which should probably be related).

TYPE III: The Divisional Model. The corporation is now organized horizontally by product areas, each division operating with relative autonomy and controlling its own independent functional areas. As companies diversify products and expand distribution, administrative pressure is put on Type II structures. Interests between competing products collide and senior management cannot adjudicate all the conflicts. By decentralizing decision making and control, by making each division a profit center, the central or head office is freed to focus on finance, research, and overall corporate strategy.

Medium-sized companies are ripe for crisis when moving from Type I to Type II and then from Type II to Type III. The transition from entrepreneurial-founder to professional management is especially traumatic. Howard Head's self-insight at the Head Ski Company is well known to a generation of business students:[10] "I finally developed the ability to take on a general manager," he said, then admitting, "It was hard for me to operate under this framework." Head moved himself into a "consultant" role, agreeing to "operate through the president"—though his addendum—"Of course . . . I must exert authority"—echoes the eternal entrepreneurial battle cry. Few entrepreneurs are ever ready to retire, and fewer still can give up the reins without a fight.

Suffice it to say that no top-performing medium-size company has failed to negotiate itself through the mine field-like crisis of delegation and the requisite installation of a professional management team. This does not mean, however, that the entrepreneurial instinct was snuffed out when the founder stepped down. Just the contrary. The most successful mid-sized firms were those that could simultaneously encourage venturesome excitement while building corporate controls.

LEVERAGING INDEPENDENCE

In the ten years between 1971 and 1981, the Shaklee Corporation, manufacturers and marketers of nutritional, household, and personal care products, jumped from $44 million in revenues and $1.9 million in profits to $454 million in revenues and $24.5 in profits (1983 revenues, $534 million; profits, $35 million). Return on equity averaged about 35 percent, only once lower than 15 percent and three times higher than 50 percent. For Shaklee, though timing was good, organization was better.

Increasing public interest in health foods and supplements cer tainly was important. Each of Shaklee's products—nutritional products such as vitamins, protein powders, fruit and energy bars; household products such as laundry soaps and cleaners; and personal care products for skin, hair, and beauty—exemplifies, according to the company, "commitment to quality and harmony with nature." Shaklee caught the crest of the wave in health and fitness and rode it well.

But it was Shaklee's distributional system that really energized growth. Here was the fuel of the fire. The analogy to an evangelistic crusade is more than mere metaphor.

None of Shaklee's products can be purchased in retail stores (the subject of Federal Trade Commission litigation); none can be ordered directly from the company. To buy a product, you must go through a local distributor, and upon these people, paid on a strict system of commission and incentive, does the company rest. The cover of their 1981 annual report put it well: "Ultimately it is the individual in the field—the independent entrepreneur who is building a business—that is the foundation of Shaklee Corporation."

Tremendous emphasis is placed on Shaklee's field force of independent business men and women. The phenomenon is called "multilevel marketing," and the object is to recruit and motivate subdistributors under you, workers from whom you always get a percentage. (Such a pyramid-type system, subject to the criticism that only those on top can generate real money, is used by other companies such as Avon and Amway—the latter, a private company several times larger than Shaklee, is its primary competition.)

In corporate annual reports there is usually a page reserved for a summary of financial data. SEC law requires five years, though some companies report ten. The basic numbers of sales, income, assets, working capital, long-term debt, selected ratios, dividends, stock prices are traditionally given. Shaklee presents all those (and more), but then adds two others rather strange for corporate America. Right next to "Return on Stockholders' Equity," are "Number of Independent Sales Leaders" and "Sales Leaders' Incentive Automobiles"—these being the two key barometers of Shaklee's distributional system. (Sales leaders increased from 2100 in 1972 to 13,000 in 1982, and their incentive autos increased from 900 in 1972 to 6500 in 1982. The leveling off of sales leaders over the past three years foreshadows the slowing of company growth.)

Sales leaders are the key, and all company systems are designed to facilitate their efforts. Sales leaders are those whose business has reached a certain size, $3000 of purchases per month, and this qualifies them to buy products directly from the company. There are levels of sales leaders, from supervisors to master coordinators. Master coordinators are the highest rank, attained by developing a minimum of fifteen sales leaders. "MCs" receive top-of-the-line cars and commissions that can reach into the stratosphere. Most important in Shaklee's society, however, is recognition as guest speakers at conventions and featured success stories in company publications.

The Shaklee sales plan is called "truly democratic," allowing an individual to progress as far as possible. The plan provides business-building incentives and benefits—cash bonuses, bonus cars, travel to conventions, and participation in insurance programs. A computerized telephone ordering system and a staff of "counselors" respond instantly to sales leader inquiries about orders, shipments, product availability, and bonus and incentive status. Sales leaders maintain inventories to service their customers, thus providing extensive financial leverage for the company.

Shaklee, based in San Francisco, prides itself on innovative nutritional research and first-class quality manufacturing. (The charge of product contamination several years ago hit at the vitals of the company and was fought vigorously). R&D expenditures have been increased significantly in order to develop new products to feed future growth (jumping from $1 million in 1976 to $7 million in 1981). Successful new products include Sustained Release Vita-C 500 mg—the equivalent of eating one and one-half oranges every hour for five hours.

Yet nothing compares to the importance of the field force, how it is organized and how it is motivated. The system can be likened to a religious sect; few missionaries have the sustained zeal of Shaklee distributors. It's as much social structure and group motivation as financial structure and business development. Shaklee distributors are not just plugging company products, they are "preaching the gospel" of life and health. It is their guiding philosophy and it is rooted deep.

Shaklee conventions as incentives for sales leaders are held in exotic areas of the world (like Hawaii and Vienna), and the experience gives the feel of religious revival. Leading distributors are brought together to share formulas for success and to build organizational commitment. In 1981, for example, some 50,000 people attended twenty "Supervisor Success Conferences."[11]

The organization of distributors approaches a closed society, with its own lingo and trappings of success irrelevant to the outside world. Self-image becomes dependent on achievement in system terms and recognition by system rewards (e.g., "the highlight of each month's mail" is said to be "the arrival of the Shaklee Bonus Check"; the make and model of one's incentive automobile, as determined by sales success, is a major status symbol).

When the company states that "the outreach program [distributors working with customers through workshops and personal contact] is a key ingredient in the Shaklee way," the description could easily fit an evangelical movement. Both the concept of "outreach program" and "Shaklee way" are characteristic of fundamentalist fervor. "Sharing the Shaklee opportunity" is a favorite phrase, evoking images of lay preachers going door-to-door.

The importance of the field force cannot be overestimated. Shaklee's whole effort is to support them. A 1980 strategic decision to "refocus" the company on nutritional products—currently almost

75 percent of sales revenues and operating profits—was in direct response to "our Sales Leaders' desire to emphasize nutritional products in their individual businesses." Nutritional products are called "door openers and business builders" for the independent distributors, and enable better cash flow management through higher turnover.

Shaklee products are expensive. The consumer must pay for each "level" in the multilevel system, along with the basic costs and profits. "Volume incentives," the money paid out to distributors based on bulk purchases, is an income statement line item larger than 150 percent of cost of goods sold—$196 million in 1982 and $224 million in 1983 (42 percent of revenues). This is money, beyond product cost and company overheads, that end users pay for the multilevel distributional system. Prices for products, therefore, are forced to be very high. Yet, no complaints from the faithful. However expensive, and however similar competing products, Shaklee is like religion to its adherents. (A nice business, religion. Religious belief is "price inelastic"; increasing cost does not dampen sales in proportion.) Shaklee's products (like Amway's) have the same character.

Sales in North America and Europe went down between 1981 and 1982; it was only a 45 percent increase in business in Japan (to $83 million) that generated the overall sales increase. The Japanese expansion is extremely important for Shaklee. Profitability is high since basic costs are already covered. In 1982 operational income before corporate expenses, interest, and taxes was 34 percent in Japan, better than double the 16 percent in North America and Europe. The Shaklee name, claims the company, is well recognized throughout Japan as "the leading provider of quality nutritional products."

To Shaklee's credit, it allows each international company "to be true to its own national identity" while adhering to "the constant and universal commitment to quality and products in harmony with nature and good health." One example is a tiny vitamin C breath freshener, in tune with Japanese customs of using these mintlike tablets frequently throughout the day.

Shaklee's long-term goal is to become "the world's leading nutritional products company." Realistic? Yet the recent slowing of growth suggests that the company may have reached its peak, and any further expansion efforts could be counterproductive.

The classic mistake of successful medium-sized companies is to assume unending growth, projecting historical trends into infinity. The truly top-performing mid-sized firm will sense its proper level and seek long-term profit maximization.

The Shaklee Corporation built a remarkable record on two of the Creative Strategies, Product Emphasis and Employee Opportunity—with additional support from Distinctiveness (even if only perceived) and Focus/Coherence. How the company handles the Growth–Profits Tradeoff is the current question.

ENTREPRENEURIAL SPIRIT

Entrepreneurship is the driving energy of a new world of business, a world encompassing a broad base of traditional organizations and innovative institutions of all sizes. The concept is no longer limited to small, start-up companies; its impact today is pandemic.

The widening scope of the field requires a broadening definition of the term. Entrepreneurship, to me, is the economic synthesis of human knowledge, the molding of physical substance and value out of mental form and concept. Entrepreneurship is the modern human analog of the original Genesis creation, when chaos and void were transformed into heavens and earth. Entrepreneurship is the process that produces something from nothing.

It is also exciting—the hope of the big hit, the tension of uncertain outcome, the suspense of expected success. What makes entrepreneurship energizing to the individual is the fuel that empowers society and drives human progress. Of the top 100 American firms in 1918, fewer than half were recognizable in 1968.

All human beings are created equal, but only a few forge the future. We now explore the entrepreneurial mind. The excursion puts us in touch with the roots of business success, the foundation of successful companies. It also sensitizes us to the corporate culture necessary to catalyze ongoing dynamism. If a "top-performing" mid-sized firm is to maintain that high status, creativity must be developed and innovation fostered.

Entrepreneurial environments are the fertile fields in which the best companies grow, and those key employees who indeed forge the future must be encouraged, protected, and kept. Whether through profit sharing, stock options, royalty rights, or personal recognition, those few must be kept.

Creativity and innovation are essential for mid-sized success; to compete against giants a smaller firm must see earlier, sense quicker, and respond faster.

The key to stimulate creativity and fire innovation? Entrepreneurial motivation, the magnetic pull of proprietary participation. Incentive generation is vital because research and innovation are not the same thing. The former can be done on demand; the latter cannot. Research can be programmed from without; innovation must be generated from within. (Research and innovation, we should stress, are not the private domain of technology-driven companies; they are essential components of all successful businesses.)

Many companies today, recognizing the need to attract and retain business innovators, are devising unusual methods of granting autonomy and giving ownership. These mechanisms are becoming an accepted part of modern corporate life—however cluttered the classic organizational chart.

"HAVE THE GUTS TO FAIL"

"Have the Guts to Fail" is MacDermid's motto, and according to its chairman, that feeling is "instilled in all our people." This small specialty chemical company ($61 million) puts its money where its mouth is, allocating some 60 percent of management's incentive income to how well they define and achieve their objectives. "We want people to try innovative approaches. If they fear failure, they never dare new ideas."

Profits have approached 10 percent on sales, and even in the depth of the recession were a healthy 6 percent (1983 earnings, $3.8 million). An interesting statistic, trumpeted by the CEO, was the $8553 in net profits after tax for each of the 501 worldwide employees in 1981, not even their best year.

The company lays heavy emphasis on flexibility and innovation, concepts the firm views as synergistic. Day-to-day operations and functions report to the president. Research and their New Opportunities Group report to the chairman. "This gives great flexibility enabling us to grasp and create opportunities for the future."

MacDermid, located in Waterbury, Connecticut, stresses its "problem-solving capabilities," "a management team that reacts to the unique needs of each customer." Whether the needs are apparent to the customer, the company continually strives to raise quality and reduce costs. Heavy R&D is allocated to producing customer-specific chemicals that are not easily duplicated. The company prides itself on going "beyond the manufacturing and distribution of specialty chemicals. We anticipate customer needs and attempt to solve their problems through creative management and creative chemistry."

Company technologists analyze customer requirements, for example, to improve production lines and supply all necessary chemicals, equipment, control instrumentation, training, and field service. Investing in "cutting edge technology" and "creating new product opportunities" are said to "precede customers' demand." Senior management states forcefully that the company does not "merely respond to market or competitive driven strategies."

MacDermid claims to field the broadest base of products in its industry, some 600 specialty chemicals. It stresses "surface technology." The company develops, compounds, sells, services, and reclaims proprietary chemicals that form, protect, or enhance metal and plastic surfaces. MacDermid believes that its "independence" has allowed it to "remain flexible and responsive in filling the needs" of various industries.

MacDermid uses its technology efficiently, transferring knowledge from one area to another. These "building blocks" of science develop products and processes for different industries. For example, similar chemical technology used to strip copper from a single copper-plated steel part after heat treating can be applied to strip copper from a sophisticated printed circuit board used in computers. Such building blocks of specific chemistry are combined to produce most of the specialty chemicals offered to automotive, construction, and electronics companies. "Quick response to the challenges from our customers" is based on this "store of knowl-edge." The company boasts that "We won't tell a customer, 'It can't be done.'"

MacDermid is making a major commitment to serving the elec-tronics industry. It claims to be the only company to produce specialty chemicals that serve all primary processes used in pro-ducing printed circuits: etchants that remove the copper and define the circuit; plating chemicals that provide conductivity and protect the circuitry; ink resists that provide the correct circuit image. More recently, the company has developed a line of chemicals for the production of microelectronic chips or integrated circuits.

Employees are called "innovators and entrepreneurs," "highly motivated service-oriented professionals who thrive on the challenge of making their dreams real." "Investing in People" is a prime company commitment. Substantial sums are spent on recruiting, hiring, and training; and an extensive evaluation program puts a ceiling on employee rewards only "as high as their individual accomplishments."

The importance of personnel commitment is exemplified by the fact that employees own 15 percent of the company (exclusive of personal holdings). This intimate involvement, says senior man-agement, gives MacDermid "a competitive edge in a marketplace where many of our competitors have been purchased by larger companies who do not understand the chemical specialty business."

The leading Creative Strategies? Focus/Coherence. External Per-ception. Employee Opportunity. Efficient Innovation.

ENTREPRENEURIAL STYLE[12]

While mid-sized firms are not entrepreneurships in structure, the best of them must be entrepreneurial in spirit. And to understand what makes these top performers tick, we must feel the pulse of the entrepreneur.

Human beings are strange creatures. Just scribble a person's name on a contract giving legal ownership or proprietary position, and he or she will work longer hours, endure more hardships, suffer more abuse, absorb more stress, and earn less money. Why?

Merely the prospect of making more money in the long run. That's part of the answer, sure, but only part.

Most people would love to run their own business, to be their own boss. They imagine going to work in the morning without superior to serve or time clock to punch. A rugged individualist is the image, a person cutting his or her own path, determining his or her own destiny. Of those who take the plunge, a few prosper, most fail, all struggle. And yet the glamor remains: It's the chance of a lifetime, the Great American Dream. (Today more top business school graduates opt for entreprencurial endeavors than ever before.)

More than dollars are involved. Personal achievement more than organizational security motivates the typical entrepreneur. The business must become the most important thing in the world. It must *be* the world, at least for a time. The day must begin and end with the daily sales report, the monthly P&Ls, the new-product introduction, the almost-working prototype. The entrepreneur must burn with his idea, be obsessed with its success, and consumed by its passion. Wholehearted commitment, monastic dedication, intense energy, great perseverance—these are the critical success ingredients. Running your own business has been compared to keeping an ever-demanding mistress content.

There are, of course, no cookbook recipes for entrepreneurial triumph. Add everything conventional wisdom requires, and failure is often the outcome. Leave out the commitment, dedication, energy, or perseverance, and disaster is almost surely the result. When dealing with new ventures, it is far easier to predict failure than prescribe success.

Starting a new business is a life-affecting decision. It will dominate your every working hour and absorb most of your waking ones. Recent research on entrepreneurs reveals some interesting, perhaps startling, characteristics. In general, independent successful businessmen are not necessarily the smartest (cerebral types are more interested in theory); not necessarily the best students (some had dropped out of school, some had even been expelled); not the most stable employees (many had been fired from previous jobs); certainly not comfortable around subordinates (they only trust other entrepreneurs); and not viewers of spectator sports (they are active, not passive, and prefer to participate). All in all, an entrepreneur is one rare bird.

John Welsh, director of the Caruth Institute of Owner-Managed Business at Southern Methodist University, has identified eleven characteristics of successful entrepreneurs.[9]

1. *Good Health.* They maintain heavy workloads for protracted periods of time; they will themselves well; even those with chronic problems are sick less frequently.

2. *Basic Need to Control and Direct.* They require freedom and authority; they enjoy creating and executing their own strategies; they are oriented toward results and consumed by accomplishment; achieved goals are superseded by greater goals.

3. *Self-Confidence.* They are relentless in pursuit of objectives, as long as they are in control; they like to be held accountable; they firmly believe that nobody can do the job better.

4. *Never-Ending Sense of Urgency.* They thrive on activity and excitement; they have high energy levels and are always committed toward accomplishing objectives.

5. *Comprehensive Awareness.* They maintain constant awareness of the big picture and how each event fits together; they see both the forests and the trees.

6. *Realistic.* They accept things as they are; they seek firsthand verification; they want to measure and be measured; they are honest and assume everyone else is also.

7. *Superior Conceptual Ability.* They sense relationships in the midst of complex and confused situations; they identify problems quickly and achieve solutions rapidly.

8. *Low Need for Status.* They focus externally, preferring praise for their businesses rather than themselves; they are not embarrassed to admit ignorance; they subordinate luxurious trappings of success to current business needs.

9. *Objective Approach to Interpersonal Relationships.* They are more concerned with results than feelings; they maintain psychological distance; they eschew lines of authority; they are not good team builders.

10. *Sufficient Emotional Stability.* They have considerable self-control; they are challenged, not discouraged, by setbacks; they have difficulty with personal feelings.

11. *Attracted to Challenges, Not Risks.* They play for high stakes but prefer situations in which they can influence the outcome; they calculate risks and like odds to be interesting but not overwhelming.

Finally, a word of caution. Good entrepreneurs and good businessmen are not necessarily the same animal. There are substantial skill and personality differences between innovators on the one hand and managers on the other. Each group, of course, can produce its share of commercial successes. Indeed, some innovators make good managers, but this is often not true. To run your own show you need fire in your belly as well as brains in your head. To sustain an ongoing operation you must be skilled in organizational control and sensitive to human relations. We shouldn't get mixed up; we shouldn't blend the two together. If we become so intoxicated by the entrepreneurial side that we neglect the business side, we will be washing both good money and good ideas down the same drain.

Test Your Entrepreneurial Quotient

Think you have entrepreneurial instincts? Want to check your "EQ?" Try answering the following questions:

1. Which do I prefer, job security or personal independence?
The entrepreneur is willing to risk abject failure—personal bankruptcy and public embarrassment—in order to play his or her own game.

2. Is my business the most important thing in my life?
If not, you could be in big trouble striking out on your own.

3. Am I willing to work sixty hours a week for poor wages for long periods of time?

You had better plan on working many more hours than that for a lot less pay, at least at the beginning. Work, for the entrepreneur, is its own reward.

4. Can I take full responsibility for meeting my payroll and paying my bills?

If you answer "no," you should work for someone else, not yourself.

5. Do I like to think about business at home?

You should if you are going into business for yourself, since that is exactly what you'll be doing a lot of.

6. Does my business product have something unique about it: some new technology to use it, some special method to make it, some different way to sell it?

If not, you'll be forever running uphill.

7. Do I have to be told what to do?

If so, you need to be under a boss, not be one.

8. How badly do I want to be my own boss?

The answer should be "Plenty Bad." You'll be putting up with many irritating aggravations for little immediate reward.

9. Which is more important to me, achievement or power?

A typical entrepreneur would rather market his or her own product from a rundown garage than manage a large corporate division from an eight-window corner office.

10. If given the chance to go out on my own, would I hesitate?

Most entrepreneurs wouldn't hesitate a microsecond, but then again, most of them would fail.

Now, if you still want to run your own business, but have failed to meet any or even all of the above criteria, take heart! Entrepreneurs, remember, don't make the mold; they break it!

CHAPTER 6

WATCHING FLOURISHERS

Sorting Types, Sensing Spirits

We now move beyond individual cases. We bring in larger groups. The specific situation is vital—the backbone of our analysis—but we must examine a data base to generate confidence in conclusions. We conduct a "case search" of a healthy number of top-performing medium-sized firms, those companies that consistently outperform their larger-sized rivals, those mid-sized firms that "flourish among giants."

We seek guiding principles, concepts that apply generally, strategies that explain success. More than 130 leading companies are put under the microscope, and one or more outstanding characteristic is sighted and labeled in each. Strategic position and organizational structure are stressed.

We begin by describing a sample of top-performing mid-sized firms. For each company in this select society, we uncover the "critical success strategies" that underlie competitive victory, that made the firm a winner. This judgment must be perceptive ("arbitrary" would be the more rude adjective).

To begin, we generate a list of critical success strategies for all mid-sized firms in this best-performing group. Then we collapse the specific statements into general categories, trading off, as one must, the individual for the collective, the clear-cut for the abstract, sacrificing primary detail for higher-order understanding. We investigate "the particular" in search of "the general." Our goal, always remember, is practical strategies applicable for every company of medium size.

"Content analysis" of corporate publications—annual reports, SEC filings (10-Ks)—is used to assess and compare companies.[1] In highlighting critical success strategies for each top-performing firm, we do it in two ways: first from the viewpoint of internal management, and second from the viewpoint of external analysts. We then play the emergent principles back over the entire sample and assess their explanatory strength and predictive power. (Chapter 6's qualitative or case-oriented methodology complements Chapter 9's quantitative or numerically oriented methodology.)

QUALITATIVE ANALYSIS OF CASES

Qualitative or case analysis is essential for understanding complex organizations.[2] There is no way that statistical analysis alone, no matter how accurate the numbers or how large the data base, can generate understanding of corporate strategies. Qualitative analysis of corporations is concerned with understanding human behavior from the actor's frame of reference,[3] so that we can see the situation as the actors see it.[4] The key questions we ask in the qualitative approach are: What's going on here? What are the forms of the phenomenon? What are the variations of this phenomenon?[5]

It is in the ever delicate matter of determining "causation" that qualitative techniques become esssential. Quantitative or numerical methods cannot deal meaningfully with two-way flows—"chicken" or "egg" questions—the ambiguities and parallel pathways of the causation process. The most significant correlations, armed with astronomical statistics, cannot dictate direction of cause and effect. Numbers alone are bereft of fundamental capacity to determine root reasons. "Quantitative methods by themselves may ignore much of the process phenomena associated with a particular research question so that a real understanding of what's happening may not exist."[2]

Indeed, many uncertainties of cause may later develop from apparently "obvious" correlations. For example, do firms with large market share *become* more profitable or do more profitable firms *achieve* large market share? The direction of causal relationship, especially when common convention is assumed, can offer nasty conundrums for those who seek positive corporate action.

CONTINGENCY STRATEGIES

No strategy works everywhere. There is no business principle applicable in all situations. Exceptions exist to every conceivable recommendation. No one is "willing to admit the possibility that there exists some strategy or set of strategies which are optimal for all businesses no matter what their resources and no matter what environmental circumstances they face—an assumption that [would be] inconsistent with all research studies on business strategy conducted to date . . . [therefore] any theory of business strategy must be a contingency theory."[6]

"Contingency theory" is important for strategic management; it is a conceptual tool especially useful in moving from descriptive strategies of what "is" to prescriptive strategies of what "should be." Some examples of contingency theory: The findings that high R&D expenditures depress return on investment when market share is weak but increase return when market share is high; heavy marketing expenses depress return for low-share businesses; comparative quality of products is most profitable when the purchase frequency is low, market growth is medium to high, the production cycle is long, and capital intensity and vertical integration are low.[7]

Contingency theory builds effective strategies for mid-sized firms. But be prepared for more than one "order" of action here. A "first-order" contingency would assume that strategies for medium-sized companies might differ from strategies for large-size companies. A "second-order" contingency would assume that medium-sized firms, say, in capital-intensive (or low-growth) industries should optimally behave one way, while their counterparts in non-

capital-intensive (or high-growth) industries should optimally behave another way.

In an early application of contingency theory, R. L. Katz proffered
three sets of strategic propositions for companies; one universally
applicable, one for large companies, and one for small companies.[8]

Universal Propositions.   Always lead from strength. Concentrate
resources where the company has (or could develop readily) a
meaningful comparative advantage. The narrowest possible product–market scope should be chosen for each discrete business unit
consistent with that unit's market environment, resources, and
strengths. A unit whose future stream of anticipated earnings (when
discounted at the corporation's current cost of capital) is less than
its value in liquidation should be sold off.

Large-Company Propositions.   Planning is critical. Give up the
crumbs and dregs—set a minimum size for products or divisions.
Preserve company strengths and safeguard company stability.

Small-Company Propositions.   Attack when the enemy retreats.
Take advantage of opportunities. Be and remain as inconspicuous
as possible. Respond/react quickly. Retreat when the enemy attacks.[9]

CRISES IN THE MIDDLE

Organizations, like people, have mid-life crises. The trigger, however, is often not age. How long a firm has been around has little
direct meaning; time in existence has scant impact on executive
perception or corporate culture.

What matters is *structure*: how the company is set up, who reports
to whom, what the organizational chart looks like, the kinds of
positions running the place. *Strategy*, too, has its hand on the
throttle. Company goals and the means to achieve those goals
exert substantial influence over the social setting. Strategy and
structure, as players and partners, share top billing in shaping the
internal environment.

When does "mid-life" begin? When does a company undergo
its rite of passage from one stage to another? Organizational size
more than chronological age determines when a firm enters transition. In most cases structural change occurs when the company

is intermediate in size. The time of transformation often occurs at both ends of the medium-sized spectrum, first when the firm is maturing out of its entrepreneurial stage, and next when the firm is establishing its large organizational posture. Medium-sized companies, in general, are particularly susceptible to structural turbulence.

Thus the "mid-sized" crisis for companies is analogous to the "mid-life" crisis for people. What are the danger points? Where are the hot buttons? Which are the warning signs? These are issues we continue to explore.

STRATEGIES OF SIZE

A 1967 study analyzed strategies selected by smaller companies in competition with larger companies in similar product markets. (Nineteen successful, two borderline, and two unsuccessful smaller firms were examined.) "The impression that small manufacturing companies compete directly with large corporations is erroneous. Rather, these companies probed for soft spots and gaps in the market—the neglected or untried products. They adopted unconventional methods and met requests for custom-made products or quick delivery. They gained advantage from the technical skills of scientists and engineers attracted to small firms. . . . The management in these companies concentrated on particular skills of functional strengths."[10]

Approaching the problem in reverse, a 1976 paper defined "three principal areas of weakness in small businesses that cause trouble, all of them management centered": growth for growth's sake, inadequate cost analysis, lack of balance sheet concern.[11]

The target of a 1978 paper was the commonplace tendency to submit slavishly to the "received dogma" that profitability is largely determined by market share. Although agreeing that "in general market share and return on investment go hand in hand," the authors warn that "many of the inferences that both managers and consultants have been drawing from this finding are erroneous and misleading."[12]

Castigating these "sweeping generalities [which] offer little consolation to those businesses that, for one reason or another, find themselves in a poor market position," it is claimed that the simple classification system of industry growth versus market share defines strategy "at such a high level of abstraction that it becomes meaningless." (See Chapter 2, Figure 2.2—the essence of the Boston Consulting Group's publicity if not philosophy.) "A successful business must be specific, precise, and far-ranging. . . . By taking the attention of corporate executives away from these essential details and instead focusing their attention on abstractions, many planning systems do a great disservice."[12]

In the above study the three low-market-share corporations that outperformed the other much larger market share companies in their industries—Union Camp in forest products; Crown, Cork & Seal in metal cans; and Burroughs in computers—all exceed our boundary limits for mid-sized firms. Nonetheless, the authors' conclusions—the identification of four important characteristics that these successful low-market-share businesses have in common—become part of our story.

- ☐ The companies compete only in areas where their particular strengths are most highly valued.
- ☐ The companies make efficient use of limited research and development budgets.
- ☐ The companies eschew growth for growth's sake.
- ☐ The companies are led by chief executive officers whose influence is all-pervasive and who are personally willing to question conventional wisdom.

These themes—segmentation, efficiency, controlled growth, CEO commitment—as if leit motifs in a Wagnerian opera, we shall hear continuously.

We now consider size of corporate home. What are the mental attitudes generated by conglomerate ownership versus corporate independence? Consider two medium-sized businesses, one independent and the other a division of a larger corporation. What are the mental or cognitive differences between the divisional general manager (DGM) and the chief executive officer (CEO)? (We make the assumption that the DMG's division is the precise operational equivalent of the CEO's company in every respect except ownership.)[13]

Management theorists postulate that the "administrative regulation" compelled by the force of sheer size biases the strategic choices of the DGM with respect to his CEO counterpart. The DMG, all things being equal, sees a shorter time horizon for achieving results; he has a greater tendency to adopt strategies that have more certain outcomes and are more easily explainable to uninitiated higher-ups. The DMG places less weight on psychic, personal, and professional payoffs, and more weight on financial ones. The consequences are predictable: Aggressive corporate postures, such as innovation, usually thought to be enhanced by company size and diversification, become cognitively crushed by the pressure of administrative bureaucracy.[13]

The implications for executive behavior appear to be reinforced by the data (albeit scanty) showing innovation to be maximized in companies with a 5–20 percent market share, that is, mid-sized firms. These behavioral deductions suggest definite and distinct areas of comparative advantage for medium-sized companies, characteristics of operation having (potentially) the force of natural behavioral law rather than the constraints of artificial government regulation.

How to take advantage? Mid-sized firms, for example, can seek opportunity to optimize longer time horizons, all things being equal. Longer time horizons, we should note, need not only imply technological R&D. It could just as easily include, say, the development of more customers and buyers in the long run through reduced prices and profits in the short run. There are many other techniques. Higher-quality products can be sold at competitive prices; more extensive distributional channels can be established; more responsive service can be offered; and so on. Of course, such a comparative advantage for mid-sized firms would be slight; but, if valid, it could increase probability of success. Loading the dice ever so slightly in the medium-sized thrower's favor is the only way to fix this high-stakes game.

The title of a 1981 paper put it well, "A Small Business Is Not a Little Big Business."[14] (Although the paper targets companies smaller than our mid-sized firms, the critical point made is that managerial differences are size related.) The authors argue that the traditional assumption that small businesses should use the same management principles as big businesses, only on a smaller scale, is essentially wrong. "Resource poverty" changes both the character and content of management. Small businesses tend to be clustered in highly fragmented industries prone to low entry barriers and excessive price cutting. The differences between profits and cash flow, particularly, can be devastating to the smaller company without financial clout. Seasonal variations can exacerbate problems. Liquidity, conclude the authors, is a matter of life or death for the small business. "A small business can survive a surprisingly long time without a profit. It fails on the day it can't meet a critical payment."[14]

The above "strategies of size," we must stress, are just ideas and lists. They are not organized, not verified, not efficient, not sure. They are only a start.

Lists can make effective checks of procedure and monitors of behavior, but only constructs and models can bring pattern to data and order to chaos. But the mechanisms for forming constructs and making models cannot be ivory-tower theory. One must get into the unsimplified business world of real companies meeting real competition in real industries. That is why studies of individual corporate cases comprise such a large proportion of this work. We seek models, but models built on fancy are models built on sand.

TOP-PERFORMING SAMPLE

The 128 companies selected for the top-performing mid-sized firm sample represent seventeen broad industry groupings.[15] The year chosen was 1978, a time of near normal economic activity and industrial performance. Individual companies range in revenues from $16 million to $601 million, the mean being $163 million (in 1978 dollars, remember). Of the firms, 87 percent had gross sales below $300 million, 94 percent below $350 million, and 96 percent below $400 million.

The average return on stockholders' equity (ROE) was about 24 percent,[16] giving about a 7 percent "premium" over the median ROE for the largest corporations in the same industries.[17] *Each of* the mid-sized firms in our sample had a higher ROE than this median ROE of its giant competitors.

FLOURISHERS ALL

In this section we sample the sample. We select several companies from the 128 top-performing mid-sized firms that form our data base. We seek the prime generators of their individual success. Then, in the next section, we consider the sample as a whole. (Each company, remember, competes in an industry with much larger rivals.)

Great Lakes Chemical

This company concentrates on one class of products and uses it to serve several different markets. It has steadily built market share in a relatively flat industry. Great Lakes is the world's leading producer and marketer of bromine and brominated specialty chemicals. Its products fall into the following functional categories: fire control (fire extinguishing agents and flame retardants used in high-performance resin systems for electronics, appliances, construction); agricultural specialties (pesticides and other agri-chemicals); industrial and specialty chemicals (e.g., water treatment, oil and gas drilling, cleansing agents, dyes); specialty lubricants (broad line). The company is the acknowledged leader in developing, manufacturing, and marketing brominated flame retardants worldwide (accounting for 31% of total revenues).

Great Lakes has enjoyed a ten-year compound growth rate of over 25 percent. Its 1983 revenues were $228 million on which it earned $23.8 million, a full 10 percent after tax. (The first half of 1984 evinced increases of 41 and 73 percent in sales and profits.) Net return on sales has attained a hefty 15 percent three times in recent years, and exceeded 14 percent six years in a row—falling below 10 percent only once in the past twelve years (9.4% in 1982 when it far surpassed the chemical industry in general).

Great Lakes is located in West Lafayette, Indiana. It combines coherent focus with innovative expansion, both of which are exemplified by its two 1982 acquisitions. By purchasing majority interest in the leading independent marketer of bromine-containing "clear fluids" for oil field services, Great Lakes is now involved in what they expect to become "the biggest-ever consumer of bromine." (Although it has grown to become a $180-million industry in only a few years, the application of clear-fluid technology is employed in less than 5 percent of the wells that would benefit from its use.) The synergy between Great Lakes' manufacturing–technical expertise and the new acquisition's proven marketing skills "assures us a prominent place in this fast-growing market." (Coherent focus was also the theme of its 1981 acquisition of another brine and flame retardant business, adding important reserves, $20–$25 million of sales, and excellent synergies.)

The company is also willing to explore new vistas. The majority interest acquisition of a newly formed biotechnology corporation puts Great Lakes into the business of selling enzymes consumed in the production of high-fructose corn syrups. They anticipate building on this new specialty chemical area by generating "specialty enzymes for dairy, brewing and other biogenetic engineering applications."

Two interesting items stand out in Great Lakes' 1982 annual report, each indicative of company attitudes. Normally one does not expect to read much about competition in company propaganda—nothing more than general platitudes, not in a prominent position, and never with specific names. Yet right upfront in the president's letter to stockholders is a section called "Competition Update." The material listed on three firms—the primary foreign competitor (Israeli), the primary domestic competitor (Dow), and a large new entry in flame retardants (Ethyl Corp.)—is informative, interesting, detailed, and surprising. To the frequent reader of annual reports it stands tall. Where one usually slides by trite phrases, Great Lakes gives hard facts. No questioning the External Perception of this company.

Then there's a "people page," a presentation of the backgrounds, educations, and careers of the seven senior executives of the company. It is an impressive group.

Guilford Mills

Value Line (the investment service) calls Guilford "a standout," "the gem of the textile industry." Kurt Salmon Associates, the textile industry's most respected consulting firm, taps Guilford as the number one performer in three key financial criteria: return on total equity, return on invested capital, and net income on sales (topping forty-eight publicly traded textile firms over five years).

Textile companies are considered good if they earn 10 percent on stockholders' net worth per year. Guilford (based in Greensboro, North Carolina) earned 15 percent in the recent recession and has averaged 27 percent over the past five years (three years over 30 percent (1983 sales, $255 million; net income, $15 million). A look at the balance sheet shows that these impressive equity returns were generated without using much financial leverage. Long-term debt accounts for only about 12 percent of invested capital today and has averaged just over 20 percent for the past five years.

Why is Guilford so consistently profitable? We highlight four basic reasons.

1. *Dominance in Warp Knitting.* Guilford controls about 25 percent of this $1 + billion market. The company is no bigger than medium sized in the entire textile industry (of seventeen firms that are larger than Guilford on the Kurt Salmon roster, ten are more than double its size, three more than four times), but by concentrating on one segment of the industry it achieves competitive advantage.[18]

2. *Production Efficiency.* Guilford is one of the premier low-cost producers in the industry. The company invested in new machinery and has in its four plants, all in North Carolina, some of the most advanced facilities extant. Its manufacturing base is one of the strongest and most versatile in the United States and, with its United Kingdom subsidiary, in the world.

3. *Styling and Fabrics.* Guilford is a design leader, tracking the trends in a rapidly changing market. It was right on top of, for example, the recent growth in athletic wear and jogging apparel. Scores of new fabrics are developed each year through extensive R&D; many of the major fabric programs being sold today did not exist two years ago. Creating "new dimensions in durable luxury" for the "demanding American consumer" is the company objective.

4. *Sales and Marketing.* Guilford's own internal sales force, one of the industry's most productive, sells about four-fifths of company output. Many of its finished fabric lines are branded, such as the high-styled "Dynasty One" collection of sixteen fresh fabric styles for robewear and loungewear, and the feather-weight "Activa II" running gear fabrics that are strong and durable with excellent moisture absorbency and antistatic qualities. Guilford's "Performance Rated Warranty Program," covering over 23 million garments, is the first ever offered by a fabric maker direct to the consumer.

Guilford derives about 80 percent of its sales from the apparel industry, and apparel will continue to be the company focus. A little more than 10 percent of sales is derived from industrial sales (fabrics for automobiles such as upholstery velvet and suede; fabrics for health care such as flexible bandages and surgical masks; substrates for luggage, shoes, and toys). A little less than 10 percent comes from home furnishings (heavy-duty velvets; mattress, sheet, spread, and comforter fabrics; thermal drapery).

Some 3000 garment manufacturers comprise the company's customer base; they are mostly medium-sized, privately held manufacturing companies in the $10–$25 million annual volume range. These firms are in every aspect of apparel manufacturing: sportswear, outerwear, career apparel, swimwear, loungewear, sleepwear, robes, dresses, lingerie, and the like.

Guilford strives to pioneer important apparel products, such as the first machine-washable velvet construction in the United States; thermal lining for athletic apparel and jeans; and flame-resistant, chemical-free fabric for children's sleepwear. (The company claims to be "the largest producer of flame resistant fabrics in the entire industry.")

Noxell

What do Noxzema skin cream, Cover Girl Cosmetics, and Lestoil cleaning fluid have in common? They are the products of Noxell, a very successful mid-sized firm in a highly competitive industry of marketing giants such as Revlon and Procter & Gamble.

For Noxell 1983 was its 28th consecutive year of sales gains. Revenues were $304 million and net income was $23 million. Net returns on sales have been remarkably consistent, varying within *one-half of one percentage point* over the six years from 1978 through 1983—7.6, 7.4, 7.2, 7.2, 7.1, and 7.6 percent. The company has no long-term debt and equity is better than 70 percent of total assets. (1984 first half revenue, $187 million; earnings, $15.5 million.)

Cover Girl Cosmetics are clearly the core and future of this Baltimore-based company. Cover Girl sales have been rising steadily (25% in 1983, 27% in 1982), and its percentage of total corporate sales now stands at about 57 percent. Strong Cover Girl momentum is attributed to a growing market coupled with increasing market share—every product line posted a new sales record in 1983.

Marketing, of course, is critical and the Cover Girl image is perfect: "clean, healthy all-American beauty" portrayed through the use of models such as Cheryl Tiegs and Christine Brinkley and actress Stephanie Powers. Advertising is prime-time television and major magazines, and consumes a prodigious 20 percent of annual sales. (Massive advertising expenditures are characteristic of the industry, as are low costs of goods sold. Noxell's fat 60 percent gross margin is required to sustain high profitability.)

Noxell is a marketing pioneer. In the early 1960s the company introduced the selling of cosmetics to supermarkets, drugstores, and discount centers in addition to the traditional outlets in department stores. The company also defies conventional wisdom by limiting the number of shades offered for its Cover Girl products (lipstick, nail polish, eye and facial makeup). Most cosmetic companies dazzle consumers with an overwhelming assortment of colors, choices and variations—thereby demanding large inventory allocations for both manufacturer and retailer. Noxell's restricted selection holds down inventory carrying costs and generates the fastest turnover of any major cosmetic line on the retail level— thereby improving profitability for the retailer and encouraging the promotion of its Cover Girl brand.

Noxell's fundamental formula has been to build consumer confidence in a brand name and then introduce new products bearing the same name. The famous Noxzema skin cream—marketed for sixty-nine years, it is the leading facial-cleansing cream in the United States —has been expanded into a whole line of toiletries including shaving foam, antiseptic skin cleaner and pads, facial lotion, and so on. The "Cover Girl" name now sports a host of products: MakeupMates, Luminesse Lipstick, Eyes, NailSlicks, Pro-Lining Pencils, and so on. (The recent acquisition of Caliente Chili, a seasoning manufacturer, signaled interest in the premium-priced segment of the specialty food business.)

Keystone International

When Keystone reports that it had "a difficult year" in 1982, don't feel too bad. It means that the company only earned 9 percent after tax on sales rather than its usual 14–15 percent. From 1970 through 1981 return on stockholder equity moved between 23 and 35 percent every year (sales increased from $17 million in 1970 to $132 million in 1982). It is no surprise that Keystone has been one of the best-performing public companies over the past ten years.

Keystone (based in Houston) calls itself "a worldwide leader in the manufacturing and marketing of automated flow-control products and technology." It serves numerous industries and geographical areas with the same products and technology—valves, actuators, controls, and the like. It is committed to the development of state-of-the-art flow-control products and systems that regulate the bulk movement of liquids, gases, and solid materials. Operations range from food-processing and pharmaceutical production to waste treatment facilities and naval defense fleets. Keystone is currently planning microcomputer interfacing.

The company has clear focus: A single product and technology, applied in every possible situation. (Indicative of the reemphasized focus, a truck equipment subsidiary was spun out in 1982). Keystone claims to be the low-cost producer and to have the dominant market share position, both derived from "standardized manufacturing efficiencies."

The real test of a company, however, is not ever-higher growth but unexpected downturn. In 1983 sales from continuing operations dropped 15 percent to $100 million. Yet after-tax net profits main-

tained a healthy 11.4 percent of sales. Taking the third quarter as
an example, Keystone earned $3.3 million (12 percent) on $27.6
million in sales versus $3.6 million (11.5 percent) on $31.2 million
in sales the year before. It is remarkable to sustain such a high
return on sales in the face of such a steep falloff in revenues. (The
first half of 1984 continued the trend of squeezing more profits
from the same dollars. Sales were up 10 percent to $61 million,
while profits were up 29 percent to $7.6 million; returns on sales
increased from 10.5 to 12.4 percent.)

Henredon

"Difficult," as Henredon described fiscal 1983, is a relative term.
Sales slipped for the first time in thirteen years, a 12 percent drop
to $111 million. Yet after-tax profits were a robust 10.5 percent
($11.6 million), just above the ten-year average for this Morganton,
North Carolina company. Over the past decade, returns on equity
ranged from a low of 17 percent to a high of 22 percent—other
than 1983 (13 percent).

What makes these returns on equity particularly strong is the
very high percentage of equity to total assets—a remarkable 83
percent! The current ratio is 7.6; there is almost three times as
much *cash* as total current liabilities.

Now, some might criticize the company for *too* conservative a
financial policy, for letting cash sit idle earning only market interest—especially since the company paid out dividends of barely
more than one-third of net income. Sure we remember those lectures
on "optimum" debt structure to maximize return on equity, eloquent
discourses on how companies should use financial leverage to
enhance profit performance. Yet the fact remains that such extremely
sound (even "overly sound") balance sheets are characteristic of
the best-performing medium-sized firms. Which way the cause–
effect relationship flows is moot. The powerful correlation carries
its own message.

Henredon's business? The furniture industry, in which it is a
quality leader. The company manufactures and markets fine wood
furniture (e.g., dressers, beds, chests, cabinets, chairs, desks) and

upholstered furniture (e.g., sofas, love seats, chairs, ottomans). Wood products contribute some 60 percent of sales, and prices are in the medium-to-high range. Although Henredon's products are designed primarily for homes, many of its pieces are purchased for banks, offices, hotels, clubs, and other commercial establishments.

More than 2000 different items comprise the company's line. Most of Henredon's furniture is designed by its own staff, who develop new styles to meet changing consumer tastes and needs. Collections (or coherent groups) of furniture currently being offered include a variety of related designs based on fine furniture of different periods, including French, Spanish, and Italian traditional pieces, and pieces of contemporary design. While each of these collections is complete in itself, they are fashioned so that a customer can purchase compatible products from different collections.

Henredon fields its own sales force, most of whom are compensated on a commission basis. No one customer accounts for more than 4 percent of sales, indicative of the wide revenue base. Although the furniture industry is highly competitive, there are fewer manufacturers in the upper end of the business where Henredon's perceived position is strong.

Indicative of company character is the strength of its public presence—the open, confident dignity of its advertising; the clean, consistent format of its annual report. This is a quiet, elegant company that cuts a distinct image with coherence and product focus.

CATEGORIES OF CRITICAL SUCCESS STRATEGIES

One garners numerous impressions from coursing through scores of top-performing mid-sized companies, of which the above five are representative of the 128-firm sample. The flow is full, the reading rich. Nonetheless, a few overriding concepts stand out clearly, as strong signals emerging from diffuse noises: product orientation, segment dominance, corporate coherence, business distinctiveness, CEO commitment.

At this juncture these categories must remain mere impressions, intuitive ideas that popped above the others. Our objective is to transform these qualitative notions into quantitative expressions, to convert ideas into numbers.[19]

Where are we headed? The trick is to enumerate a modest number of strategic categories that could represent, effectively and efficiently, the strategic concepts of the sample. Which, in other words, are the generators of success expressed by our 128 top-performing mid-sized firms? The procedure of development was iterative and intuitive, with various combinations of categories stated and tested, and then restated and retested.

It was only after struggling through many such cycles that it became apparent that we were confronting an incongruity. The strategic categories chosen seemed awkward when taken together; they did not articulate well as a group, and no subtle change of wording could help.

The resolution to the problem came with the realization that we had embedded a dichotomy within the primary strategic categories. On the one hand, some strategic categories chosen represented the companies' critical success strategies as seen from the companies' or management's own *internal* point of view; and on the other hand, some strategic categories chosen represented the companies' critical success strategies as seen from an observer's or analyst's *external* point of view.

Whether in fact this observation was obvious or trivial, it seemed important at the moment, and it did catalyze some action. We thus set about the task of developing *two* sets of categories for corporate critical success strategies, one from the company viewpoint (labeled Strategies Inside-Out), and one from an observer's viewpoint (labeled Strategies Outside-In). Though admittedly impressionistic, the division resolved some conflicts and gave a good ring.

Two listings of mid-sized critical success strategies were compiled; then each of the 128 mid-sized companies was evaluated for each listing. Ground rules were established to contrast methodology as well as orientation: Each of the sample firms could be placed into only one of the Inside-Out categories, but into as many Outside-In categories as appropriate. (Judgments were based solely and directly on what the company and its CEO said in the firm's annual report. See Chapter 9 for validation of using annual reports to assess content.)

TABLE 6.1. Mid-Sized Firms' Critical Success Strategies: Strategies Inside-Out[a]

Category	Number of Firms	Percent
Product leadership	24	19
Product focus	21	16
Product innovation/technology	19	15
Customer orientation	13	10
Product quality	11	9
Product brand name	9	7
Product nature	7	5
Owners/management/employees	7	5
Internal self-sufficiency	4	3
Financial strength/acumen	4	3
Environmental awareness	4	3
Flexibility	3	2
Aggressive marketing	2	1+

[a] From the perspective of company management (sample size = 128 top-performing companies).

Tables 6.1 and 6.2 present the results. The two approaches should be considered independently first, and then comparatively.

STRATEGIES INSIDE-OUT

From the perspective of company management (normally the CEO), the primary critical success strategy was overwhelmingly *product related* (Table 6.1). Of the 128 firms, 91 (71 percent) specified some aspect of the company's products as directly causative of their continued success. This result was expected in concept, but surprising in magnitude. We had thought more companies would tap "management," "production," "efficiency," or "financial acumen" as the primary reason for their success. (It would be interesting to compare a content analysis of top-performing large-sized firms. Would the emphasis be as heavy on "product"?)

What unifies the six strategic categories that include "product"—leadership, focus, innovation/technology, quality, brand name, nature? It is the *proprietary essence* of the product, the unique or distinctive aspect of the product particular to each firm, that is deemed essential for corporate success.

The two strategy categories at the top of the list deserve additional comment and provoke two questions. "Product leadership" was an astonishing winner in that we had not expected so many mid-sized firms to boast that they were the "largest" or "leading" firms in their fields. It sounded contradictory, certainly paradoxical. The first question, of course, is one of market description and product boundaries, and the obvious answer is that these mid-sized firms simply define tighter markets and closer boundaries than is usually done in common business–economic practice.

The second question is the "chicken–egg" conundrum again: Which came first? Did the product leadership "cause" the firm to become successful? Or did a firm that was intrinsically successful for other reasons then "attain" product leadership simply because it was so successful? The latter seems the likely choice in several of the companies.

"Product focus," the runner-up, begins to suggest how success may be derived, a derivation in line with both previous research and practical experience.

STRATEGIES OUTSIDE-IN

From the perspective of observers/analysts external to the company, and allowing companies to be assigned to multiple categories, a different picture is drawn—but the pattern differs more in order than in kind (see Table 6.2 for the data, Table 6.3 for the definitions). Remember, firms were placed only into those categories noted in the firm's annual report as underlying company success. The strategic judgment was based solely on what management chose to explicitly communicate.[20]

"Coherence" is at the top of the list, a clear winner with 82 percent of the companies included. What this means—whether it is even meaningful—is another issue. The overwhelming number sends caution warnings about hasty conclusions. This entire exercise, remember, is founded on the qualitative method of case

TABLE 6.2.   Mid-Sized Firms' Critical Success
Strategies: Strategies Outside-In[a]

Category[b]	Number of Firms	Percent
Coherence	105	82
Commitment	79	62
Dominance	78	61
Distinctiveness	71	55
Relevance	70	55
Progressiveness	64	50
Clarity	58	45
Perceptiveness	57	45
Consistency	42	33
Fulfillment	29	23
Flexibility	25	20
Efficiency	20	16

[a] From the perspective of an observer/analyst (sample size = 128 top-performing companies).
[b] Formal definitions of strategy categories given in Table 6.3.

analysis. No attempt has been made to "control" the experiment, to compare these top-performing mid-sized firms with not-so-top-performing mid-size firms. (This we do in Chapter 9.)

Again the most striking result was the large number of firms that claimed "dominance" of their particular product–market. A full 61 percent of the sample asserted that they were *the* largest producer of product X or gadget Y, and this assertion was usually made directly and boldly. Even compensating for the fact that each company is perfectly free to define and bound its own product–market as it chooses, the number of *mid*-sized firms that boast "dominance" as a company characteristic is fascinating and significant.

Finishing second (62 percent) was "commitment," the sense of corporate resolve and executive determination. One might cynically expect such commentary to bloat annual reports, and thus dismiss such spoutings as platitudes and palaver devoid of real meaning. (Again, the control matchings of Chapter 9 are needed.) Nonetheless, one is struck by the sincerity as well as the ubiquity. One can readily believe that the chief executives of these top-performing

TABLE 6.3. Mid-Sized Firms' Strategies Outside-In[a]

Coherence: A composite measure of the corporation's focus/relatedness of business(es) and coherence of goals/objectives/strategies.

Commitment: A composite measure of organizational determination and individual dedication on behalf of CEO, directors, executives, and employees.

Dominance: A composite measure of the corporation's high market share within its own tightly defined corporate niche, and the sales growth and selling/marketing orientation required to enhance that position.

Distinctiveness: A composite measure of corporate uniqueness, significant aspects of the firm's interaction with the external environment that set it apart from competitors.

Relevance: A composite measure of the corporation's (or the corporation's products') degree of "perceived need" in the minds of customers.

Progressiveness: A composite measure of the corporation's internal growth and development, its orientation toward new products and innovation, and its current expenditures for future progress.

Clarity: A composite measure of the corporation's conception of its own operational activities and strategic goals/objectives/strategies.

Perceptiveness: A composite measure of the corporation's appreciation of the external market/industry environment, and its sense of internal strengths and weaknesses in relationship to that environment.

Consistency: A composite measure of the corporation's stability—stability in profits, production, organization, and strategy.

Fulfillment: A composite measure of the degree of personal satisfaction and job-related enthusiasm on behalf of the CEO, corporate executives, and all employees.

Flexibility: A composite measure of the corporation's capacity/ability to change its current direction in order to take advantage of new opportunities and/or avoid new threats. (The inverse of corporate inertia.)

Efficiency: A composite measure of the corporation's proficiency in producing the most output from a given quantity of input.

[a] Category definitions from the perspective of an observer/analyst.

mid-sized companies are more "committed" to their companies, that this commitment is more than a by-product of business success and financial gain, and that in many cases the commitment came first and is cause, not effect.

Lending support to the importance of commitment as a cause (rather than an effect) of mid-sized success is the recurrence of family-controlled (and often family-operated) firms in the top-performing sample. The "family factor" correlated high with commitment for those CEOs who either had founded the company themselves or were the direct descendants of the person who had. There was a sense of personal pride, of extended self-identification, of transcendent responsibility to employees, stockholders, customers, and communities.

In their book *The Firm Bond: Linking Meaning and Mission in Business and Religion*, Kuhn and Geis define commitment as the critical link between personal meaning and company mission.[21] They show how the individual commitment strength of employees determines the collective goal achievement of companies. (This is particularly true, as the data here show, for chief executive commitment.)

Businesses have much to gain from personnel dedication and should seek ways and means to enhance it. Employee commitment is one of the clearest characteristics of the most successful companies. How can such commitment be built? How is it often destroyed?

As Kuhn and Geis portray in detailed case histories, commitment *builders* are powerful: identification (the melding of interests between employee and company), confidence (employee belief in company trustworthiness), momentum (company forward movement), responsibility (personal position and trust), and accomplishment (employee sense of reaching and attaining concrete goals).

Commitment *breakers* are equally potent: alienation (estrangement between employee and company), powerlessness (employee belief that company events are beyond personal control), meaninglessness (employee sense that nothing about the company has any import or interest), worthlessness (employee sense that company activities are devoid of benefit or reward), and anxiety (employee unease caused by apprehensions of ill). The best companies develop the builders and avoid the breakers; they make commitment a top priority.

So while the word "widow" is more frequently associated with cursors on computers than with tackles on television, other words such as "care," "teamwork," "confidence," and "trust" score high in content analyses of managerial conversations. "People" are what executives are talking about.

A comparison of the two sets of mid-sized critical success strategies—inside-out and outside-in, each derived from a different perspective—shows some categories to be identical. It is apparent that "product focus" and "coherence," and "product leadership" and "dominance" are important in the strategic structure of top-performing mid-sized firms.[22]

CHAPTER 7

STRATEGIC MANAGEMENT

Learning Methods, Using Frameworks

"Strategy" describes the relationship between an organization and its environment. It is the key linkage between mission and goals above and operations and functions below. It is the vehicle for arraying alternative choices and driving the resource allocation process (see Figures 7.1 and 7.2).

Strategy is the process by which company mission and goals are translated into objectives and projects. Finding effective strategies is the search for *competitive advantage*, areas of the business environment where one firm has or can develop the strongest market position relative to all other firms. Competitive advantage seeks to capitalize on the *distinctive competencies* of the organization, those functional areas of the company—whether products, technology, distribution, brand name, customer loyalty, finance, and so on—where it excels or can excel compared to its rivals.

Strategy is an ancient term derived from warfare under which a host of company–industry and product–market interactions can be classified. Definitions are as numerous as authors, but certain elements are common to all. Thus the ruling troika of strategic

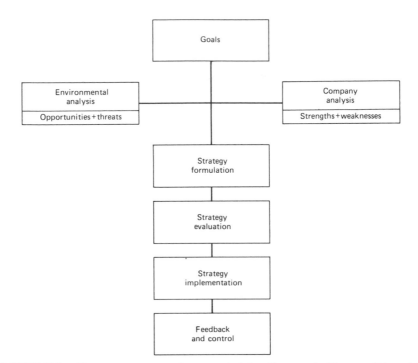

FIGURE 7.1. Corporate strategy framework (after Bowman). (*Source:* Edward H. Bowman, "Epistomology, Corporate Strategy, and Academe," *Sloan Management Review*, Winter 1974.)

thinking is: industry opportunities and threats, company strengths and weaknesses, and managerial choice. But strategy is still "academic"—in the worst sense of the word.

How is corporate strategy formulated? The ideal process is by mapping a firm's strengths and weaknesses onto market opportunities and threats in order to accomplish long-term goals and short-term objectives. The primary output is the generation of alternative policies, different possibilities of company direction for executive consideration. These policies are then evaluated for probable outcomes, and the best are chosen for implementation. Internal consistency, especially with company mission and goals, is a prime test in the evaluation of each alternative strategy. *Creativity* is the touchstone for strategy formulation, just as *consistency* is for strategy evaluation, and *structure* is for strategy implementation.

The relationship between strategy and structure is one of the principal advances in business understanding of the past several decades. Certain kinds of corporate strategies demand certain kinds of organizational structures, and conversely, if these same organizational structures are in place first, they will exert pressure for their complementary corporate strategies. (The classic example is the relationship between a multiproduct or multinational strategy with a "divisional" structure. In a divisional structure, each division

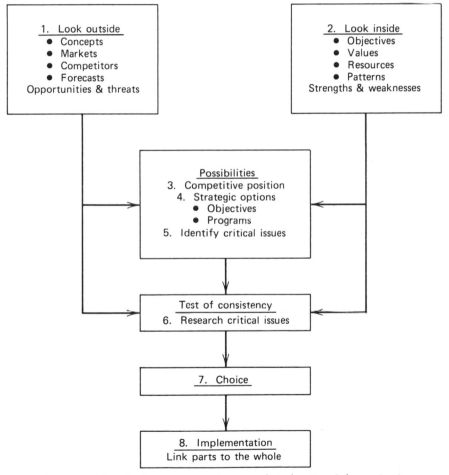

FIGURE 7.2. Business strategy framework. (After Kurt Salmon, Inc.)

is responsible for a distinct product line or geographic area and maintains internally its own functional departments—marketing, manufacturing, finance, etc.)

Peter Drucker's simple 1954 question—"What is our business? And what should it be?"—is an ultimate summary of strategy, however sophisticated the later incarnations.[1] Two primary thrusts are embedded implicitly in strategy—the strategic ends or goals, the organizational grand design, where the firm wants to be in the future; and the strategic means or processes, the ideas, actions, and activities necessary to achieve those goals. Alfred Chandler combined both thrusts in his 1962 statement that strategy is "the determination of the basic long-term goals and objectives of an enterprise, and the adoption of courses of action and the allocation of resources necessary for carrying out these goals."[2]

H. Igor Ansoff called strategy "a concept of the firm's business which provides a unifying theme for all its activities."[3] Strategy, he says, is "a type of solution to a problem, but not the problem itself. The problem that gave rise to this particular type of solution was a product/technology mismatch between the firm and its newly turbulent markets." Ansoff poses the strategic question: "How do we configure the resources of the firm for effective response to unanticipated surprises?"[4] But in the "real world," is strategy more corporate fad than company fact?

It has been said that most corporate planning is like a ritual rain dance; it has no effect on the weather that follows of course, but it does make those who do it feel they are in full control. Most of the time we use "models" in corporate planning, we are laboring to improve the dancing, not the weather.

STRATEGIES FOR BITS

It was sometime in the early 1970s that "strategic planning" emerged with flourish and fanfare on the corporate scene. At first the arcane instrument of a new breed of business theorists and technical managers, "strategic planning" soon became the in word of the decade, monopolizing executive-suite meetings and consuming board-level symposia. Here was the managerial means to deal with uncertainty, the technical tool to handle a future suddenly laden with doubt.

But words alone can work no wonders, "strategic" as an adjective is no panacea, and mouthing "strategic planning" makes no miracles. To understand something of the problem, compare the 1981 and 1982 annual reports of the Hughes Tool Company, the world's largest manufacturer of bits, joints, and tools for oil-well drilling.

Hughes's 1981 annual report lauded its remarkable nine-year record—sales skyrocketing almost twentyfold from under $100 million in 1972 to almost $1.8 billion in 1981, profits vaulting even higher from $10 million to over $255 million in the same time period. Such spectacular growth, continued the commentary, could be attributed to "effective planning."

Based on 1981 operations, Hughes Tool ranked 213 among the Fortune 500 in order of sales, 76 in net income, and 10 on the basis of net income as a percent of sales. The company has been one of the best performers in American industry, and as such an interesting firm to study. It is, of course, a large-sized company, but let that not deter us. There's no discrimination here. In fact, we should put one of the enemy under analysis—especially in light of the strategic problem it faced, and the strategic solution it found.

"Effective planning," claimed Hughes in an especially prominent position on the inside cover of its 1981 annual report, is "one of the most common factors among the most successful corporations of today. A logical plan for the future is of particular importance to companies involved in a growth industry; objectives and strategies must be carefully formulated and implemented in order for a company to grow with the industry it serves."

There is surely no public relations advantage in claiming that company success is based on economic conditions, industry growth, high demand, inelastic pricing, or, as is often the case, just plain luck. A company must give the impression that its success record is self-generated, that its good fortunes are the product of managerial intelligence—and therefore likely to continue. (One appreciates the remark attributed to Thomas Watson, Jr., of IBM. When asked the primary reason for his enormous success, he is reputed to have said, "Because my father didn't start no meatpacker.")

Then, thud! came one of the oil industry's worst slumps ever. Hughes's 1982 annual report blames "numerous economic and petroleum industry conditions" for the company's precipitous 42 percent decline in earnings. The company reported its first loss in fifty years in the first quarter of 1983, and the first-half net loss was $21 million. (For calendar 1983, Hughes lost $91,000—essentially breakeven—on revenues of $1.16 billion, a drop of 36 percent from 1981. Losses continued in the first quarter of 1984—$14 million—but profitability was predicted thereafter.)

The 1981 annual report presented a glowing strategic forecast for 1982: 4500 rotary rigs was the average number of drilling wells expected to be in operation over the year (the driving statistic for Hughes' oil field businesses), a projected increase of 13 percent over the previous year. Hughes's experts predicted that "the most important factor is that we expect the average rig count will continue to grow. We could see 8500 rigs running worldwide in 1986 assuming only a 9% annual increase. Now the growth level won't be at the levels we had in 80 or 81 in the U.S. But we will predict this substantial growth, with the number of rigs increasing each year."

The 1982 annual report states that the active rotary rig count averaged 3105 in 1982, *down* 22 percent from 1981. October 1982 saw only 2379 rigs running, a dramatic drop of 47 percent in barely nine months, and the lowest level in decades.

The 1981 annual report stated that the strategic forecasts of industry activity are vital parts of the planning process at Hughes Tool, a critical method of "identifying and anticipating the demands of our various markets for [oil field] tools, equipment and services," "a framework for determining key elements of both the annual and five-year plans."

The 1982 annual report focused on the decline in U.S. drilling activity and the problems of managing a downturn.

The Hughes Tool Company, without question, is a superbly run organization; its engineering technology is state of the art, its managerial technology second to none. Yet with all the sophistication, all the expertise, all the experience, it missed and missed badly. Its experts made the cardinal error of assuming that "extrapolation" is the essence of strategic forecasting, that the future, in some form, will always imitate the past. What Hughes did— and how it adapted—makes an interesting story for readers, and an important one for businesspeople.

Strategic planning—what it is, and what it is not—is critical to understand. A predictive technique, even the best of them, is never managerial magic. So Hughes blew its primary projection, one in which we can assume the active participation of several dozen economists, industry analysts, statisticians, and planners. Hughes, of course, was not alone; its forecasting failure was the rule, not the exception, in an industry humbled by declining oil prices, decreasing demand, changing tax laws, stricter lending policies, and the general recession.

Hughes reacted well, perhaps exceptionally so. It made the tough decisions and took the necessary cutbacks, moving quickly to stem the financial collapse at acceptable levels—yet all the while preserving capacity to take advantage of demand resurgence and developing technology to assure competitive edge. This, too, is part of the story. Anyone can look like a hero when the going is easy, when industry growth spirals upward; it's what happens when demand turns sour, it's the bad times that test good management.

In 1982, despite the most drastic decline in drilling industry history and in the face of increased price competition, Hughes Tool recorded its second best year ever. Several divisions of the company—those engaged in the manufacture of production-related tools—were even able to increase sales and maintain margins near 1981 levels. But then came 1983, and the newly written rules had to be rewritten again.

In 1909 Howard Hughes, Sr., a graduate lawyer, invented the rolling cutter rock bit for drilling oil wells and revolutionized the drilling industry. It was this one patent that spawned the Hughes Tool Company, indeed the entire "Hughes Empire" that the ephemeral Howard Jr. later developed—aircraft, technology, defense, airlines, even Las Vegas hotels. Howard Sr. died in 1924 and his quixotic, soon-to-be-famous son took over. The flamboyant younger Hughes allowed the "tool division" to operate independently, though he milked it for cash by not allowing either its equipment to be kept modern or its management to acquire and build.

In December 1972, with Howard worrying about larger issues in life (such as the TWA lawsuit and becoming a recluse), the tool division, still concentrating solely on drilling, was carved out of the Empire and taken public. "Now," according to Chairman and Chief Executive Office James R. Lesch, "we could be more in control of our own destiny. We decided to diversify and expand, getting involved in production."

Quite a statement, that. The new businesses, acquired for their proprietary technology and then developed internally, now contribute 55 percent of company sales, with growth rates exceeding the original businesses. Capital expenditures, indicative of company commitment to the future, increased 54 percent on an average annual basis since 1972, aggregating well over $1 billion. And even after the sequence of acquisitions and subsequent investments, Hughes' balance sheet remains one of the strongest in the industry— as of December 31, 1982, Hughes's current ratio was an impressive 3.78 and stockholders' equity accounted for over 53 percent of total assets. (Nonetheless, Hughes's year-end debt-to-capitalization ratio was higher than usual, and steps are being taken to reduce debt with positive cash flow after funding the streamlined capital programs.)

From his elegant though not massive office, paneled in dark woods and perched high atop a breathtaking skyscraper in downtown Houston, CEO Lesch reviewed the strategy that brought such success to Hughes. "We wanted to strike a balance between 'drilling tools and equipment' and 'production tools and services'; we sought vertical integration within the drilling-oriented segments and horizontal expansion into oil field products and services."

With its series of acquisitions, Hughes has almost achieved 50– 50 parity in sales and identifiable assets between the drilling and production groups, though profits are still skewed toward drilling operations due to widespread price discounting and underutilization of capacity in production. When asked about conglomerate-type diversification moves, the chairman smiled and said, "We've been shown some things, but our answer has always been 'No, we'll stick with what we know.'"

In the ten years Hughes has been a public company, management's guiding strategy has positioned the company where it is no longer dependent on any single phase of the petroleum industry, thereby reducing the impact of violent market swings or worldwide political crises. Furthermore, in each product area, Hughes has sought technological strength, seeking synergy among its divisions by providing customers with a full range of products and services.

Hughes has over 17,000 employees (50 60 percent in Texas) and thirty-three manufacturing plants worldwide. Distribution stockpoints and service centers are located in areas of drilling and production activity throughout the United States. Internationally, Hughes markets its products and services in almost all oil-producing countries, whether directly or through licensees, sales agents, or distributors. (The company is active on the Chinese mainland, representing other companies as well as itself.)

Hughes is organized in two ways, one by structural group, the other by functional application. Each of the groups is composed of self-contained divisions, each headed by a president/CEO with all requisite staffs and functions for independent operations. Hughes maintains lean corporate support, though it actively encourages interdivisional efficiencies.

The six divisions in the Drilling Tools and Equipment Group are primarily interested in "making hole," whether drilling for oil and gas (by far the largest), water well and mine blast holes, or construction shafts. The company's largest division—Hughes Tool per se—is the world's leading supplier of rock bits, tool joints, and related drilling tools. Its products include both carbide and steel tool rock bits, solid-body bits with polycrystalline diamond cutters, replaceable blade drag bits, and the like—some 200 basic sizes and types of drilling bits, ranging in size from 3¾ inches to 26 inches in diameter, each designed for specific types of rock formations. Hughes claims 40 percent of the domestic market and 50 percent of the free world.

The eight divisions that comprise the Production Tools and Services Group market their products to companies that produce oil and gas. BJ-Hughes Services (the largest piece of that first acquisition with revenues over $400 million) provides oil and gas well cementing, acidizing, fracturing, sand control, drill stem testing, and nitrogen stimulation services. BEST-Hughes supplies hydraulic workover services. Brown Oil Tools manufactures linear hangers and other downhole equipment, including "fishing tools" for removing equipment lost or stuck in the hole. (Brown's founder had over 350 patents and a reputation for finding ingenious solutions to customers' problems. Brown's own problem, however, was an inability to fully exploit what it had. Three years after joining Hughes, sales had doubled.)

The Corporate Technology Advisory Council, made up of research and engineering managers from the various divisions, forms the core group of a continuing R&D effort. They meet regularly to exchange information, seek new ideas, and assure companywide R&D efficiency. Hughes allocates over $25 million every year for research and development. The company owns over 650 patents, of which more than 300 are in active use. (Two critical patents are currently being contested in the courts.) The chairman emphasizes that Hughes's R&D programs, more than the patents themselves, are the reason for the company's success. Every major advance in rock bit state-of-the-art, he claims, has come from Hughes, and, he adds, almost every division has recently or will soon bring new or improved products to market.

Jim Lesch personifies his company. A 1946 graduate of the University of Oklahoma, Lesch spent six years as a field engineer in the Rocky Mountains. He then returned to Oklahoma as a regional engineer, coming into sales management in Houston in 1958. He became a vice-president in 1962, joined the board in 1964, became a senior vice-president in 1968, and was president and chief operating officer when Hughes went public in 1972. When the then chairman and CEO, Mr. Raymond M. Holliday, retired in 1979, Lesch was promoted to the top spot. A kindly man with the look of a seasoned veteran, Lesch travels a great deal and enjoys working through subordinates. (As a matter of interest, though Lesch was president and chief operating officer of the company while it was still owned by Howard Hughes, he never met the man. Even Holliday, frequently in touch with the Boss personally until the late fifties, only communicated by memo thereafter.)

Quality and integrity, according to Lesch, are the watchwords of Hughes. "We get the most mileage," he says, "out of assisting our customers with their problems." The same holds true for the local community, part of the extended constituencies of a modern corporation. Hughes, for its part, is involved in the renovation and redevelopment of Houston's east end, and Lesch is active in civic affairs (he was president of the chamber of commerce in 1977–1978).

Looking ahead, the chairman sees brightness. Hughes, he states, seeks maximum participation in each of its current activities. Oil and gas, he is confident, will be the world's primary source of energy well into the next century. Contrary to public perceptions, only 4 percent of the United States' continental shelf has been explored. Furthermore, he notes, subsea and riser technology is progressing to the point that wells can be sunk in 5000–7000 feet of ocean.

A corporate assessment from the CEO goes something like this. *Strengths*: People, R&D, customer base and relations, manufacturing facilities. *Weaknesses*: Difficulty in penetrating high-tech areas of measurement and modeling and, of course, the inability to control level of activity and that number of active rigs.

Strategy, remember, is devised by mapping company strengths and weaknesses onto market opportunities and threats in order to generate alternative policies consistent with overall goals. The strategic process sets objectives, assesses data, formulates potential solutions, and evaluates divergent alternatives. Strategy "positions" the company, choosing markets to attack and products to provide. Strategy—bottom line—determines where a company spends its money.

When it became certain that drilling activity would continue to decline, Hughes made the hard decisions. In every case, however, careful consideration was given to the long-term consequences of proffered moves. Such thinking is the essence of strategic decision making—when company goals are given priority in choosing among alternative policies. (The opposite approach is called "incremental decision making," when only an immediate solution to the problem is sought, with minimal deviation from the status quo a prime consideration. See below.)

Capital expenditures were curtailed, cost-reduction programs implemented, and manufacturing and service facilities consolidated where feasible. The 1982 capital budget was cut almost $50 million, or 14 percent below 1981 levels; and with capacity adequate and all plants modernized, the 1983 budget was earmarked primarily for replacement costs—down more than two-thirds from the $350 million originally budgeted for 1982. Plans to build two new plants and expand eight others were canceled. Nonetheless the more than $1 billion invested over the past five years in production-efficient modern manufacturing gives Hughes opportunity to gain market share during depressed times.

Though concerned about loyal employees, Hughes laid off over 4700, more than 35 percent of its U.S. work force. Care was taken to maintain personnel necessary to meet upswings in demand. Protective emphasis was put on keeping a tightly knit, responsive sales force in place throughout the company—important to build market share in the long run as well as to shrink inventories in the short run.

Tighter management of working capital was stressed. Inventories of raw materials and finished products were reduced by a materials requirement planning system that evaluates market conditions rapidly and optimizes response to demand. All divisions were advised to weed out marginally profitable products, which not only thins out inventory immediately but positions the company for higher profitability when conditions turn positive.

Special cost-reduction programs were instituted in every area of the company. For example, there was increased emphasis on standardization and modularization of parts, thus allowing more subassembly of inventory and consequently faster turnaround time for customer orders. The Hughes Tool Division began a robotics program for assembly line functions, a good example of common ground between short-run cost savings and long-run competitive advantage.

In addition, every effort was made to reduce administrative costs. Purchasing procedures were tightened, and advertising, travel, and entertainment expenses were curtailed. Priority was given, in each determination, to maintain target-market thrusts.

Each step of the cutbacks was made in line with strategic objectives. Improvements in product performance and new-product development must continue unabated during a downturn in order to maintain a competitive edge in the future. Projects with significant potential, even if uncertain, must not be touched—for example, Hughes's development of capabilities to drill huge 20-foot shafts down to 2000 feet (applicable to hazardous waste disposal).

So Hughes's failure in forecasting, in retrospect, has not been a failure of strategic planning; rather the estimate error has highlighted the robustness of *strategic management* as the mode of modern managerial thinking: Solving short-term problems with long-term solutions.

STRATEGIC VERSUS INCREMENTAL

Strategic planning is not a black art; strategic prestidigitation will not conjure up instant profits. Strategic management, as the more general concept is now labeled, is a way of thinking about the entire enterprise. It can best be understood in contrast to its opposite, "incremental" management.

Corporate planning has essentially two modes, two approaches to the process—the "incremental" and the "strategic" (see Figures 7.3 and 7.4). Operating in the incremental mode, the manager begins *reactively* by recognizing a problem, some unexpected shock, whether internal or external, large or small, opportunity or threat. He then searches selectively through a restrictive variety of potential solutions, making marginal deviations from the status quo, analyzing and evaluating each possibility in sequence. Deviations from the current policy are considered sequentially and widened progressively until the first satisfactory solution is found. It is accepted immediately and all other alternatives, even if potentially better, are ignored. Herbert Simon's idea of "bounded rationality" is the controlling concept here. The executive can't ever know *every*thing; so if he wants to do *any*thing, he must replace "optimizing," finding the best answer, with "satisficing," finding an acceptable answer. In the real world, according to "bounded rationality," problems need only be solved satisfactorily, not perfectly.[5]

Operating in the strategic mode, the manager begins *proactively* by defining general goals and setting specific objectives (Figure 7.4). He scans the external economic environment seeking opportunities and threats, and analyzes the internal company milieu discerning strengths and weaknesses. He then maps the latter onto the former in a search for distinctive competencies and competitive advantages. What emerges is a set of comprehensive, even exhaustive alternative policies. Each is then evaluated and assessed for probable consequences. Strategic choice is made with the touchstone of "internal consistency": Which set of alternative pol-

Incremental Planning Mode

1	2	3	4	5	6
Problem Recognition	Sequential Consideration of Policy Alternatives	New Policy Tested	New Policy Revised	New Policy Tested in Revised Form	Revision of Objectives
Unexpected shock to organization (internal or external) Sudden recognition of new opportunities and/or threats Uncertainty and risk perceived	Search for policy alternatives focuses on specific problem(s) surfacing Marginal changes in policy considered first. Minute deviations from current position The first satisfactory solution accepted; other alternatives ignored. "Satisficing"			Changes minute, on the margin	Continual revision of objectives and policy as progressively more is learned about interaction between environment and policy alternatives

Strategic Planning Mode

1	2	3	4	5	6	7	8	9
Definition of Purpose, Mission	External Strategic Intelligence	Internal Strategic Intelligence	Strategy Alternative Generation	Strategy Evaluation	Strategy Choice	Time/Step Sequencing	Strategy Feedback & Control	Strategy Review
Concept of firm Grand design Mid-term goals Short-term objectives	Information: data, ideas, questions, insights, hypotheses, evidence, etc. Environmental analysis: industry & competitive Opportunities & threats Forecasts	Organizational profile Organizational analysis Strengths & weaknesses	Development of a comprehensive, even exhaustive, list of policy alternatives Formulate strategy based on mapping firm S&W upon environment O&T	Assess probability of results for each alternative Map each set of results upon firm purpose & mission	Test of consistency Selection of internally self-consistent set of policies which best match corporate resources & purposes.	Designation of timed sequence of conditional moves Implementation Order of action steps	Information system Results tied to strategies	Overview of strategy content & process Each part connected to whole

FIGURE 7.3. Incremental planning versus strategic planning. [*Source:* Derived from *Instructor's Guide for Policy Formulation and Administration*, C. Roland Christensen, Norman A. Berg, and Malcolm S. Salter (Homewood, IL: Richard D. Irwin), 8th ed., 1980).]

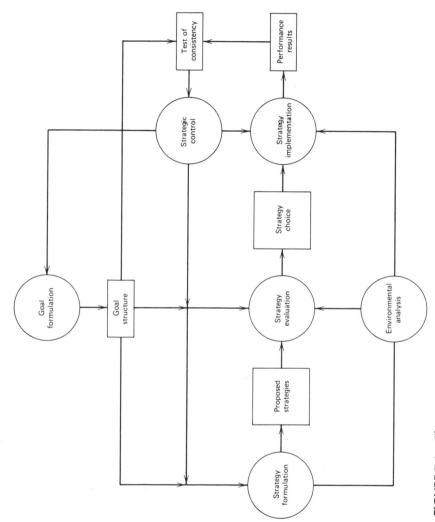

FIGURE 7.4. The strategic management process. [*Source:* Dan Schendel and Charles Hofer, *Strategic Management* (Boston: Little, Brown, 1979.]

icies best matches corporate resources and purposes? Implementation (including step and time sequencing), feedback, and control systems complete the process.

It is a common misconception to judge incremental decision making "bad" and strategic decision making "good." *Each* is good, but in its own arena. One would not resolve an urgent inventory crisis in the strategic mode, just as one would not formulate a five-year plan in the incremental mode. Creative and innovative managers, however, should function in *both* modes. While the strategic process lends itself to original thinking in devising alternative choices, the incremental mode can be fertile soil for the spontaneous sprouting of "Ah-Hah" insights.

Strategic thinking, to be truly strategic, must deal with surprise. The unexpected must be expected; the unforeseen, seen; the unimaginable, imagined. If everything is assumed to be known, if the future is anticipated to emulate the past, then the process is "trending"—and strategy, *qua* strategy, is playing no part. Strategic management must deal with more than uncertainty, more than ambiguity; strategic thinking must deal with *discontinuity*, step-function breaks from past trends, radical twists from current paths. (Hughes Tool, we surmise, has learned this distinction.)

Strategic thinking is good for people as well as companies. Individuals can apply the thought processes for planning their private lives and making their personal decisions. It is entirely appropriate to use the strategic method to resolve, for example, whether to change jobs or which job to select. An honest evaluation of personal strengths and weaknesses in light of employment opportunities and threats can be a critical part of the process, and a meticulous weighing of all alternatives in light of overall lifetime goals is well worth the effort. (One would not, of course, need strategic thinking to make the vast majority of daily decisions. "Lifetime goals" are irrelevant for choosing which movie to see.)

DEATH, HEALTH, AND TRAVEL

Death, health, and travel? Whether the trio makes literary sense is irrelevant; it makes strategic sense for Hillenbrand Industries and that's the bottom line.

If one had to construct an "ideal" mid-sized conglomerate, this company from Batesville, Indiana might be it. Hillenbrand earned $36 million on sales of $433 million in 1983. It has maintained a net return on sales between 7.5 and 8.6 percent for six years. Return on equity has averaged between 17 and 19 percent. Five-year compound growth has been 13.5 percent.

When compared with the financial performance of *Forbes* magazine's top 1008 public companies (sales over $450 million), Hillenbrand placed in the top 25 percent for five-year return on equity and the top 23 percent for ten-year sales growth. Dividend growth rate has average 14.5 percent per year over ten years, ranking 174th out of the 4000 public companies covered by Moody's Investor Service. Stock market performance has been even more impressive—a five-year increase of 212 percent (1978–1983), placing it in the top 18 percent of the *Forbes* companies.

Hillenbrand Industries consists of three wholly owned, autonomously operated subsidiaries. All three have attained leadership positions in their divergent industries, two of them maintain dominant market share.

Health Care. Hill-Rom is the leading manufacturer of electrically operated hospital beds, patient room furniture and related equipment, and prefabricated headwall service systems. The company markets to some 6000 short-stay hospitals, and its electric beds account for more than half the industry's total sales. Hill-Rom is considered the innovator in the hospital equipment industry. Operating profit in 1983 was $33 million on $132 million in sales.[6]

Funeral Service. Batesville Casket is the world's leading producer of metal and hardwood burial caskets. Protective caskets, made of steel, copper, and bronze, are designed to resist the entry of air and water. The company is by far the lowest-cost producer in the industry, and markets to some 15,000 funeral directors. Its sales of quality metal and hardwood caskets exceed the volumes of the next five largest competitors *combined*. Operating profit for 1983 was $40 million on $229 million in sales.

Luggage. American Tourister is the nation's second largest manufacturer of luggage and business cases. A wide variety of durable and affordable hard-side and soft-side luggage is sold in the medium price range. Operating profit for 1983 was $3 million on sales of $71 million. (Only American Tourister was seriously impacted by the recession—sales off 19 percent, profits off 58 percent from 1981. Clearly the weakest hitter in the Hillenbrand lineup, Tourister's strategy is to lower production costs, redesign the product line, place heavier emphasis on high-margin soft-side luggage, and increase penetration of the department and specialty store market. It was still struggling in 1984.)

Hillenbrand Industries, run by the Hillenbrand family (Chairman/ CEO Daniel; President W. August), stresses the market position of its operational subsidiaries. Maintaining market share is literally an obsession. The cover statement of the 1982 annual report states it clearly: "By focusing on our strengths we expect to continue to improve our leadership position in each industry we serve." Batesville, the company proclaimed, "continued to grow market share against less efficient competitors."

Corporate policies reflect an interesting mixture of corporation-wide attitudes and operating company strategies. All three companies stress efficient, high-quality production and assembly systems, "including robotics and state-of-the-art finishing technologies." The casket facility is considered the most modern in the world. Each company maintains a trained, professional field sales force. Only American Tourister strives for high level of brand recognition, using extensive consumer advertising.

Operating efficiencies are watched closely. The company was proud that in 1982 it increased sales 5.7 percent while decreasing inventories 3.7 percent and holding receivables constant. In 1983, with sales up 11 percent, inventories were down 5 percent and receivables down 3 percent. The balance sheet is perennially strong: the current ratio is 3.3 to 1; equity is better than 60 percent of assets. The debt-to-equity ratio has been coming down, and stands at about 20 percent.

Hillenbrand's analyses of each operating company show significant attention to market trends, including demographic data and sociocultural shifts. Batesville, for example, pays more attention to industry activity than competitive pressures.

The market for burial caskets, the company states, is limited by two factors: (1) The number of deaths, which has been nearly static in recent years and is expected to grow at an approximate rate of 0.5 percent per year for the next several years and (2) the number of noncasketed deaths; cremations currently account for approximately 11.7 percent of deaths and have been rising at about 9 percent per year. Twenty-three percent of all cremations involve a casket in the funeral service. Batesville believes that the latter percentage will increase in future years, thus softening, to some extent, the increasing impact of cremation on the casket market. Based on extensive research, 75 percent of all consumers believe in the importance of the funeral—a percentage unchanged for a decade.

"Virtually all meaningful innovations in the casket industry in the last 40 years," claims the company, "were originated by Batesville." The first real breakthrough was the invention of a gasket and closure mechanism that made it feasible to actually seal a metal casket so that it would resist the entry of air and water. Obviously such a concept could not work with wood.

The invention catapulted the rise of metal caskets, which had important production advantages as well. The casket shell, for example, could be stamped in quantity and mass produced with considerably less labor and far better quality control than wood. The latest product innovations are "reversible interiors and insertable cap panels, which effectively multiply the appeal of the product through personalization."

Batesville is committed to vertical integration, claiming "scale advantage resulting in higher margins than our competitors." While other manufacturers grew through acquisition of diverse casket companies with differing production processes and differing market systems, Batesville has relied on internal growth. "We believe in manufacturing everything that is feasible. . . . For example, all of our hardwood is made and plated in our own hardware plants. We even slit our steel, formulate and manufacture our gaskets and process our wood."

The economics of the funeral business is critical to the company, and it is well understood. Most of the country's 22,000 funeral homes are individually owned and operated, though there is a growing trend toward investor-owned chains. Each funeral home is a capital-intensive small business with significant investment in real estate, rolling stock, and personnel, all of which is idle except when preparations for a funeral are in progress. (The average number of caskets in a funeral home selection room is twenty, which is the major purchased product of the business.)

The casket market is segmented by price: 15 percent high (copper, bronze, rare woods, heavy-gauge steel); 50 percent medium (medium-gauge steel and hardwoods); 35 percent low (light-gauge nonprotected steel and cloth-covered wood). Batesville owns the high end and has made substantial inroads in the middle.

The objective of all casket manufacturers is to have their products occupy as many "spots" on the funeral home's floor as possible, thereby obtaining as much as possible of the funeral home's business (the analogy to "shelf space" for a packaged goods manufacturer is direct). The casket business is nonseasonal, although there is a slight rise in the death rate during the winter months. It is also recession proof and fashion stable—death is never out of work and never out of style.

Batesville calls its sales department "one of our great strengths." Salesmen work on straight commission, but do more than sell caskets. They actually work with funeral directors and help them succeed in their business, giving advice on financial management and community marketing. Batesville customers conduct over 75 percent of the funeral business in the United States.

"In many companies the procedure for becoming 'somebody' is to start as a salesman, then work up into an office job. At Batesville, the procedure is frequently reversed. Here, to succeed means becoming a Batesville salesman . . . and many aspirants earn the opportunity only after years of working in the office, learning the business."

The company prides itself on rapid response time. It operates fifty-three regional warehouses and service centers in which an inventory of caskets is maintained. Nearly all Batesville caskets travel by company-owned and operated trucks. Two fleets of hundreds of vehicles are in constant use—one to bring caskets from factories to warehouses and another to deliver them from warehouses to funeral homes. This internal transportation system assures "more timely, reliable, damage-free delivery than could be provided by common carriers." Total integration, from cradle to grave (so to speak), is the Batesville strategy.

In early 1984 Hillenbrand entered a fourth industry, in complete accord with their strategic planning. Medeco Security Locks is the leading manufacturer of high-security locks for commercial, industrial, and residential applications. It earned $2.2 million on annual sales of $18.7 million. (In the first half of 1984, Hillenbrand increased sales 14 percent and profits 26 percent.)

Hillenbrand, in sum, exemplifies the essence of strategic management. The key Creative Strategies at work? Dominance. Product Emphasis. External Perception. Distinctiveness. Bullseye.

HIERARCHIES OF STRATEGY

Although "strategy" is considered a senior management function, controlled out of the CEO office, there are in fact various levels of the organization at which strategic issues are considered and strategic decisions are made. We call these levels "hierarchies."

Corporate Strategy. Corporate strategy is the conceptual overview of the entire company, answering the fundamental question, "What business(es) should we be in?" and "How should they work together?" Here the various business strategies of divisional or product–market areas are pulled together in a unified, synergistic framework. The object? Compose the grand design of management and maximize the financial return for stockholders. (For example, divisions generating short-term cash with little long-term potential should feed other divisions showing long-term promise and needing short-term investment.)

Business Strategy. Business strategy is the purposes and plans for a specific division or product–market segment, answering the questions, "How do we compete in this area?" "What are our distinctive competencies to exploit?" and "How do we maximize our comparative advantages in the competitive business environment?" Variables under managerial control include segmentation options, scope of product line, level of technology, means of marketing, channels of distribution, financial planning, production planning, manpower, and so on.

Functional/Operational Strategy. Functional/operational strategy is the specific optimization of available resources, answering the question, "How can we accomplish our given objectives most effectively and efficiently?" Issues of primary concern: the maximal use of company assets, taking full advantage of internal systems and capabilities (marketing, production, distribution, etc.); interdivisional synergy, getting the most out of different divisions working together; the building of distinctive competencies on the micro level, such as the development of new technologies and products.

Though not often used, there are two higher-order levels of strategy:

Enterprise Strategy.   Enterprise strategy deals with the political legitimacy and integrity of the organization. (Charles Brown, the chairman of AT&T, dealt with little else for the years prior to the breakup.)

Interorganizational Strategy.   Interorganizational strategy is concerned with the supracompany issue of industrywide viability within the guidelines of federal regulations. Industry associations, for example promoting protectionist trade barriers in automobiles, steel, and textiles, seek industry survival in light of foreign competition. The new research consortium in the computer industry—Microelectronics and Computer Technology Corporation (unifying twelve major companies such as Control Data, RCA, Honeywell, Motorola, and several upper-end mid-sized firms)—is the most innovative example of interorganizational strategy.

CONNECTIONS WITH PROFITS

Molex makes connections—the pins, cables, conductors, sockets, sprockets, switches, terminals, and boards used in electronic manufacturing, from home appliances to medical instruments. Nothing high tech about the products. Nothing low return about the performance.

Over the past ten years net profit margins averaged 11.8 percent after tax. Return on stockholders' equity approached 30 percent. During the decade of the 1970s, sales increased 38 percent per year, growing from $9 million to $100 million. For the fiscal year ending June 30, 1984, sales were up a dynamic 43 percent to $252 million, and net profits were up a whopping 74 percent to $32 million—hitting a stratospheric 15 percent of sales. (For calendar 1983, Molex earned $22 million on $176 million in revenues.)

Molex claims "an enduring entrpreneurial spirit," and says the true interests of the company are best served by "measured, persistent progress into the future rather than by settling for immediate, short-term gains." This guiding philosophy is reflected in everything from product design to employee training. (Employee Opportunity and Growth–Profits Tradeoff, Creative Strategies 6 and 9, are major energizers of Molex's extraordinary success.)

The company has built a substantial international business; a full three-fifths of its revenues is generated outside of the United States. Only six of Molex's manufacturing facilities are located in the United States; five are in the Far East, four in Europe, one in Mexico, and one in Brazil. Molex does almost as much business in the Far East as it does in the United States ($79 million versus $83 million).

Molex is a family-controlled, family-operated company, headquartered in Lisle, Illinois. John Krehbiel, who founded the company in 1938 as a fledgling plastic molder, is chairman of the board; one son is president, the other executive vice-president. (The family owns 49.8 percent of the common stock, and 86.6 percent of Class B Common—which has strong voting rights. Asked about his family's stock, worth almost $400 million on the market, Mr. Krehbiel says simply, "It's hard to believe.")

One of the original pioneers in developing pin and socket connectors, Molex today manufactures more than 20,000 products worldwide. Components can be found in many well-known products, including Radio Shack computers, Xerox copiers, Chrysler engines, Canon typewriters, and so on.

Molex serves an incredibly broad customer base, marketing connector components to original-equipment manufacturers in diverse industries:

Consumer Goods. Televisions, stereo systems, organs, tape recorders, video recorders, home computers, electronic games, ranges, microwaves, refrigerators, freezers, dishwashers, clothes washers and dryers, disposals, and air conditioners.

Office Equipment. Business computers, computer peripherals, calculators, copiers, and dictation equipment.

Industrial Equipment. Automobiles, trucks, farm machinery, leisure-time vehicles, medical instrumentation, scientific instruments, communication equipment, and vending machines.

Marketing is conducted through 50 direct-sales offices, 40 representative organizations, and more than 120 distribution centers around the world. Molex's geographic scope enables it to handle those companies that are "introducing the newest ideas in electronic design and packaging, companies like IBM, Xerox, Sony, Phillips, Hewlett-Packard, Atari, Apple, and Olivetti; companies which design and develop their products in one location and manufacture them in another."

Molex is striving to serve its customer base more effectively, advancing the art of "connections" in the new world of microelectronics, assisting customers in lowering their costs and raising their quality. Miniaturization is the most critical design requirement, and Molex engineers are working to reduce the circuit spacing in both crimp and insulation displacement connectors. Some 210 employees, 7 percent of the total, are engaged full-time in R&D, and more than 6 percent of sales is invested in new-product research. New products are focused on "target" industries. "We must stay ahead," says the chairman, "just to keep abreast."

Molex claims that it makes more than just quality electronic components. "We feel our primary task is to develop fully integrated solutions to our customers' problems. For this reason, we get involved early in the development of a [customer's] new product."

Molex takes pride in being "extremely people oriented," for having a "very special 'family' feeling." Molex encourages recreational, social, and athletic activities among employees. From picnics to sports days, a company spirit exists.

The company strives to attract and retain "creative, industrious people who share our working philosophy." A great deal of time, effort, and money is allocated to recruit, train, and develop employees. The Advanced Management Training Course, for example, is a companywide program to make managers aware of the latest general business techniques and give them an overview of company operations. Such intensive training goes on at all levels. Classes usually number about thirty and are taught by professors from the Harvard, Stanford, and Chicago Schools of Business.

Another highly successful program is the "annual employee exchange" wherein workers, selected from manufacturing facilities around the world trade places with their opposite number in other countries. Molex believes that performing one's regular job outside one's own country gives better understanding of different cultures and manufacturing procedures. Molex credits its employee development program for producing a work force "with a record for productivity that is one of the best in the electronics industry."

Creative Strategies are found in abundance here. The standouts must include: Focus, Product Emphasis, Employee Opportunity, Efficient Innovation, External Perception, and Growth–Profits Tradeoff.

COMPONENTS OF STRATEGY

Strategic management, at its roots, is the application of the scientific method to business thinking.[7] As such the component elements are derived from a logical appraisal of situations—the gathering of information, the arraying of alternatives, the testing of alternatives, and the feedback and reevaluation. Each step of the process flows freely from the previous one.

Strategic management is a major field of contemporary business. Its elements (Figure 7.1) require and deserve treatment well beyond the scope of this chapter. We can only highlight them here, though we put some emphasis on "goals"—the driving energy of strategy. We stress practicality. What follows, then, are the fundamental tools of strategic analysis; these form the foundation for the application concepts we call Creative Strategies.

CORPORATE GOALS

Goals are what every company wants but few understand. When senior managers take advanced business courses, goals are often overlooked as obvious and simple and not worth worry or concern.

Strategy and tactics are studied, but strategy and tactics to accomplish what? The setting of company goals, not so obvious and not so simple, demands a good look.

What are goals? Definitions abound. Goals are overall purpose; the establishment of long-term mission and short-term targets are prime corporate requirements. ("Goals" may be contrasted with "objectives" in that most consider the former long term and the latter short term.)

Goals can be defined as a "planned position," "a result to be achieved," or "a desired situation to be attained." By definition or default, an organization must have goals. If a company does not set formal goals, they are set nonetheless—by neglect. Every organization has goals, whether defined or not, clear or not, attainable or not. The smart company, to be smart, will define goals, making them clear and attainable.

Why should a company set goals? For guidance, planning, direction, motivation, evaluation, and control. Goals serve several simultaneous purposes:

1. They are guidelines for strategic decisions.
2. They are guidelines for operational directives.
3. They give internal systems direction.
4. They focus subsystems on compliance and coordination.
5. They shape structure and staffing.
6. They motivate and guide subordinate behavior.
7. They are yardsticks against which results can be measured.
8. They provide the basis for organizational control.

All goals can be dissected into their component parts:

1. Position: Where in the hierarchy does the goal fit?
2. Content: What is the nature of the goal?
3. Measure: What is the indicator of the goal?
4. Level: What is the number of the goal?
5. Period: What are the time constraints of the goal?

Category	1	2	3	4	5
Position	Corporate	Divisional	Marketing	Manufacturing	R & D
Content	Financial return	Absolute dollars	Product scope	High quality	Innovation
Measure	Return on investment	Contributional income	Increase in market share	Rejection rate	New products
Level	19%	15%	3%	0.07%	3
Period	Year	Year	Season	Monthly average	24 months

FIGURE 7.5. Company goals: Categories and components.

Some examples are diagrammed in Figure 7.5.

1. A corporate goal might be a 19 percent return on investment every year.
2. A divisional goal might be a 15 percent increase in contributional income this year.
3. A product goal might be a 3 percent increase in market share the first season.
4. A manufacturing goal might be a rejection rate of no more than 0.0007 (averaged monthly).
5. An R&D goal might be the development of three new products in the next twenty-four months.

How can "good" and "poor" goals be differentiated?

The *content* of good goals is: clear, not vague; specific, not general; consistent, not discordant; measurable, not boundless; difficult, not easy; achievable, not impossible (see Figure 7.6).

The *process* of good goal setting includes: commitment by everyone, especially superiors; belief in the meaningfulness of the outcome; easy communication up and down the corporate hierarchy;

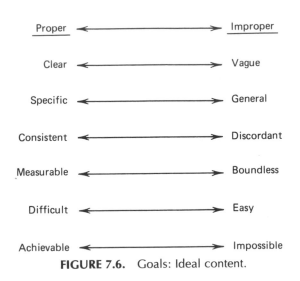

FIGURE 7.6.   Goals: Ideal content.

feedback of results; healthy and spirited competition among subordinates and peers.

In recent years new concepts have changed the way we look at corporate goals. Gone is the fiction that goals are set rationally and logically. Recall Simon's "bounded rationality"—optimizing is replaced by satisficing, the realization that problems need only be solved satisfactorily not perfectly.

Next, we no longer believe that the only "rational" goal is to increase shareholder wealth. Society has come to realize that business corporations are complex social instruments, with responsibilities extending beyond owners. "Constituency analysis" seeks to define the various groups who are "stakeholders" in corporations, and to recognize their part in setting organizational goals. A company's constituency would include the following groups: shareholders, senior management, middle management, workers, families, suppliers, customers, industry, community, local government, national government, and society.[8]

What about the goal formulation process? Is it rational? First, if one studies the real-world framework of the organizational environment, not academic theory, some interesting results emerge. Rationality, one learns quickly, rarely dominates; often, it can be hardly found. Goals are set in companies, like everything else that happens in companies, on the basis of power and position. Corporate politics has been pulled out of the closet and put under the microscope.

John French, Jr., and Bertram Raven distinguished five categories with which a person (P) can be controlled by a social agent (O), whether another person, group, or part of a group. The relevance here is direct. How are those who formulate goals in companies, the Ps, influenced by the various corporate Os?[9]

1. *Reward Power.* P's perception that O can mediate positive value (whether financial, promotional, personal, social, or psychological)—for example, the executive vice-president gets his divisional VPs to support his goals on the basis of his discretionary authority over their upcoming bonuses.

2. *Coercive Power.* P's perception that O can mediate negative value (whether financial, promotional, personal, social, or psychological)—for example, a geographical vice-president influences the president to increase advertising in his area since his sister is the president's wife.

3. *Legitimate Power.* P's perception that O has a proper and appropriate right to prescribe behavior for him—for example, the president respects the opinion of the financial vice-president in setting return on investment goals.

4. *Referent Power.* P's personal identification with O—for example, a president who never graduated from college respects his young assistant who has several advanced degrees.

5. *Expert Power.* P's perception that O has some special knowledge or expertise—for example, the vice-president for research listens to his chief scientist.

Politics is king in organizational life. Whoever has the boss's ear has a good grip on the company soul. Jockeying position and maneuvering people is the corporate bargaining game, and it's played heavy and hard in the goal formulation process.

Familiar with the "organizational politician?" We all know him. But what's he up to; what makes him tick? At the top of the list, this fellow has consummate knowledge of company systems and people—not how they work on paper but how they work in reality, the *informal* relationships. He tracks opinion of superiors, senior managerial successors, even current sleeping arrangements. His favorite position? He likes to control the flow of information. He's not too big on line authority; responsibility too soon can get you knocked out of the box. He is always seen with the right people—luncheons are important. Finally, he chooses his tasks carefully, taking only those that will work and win.

Divisions and departments, too, are creatures of politics. They act as if animate. Mere boxes on organizational charts, they have an uncanny sense of their own existence. It does not matter who is operating the shop, there is constant pressure to sustain power and position, to do things according to "standard operating procedures," to maintain the established routine, to perform the accustomed repertoire. Departments and divisions will do anything to maintain their mystical being.[10]

ENVIRONMENTAL ANALYSIS

How does one do "environmental analysis?" What does one look for? The key is the search for early signs of opportunity and early warnings of threat. (*Opportunity* and *threat* are relative terms; what might be a threat for a chemical plant, say, strict pollution regulations, may be an opportunity for a company making filters.)

Some forces affecting the company environment? Check the following:

1. *Economic.*   The shape and trend of the general economy. Are we headed up or down; are we tenuous or robust?

2. *Demographic.*   Patterns of people, projected by age, sex, geography, and so on. (For example, as the post-World War II "baby boom" bulges through the population, business is affected—cribs in early years; colleges in late teenage; home builders in the early thirties; luxury items in middle age; retirement villages in senior years; caskets, face it, thereafter.)

3. *Technology.*   The direction and time frame of progress and breakthroughs from R&D. Two new trends, for example, are the impetus from commercializing defense-related technology[11] and the growing strength of innovative countries, such as Israel, to compete in the international marketplace for science-based industry.

4. *Sociocultural and Psychological.* The changing attitudes and orientation of society. [The astute businessman can find much potential here, for example, the health and fitness boom accelerated Shaklee's nutritional products and Guilford's running apparel. Other examples include the sexual revolution (e.g., *Playboy* and *Penthouse* empires), women working, convenience stores, designer jeans.]

5. *Legal and Governmental.* Regulation and regulation reform, such as environmental protection, worker compensation, antitrust, and so on.

6. *Industry Structure.* The competitive analysis of markets and companies—the intensity of interfirm rivalries, the height of entry barriers, the potential of substitute products, the relative strength of suppliers and buyers.[12]

COMPANY ANALYSIS

Assessing a firm's strengths and weaknesses is the essence of company analysis. Each of the functional areas—for example, finance, marketing, manufacturing, R&D, public image, general management, and so on—must be examined and judged. Such judgments should be in two parts, the first independently, the second collectively. Facts, data, interpretation, opinion, projection, and insight must be distinguished from one another, and then woven together. The process should discern strengths and weaknesses relative to the company itself and relative to other companies.

What, for example, are Marion's strengths? Clearly its highly efficient "Search" R&D combined with perceptive, knowledgeable marketing.

What might be Molex's weakness? As microprocessors become more dense and integrated circuits become more sophisticated, the need for external connectors may diminish.

How about Noxell? Noxzema and Cover Girl are great names. Lestoil, on the other hand, is competing against the giant consumer goods companies and is losing market share.

Assessing corporate strengths and weaknesses is complicated by cross-currents of psychological and sociological pressures.

Consider the experience of one corporate executive running his firm's "Strategy Assessment Weekend."

"On Friday night, we filled up two columns on the blackboard, one 'Strengths,' the other 'Weaknesses.' We felt that we really understood our position, that we had good control of the company. We slept soundly. On Saturday morning we discussed Strengths; on Saturday afternoon Weaknesses. By Saturday evening we were seeing some problems with our Strengths, and some advantages to our Weaknesses. We slept lightly. By Sunday morning we realized that our Strengths weren't so strong, and our Weaknesses weren't so weak. When we left Sunday afternoon, we didn't know where we were."

When studying strengths and weaknesses, especially of one's own company, it is difficult to overcome natural biases. The kind of job you have, and the level of your position within the hierarchy, will influence your analysis of the firm. How one carries out the process of defining strengths and weaknesses cannot be divorced from position and responsibility. Thus personnel and financial concerns—whether considered a strength or a weakness—peak at senior managerial levels, while marketing and technical concerns peak at middle managerial levels. Objective assessment is difficult and one should never assume otherwise.[13]

STRATEGIC FORMULATION

This is the creative part, the time for expansive ideas and explosive excitement. When one is generating alternative strategies, there should be no worry about logic, no concern for consistency. Just have at it! The concepts produced should be numerous and novel, fanciful and fresh. If you don't uncork some wild ones here, you're missing the boat. Explore limits; push boundaries.

In developing lists of alternative strategies it is important to be exhaustive and mutually exclusive, exhaustive in encompassing all possible approaches, mutually exclusive in providing for real choice. (If all alternative strategies could be chosen together, they are not "alternatives." Such an approach is self-limiting.)

Following are some strategy categories to consider.

Product Strategies

Concentration   Focus on a single industry or product (Molex, Great Lakes, Guilford, Russell, Henredon, Stephen Cannell Productions).

Vertical Integration.   Backward integration into production (Hillenbrand) and forward integration into distribution (Shaklee). Also Tandon; the Martinsville sweat shirt manufacturers.

Horizontal Integration.   Expansion of lines for similar products (Great Lakes, Gould Pumps) and geographic expansion for same products (Molex, La Quinta Motor Inns).

Diversification.   Concentric, based around current products and skills (Plenum, Premier, Maytag); conglomerate, independent of current businesses (Hillenbrand, Ametek).

Business Strategies

Share Building.   Increasing market share of products (Hillenbrand, Noxell, Neutrogena).

Share Harvesting.   Allowing market share to fall in order to "milk" for cash (Simplicity, pre-Hurwitz).

Turnaround.   Taking a losing business and making it profitable (Eagle).

Retrenchment.   Pruning back a business in order to revitalize it (Scripto, Dr. Pepper, Bandag).

Liquidation.   Determining that the company is worth more dead than alive; that the parts independently will be more valued than the parts collectively. (Examples: UV Industries, in mineral operations, saw its share price increase from $19 to $30 upon the liquidation announcement. The Heizer Corporation, with investments in companies such as Amdahl and Fotomat, and selling at a discount on the market, was voted into liquidation to maximize stockholder value.)

Functional Strategies

Marketing.   Stress channels of distribution (Marion, Premier, Noxell).

Manufacturing. Be the low-cost producer (Tandon, Guilford, Hillenbrand); be the low-cost buyer (Eagle/April-Marcus); provide a specialty service (J.L. Clark).

R&D. Pioneer state-of-the-art products (Genentech in biotechnology, Dynatech, Ametek, Galram—see Chapter 10).

Financial. Emphasize returns and ratios (few top-performing mid-sized firms use this strategy).

Financial Strategies

Growth. Trade off short-term profits for long-term position (numerous technology companies, e.g., Apple; La Quinta).

Profits. Stress short-term returns and sacrifice long-term position (no companies will admit this approach).

Asset Reduction. Generate current revenues/profits from a smaller asset base, thus improving returns (e.g., inventory reductions, generating higher inventory turns and better efficiency—Hillenbrand).

Cash. Limit investments back into the company (curtail R&D, advertising, modernizing manufacturing equipment).

Transactional Strategies

Internal Development. Using corporate staffs to create new products and processes (IBM, Hewlett-Packard).

Internal Venturing. Devising innovative corporate structures to develop new products and services (intrapreneurship); use techniques of entrepreneurship and venture capital to stimulate corporate creativity (Control Data, 3M, MacDermid).

Acquisition. Building the company by buying other companies (Simplicity, Ametek, Dynatech, Tyco).

Divestiture. Selling off parts of the company that do not fit with current corporate strategy (Keystone selling its truck equipment division).

Joint Venture.   The combination of two or more companies to form a new project or company (Dow-Corning in silicon products, Warner-Amex in cable TV, Galram in commercializing defense-related technology).

STRATEGY EVALUATION

Now we shift gears; we go from intuition to analysis, from freeform expansion to rigorous reduction. (In the language of brain research, we jump "hemispheres," leaping from the "imaginative right side" to the "rational left side.") Evaluation should consider both quantitative and qualitative criteria, numbers and concepts, embedding all data and values.

The objective of strategy evaluation is to subject each alternative strategy to rigorous analysis. One should have reasons for either keeping or changing strategies—and although more energy is required to alter accepted policies than retain current ones, the status quo should be tested *de novo* from time to time.

Strategy evaluation is often submerged into strategy formulation. The two are very different, however, cognitively and substantively. The importance of the evaluation part cannot be overstated. Choosing is critical. Consider the classic strategic maxim that "It is better to do the right thing wrong, than the wrong thing right." (In other words a company would make more money managing a network television station poorly than operating a massive steel mill well.)

We should differentiate the *process* of strategy evaluation from the *content*; the former is mechanism, the latter substance. It is important to appreciate process in order to analyze content.

What are some key criteria for strategic evaluation? Cost. Timeliness. Validity. Reliability. Verifiability. Flexibility. Popularity. The fundamental issue for strategy evaluation is to be sure that the chosen strategy can achieve corporate goals consistent with environmental opportunities and threats and company strengths and weaknesses.

Internal consistency is perhaps the primary test of the evaluation procedure. Suppose marketing is selling the eyes off its new product;

what is the good if manufacturing can't make it and finance can't pay for it?

Richard Rumelt frames strategy evaluation in terms of discovering "asymmetries," or exploiting advantages. "Under conditions of pure rivalry (i.e., symmetry) . . . no one can predict which of two identical armies or corporations will prevail. . . . the winning strategy is always the same—play only those games in which you have an advantage. . . . one wins games by exploiting asymmetries that make a difference." He poses a powerful "rejection rule": Any strategy that does not either create or exploit an asymmetry in the environment constituting an advantage for the firm must be rejected.[14]

In the evaluation procedure, Rumelt uses four tests.[14]

The Goal Consistency Test

Is the strategy internally consistent? Any strategy that contains goals, objectives, and policies that are mutually exclusive, that in any way contradict each other, must be rejected. Thus the goal of "growth" is often incompatible with "maintaining personal control over all functional areas."

The Frame Test

Does the strategy deal with important areas? Any strategy that does not deal with relevant subjects must be rejected. The distinction between solving pressing problems and facing important issues is germane in all decision situations, but especially so in strategy-making ones. The frame test is directed toward highlighting the relevance of issues, not the solving of problems. One must be sure the "right subjects" are being addressed. Discriminating between importance and unimportance is the essence of strategic "wisdom." For example, size in the automotive industry, location in retailing, and image in the liquor business are pure frame theories "in that they indicate what one should have as an objective rather than how to accomplish it." (Note that most of our Creative Strategies fit the frame model.)

The Competence Test

Is the problem properly factored to enable strategic solution? Any strategy too general or too cumbersome must be rejected. Unless a strategy assumes subproblems that are solvable—understandable enough and simple enough—one is simply substituting one ill-structured situation for another.

The Workability Test

Is the strategy likely to "work?" Any strategy not expected to be implemented successfully must be rejected. Determination is based on two general categories: (1) the adequacy of resources available and the ease of proper deployment and (2) the accuracy of probable outcomes associated with each particular action.

Traditional forms of evaluating strategies include the following:

Classical Models. Strategy as a "set of goals and major policies" stressing consistency, risk, timing, and adequacies.[15]

Life Cycle Models. Strategies contingent on different phases of the product–market life cycle—preparation/R&D, introduction, growth, shakeout, maturity, and decline.[16]

Cross-Sectional Models. Strategies driven by the collective experiences of numerous companies in diverse industries, such as the direct relationship between market share and return on investment.[17]

Strategic Group Models. Strategies based on a company's competitive position within industries. Since industries are heterogenous, probable success patterns depend on different structural locations.[18]

Experience Curve Models. Strategies tied to economies of scale in cumulative production. (Costs of value added drop 20–30 percent each time the number of units manufactured over the lifetime of the firm/plant double.) Companies are advised to "ride down the learning curve," even by buying market share through taking short-term losses, so that lowest costs will eventually generate highest profits.[19]

The following is a series of test questions, exploratory probes for the strategic evaluation of each specific alternative strategy.

1. Is the strategy identifiable and clear?

2. Is the strategy workable and practical?

3. Does the strategy develop or create competitive advantage, maximizing distinctive competencies, playing up company uniquenesses?

4. Is the strategy internally consistent—consistent with company goals, strengths and weaknesses, functional capabilities, resource availabilities, and timing requirements? (If not, can company resources—human, physical, financial—be obtained in the proper time frame?)

5. How does the strategy affect current strategies? Will it require any radical change or restructure?

6. What is the risk–reward tradeoff? Are the risks acceptable in economic and personal terms?

7. Are the personal values and aspirations of senior management being satisfied?

8. Does the strategy consider adequately the diverse constituencies of the company?

9. What competitive responses might the strategy trigger?

10. Does the strategy stimulate managerial effort and engender corporate commitment?

11. Can the strategy be implemented with the present organizational structure or with a planned altered structure?

12. How can the strategy be assessed? How can its viability be checked? Can it be quantified and measured?

13. Are there flash feedback mechanisms, early indicators of results (e.g., market responsiveness)?

14. What is the time sequencing of strategic components, and are they realistic?

15. Does the strategy provide sufficient flexibility, enough room for subsequent modification?

STRATEGIC IMPLEMENTATION

Now comes the hard part: making strategies work. This is the moment of truth when words and papers are transformed into deeds and action. This is when machinery gets rolling and hands get dirty.

There are three general categories to consider. We highlight each, a full discussion being beyond our scope.

Structure. Structure is the mechanism that implements strategy, and strategy is the motivation that changes structure. The two are intimately related, with each affecting the other recursively. (As noted, a multinational strategy will force a divisional structure, whether intended or not.)[20]

Control. The object is to establish systems that will be self-generating and self-policing, requiring minimal external intervention by senior management. Executives can't always watch, and shouldn't spend the time if they could. Personnel must be organized and motivated so that they will intrinsically seek to accomplish management's policies. Employees must fulfill company needs by promoting their own interests.

Inertia. When strategies change, ways must be found to break tradition. Previous patterns well ingrained must be shifted and reformed. Generating momentum is the boss's task.

KEEPING STRATEGIC PERSPECTIVE

A word of caution. Strategic management is a powerful management technique, overtly so. As such, one must keep in mind its weaknesses and avoid easy misuse. Most important, one must not forget that generalized strategic advice that works is hard to find and harder to apply.

Don't ever allow simplistic solutions, however glib the words and smooth the show, to affect complex corporate decisions. Almost everything strategic is "contingent," that is, subject to variation and change depending on specific circumstance. What is ideal for one company may be disastrous for another, though the two firms may appear outwardly similar—one apparently minor difference is often all it takes to turn right into wrong.

We conclude by rooting ourselves in the real world, by hearing from one who must "hack it" every day. He is a planning executive in a large multinational company with over thirty years' experience. In responding to a group of academic strategists, he was candid: "I have a hard time understanding what you are really talking about . . . fancy language and 'scientific jargon' do not cover up poor thinking. . . . Plans are, bluntly speaking, strictly for the birds; once you have a written plan you may as well throw it out, because most of the time it is going to be absolutely wrong. The great importance of planning lies in the fact that it is a *continuous learning and decision making process*. As such, it is invaluable in any corporation worth its salt."[21]

The typical MBA-type response, of course, is cramming more data into models and stuffing more information into people. But as Ackoff says in one of his fables, "the less we understand something, the more variables we require to explain it."[22]

CHAPTER 8

CREATIVE MANAGEMENT

Catching Visions,
Jumping Gaps

"I'm Sam Barshop, *former* Regent." That was how the chief executive of La Quinta Motor Inns, one of the nation's most successful lodging chains, introduced himself at a formal meeting at the University of Texas School of Business—and it said much about one of the most creative men in his field. Much about his interests. Much about his self-image.

It was a very funny remark, dry and pungent, but one has to dig into the depths of Texas politics, a maze of mystery and dark sayings, to understand the humor. First of all, one must appreciate the importance of the Board of Regents in Texas. Its eight members control what has become one of the truly great universities in the world. Its endowment is over $2 billion, soon to surpass Harvard as number one—and it still owns 2 million acres of oil-producing lands in west Texas. Texans idolize their university, as well they should, and it is said, only half in jest, that "a Regent's power is only slightly more than a Governor's."

Sam Barshop had been appointed by Governor Bill Clements, and a better, more nonpolitical choice he couldn't have made. Barshop was one of the most active supporters of the university, giving not only his money but his time, energy, and spirit to build his alma mater. He led the endowment campaign for the business school, supporting Dr. George Kozmetsky, the legendary former dean, in moving the school, already the largest in the country, to one of the finest. The business school's endowment, on its own, is larger than that of many universities. As for the credit, give Barshop a good hunk.

Barshop's appointment was applauded at the university, which had a checkered history of enduring regents with more interest in influence than academics. So what happened? How does this sweet story turn sour?

Well, qualifications were swamped by politics. The problem was that Governor Clements, defeated in his reelection campaign by Mark White, had made the appointment during his "lame duck" period. (The campaign was particularly virulent, even for Texas. Clements, by the way, had also appointed as a regent former governor John Connelly, a political ally.)

Governor White is an extraordinarily able individual, with profound understanding of intellectual resources and demonstrated dedication to academic excellence.[1] Yet, the new administration had to eliminate vestiges of the old—and unfortunately Sam got swept into the swirling vortex. A battle raged in the state Senate. Sam, so apolitical and so perfect, was the toughest to knock out, but knocked out he was. Pressure and patronage had overwhelmed competence and commitment. It was not Texas' finest hour.

So Sam had been a regent for a few weeks, and it was his proudest moment and fondest role. (His "former Regent" remark was made the day after his nomination was overturned, and it broke the room up.) For a political amateur, Barshop ran an impressive campaign—with grit and intensity he told his story. He became the hot topic of political gossip and media coverage, and the vote was closer than expected. Several state senators defied political common sense to vote for Barshop. Sam was so impressive that some would push him for elected office. But that's not his style.

Sam Barshop, a large, kindly man in his early fifties, would rather be known as a supporter of the university, and as a developer of his beloved San Antonio, than even as a financial innovator and extraordinary corporate leader. He is in fact all four.

La Quinta Motor Inns is the nation's fastest-growing motel chain; it is the marvel of the industry, having rewritten the rules. Coming from nowhere, it manages almost 20,000 rooms. La Quinta's occupancy rates have exceeded the industry average by 10–15 percent over the past five years.

Its marketing concept is simple: To provide guests with quality accommodations and essential services in convenient locations at reasonable prices. Clean, comfortable rooms are offered at highly competitive rates. By providing only those services and facilities most preferred by business travelers (24-hour messages, same-day laundry, cable TV, free-standing restaurant), and by eliminating such nonessentials as banquet facilities, extensive public areas, and large meeting rooms, La Quinta can outprice the traditional convention or resort-oriented lodging establishments.

Barshop believes that "our market share will continue to grow as more companies and travelers discover La Quinta is an attractive alternative to expensive full service properties." Yet, sensitive to the discontinuity thinking that good strategic management demands, he adds some wise caution: "Our industry is dynamic and we recognize the need to continually evaluate our concept and its execution. We must fit the future marketplace, not the other way around."

La Quinta concentrates on its one business, expanding horizontally into new territory, always maintaining the same focus. Its Motor Inns are strategically positioned between budget and luxury hotels, and geographically located on major traffic arteries near business districts, airports, and universities.

At the end of fiscal 1984, La Quinta was operating 125 inns and licensed the operation of 13 others in twenty-five states, principally in the Sun Belt and Rocky Mountain areas. Daily rate per occupied room averaged $32 in 1984 ($28 in 1982), quite a bargain as any traveler can attest. Occupancy rate, the vital sign of hotel health, maintained a sturdy 73 percent in 1984, a weak year, down from a two-year average of 80 percent in 1981 and 1982.

Typically a La Quinta motor inn has 106–138 rooms, with a distinct Spanish-modern architectural style topped by a red-tile roof. Individual units are usually managed by husband and wife teams who live on the premises, supported by about fifteen in help.

"We like having couples as managers," comments Barshop. "Generally they are second career people who treat our guests as if visitors in their home—which they are."

Because La Quinta's management couples do not have responsibility for food service, they are able to devote their attention to providing clean and well-kept facilities, courteous and friendly guest service, and accurate and timely operational reports. (Cleanliness is almost a fetish to La Quinta. "Men are more finicky about a clean room than women," observes Barshop. "They'll check under the beds, run their fingers along the window sills, even look in the toilets. They'll forgive anything, even surly clerks, but never a dirty room.")

"We leave food service to the experts," continues the soft-spoken Barshop. "Our first inns had in-house restaurants and bars—until we discovered we were spending a lot of time and energy doing something we didn't do well. We could be more successful doing what we do best, which was simply selling beds. Today all of the restaurants are operated by national chains. We wanted our managers to concentrate on keeping our rooms clean and our guests happy. I've always admired the philosophy of keeping things simple. Simplicity isn't easy when you're growing as fast as we are. There are constant temptations to add services or change things. Why have bells, whistles and waterfalls when all our guests want is a good night's rest?"

Barshop's "simple little system" cuts to the core of creative strategies for mid-sized firms: (1) Define your market and concentrate on serving it; (2) keep it simple; and (3) when you find something that works, keep doing it.

And "doing it" he does. Five-year compound growth rates (1978–1983) were 23.7 percent in revenues, 29.3 percent in profits, and

31.7 percent in working capital provided by operations. The San Antonio-based La Quinta earned $13.5 million on revenues of $113.4 million in 1983, and $12.8 million on $136.8 million in 1984. Yet the period was called "the most difficult time in our corporate history," the Southwest being hit by oil price declines and peso devaluations. Barshop responded by aggressively controlling costs, strengthening his management team, accelerating development activity, and placing increased emphasis on long-range planning.

The "accelerating development" is the most interesting part; it's not something you'd expect in a downturn. Barshop decided to expand rapidly "in spite of the short-term negative impact on earnings." He made this decision "to take advantage of stabilized or reduced construction costs." By May 1984 approximately one-third of La Quinta's inns were less than three years old. For fiscal 1985, the company anticipates opening 22 new properties, primarily in the Sun Belt. "We are confident these new inns will be a significant long-term advantage as we seek to increase our market share."

Yet there is constant pruning. All properties not meeting La Quinta standards in quality or performance are put on the block. Two inns were sold in 1982 and another two in 1983, resulting in pretax gains of $3 million and $3.5 million, respectively. Barshop is a master of financial strategy, and asset redeployment is an important tactic.

Coordination is vital when two dozen or so buildings are being constructed at the same time. La Quinta uses standard plans and specs; they are adapted for each site by local architects familiar with local building codes and requirements. The company generally contracts with third parties at fixed prices, and the all-masonry construction is structurally sound, fireproof, and energy efficient. The buildings are prefabricated, more than half built in a factory, not on the site. Company managers handle five projects simultaneously. (Average construction time for the eighteen new inns opened in 1983 was less than ten months, and the final cost was within 5 percent of budget. Construction costs average about $37,000 per room, comparing favorably with the $42,000–$65,000 at rivals like Marriott or Holiday Inn.)

During 1983 La Quinta began a more formalized approach to strategic planning. Actual and potential competitors, nationally and regionally, were identified and monitored continuously. An extensive remodeling/refurbishing program was begun to bring older units up to newer standards. Special attention was allocated to nine inns performing below par. A flexible five-year plan for geographic expansion was begun.

The company contemplates over 300 inns by the end of the decade. Additions include 43 in California and 19 in Florida—decreasing the economic vulnerability of regional concentration (reducing Texas-based inns from 48 percent to 27 percent). La Quinta is penetrating major city markets—Chicago, Phoenix, New Orleans, Atlanta—and targeting Virginia, Maryland and Washington, D.C. for initial entry into the East Central Region.

How can La Quinta afford to finance such rapid expansion, especially the high capital costs? This is the creative part. It involves an innovative financial mechanism developed by Mr. Barshop and works like this. A joint venture (or partnership) is established in which La Quinta and a co-venturer (or limited partner) share ownership of one or more motor inns, each typically owning a half interest. The company's partners provide equity and long-term debt, or land. La Quinta operates the motor inns and receives development and management fees. The co-venturers share profits and losses and any residual value in the motor inns (at the time of sale) in the same ratio as their ownership interests. So simple, and so effective. Financial strategy, clearly, is a major thrust.

"We get tremendous leverage," states Barshop, "while decreasing our financial risk at the same time." Not only are the dangers of new property development diminished, but the joint-venture arrangements provide other advantages: They make available certain choice sites; they enable equity and debt financing on more favorable terms (often two to three points below conventional mortgage rates); they facilitate more rapid expansion while maintaining operational control (much more than would franchising). Now that's creativity!

Today, the Prudential Insurance Company is a joint-venture partner in some thirty-six motor inns and twenty free-standing restaurants, having put up over $100 million. The relationship was begun in 1971. "We were conservative," recalls Barshop. "We opted not to go for short-term funds from the real estate investment trusts, though people at the time thought we were foolish for giving up half of our project in order to get the long-term money. Then came the economic crunch of 1973–74; when a lot of people were hanging by their fingertips, there we were sitting with long-term permanent financing in strong joint ventures. We're willing to sacrifice short-term profits for security. The same is true today."

Barshop's financial genius is to mix conservative strength with dynamic innovation. He won't turn a spade for a new property until the funding has been arranged. Of the $200 million committed for new construction in fiscal 1983 and 1984, $76 million was cash in the bank (including new public debt and equity), $77 million from the sale of industrial revenue bonds and $47 million from joint-venture arrangements. Barshop anticipates raising $1.5 billion over the next ten years. Based on his record, investors line up, checks in hand.

Barshop calls for continued growth. ("We're only in about 20–25 percent of the markets with over 100,000 people, and haven't even saturated those.") He articulates four prerequisites:

1. Securing the best locations. "We will pay a premium price for a prime location. You can change everything else about a motor inn—management, bed spreads, drapes—but you can't move the building."

2. Securing innovative joint-venture financing. "We'd rather own half of another 100 inns than all of 50."

3. Internal communications and control. A computerized management information system will link all inns with regional offices and headquarters; the system will provide data and controls, allowing the mom-and-pop managers to concentrate on running the property and serving the guests.

4. Quality and depth of management. "One analyst said we have a management team capable of running a company twice our size. I consider that a compliment because we *will* be twice our size in the near future."

Expansion is planned by "clustering" in larger markets, and then going back and filling in the smaller markets where La Quinta's streamlined operations are well suited. Forays from their Southwest homebase are in 300-mile increments (so that "our reputation and name identification can precede us".) Sam likened La Quinta growth to cookie-cutting: "You keep cutting," he said in his easy drawl, "until there's no more dough left."

Sam and his brother Phil grew up in the real estate business started by their father, a banana importer. When they opened their first La Quinta in 1968 (the name means "a country home" in Spanish), they were only expanding their real estate holdings. "We had no plans to become motor hotel operators," recalls Sam with his unassuming stance and infectious grin, "much less a national chain. In fact Phil has gone back into real estate, but running La Quinta is what I enjoy." (A security analyst once asked Sam when would be a good time to sell La Quinta's stock. His reply: "When we build a high-rise hotel in New York.")

Sam takes out a cigar and confesses, "I wouldn't know how to check someone in or out of a motel if my life depended on it. I handle the real estate and financing side of La Quinta. I'm good at it, and love it. Operations are handled by three first-rate senior vice-presidents. I delegate a ton of responsibility and pay them very well."

Which Creative Strategies stand out? La Quinta is certainly Distinctive, from architecture to room pricing to financing. The company is completely Coherent; it does one thing and does it best, Dominating its niche. It has superb External Perception, knowing its customers and what they want. Sam Barshop cuts a High Profile as chief executive, and he enjoys giving employees substantial Opportunity.

The future for Sam? Surely to build La Quinta into a major national chain, giving the giants a good run. He would also like to "give something back to San Antonio," and has plans for fascinating developments and projects ("the most beautiful mall in the country"). Though he dismisses any notion of public office himself, he is close to San Antonio's dynamic young mayor, Henry Cisneros, whose political future, pundits feel, should assume national proportions. Meanwhile, Sam Barshop and his wife, Ann, enjoy a life of accomplishment and civic responsibility. And should any future governor opt for competence and commitment in appointing a regent. . . .

CREATIVE AND INNOVATIVE MANAGEMENT

The emergence of a new mechanism for management, like the eruption of a supernova in astronomy, is an event of remarkable impact, bold and beautiful in form, stark and stunning in content. In the 1950s it was management science, the application of quantitative methods to solve business problems. In the 1960s it was behavioral science, the employment of psychological theory for organizational understanding. In the 1970s it was long-range planning, the use of formal methods for forecasting the future and simulating corporate response. In the 1980s it is creative and innovative management, the generation of novel solutions for complex problems.[2]

Human civilization is founded on social groupings, the gatherings of individuals in organizations and institutions of all kinds. The running of these transpersonal bunches, the capacity to develop and maintain cohesive order, is what "management" is all about.

From despots to deputies, "managers" have historically made groups go. "Good" management was always defined operationally by "success," whatever success meant for each particular group. Managers were chosen by instinct and survival, and information was transferred by observation and osmosis. The system worked for generations, for millennia (though even Moses was advised to "delegate" by his father-in-law Jethro).

The world today is very different. As much as we have gained in technology and sophistication we have lost in robustness and stability. While we have progressed in collective power, we have retrogressed in individual control. A manager just cannot assimilate the incessant barrage of high-density data that are the nervous impulses of modern organizations. Internal triggers and external shocks overwhelm analytical capacity. Frameworks are needed to simplify and reduce, trading off precision for accessibility and accuracy for comprehension.

Management concepts and administrative systems develop more by necessity than by design. Always, it seems, what comes about is what is already essential; there is no time to nurture the developing process. The history of management in this century—from Taylor's scientific management to functionalization to operations research to organizational structure and strategy—is the story of theory striving to keep pace with practice, of academics trying to formalize for executives what the best ones were doing by the feel of their gut.

Once more we are at an impasse. Even strategic planning, having promised to forecast and guide, has too often extrapolated the past and missed the future. What will happen is no longer governed by what *has* happened. Problems exist today that are difficult to factor into component parts, much less solve. Decision support systems and the like notwithstanding, what we need now is more than a new form of management; we need a new form of thinking!

Creative and innovative management, in Dr. George Kozmetsky's vision, must become the focal point of "nonroutine pursuits" and "nonprogrammable administration." Strategic management, of itself, has failed. Coordinating myriad quantas of data is beyond anyone's capacity to analyze fully, but decisions can be made with confidence when data reduction is combined with directed insight. Creative management, almost by definition, defies upfront quantification and early verification. Creative solutions are often suboptimal when measured by conventional yardsticks. Yet such "suboptimal" initiatives can often overwhelm reason and blow out logic. These startling mental processes are performed constantly without awareness by first-rate corporate executives.

Creativity is the input to innovation, the raw material of which revolution is built. At this time in human history, we need such a revolution; not a political one (we've had enough of those), but an administrative one. The issue before us becomes one of *leveraging* creativity, of maximizing its appearances and applications. We must generate families of fresh ideas, clusters of original alternatives, so that in the analytical/evaluation phase best choices can be made.

DYNAMIC DIVERSITY

"We attempt to capitalize on change." So states the president of Dynatech, a diversified high-technology company that earned $11 million on $147 million in sales in fiscal 1984. The company has combined a long-standing R&D strategy with an aggressive acquisition strategy to become a top-performing mid-sized firm. It is one of the few not focused on a single product/market.

With headquarters in Burlington, Massachusetts, Dynatech is composed of some *two dozen* operating companies, no one of which has more than 285 people. These companies manufacture and sell electronic-based test and measurement instruments for special segments of three major markets—telecommunications, broadcast communications, and medical diagnostics.

For the past five years Dynatech has maintained an impressive compound annual growth rate: sales, 28 percent; income, 30 percent; earnings per share, 26 percent. In fiscal 1983 (revenues, $99 million; earnings, $7.4 million) the firm generated about 30 percent return on invested capital for the eleventh consecutive year. (Only foreign sales, normally 20–25 percent of the business, was flat.)

"We consider broad definitions of businesses we want to be in," the president commented. "We try to gain significant representation in high growth, high technology niche markets. We are flexible in choosing the niches."

In data communications Dynatech does not make mainframe computers, front-end processors, or terminals. They target tighter; that's their game. They make the diagnostic and switching equipment that enables pieces of digital equipment to "talk" with each other from remote locations. "Network management" is their specialty. Customers include the New York Stock Exchange (stock transactions), the Federal Reserve Board of Chicago (wire transfers), and the Southern California Rapid Transit District (schedules for 2400 buses and 7000 drivers).

In clinical diagnostics, Dynatech specializes in immunology and bacteriology testing, where "our test procedures [using enzymes and fluorescing materials instead of radioactive isotopes] are the safest, most reliable and cost effective in the market."

In broadcast communications Dynatech's computerized newsroom automation system is expected to revolutionize radio and television news reporting. Free of telex machines and typewriters, news staffs will work with electronic data that can be fed into, retrieved from, and stored in dedicated terminals. (Sales for the first three months were $2 million.)

Dynatech was founded twenty-five years ago as a research and development firm by two professors from the Massachusetts Institute of Technology. (Since the beginning, J. P. Barger has been president and Warren Rohsenow, who retains his MIT professorship, has been chairman.)

The character of the company changed in the mid-1960s when it shifted from contract R&D, which is self-limiting, to proprietary products, which can generate operational leverage. The original market was medical diagnostics. In the early 1970s the company expanded into electronics diagnostics (e.g., monitoring and simulating entire networks). Since then, the focus has been increasingly on electronics and microprocessor-based technologies (which today accounts for more than two-thirds of company revenues).

Dynatech invests heavily in product development, consuming over 8 percent of sales in R&D. The next generation of new products is intended to propel the company to $200 million in sales.

While the communications group is the largest, fastest growing, and most profitable business segment, no one product dominates. Dynatech claims that "diversity of products and markets is a major strength of the company." Why does this strategy work for Dynatech when "product focus" is a primary strategy for most top-performing mid-sized companies? The simple answer is narrowcasting of markets combined with first-rate R&D—an expertise applicable to all subsidiaries.

"To keep ourselves lean and ready for more changes," the president continued, "we have kept investment in fixed assets on the light side." Dynatech's financial strategy is to maintain consistent, rapid annual increases in sales and earnings per share. Growth has been financed largely through internally generated funds, amplified by acquisitions. The low investment in fixed assets, combined with a strong return on sales, enables excellent return on investment.

Dynatech's expansion has been fueled by buying small companies: four in fiscal 1982 (air purification, temperature measurement, broadcast switching, and analog signal products)—total volume $5 million; seven in fiscal 1983 (pressure measurement, computer graphics for weather broadcasts, lightning detection, fluid handling for medical diagnosis, newsroom automation, integrated circuit handling, and temperature measurement)—total volume $7.7 million. A larger acquisition took place in fiscal 1984—

Controlonics, with $20 million in sales, specializes in signal processing for the specialty consumer (it is the leading manufacturer of "Whistler" radar receivers). Dynatech uses its skills in managing R&D to increase the value in its purchases. Acquisitions are made generally for stock.

"While we recognize that with change comes risk, we also know that not to change occasions even greater risk." The company, for example, is building up its direct sales organization in order to increase its sophisticated systems sales, thus incurring increased marketing expenses. Dynatech's senior financial officer sees an advantage: "We can get higher gross margins on this kind of business."

Dynatech conducts its diverse activities by balancing strong leadership at the corporate level with great autonomy for operating managers and technical experts. A high degree of independence and incentive is given to create and manage technological innovations. Presidents of subsidiaries run their businesses as profit centers with advice and counsel from group vice-presidents. Allowing people to "develop their own ideas" is part of Dynatech's strength. "Underlying our business approach is our belief in nourishing the entrepreneurial spirit."

COMPUTERS VERSUS BRAINS

How do chief executives plan corporate directions? Though attention has focused on the new tools of decision technology—data processing, statistical analysis, modeling, forecasting—the real story is what happens next. How can enormously complex problems—involving competing and interwoven social, cultural, ethical, and personal issues as well as economic ones—be integrated into coherent wholes? Considering the large numbers of people often involved, and the compressed periods of time for finding solutions, the situation becomes baffling.

Will computers help? Will electronic circuitry be making more strategic decisions? For certain operational issues, computers are essential: record keeping and data base management, minimizing costs of ingredients and inventory levels, maximizing efficiency in component scheduling and travel routes, and so on. Even for the organization and integration of long-range planning, computers are vital. But here, they are only a notebook. True strategic management demands creative insight.

The executive computer, symbolizing not money but knowledge, represents the new wealth of a new world—information. But who wants all that data? Who needs all those numbers? Today's most critical need is not more information but *less*. We need data reduction techniques, systems of selection and discernment, the intelligent search for meaning. We have enough numbers; what we need is understanding.

Computers are deterministic, preset by circuit and code; though the software be intelligent, electronic pathways are still hard wired to spark a known output. Brains are probabilistic, patterned by design and chance; in the gray matter of the cerebral cortex semi-random processes can trip new thresholds. It is impossible to program computers, however large the data base and however expert the system, to make strategic decisions—that is, decisions that are original in essence and unique in vision. The two dimensions are forever incompatible. Computers can crunch vast numbers and sift complex algorithms by brute force, but only brains can search imaginatively for order and innovation amidst chaos and tradition.

Brains do one conscious thing at a time, generally not more. But they can shift rapidly from one to another, like time-sharing in a computer. The neural apparatus (called the reticular activating system) highlights and habituates information, directing our attention. Furthermore, electric splashes of sensation can be traced throughout the brain, appearing not only in the specific conscious areas of the cerebral cortex but also in the unspecific (or association) areas of the cortex and in the lower subconscious centers. Among these brain areas, data passes back and forth furiously and incessantly, being synthesized and transformed in the process. Waiting some time to make a crucial decision could give these subtle systems a chance to work their loomlike magic.

RATIONAL VERSUS NONRATIONAL

Rational inquiry and nonrational insight should be complements, not antagonists, in seeking solutions to complex problems. Modern brain research has shown that one side of the cerebral hemisphere, usually the left, is logical and cognitive, while the other side, usually the right, is holistic and affective. The left brain, the one that speaks, dissects the pieces; the right brain, the one that visualizes, synthesizes wholes; the left operates deductively and rigorously, the right by patterns and images.

Creative decision making involves the exquisite interweaving of programmable logic and nonprogrammable impression. An executive requires both hemispheres active; he must see both the forest and the trees.

Personal opinion and values used to be deemed irrelevant. Of course, they could never be avoided. Now we take a different tack. We consider individual desire and intent perfectly respectable inputs for the decision maker. Intuition has come out of the closet.

There is new appreciation for the art of conceptualizing decisions amidst the science of analyzing them. A manager's subjective feelings should not be intimidated by so-called objective tests. An executive should not be afraid to contradict the computer. But neither should she leap to arbitrary conclusions without concern.

Try this procedure for creative thinking. First assess the problem intuitively. One should not too quickly call upon expert advice or embed oneself within traditional trains of thought. Such isolation allows the psyche minimum creative coercion, lessening the likelihood of interference from preset concepts and long-standing lines of logic.

On the other hand, wholly intuitive decisions can be dangerous if quantitative input is ignored. Executives should make a nonrational decision—that is, a "creative" one—only after they clearly understand the rational alternatives and the logical implications of the "innovative" choice. Intuition and analysis must be tested against each other constantly in a recursive process, with each cycle bringing greater confidence.

DECISION MODIFIERS

What is creative management? More, to be sure, than external analysis and internal intuition. Psychological motivation and political positioning are also involved. "Stakeholder analysis" is a qualitative technique that segregates the relevant parties and projects the personal attitudes of each. What are everyone's driving motivations, his or her "stakes" in the matter? Crucial here is an assessment of individual feelings and hidden agendas. What's the private bottom line? Potential political standing and perceived career paths are often lurking just beneath the surface and must be considered in all creative management decisions.

Are most executive decisions made rationally? If "yes," that's not necessarily good; if "no," that's not necessarily bad. Decisions are made by people, and people are constrained by company traditions and manipulated by political bargaining. The inertia of functional departments to do things the way they have always done them, according to "standard operating procedures," is a potent regulating mechanism, just as the influence of powerful personalities is a reality of the corporate hierarchy.

The pervasive strength and profound pressure of long-set bureaucracies—formal staffs, assistant to's, budget directors—are more a focus of serious study than the butt of sarcastic humor. "Networking" a company—discovering channels through which influence flows—often shocks top management. How real power patterns are structured can differ markedly from official organization charts. (Watch the executive secretary!)

DECISION SETTINGS

Devising creative strategies must take into account the nature of the organization. How to "cut a company" is essential for understanding the strategic process and making the innovation ring right. Numerous dimensions are involved. Strategic decision making is a function of the social structure and corporate culture. Is the sector profit-making or not-for-profit? The organization large or small? The product original or repetitive? The level of managerial decision top or middle? The personalities assertive or passive? The procedure individual or collective?

For example, in a high-technology company, how should the chief operating officer direct the key research scientist? In a charitable foundation, what dollar value should be placed on subsidized concerts for poor children? In a manufacturing firm, what level of losses can be sustained before a division is dispatched? In the media, should a magazine publisher stop his editor from printing a story critical of a top advertiser?

Each of these creative decisions, while similar in superficial form, differs in fundamental substance. The scientist is an inventive sort, perhaps not taken to close supervision. The artistic enrichment of the kids defies quantification. The manufacturing division may become a vital resource in future years. The magazine may not exist without editorial freedom.

Compromise, said to be golden, is sometimes a weak manager's failure to choose between contradictory positions or people. As such, the "in-between" solution can be worse than either of the extremes—and be no solution at all. To allocate to each of two competing projects half the money requested dooms both to certain disaster. Collaboration, on the other hand, brings the opposing parties onto the same side, encouraging interaction and establishing conditions for innovation. The dialectic of dissent, carefully controlled, is a marvelous antidote for the poison of group-think.

Models can be used as classification frameworks, as long as one doesn't take them too seriously. For example, consider "information required" and "dimensions of thinking" (see Figure 8.1). If the

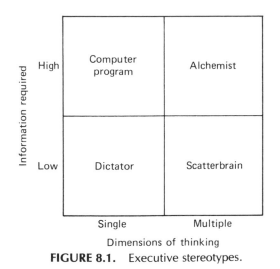

FIGURE 8.1.   Executive stereotypes.

decision maker uses low information and thinks in only one dimension, he's decisive and independent, a "dictator." If he uses high information and thinks in one dimension, he's analytical and rigorous, a "computer program." If he uses low information and thinks in many dimensions, he's flexible and fleeting, a "scatterbrain." If he uses high information and thinks in many dimensions, he's transformational and synthetic, an "alchemist." (The integrated attitudes of the last fellow would seem to make the most effective executive under normal circumstances—although a company nearing bankruptcy might need a dictator, a mutual fund might want a computer program, and an advertising agency might like a scatterbrain.)

CREATIVE VERSUS STRATEGIC

Creative management decisions begin novel in character, vague in structure, open ended in process, and ambiguous in content. Complex decisions in unfamiliar areas must be factored into simpler subdivisions in familiar areas. Only then can strategic routines and procedures be applied: problem recognition, problem diagnosis, solution search, alternative generation, alternative analysis, preliminary screening, serious evaluation, final choice, authorization, feedback, and review.

The critical test of strategic management, remember, is *internal consistency*. Does the overall plan make common sense? Does it resonate well with all issues and areas? Is, for example, the decision to launch a new product consistent with all functional departments: Is production ready to make it; marketing ready to sell it; financing ready to pay for it? (How often does an ever-eager sales force promise delivery months before the plant can produce the stuff!)

One often associates "creativity" with the arts and "innovation" with technological inventions. While appropriate in these contexts, "creative and innovative management" attains its potential as a *strategy*-making mechanism even more than a decision-making one. Thus a difference emerges between "strategy making" and "decision making," the former subsuming larger scope and complexity. More than the traditional tradeoffs between "optimizing" and "satisficing" reside here. Corporate power and prosperity are the chips being bet. Creative and innovative management, desirable for decision making, becomes essential for strategy making. If the game we play is management, the stakes we gamble are the highest.

MINIMILL PUNCH

American pundits have written off American steel. "The U.S. should get out of the business altogether," they spout. "We have lost comparative advantage and can no longer compete in world markets."

Before spouting they should come down to Charlotte, North Carolina, and take a look at a company called Nucor. The offices won't impress them, but the profits will.

Nucor is a revolution. In an industry where the giants are hemorrhaging red ink, closing plants, and diversifying, this mid-sized firm is a whopping winner. It changed the game by rewriting the rules.

Any American steel manufacturer making *any* money is news. In the three years 1978–1980, Nucor returned over 9 percent on sales and 33 percent on equity, earning $42 million on 1979 sales of $429 million and $45 million on 1980 sales of $482 million. For a decade earnings grew at over 40 percent a year; profits increased 1500 percent between 1971 and 1980. (Even in the worst year of the recession, 1982, when industry shipments plunged to their lowest level since the Depression, Nucor made 4.6 percent on sales of $486 million, rising to 5.1 percent in 1983 on sales of $542 million—that's profit, remember, not loss. First quarter 1984: revenues, $152 million, up 27 percent; earnings, $5.3 million, up 52 percent.) These numbers would be the envy of even high-tech companies; for a mid-sized steel company they're spectacular. What's more, Nucor is taking market share *away* from Japan and Taiwan.

Nucor is the low-cost producer, combining outfront technology with innovative incentive systems. The results, almost paradoxically, are some of the world's most competitive steel products and most productive steel mills—and some of the South's best paid workers. Now that's a creative hat trick.

Nucor manufactures steel products in two divisions:

1. Nucor Steel Divisions produce bar, structural, and special steel products used mainly in construction. They operate scrap-based steel mills in four locations. All have been constructed in the past fourteen years. These mills utilize modern steel-making techniques and produce steel at a cost competitive with any plant anywhere in the world.

2. The Vulcraft Divisions are the nation's largest producer of steel joists and joist girders, used for structural support in industrial, commercial, and institutional buildings. The divisions also produce steel deck for floor and roof systems.

Nucor's formula combines unusual labor practices, state-of-the-art technology, and aggressive marketing. The company carves out product niches and beats the integrated giants on both domestic and foreign fronts. "It's the closest thing to a perfect company in the steel industry," commented a Merrill Lynch analyst.

Productivity is the goal, and "minimills" are the key. These are smaller, more limited, more efficient plants that produce certain types of steel products more quickly, with fewer people, and at less cost. Their technology is leading edge and they are multiplying, expanding, and stealing market share. Minimills now ship over 20 percent of domestic steel, up from 10 percent in 1970.

Minimills start with scrap steel and produce simple steel products, in contrast to the integrated mills (like U.S. Steel and Bethlehem Steel) that convert raw ore into larger and more complex products.

"The minimills are a thing of the future," said an industrial economist with the World Bank. "The big integrated steel makers always had it in their mind to build everything in their plants — mills, furnaces, coke ovens. They built the Cadillacs of the industry. But the minimills said, 'We don't need all this.' They build the Honda Civics of the industry. And they're winning."

Projections go even further: Minimills are estimated to take between 33 and 45 percent of the market by the turn of the century. "The steel industry," says a Shearson analyst, "is being born outside the steel industry."

There are three building blocks for Nucor's competitive advantage:

Latest Technology.   Due to smaller size and output—less than 1 million tons per year—a minimill can use electric arc furnaces to melt scrap into molten steel, avoiding the need for coal, iron ore, coke ovens, and massive blast furnaces. The molten steel is poured into continuous casting billet systems. Highly sophisticated rolling mills convert the billets into angles, rounds, flats, and other products.

Cheaper Labor Costs.   With plants located away from traditional steel centers, the minimills tend to be nonunion and hence more flexible. Nucor's low base wage and large bonuses tied to productivity are part of the revolution.

Efficient Operating Methods.   Plants are designed for cost-effectiveness; there are no frills here. The result is lower capital costs and higher productivity. Constructing a 1-million-ton wire rod plant might cost a minimill $286 per ton of annual capacity, while an integrated steel maker would have to allocate about $625. The total cost of all four Nucor plants, including expansions, improvements, and modernizations, averaged less than $135. Productivity tells the same story. Operations in the minimills are highly automated and require fewer employees than conventional mills. The 1-million/ton minimill needs only 1.9 man-hours to turn out a ton, while the mammoths require 3.5. Minimills produced steel for $263 per ton shipped in 1981; that's almost 30 percent cheaper than the integrated mills at $366 per ton. The average Nucor employee produces about 700–800 tons of steel a year, double the 350 tons per employee at the large integrated mills. Wages average about $48 a ton at Nucor, less than one-third of the $185 a ton at the majors.

Nucor's 300,000-ton plant in Plymouth, Utah, is a low-cost producer. It started generating profits soon after start-up. It took the Japanese head on. They had had 50 percent of the market for "merchant bars" used in heavy construction and equipment. A year and a half later, the Japanese share had been eroded to 10 percent. "Nucor really went in there and took them," said Kim Clark, a Harvard Business School professor. "The minimill may actually be more productive than the imports."

Nucor's aggressive marketing is a fundamental part of its strategy. The common pricing structure in the steel industry is complicated.

Nucor opts for a simpler system. All customers ordering the same quantity are charged the same price—no exceptions. Nucor Steel has positioned products very competitively. For several years its prices have been equal to or lower than the imports. A considerable proportion of Nucor's growth has come at the expense of foreign producers.

Nucor developed its steel business almost by accident. It was an offshoot of a near bankruptcy—the old Nuclear Corporation of America. Producing steel was only a way of providing raw materials for its main business, which was then making steel joists. Being the novice, Nucor was not misled by the "wisdom of the wealthy." Today, whenever the minimills go after a product, the integrateds back away. It's no compete.

Personnel policies are a central strategy, a major factor in Nucor's success. Company controller Jay Bowcutt is blunt: "We really don't want laid-off steel workers. They have a philosophy of unions and big steel ways. Our people aren't tainted with those backgrounds." It is said that the word "union" is a pejorative term in these small towns, and big-city steel mills hold no allure.

"The rural areas provide one of the really great untapped labor resources," said F. Kenneth Iverson, Nucor's high-profile president. "Farm workers are high productivity workers and are basically mechanical."

Management–employee relations are founded on four principles: (1) earnings according to productivity; (2) job security for proper performance; (3) fair and consistent treatment; and (4) easy and direct avenues of appeal.

Nucor believes that "money is the best motivator." The wage system is incentive oriented, highly so, with those incentives tied directly to productivity. The base salaries are low, about $6 an hour. But productivity bonuses can add between 50 and 100 percent to total compensation—with no upper limit. When plants are running at full capacity, workers can make over $30,000 a year in a region where half that might be the norm. (And the company doesn't artificially raise standards, as do some companies, when workers consistently beat them.)

All Nucor mills have high productivity, which results in labor costs less than 20 percent of sales—well lower than competitors.

Nucor stresses that job security is "enhanced by added productivity," not threatened by it, and as a result, employment turnover is low.

All employees have a significant part of their compensation based on productivity. All incentive systems are designed around groups, not individuals. This applies to everyone from production workers to clerks and secretaries to senior officers.

In the production incentive program—probably the most important—the groups range from fifteen to thirty people, and there is stiff competition among them. The program, the company explains, must be easy to understand and the rewards must be rapidly received. Group operations are definable and measurable, and bonuses are paid promptly. In this way employees can relate increased effort and productivity directly to increased reward and compensation. This additional compensation has no maximum, recall, and it is not unusual for production bonuses to double base pay. Characteristic of the company, foremen receive the same bonus as employees they supervise.

Nucor's attitude is that each bonus group is in business for itself. Nucor provides the building, the equipment, the know-how, and the supervision. But what each group earns is dependent entirely on how much they produce.

In one operation, the joist production line, bonuses are based on roughly 90 percent of the historical time it takes to make a particular joist. If during a week a group makes joists at 60 percent less time than the standard time, they receive a 60 percent bonus. The bonuses are included with their very next regular pay check. (In melting, casting, rolling, and straightening, bonuses are based on good tons produced per hour.)

Yet production rules are strict—if a machine breaks down, everybody suffers; workers revert to base pay until it is fixed (which, you can imagine, is fast). If a worker is more than a half hour late, he loses his bonus pay for the day; more than an hour late, for the week. Nucor, we expect, has no problem with tardiness.

Productivity is not limited to workers. Nucor demands a lean executive staff—there are only four layers of management, just three steps from president to lowest level. A scant fifteen people, including clerks and secretaries, work in Nucor's unassuming offices. "Jack Benny would like this company," smiled one security analyst. "So would Peter Drucker." (Nucor executives like to quote Drucker's line that "it is a symptom of a sick organization to rely on coordinators, assistants and other such whose job it is not to have a job.")

Spartan offices reflect the absence of corporate perquisites. Though Nucor is one of the most successful American companies, there are no company planes, no company cars, no country club memberships, not even reserved parking spaces. Everyone, including the chief executive, flies coach. All employees receive the same insurance, holidays, and vacations. Yet there is an array of benefits for workers. Nucor contributes $1200 a year toward college or vocational education for every child of every employee. The annual bill rings up more than $200,000. ("It's hard enough to get good productive people," said Iverson. "When we get them we want to keep them.")

Managerial bonuses are based on return on assets; since Nucor is a capital-intensive business, this is the best test of managerial productivity. In an operating division these bonuses can run as high as 50 percent of base salary. In the corporate office it can run up to 30 percent of base.

Executive compensation is interesting. First, senior officers do not have employment contracts. They receive no guaranteed profit sharing, pension plans, or other normal executive perks. More than half of each officer's compensation is based directly on company earnings. Base salaries are set at 70 percent of what individuals in comparable positions with other companies would receive. If Nucor produces below par, that's all they get. Bonuses above base are coupled to an 11 percent return-on-equity trigger. If that minimum standard is not met—as it wasn't in 1982—remuneration is cut dramatically. (Iverson's total 1982 compensation was $106,716—one of the lowest for a Fortune 500 chief executive.) If minimums are achieved, half the bonuses are paid in cash and half deferred.

Management maintains an open relationship with workers. They tell employees everything about the company—failure and success, the bad with the good. "We emphasize the fact that management does make mistakes," said the personnel manager. "Probably 40 percent of the decisions made by a good manager could have been better."

"I wouldn't think of working in one of those integrated steel plants when I could work at Nucor," said a minimill manager. "Their plants are old, outdated. They're on the skids. Unless they throw me out of here, I'm staying."

Nucor was selected by NBC to be included in a documentary on productivity entitled, "If Japan Can, Why Can't We?" American workers are willing to work, concluded Nucor's personnel manager, but "too many times management gets in their way."

Though they beat out the integrated and foreign competitors, Nucor's easy ride is over. Other minimills have entered the industry. The rapid growth of the past decade is simply not repeatable. Nucor has saturated its current product areas and is technologically unable to produce the flat rolled steel used in automobiles and the heavy structural steel used in construction—where the tonnage is massive and the margins are higher. Minimills produce only small, bar-type products—rods, angles, and squares—used in modest-sized constructions from engine components to basketball hoops.

"We're now head-to-head against much tougher competition," said President Iverson. "It was no contest when we were up against the integrated mills. Now we are facing minimills who all have the same scrap price, the same electrical costs and the same tech-nologies."

The primary limitation of electric arc furnaces is their size—they cannot attain the economies of scale needed to produce flat rolled sheet, the steel needed for 50 percent of domestic production. An executive of a major commented, "We've concentrated on the more sophisticated products where they [minimills] can't compete, and we've dropped the inefficient product lines to them."

But some say sophisticated minimill technology may be only five years away, and then the whole market will lie open for them. "It's just a matter of time," said Samuel Siegel, a Nucor vice-president, "and then the big mills will be in hot water."

Ken Iverson is a legend at Nucor. The manager of personnel recalls an early encounter: "When I first started to work for Nucor, Ken told me: 'John, you are going to make at least three mistakes in your first few years. Each of these mistakes is probably going to cost us $50,000. I want you to be aggressive and make decisions. Just one word of caution. We don't mind you making the mistakes, but please just don't make them all in one year.'"

Iverson opposes government intervention in world trade, including steel. "I am," he says, "an uncompromising advocate of the free-enterprise system." Mr. Iverson was selected as the best chief executive in the steel industry for 1980 and 1982 by the *Wall Street Transcript*.

But for Iverson to make good on his promise of 15–20 percent growth per year, Nucor must be constantly expanding its product lines. Whether he can do it is not the point. Nucor has proven that not only can mid-sized firms compete with giants, they can revolutionize an industry and catalyze economic revival. Companies need not be huge to be winners, nor must America concede basic businesses to foreign megaliths. We just need fresh faces and strong voices.

Thus creative management is more than science and technology, research and development. It is an attitude toward doing business, toward treating employees, toward moving the company. It is the frame of mind that builds successful firms of all sizes. And it doesn't need the crutch of government largesse.

INDUSTRIAL POLICY VERSUS CREATIVE MANAGEMENT

"Industrial Policy," the new call among political partisans, tickles our ears in an election year. It is, we are told, the national economic panacea for international competitive sickness. "IP," to those on the in, would direct and control from Washington the thrust and focus of American industry. IPers believe that the free-market system is no longer efficient and that the government must intervene to prop up business and support jobs. Coined by intellectuals and caught by politicians, IP is a symptom of economic illness and political fever.

One cannot deny the appeal to industries suffering decline and workers without work. Nor can one negate the fact that in a tightly wired world foreign governments can shift the commercial balance of power by giving home-grown companies unfair advantage. So IP sparks the hope that federal funds might aid outmoded and out-priced companies regain former glory.

But numerous industries will vie for the golden tap. Which to promote and which to protect? Which to ignore and which to forget? When the government picks "winners," it must, by that same decision, also pick "losers." To sustain one, we must shun another. An increase of jobs here must result in a decrease of jobs there. If automobiles are chosen, why should textiles be condemned? Who is to decide that employment in the Midwest should go up while employment in the Southeast should go down? Why should large steel mills in the North be subsidized if small steel mills in the South can be so profitable? One conjures up tortuous visions of procedural miasma, politicking, and lobbying of unprecedented magnitude. Resources, we have come to learn, are not unlimited; available subsidy is only finite. (What, by the way, happens to IP when favorite industries do not make the Federal Hit Parade?)

Socialism, it is said, is a wonderful concept; the dream of economic equality and financial fairness is utopian. The only problem, of course, is that it just doesn't work. Theoretical idealism breaks up quickly against the rocks of pragmatic realism. Human beings function best when they are controlled least, when they prosper in proportion to personal initiative and self-driven intensity.

American business is still burdened by archaic regulations codified two generations ago. There were right and rigorous reasons then. We were fast becoming, in those heady days, the world's premier industrial power; our growth was unimpeded, domestic markets were burgeoning and foreign markets beckoning. Industries and industrialists became intoxicated with their new-found powers, and consumers and workers, at the mercy of these quick-born mammoths, needed protection. Yet times shift and paths twist. What worked then won't work now.

Is passivity the answer? Is public policy perfect? Should national debate go quiescent? The status quo be bronzed? By no means. What American industry needs is simple: Not more control by government but more confidence in management. Not centralized planning by bureaucrats but aggressive leadership from businessmen. Not Industrial Policy but Creative Management. More micro and less macro.

American industry must be freed from constraints, not encumbered with more. American business must be invigorated, not suffocated. The mold for forging the future? Independent management, not centralized command.[3]

The ends of Industrial Policy are desirable, it's the means that are questionable. It is not sufficient to deny IP for American business. To critique is always easier than to construct. It is one thing to describe the illness, quite another to prescribe the remedy. Industrial Policy will not work. What will? Alternatives proffered usually stress macroeconomic manipulations, like looser money, tighter budgets, and the like. Yet something is missing. We've heard all this before.

One might believe by reading erudite arguments and counter-arguments that industrial revival in America is linked to some "new economic policy," whether monetarist and supply side on the one hand or increased taxes and government spending on the other. A cardinal mistake here—and it permeates contemporary thought—is the notion that economic solutions to industrial problems will yield business success and competitive advantage. Macroeconomics surely has its place, but not the whole place. Macroeconomics is vital in defining and modulating the pace and proportions of the economy, but it is deficient in securing and prospering individual firms. It's like trying to coach a basketball team by determining the theoretically proper mix of heights, weights, and talents of players without ever teaching any of them how to dribble, pass, and shoot.

Economists dominate economic thinking. Logical, at least at first. But economists, when one thinks about them, don't run companies. They don't manage budgets and don't direct staffs. They never formulate corporate strategies and never build corporate structures. P and L, personnel, and product positioning are terms they do not use. Meeting payrolls is something they do not do. Making enterprises work is responsibility they do not have.

Yet enterprises—for-profit businesses and not-for-profit institutions—are the components of the economy. Like cells in a body, they *are* the economy; and to treat the economy only by macroeconomics is to treat an epidemic only by epidemiology. Building businesses in the former, like curing people in the latter, must be addressed. To leave the economy solely in the hands of economists is to leave the sick solely in the hands of statisticians.

We must listen to the Gross National Product. We must hear the rhythms of small businessmen, middle managers, and corporate executives. We must feel the beat of individual needs, wants, and desires. The world works because some have vision and brilliance, with the tenacity and temerity to produce and provide.

Creative and innovative management is what America needs, and government policy should be directed toward building it. But this is not a topic of macroeconomics; one does not study it in doctoral programs; there is little research, no Nobel Prizes, and minor media. It is local not global, micro not macro.

Yet the stakes are big, not small: Creative and innovative management is the economic pulse of American health. It is the life blood for sustaining the strength of the economy, for improving the quality of management, for securing the robustness of business. It is the fulcrum for the final fifth of the twentieth century. If America is to build a strong national economy, benefiting all citizens and leading the world, the mechanism must include creative and innovative management.

Though words flow easy, precise definitions come hard. *Creativity* is the process by which novelty is generated, and *innovation* is the process by which novelty is transformed into practicality. Creativity forms something from nothing, and innovation shapes that something into products and services. To nurture and develop creative and innovative management is to engender America with the power to prosper.

Both collective policy and individual business are involved. If creative and innovative management can build industrial abundance in America, it will do so on two pillars: the macroeconomic environment and the micro business structure—macro and micro. But such flourishing will not happen by accident. It is a way of thinking new and hard. No one risks for little reward. Only within a proper environment will American management make the right moves and take the right risks. This environment has two elements: (1) An economic climate responsive to creativity and innovation and (2) a corporate culture conducive to such novel management.

CREATIVITY AND THE ECONOMIC ENVIRONMENT

1. *Encourage Risk by Strengthening Reward*

Proprietary ownership is a powerful human motivator; it is capitalism's great advantage over communism, and we must pound it without pause. We should strengthen our patent laws, to include new forms of invention in the information and knowledge-based sciences. Government contracts should be structured to encourage recipients to reach and to risk—whether defense contractors, university science departments, or government laboratories. Institutions and individuals must benefit from their toil. Federal R&D funds, perhaps our nation's chief asset in building comprehensive national security, should embed economic as well as military forces, deriving optimum value from each. Government contracts, for example, might be awarded to firms that generate original ideas or products, or firms adept at commercializing defense-related technology, whether the firms be large or small.[4]

2. Facilitate Information Transfer

Creativity and innovation are resources that increase with use: The more you use it, to quote George Kozmetsky, the more you have it. To enhance applications, we must publicize and promote. Although creativity and innovation are private processes, they can be fostered by information sharing and situation setting. Centers for innovation and invention should be established, funded by state and federal governments, and administered by colleges and universities. National data banks can enable active researchers and potential entrepreneurs to access ideas and information.

3. Focus Government Fiscal and Tax Policy

Many words are spoken in Washington; millions every year are written into record and law. None is heard more clearly, none is read more carefully, than those dealing with taxes. By tax law the federal government directs public policy. A clear message for developing creative and innovative management will be given only when tax policy is the medium. We should reward creative and innovative companies through lower taxes, rather than penalize their profits with higher taxes. Tax credits for incremental R&D is a first, albeit halting step in the right direction. We might consider, say, tax credits for new patents, for new products, for R&D expenditures above industry norms. Capital gains, as another example, might be dropped further, perhaps to zero, but only if, in my opinion, the holding period is increased. (*Reducing* the holding period to six months, while personally productive, is socially counterproductive; it flies off in the wrong direction by encouraging financial manipulation, not productive development.)

4. *Understand the Creative Process*

Public policy should support research and education in creative and innovative management. Studying the process should become a national goal—not a curiosity, a necessity. America's finest researchers should be sponsored and interdisciplinary work encouraged—from organizational psychology and the decision sciences to artificial intelligence and the neurosciences. The arts, too, offer much and should not be neglected. We must stimulate creative and innovative management in our schools. Principles of creativity and innovation can be taught at every age, in parallel with enhanced math and science, from early education through high school and college. Schools of business should take the lead, instilling motivation to shift and change rather than drilling techniques to trend and continue. One danger of making business more rational, more analytical and computer based, is the subtle pressure to stifle the new and inhibit the fresh. Businessmen must be prepared to make nonrational (not *ir*rational) decisions, gambling on instinct and perception.

5. *Promote Interaction among Sectors*

Creative and innovative management is not sector specific. It occupies a unique place at the union of industry, government, and academe. Each sector must make its contribution, and critical mass can be generated nationally only when all focus their force on the interface. Intersector interaction is not just a current fad, it is the white-hot focus—and government policy should catalyze the reaction. The Department of Defense policy of rewarding companies with university ties additional independent R&D funds is an excellent prototype. State governments, too, must participate; they may, for example, offer matching incentives for state-based R&D, increasing operational leverage and financial appeal.

CREATIVITY AND THE CORPORATE CULTURE

1. *Encourage Risk by Strengthening Reward*

Most companies give mixed signals about risk. They praise new ventures with lofty words and reward failure with career wipeout. One such derailment incinerates the whole house of corporate cards. We must shift this risk–return tradeoff by decreasing the risk and increasing the reward. Incentives for originality and invention must be internalized and believed by the company underground. The organizational structure must support it; the informal networks must promote it; the grapevines must confirm it. Participating in new ventures—not just making them successful—must be the pinnacle of corporate achievement. MacDermid's "Have the Guts to Fail" should become the national battle cry. Creativity and innovation have expression, one should note, in all areas of corporate life—not just high technology and new products. Managers who look beyond the traditional, who see the unusual, who dare to be different—upon these does posterity rely.

2. *Facilitate Creative Types*

Egalitarianism, the belief that all people are equal, is a fundamental American value. While wholly appropriate in politics and society, it is artificial and awkward in economics and business. People differ in every respect, with the capacity for creativity at the top of the list. A company must respect its creative types. They are a breed apart, absorbed in their quest, dedicated to intensity, oblivious to others. Creatives are often difficult to control. They work strange hours in strange places. They don't want supervision and demand personal satisfaction for personal achievement. Proprietary participation—especially financial reward—is an essential motivation. How to find them? A word of caution. Creative and innovative people may not be the smartest or brightest; they may not be aggressive or assertive or even realize their own gifts. The best firms will treasure them.

3. *Focus Corporate Fiscal Policy*

Companies that talk innovation and invest elsewhere dig credibility gaps. Promoting creativity is no mean task. A firm must evidence its commitment, putting cash on the line. Nothing energizes more than the movement of money. You can't talk creativity and fund tradition. The resource allocation process must encourage creativity and innovation; new procedures must skew dollars to more risky ventures. Most critical, results cannot be expected quickly. Corporate executives must see beyond the horizon, beyond the quarterly reports, beyond the Street called Wall.

4. *Understand the Creative Process*

Creativity or innovation happens by itself, but not all the time. Since innovators are often not the brightest or most aggressive, the firm must find them, or, more accurately, help them find themselves. One cannot train people to be inventive, but one can develop educational programs to facilitate the process. Creativity appears with infinite variety. In a high-tech firm, for example, a person with a new method for inventory control may not think herself creative—yet the benefit to the company may exceed most scientific study. One good idea covers a lot of ground.

5. *Promote Interaction among Departments*

Scientific advance depends on constant communication among diverse disciplines. Likewise for the best businesses. When problems are attacked by divergent approaches and disparate facts, a wider range of solutions emerges. Task forces composed of different departments are not unusual in corporate life, but these are often established for coordinating current programs rather than creating new ones. Interdepartmental cooperation in companies, like interdisciplinary work in academics, is fraught with suspicion and worry about territoriality and dominance (the sociobiology of ant hills and wolf packs does not encourage creativity). A firm's new-products division doesn't want the service department inhibiting innovation; service says it's ridiculous to develop products that can't be fixed. Mechanisms must be found to break these barriers. The catalyst is often the person to whom the departments report; the boss must become actively and aggressively involved. If he or she recommends the interaction, yet does not participate personally, it will surely fail.

The opportunity is here; the time is now. What we have is nothing less than the restructuring and recrudescence of American industry. Economists and executives must work together in building both a macro/economic foundation and a micro/corporate structure. In the new realities approaching the year 2000, to achieve domestic vitality and world leadership, the American trick is creative and innovative management.[5]

Personality and Creativity:
How Creative Types Think and Act

Personalities, like fingerprints, are unique. Though composed of similar elements, the endless combinations make each pattern singular. Every human being is an aggregate sum of numerous traits, a complex amalgam of inner attitudes and outer actions. When executives build companies, when creative and innovative managers pioneer new strategies and structures, personality is a controlling factor.

The characteristics arrayed in Figure 8.2 describe how humans behave and may accent the creative process. The grouping is a fair sample, though hardly complete. As a conceptual aid, each trait is organized as a linear spectrum, with each word of the pair defining an extreme. Most people, of course, fall in the middle of all the traits, some a little more to the right on one, some a little more to the left on another. It's the combination, remember, the exquisite intertwining of elements, that makes us unique.

Inward $\longleftarrow$ — $\longrightarrow$ Outward

Independent $\longleftarrow$ — $\longrightarrow$ Dependent

Active $\longleftarrow$ — $\longrightarrow$ Passive

Intense $\longleftarrow$ — $\longrightarrow$ Lethargic

Dominant $\longleftarrow$ — $\longrightarrow$ Recessive

Competitive $\longleftarrow$ — $\longrightarrow$ Cooperative

Acquisitive $\longleftarrow$ — $\longrightarrow$ Quiescent

Objective $\longleftarrow$ — $\longrightarrow$ Subjective

Consistent $\longleftarrow$ — $\longrightarrow$ Capricious

Conceited $\longleftarrow$ — $\longrightarrow$ Modest

FIGURE 8.2. Personality and creativity: How creative types think and act.

We introduce each of the following trait spectrums with a question. What is the essence of the personality element, and how might it affect the creative process? That's what we want to stress. There is, of course, no right or wrong answer, just reflections on the way people feel. Creative types are rich with variety, and personality assessment should enhance, not limit this expression.

Inward–Outward. How would you rather spend an evening, reading at home or partying with friends? Those choosing the former are Inward (or introverted, in Jung's terminology); those choosing the latter are Outward (or extroverted). Whether one is Inward or Outward might affect the creative process in different situations; for example, working in an "open-office" environment with no private enclosures favors Outward employees. Inward people generally like more time for private contemplation, though Outward people might have a better sense of practical application.

Independent–Dependent. In taking responsibility for introducing a major new company product—with promotion promised for success and dismissal likely for failure—would you rather report to your superior frequently (e.g., daily) or infrequently (e.g., monthly)? Independent people are generally more creative; they care less about custom and more about content. Though independent people seem to have more status in society, companies would fracture with too many of them. Furthermore, a person dependent in one mode, say as corporate middle manager, might be quite independent in another mode, say as an officer in the Naval Reserve.

Active–Passive. Which job would you prefer (assuming equal salary and status), sales manager opening up new accounts or personnel manager maintaining proper paper flow? Actives are more creative, affecting their environment, not just finding a comfortable place in it. A company must have a balance between the two types: too many actives will cause chaos; too many passives will yield stagnation.

Intense–Lethargic. Would you ever work on Thanksgiving to get a critical shipment out to an important customer? If so, you're probably intense. Do you often have to be told what to do several times before you finally do it? If so, you're probably lethargic. Intensity correlates highly with creativity; the creative process demands high energy and persistent effort. Intensity is an important trait for entrepreneurs who must build from nothing, but it can be disrupting for middle managers who must maintain steady work output.

Dominant–Recessive. When serving on interdepartmental committees are you ever selected as chairman? Dominants in business, like dominants in genetics, express their traits and get their way—but too many dominants clash and cause conflicts. The revolving-door exodus of a succession of "heirs apparent" in corporations run by strong, though aging founders is a classic case of clashing dominants. Dominants are often creative, but the correlation may not be cause and effect. Recessive personalities, relatively unencumbered with people control, can allocate more effort and attention to novel ideas.

Competitive–Cooperative. Assume you work on the sales staff of a company selling office equipment to corporate clients. Which method of compensation do you prefer: (1) Each salesperson is free to approach any potential customer and is paid a commission, say 6 percent, based on his or her personal sales only? Or (2), each salesperson is assigned to cover an equal number of potential customers and is paid the same 6 percent commission based on the sales of the entire sales staff? The balance between competition and cooperation is a difficult one to keep, as when three senior vice-presidents—over administration, marketing, and finance— are all candidates for president. Creative types are often competitive, though their arena of competition may be more achievement and recognition than remuneration and promotion.

Acquisitive–Quiescent. Do you need to build and accumulate in order to feel accomplished? Are you constantly seeking new things to buy and use? The founders of companies are more often concerned with augmenting their firms' power than with aggrandizing their personal finances. "Acquisitives," of course, are high-risk personalities, often operating close to the edge of disaster. Creative managers are found on both sides of this spectrum, each with a different cast. Acquisitives are dynamos; quiescents pull the surprises.

Objective–Subjective. In selecting a new assistant vice-president, on what would you put more weight, her scores on intelligence tests and psychological profiles or your personnel director's first impressions after a fifteen-minute interview? In an age of accelerating quantification, when computers produce prodigious amounts of data, instincts and insights are under increasing attack. Others, however, speak of the importance of articulating rational analysis with nonrational perception. Creatives come down clearly on the subjective side; an objective personality is often inhibited from seeing novelty.

Consistent–Capricious. How predictable are you? Does your boss have confidence that you will do the job as she expects? In trying to win back old customers, for example, would you give everyone the same line? Do you enjoy jumping from job to job, company to company? It is rare when consistency is not a virtue, and reliable employees are considered golden. On the other hand, firms operating in rapidly changing industrial environments need a few capricious sorts, creative types who can explode with new ideas. (They must, of course, operate under control—which poses some problems when the capricious one is the entrepreneurial boss.) While creativity and capriciousness are not synonymous, regularity and repetition stifle originality.

Conceited–Modest.   Can we expect to hear all your fabled exploits every time we see you? Assuming your subordinates would never know the truth, would you rather overplay or underplay your personal relationship with the president? Society considers, if we believe convention, modesty a virtue and conceit a vice. Yet to be successful in business, we are told, one must flip those pairings around. The truth, of course, is both and neither. Few creative types hold their long suit in modesty; creatives feel their ideas are supremely important, demanding immediate recognition and instant action.

CHAPTER 9

MATCHING FLOURISHERS

How They Differ,
Why They Excel

"*Texas Business* is more than a magazine; it's an image, an idea, a vision. It represents everything that means business in Texas—it's aggressive, expansive, determined, outspoken, independent, confident, strong, proud." So states E. John ("Jack") Martin, president and publisher of *Texas Business* magazine, one of the most successful area business periodicals in the country.[1]

More than 100 publications cater to state and city business markets in the United States. It's a relatively new industry, reflecting a growing trend toward regionalization of the economy, the recognition that local factors can be as important as national ones in determining commercial conditions and company success. Yet, lacking the huge circulation numbers traditionally required for national advertising, it is difficult for these small magazines to make a good go.

Why does *Texas Business* stand out among its peers—with solid circulation, healthy renewal rates, expanding advertising, and rising profitability? What is it about this publication that commands the attention of subscribers and advertisers, and enables it to compete for readership time and advertising dollar with the major national magazines (such as *Forbes*, *Fortune*, and *Business Week*) with a fraction of their circulation and editorial budgets?

Creative Strategies at *Texas Business* stress the following:

Dominance. It is the only statewide monthly magazine in Texas focused exclusively on business.

Product Emphasis. An intense effort was made to enhance the editorial product before attacking circulation and advertising.

Focus. A clear, direct thrust toward business in Texas; stories stress Texas companies and business opportunities; national issues are dealt with only as far as they affect Texas; international reporting emphasizes Texas trade.

External Perception. The scope of the magazine is enlarged through major public events, symposia, and annual awards, which build the image and impact of the magazine.

High-Profile CEO. Clearly the key, the unifying force. Jack Martin has energized the magazine, transforming a weak flounderer into a roaring charger.

Texas Business derives great benefit from the fact that Texas as a business market is both growing and coherent. The pro-business attitude is perhaps the best in the country. There is minimum restrictive regulation. People support businesses and businessmen. There is strong enthusiasm for things Texan. State corporations are a source of civic pride. There is a definitive "Texas Spirit" pervading the commercial atmosphere. Businessmen are heros, not villains in the Lone Star State. The "Can Do" attitude pervades. (If people do business in New York to make money, and if people do business in California to have fun, then people do business in Texas because it's a good thing to do business.)

Dallas-based *Texas Business* was founded and financed by the Baker Management Company, headed by Don Baker, a tough, resourceful entrepreneur who in typical Texas style started from scratch and with his brothers parlayed a small housing publication into a strong sun belt network. His *Living* magazines now dominate the new housing markets in Dallas, Houston, San Antonio, Austin, Denver, Phoenix and Orlando. *Texas Business* was a true venture, and since few new magazines survive, a highly risky one.

The concept was excellent though untested, and the positioning perfect though undeveloped, but neither was sufficient to achieve success. Until Jack Martin took the reins, the magazine was struggling—with weak public image, low employee morale, inconsistent editorial content, sickly advertising. Red ink was spurting constantly. Jack made the whole difference. He was a human dynamo, involving himself all-pervasively in every area of the company.

A business can have everything going for it, but without management it is nothing. *Texas Business* just didn't have the spark, the presence, the distinction to entice readers. And without reader interest and allegiance, all the circulation schemes and all the advertising pitches are only blank shots into empty air. Editorial had to come first, "the book" had to be number one. And that's precisely what Jack hit in his first year.

Working with editor-in-chief Brux Austin, a publishing professional with broad national experience, Jack gave direction and generated intensity. He built the team, giving them confidence and esteem. The bottom line was anemic, and Jack knew he was expected to improve it fast. But he had the foresight and the guts not to mortgage the future for a quick trick in the present.

"The hub of our wheel is editorial," asserts Martin, making careful use of his British accent. "All else are spokes."

Editorial budgets and staffs were beefed up. Writers were given sharper focus for articles. Assignments stressed more bite and less fluff. Editing was tightened and word lengths limited. Type styles were changed. A cleaner, more modern look was developed. Consistency of product was demanded. Regular features were added to give readers easy access—leading columnists, a "Challenge" editorial, "Pipeline" (late-breaking news), "Texas Scout on the Potomac" (intelligence from Washington), "Briefcase" (short news items), and a popular "Top Drawer" style section (the best in vacations, restaurants, clothing, cars, etc.). Whereas others might concentrate on how many ad pages were sold for a given month, Jack pounded the edit side.

"Our desire to make money," comments Jack, "must be at least one millimeter behind our desire to impart useful information." Reversing the order, he asserts, will kill off both.

"We are far more than just a magazine," says Martin with force of conviction. "We have multiple associations with the business community in Texas. For example, we play a major role in integrating the graduate business schools with the major corporations. We think 'public' constantly."

Conferences were established, increasing business and media awareness of the magazine. The Texas Lyceum, co-sponsored by *Texas Business*, brings together dynamic young leaders to discuss issues for the state's future. (Upwards of 700 leading executives attend this annual event along with five Texas governors and national figures.) The Rising Stars is an annual award for upcoming leaders under 40. The magazine puts on emerging companies symposia, introducing entrepreneurial firms to sources of venture capital. In each case *Texas Business* is catalyst and sponsor. Each attracts significant interest. "We are positioning ourselves at the leading edge of business in this state," says Martin. "Our events involve the top people."

Perhaps the most significant is the Texas Business Hall of Fame, which has attracted national publicity. This is a gala occasion honoring several of the great Texas corporate founders and executives each year. "The idea for the Hall of Fame was around for three years," recalls Brux Austin. "There was a flurry of memos and conversations. Most people called it 'impractical.' It took Jack to say 'Let's do it. I don't care how.' He then mobilized the business community into a coalition. The Hall of Fame is now a state institution. When Jack Martin says we are going to do something, we do it!"

Jack Martin is an Englishman from Liverpool, coming to Texas by way of New York, and a more committed leader of Texas business you will not find. A captivating public speaker, he is a favorite among civic and business groups. While some might consider such activities as diversions from his managerial role of running the magazine, Jack positions it dead center.

Martin sees more than social responsibility here. His eye scans the strategic battlefield—not what is there today, but what might be there tomorrow. He states coolly: "Every time we produce another event; every time we get additional press and publicity—we raise the entry barriers for anyone challenging us in this market. We've made it prohibitively expensive for potential competitors. I've been like a bloody politician—running across this state—but I love it."

"Our magazine is the flagship of the business community, and we must be where the action is," Martin asserts. He takes an active role in the Dallas Chamber of Commerce, where he is chairman of their international committee. Recently he took a group, including the mayor and twenty top business executives, on a VIP trade mission to Europe, meeting leading business and government officials.

Martin lays heavy emphasis on overseas activities. He founded a section in the magazine called "International Trails," expanding the vision of smaller companies for foreign trade. Jack approaches international business with evangelistic zeal. He asserts that the changing world demands commercial activities beyond our borders. "I am not prepared to sit idly by while the global economy affects the vitality of Texas companies."

Jack is personally instrumental in encouraging Texas-based companies to expand their horizons, to become involved internationally. "I spend many hours a month at the Chamber, and it's exhausting. But not only is it my civic duty, it also produces direct benefits for the magazine. Visibility is the key. I interact with all the powers in Texas."

As publisher of *Texas Business*, Martin is often in the state capital (Austin) working with government, and he is a familiar figure around the governor's office. Says editor-in-chief Austin: "Our magazine has taken a posture of leadership in the state. When we see something wrong, we challenge it. We have identity. Both in politics and in business our influence is very strong. Our position is second to none."

Martin had been recruited by a major headhunter for *Texas Business*. He credits his wife, Pat, for cementing what everyone admits was a "big risk." ("She showed that not all English are stuffy," he recalls.) Don Baker confirms that Jack was his biggest business risk—Don checked eleven out of twelve references—but then to his credit agreed to let Jack run the whole show. It wasn't an easy decision. Baker's *Living* magazines were making lots of money, and *Texas Business* was losing most of it. The magazine was five years old, and people were wondering whether it would survive. In the magazine business, such rumors are deadly.

When analyzing his remarkably successful tenure with the publication, Martin goes right for his mistakes. "I didn't trust my own gut instincts when first assessing the staff. It took more than a year to put the right people in the right places.

"Early on, some six months after I took over, I took a strategic audit of the company. I worked with a corporate strategist with business and media experience. The effort was enlightening, the impact profound. It stressed the vital importance of 'visibility' and my becoming a 'high profile chief executive.' I remember my wife telling me every night that none of the people she was meeting had heard of *Texas Business*. We determined to go right after that.

"A critical point came when I was invited to Washington to address the Texas Breakfast Club, the oldest political club in the capital. My subject was how the West is destroying itself. I had calls from influential people requesting copies of the speech, including one from the White House. Since that time I've had invitations to speak all over Texas. We wouldn't be where we are today without this visibility.

"The most fascinating thing about our success is the real benefits of strategic thinking. We produced results more rapidly than would be expected from even the national publishers. We had to do all the right things, sure, but we also had to do something more. Some marvelous strategic insights and real commitment to our strategic plan are the keys to our success."

"Our perception of ourselves has increased dramatically since Jack took charge," says Brux Austin. "Jack can go into any CEO's office as an equal—at least an equal. Everyone knows we have the power in this state, and we use it for collective benefit."

People work hard at *Texas Business*. Finding the right people for the corporate culture is critical. "We almost have to chase our people home at night," laughs Martin. "This is the hot place to work."

Martin is a superb manager of people; this is his forte. He radiates enthusiasm and confidence, and talented people just love working for him. The magazine, under Jack's leadership, has developed a strong professional staff, unusual for a regional publication. *Texas Business* has become an extension of employee ego: Personnel feel the exhilaration and joy of producing an excellent product; they like having meaningful impact on the economy of the state. "We use the tool of encouragement," states Martin. "We create a positive environment that gives our people maximum creative opportunity."

"Only after the improved editorial product generated strong renewals and new readership could I turn my attention to advertising," states Martin. "I was able to attract one of the top advertising executives in the region. She has a national reputation and came to us not because we offered more money but because she saw that we had life and spirit, that people were talking about us, that we were going places. If I had tried to attract top people when I first arrived, I'd have been laughed out of town. I can't stress enough the importance of the editorial product and my own visibility in the state—both of which were directly derivative from our strategic plan.

"The whole profile of this publication has changed drastically over the last 18 months. Ad revenues are up over 200 percent. Every sales person has been replaced. I upgraded national rep firms in New York, Chicago, and California—and now over 30 percent of our ad revenues comes from national advertising, which is excellent for a regional publication. To get national advertising you get scrutinized pretty closely. But remember where it all comes from: Putting that initial emphasis on product—the editorial content. Our quality is superb. In fact we are told by many entering the regional business field that ours is the formula they wish to emulate."

Growth of the magazine is taken with deliberate speed; no inflated balloons are aired around here. Circulation is taken up slowly. It's now about 50,000—with an anticipated 65,000–80,000 being the ultimate ideal. (Estimated 1984 revenues: $3.8 million—the smallest of our mid-sized companies in Part One. Profits for this private company are already better than 10 percent pretax and growing.) Though these numbers seem low by national standards, the geographic focus and exceptional demographics—incomes, net worths, executive responsibility—create high advertising value. "Our readership is like a Golden Who's Who of Texas," smiles Martin, "with much influence and voltage in the state. Henry Cisneros, the popular mayor of San Antonio, says *Texas Business* magazine helps him do his job more effectively."

The magazine made its first real profit in 1983, with vital numbers trending upward. Before Martin signed on, there was real question of the publication's survival. At best, it seemed, would be a forced sale at a significant loss. In less than three years, *Texas Business* is a hot property worth several million dollars above all investments. (It is hard to quantify the public and psychic value of such a potent communications vehicle in addition to the pure economic value.) "And this," promises Jack, "is only the beginning."

Martin also initiated new products which capitalize on the distinctive competencies of the magazine. One is an office space guide (Dallas and Houston) of coffee table quality. Another is a joint venture with airlines for business travelers. Another product in conjunction with the governor's office is designed to enhance business investment in the state.

"We did the 10th year commemorative publication for the Dallas–Fort Worth Airport," says Martin. "People are now approaching us. We have the reputation for publishing products of class and style. Texas is a marvelous state. It welcomes new people. If you work hard, you can really get on here."

As for the future, Martin looks two ways: the first is vertically with new products in current geographic areas (Texas); the second is horizontally with current products in new geographic areas.

"There are some interesting small publications in the regional business market out there," says Martin. "Another possibility is a joint venture for cable television in Texas. One thing is for sure: I must create opportunities for everyone on our staff to grow. This is vital—especially for me."

ASSESSING LARGE NUMBERS OF COMPANIES

We now switch gears. We go from single firms studied individually to multiple firms studied collectively. We have seen what works for particular companies, but what about applications for all companies? How can we build confidence in conclusions?

We go for large numbers. About 100 different variables will be analyzed across a data base of 334 mid-sized firms. Which are meaningful, helpful, applicable—and which are not? Our task is to discern those corporate characteristics that best correlate with top-performing companies.

Quantitative methods have had little impact on business policy.[2] Yet numerical analysis is critical if strategic theory is to be made more robust. When major concepts are founded on few cases, one hesitates to accept generalizations, however logical. On the other hand, one must take care to ground numerical analysis on the bedrock of real-world activities. Both qualitative and quantitative methods are necessary for strategy and policy research. Qualitative analysis provides relevance; quantitative analysis produces confidence.

In order to employ standardized and accessible data, we choose annual reports and form 10-Ks (required each year for public companies) and subject them to "content analysis," a precise method for discerning imprecise information (discussed in Chapter 6).[3] Though these company-prepared documents inject bias, distortion, and inaccuracy, awareness of the problem is the beginning of safeguard.

Documentary sources have been used infrequently in strategy and policy research; thus theory has been traditionally based on small samples. Much of the classic work in the field, however insightful and revelatory, must be partially discounted due to the often limited number of supporting cases. Sophisticated techniques are sapped of their power when only a handful of companies are considered.[4]

The tradeoff is real. Large samples eliminate in-depth field work; to visit and interact with several hundred companies is not practical. On the other hand, the use of documentary sources removes the investigator from the primary source of data; it is hard to be an armchair corporate analyst.[5]

Though some may disparage the use of annual reports in strategy research, dismissing them as mere promotion and propaganda, the argument can be turned "outside-in," transforming the externally directed propaganda into internally directed probes. There is no better method of obtaining standardized data of a nonfinancial character. The common motivation underlying the preparation of annual reports yields comparative consistency. Companies design their annual reports for the same reasons: to enhance public perception, to impress stockholders, customers, creditors, and vendors. All public companies are trying to prove these same points; they all have these same objectives.

E. H. Bowman states that "annual reports can be used not only for the quantitative figures disclosed but also as a 'projective test' and as an 'unobtrusive measure.' In the same way that a Rorschach test or even an interview by a psychiatrist permits information to be inferred about an individual, so does the careful reading of the annual report allow this for a corporation, especially on a comparative analysis basis."[6]

Bowman reports two "validity tests" authenticating the accuracy of annual reports in reflecting reality, because "there may be some doubt in the reader's mind as to whether annual report discussion usefully approximates real activity." Bowman concludes that although many would relegate annual reports to the junk mail file, especially the discussions and descriptions, "sufficient careful work can turn what is apparently base metal into gold." Hence the title of his article, "Strategy, Annual Reports, and Alchemy."[6]

MATCHING THE PAIRS

Companies were chosen and matched with much effort. Several thousand public corporations were scanned, more than one thousand studied in some depth. Detailed investigations of products produced and markets served were compared with five-year financial performance.[7]

There were three preliminary criteria for the matching process: similar kinds of product/markets; similar size of sales/revenues; divergent financial performance as measured by returns on assets.[8] (Matching revenues help match market share, thus evening out this large contributor to profitability and allowing other factors to emerge.)

Some of the matings seemed ideal (see Table 9.1). Almost identical products were being produced by "pure-play" companies of almost

TABLE 9.1. Matched-Pair Analysis: Some Representative Matchings

Firm	Business/Products	Sales	Assets	Percent ROA[a]	Percent ROE[b]
Bundy	Tubing	169	115	13	13
Clow	Pipes/valves	166	109	9	7
Worthington	Steel	278	123	26	30
Unarco	Steel	275	163	12	12
Nucor	Steel	307	194	23	23
Lukens	Steel	298	199	12	10
Kennametal	Industrial tools	263	222	27	20
Warner & Swasey	Industrial tools	252	231	7	6
Cross & Trecker	Industrial machinery	298	237	20	19
Pettibone	Industrial machinery	296	256	11	11
Keystone	Flow controls	83	69	28	24
LFE	Flow controls	83	57	9	9
Waters Assoc.	Scientific instruments	57	46	27	22
Milton Roy	Instruments/controls	58	45	6	6
Fluke	Electronic equipment	104	81	23	21
Watkins Johnson	Electronic equipment	106	96	8	7
Echlin	Automotive equipment	304	226	20	17
Maremont	Automotive equipment	338	227	11	12
Bacardi	Rum	241	113	26	28
Glenmore	Alcoholic beverages	205	92	5	10

(Table continues on p. 250)

TABLE 9.1. (*continued*).

Firm	Business/Products	Sales	Assets	Percent ROA[a]	Percent ROE[b]
Salem	Carpets	170	72	22	30
Masland	Carpets	175	82	10	8
Guilford	Textiles	196	95	30	23
Texfi	Textiles	169	122	5	0
Fab	Textiles	84	49	25	22
Thomaston	Textiles	103	59	2	1
Palm Beach	Apparel (men's)	233	116	27	31
Salant	Apparel (men's)	231	119	12	10
Jack Winter	Apparel (women's)	55	52	24	13
Aileen	Apparel (women's)	58	54	0	-1
Great Lakes	Chemicals	88	78	29	24
Virginia	Chemicals	110	75	11	13
Terra	Agriculture chemicals	199	135	5	7
Beker	Agriculture chemicals	201	245	1	-36
Plenum	Book publishing/science	20	19	26	31
Allyn & Bacon	Book publishing/general	29	28	6	8
Noxell	Cosmetics	180	87	28	19
Alberto Culver	Cosmetics	190	98	8	8
Henredon	Furniture/home	94	63	26	17
American Seating	Furniture/commercial	88	56	5	4

Int. Flavor & Fragrance	Chemical/additives	366	345	26	22
Sun	Chemical/organic/inks	394	293	13	21
Marion Laboratories	Pharmaceuticals	120	98	17	13
ICN	Pharmaceuticals	85	81	1	−13
Bandag	Tires/retreads	251	182	24	16
Mohawk	Tires	222	115	11	3
Trus Joist	Roofs/floors	78	32	31	30
Riblet	Housing products	77	29	13	12
Knape & Vogt	Home products/building	55	31	23	15
Imperial	Building supplies	68	24	6	3
Goulds Pumps	Pumps	188	115	30	27
Robbins & Meyers	Pumps	127	84	16	15
J.L. Clark	Metal packaging	93	59	35	24
Plant Industries	Metal & plastic packaging	67	45	9	1
Molex	Electrical connections	98	72	34	27
Augat	Electrical connections	79	68	28	21
Dynatech	Electronics/medical	28	16	19	19
Gelman Scientific	Filters/medical	34	27	13	12
Premier	Distribution/electronics-maintenance	258	129	30	22
Kaman	Bearings/music/aerospace	263	117	14	13
Tyco	Diversified/fire-fighting-electronics	216	194	16	29
Michigan General	Diversified/building-highway	201	130	6	7

(Table continues on p. 252)

TABLE 9.1. (*continued*).

				ROA[a]	ROE[b]
Carlisle	Diversified/auto-industrial	243	119	21	18
Union	Diversified/industrial-electronics	183	129	10	7
Maytag	Household appliances	325	181	39	25
Magic Chef	Household appliances	410	357	13	12
Binney & Smith	Crayons	75	64	22	15
Hasbro	Pens/toys	104	62	6	1
General Houseware	Cookware/furniture	61	27	23	26
Mirror	Cookware/boats	132	79	9	6
A.T. Cross	Mechanical pens and pencils	73	51	42	30
Scripto	Pens/lighters	40	24	-6	-25

[a] ROA = Earnings before interest and taxes divided by total assets, 1977–1978.
[b] ROE = Net profits after taxes divided by stockholders equity, 1977–1978.

identical size (and therefore having almost the same market share); yet the two companies had sufficiently different (and consistently different) returns on assets, thereby giving the strategic investigation real meaning.

Strict adherence to the ideal, however, would have limited the sample size. Some intuitive matchings were allowed, including companies with interesting mixes of products. In some cases we chose to match firms that had similar sizes within the same general markets/industries, even though their particular products were not alike. In this manner we hoped to see some product-related characteristics emerge from the data. Would the better-performing mid-sized firm be more likely to sell a branded product, a technologically advanced product, and/or one that was focused on a special segment of the geography? These and a host of similar questions, as well as the desire to develop a large matched-pair data base, encouraged cautious departure from a policy of exact product identity.

DESCRIBING THE DATA BASE

When constructing the data base, we paid no attention to how the pairings would look as a whole. It was concern enough to match the numerous firms as closely as possible.

When the 167 matched pairs had been finalized, we then asked the critical question: Had any overt biases crept into the data base?

Tables 9.2 and 9.3, and Figures 9.1, 9.2, and 9.3, describe the distributions. Average revenues were $173 million, with 63 percent falling between $50 and $250 million. Average assets across the same sample were $119 million, with 59 percent falling between $50 and $250 million.

Table 9.3 and Figure 9.3 give some sense of size relationships. They show the "revenue ratios" of smaller-sized firm to larger-sized firm for all 167 pairs. The average ratio was 0.80, which means that the revenues of the matched pairs averaged within 20 percent of each other. (Eighty percent of the sample had a ratio better than 0.67; 46 percent greater than 0.85; 33 percent greater than 0.91; and 13 percent greater than 0.96.)

TABLE 9.2. Distribution of Mid-Sized Firms by Revenues and Assets (sample size = 334)

	Total Revenues (millions of dollars)					
Revenues:	$5–$25	$25–$50	$50–$100	$100–$250	$250–$450	$450+
Firms:	13	32	93	118	60	18

Mean revenues = $172.8; standard deviation = $145.5

	Total Assets (millions of dollars)					
Assets:	$5–$25	$25–$50	$50–$100	$100–$250	$250–$450	$450+
Firms:	40	62	92	105	30	5

Mean assets = $118.8; standard deviation = $115.3

Finally, the number of matched pairs in which the larger company was the better performer was about identical with the number in which the smaller company was the better performer (Table 9.3).

CHOOSING THE VARIABLES

Some thirty-one quantitative and sixty-eight qualitative variables were selected for the study. Which would attain significance, and

TABLE 9.3. Distribution of Matched Pairs by Relative Size: Total Revenues Ratio

Total number of matched pairs: 167

Total revenues ratio: $\dfrac{\text{Sales (smaller firm)}}{\text{Sales (larger firm)}}$

Average smaller/larger ratio = .80 (standard deviation = .15)
Percent matched pairs > .96 = 13 percent
Percent matched pairs > .91 = 33 percent
Percent matched pairs > .85 = 46 percent
Percent matched pairs > .67 = 80 percent

Number of matched pairs in which the larger firm was more profitable = 83.

Number of matched pairs in which the smaller firm was more profitable = 84.

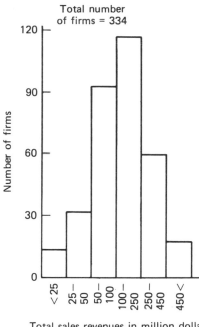

Total sales revenues in million dollars
(1977 and 1978)

FIGURE 9.1. Distribution of mid-sized firms by sales revenues.

what might they mean? It was hard to predict the former, nor was the latter always obvious.

For the quantitative variables, we included all the standard financial ratios of profits on equity and sales, asset turn, debt, current position, inventory turn, and so on. Then came some less common ratios with which we sought to approach strategic issues. For example, the ratio of net plant and equipment to gross plant and equipment was included as a test of "newness" of assets (maybe). The ratio of capital expenditures to sales was viewed as indicative of company commitment to the future. (Any ratio is subject to different interpretations, different meanings in combinations, and different significances in different industries.[9])

Choosing the qualitative variables was easier in that one could simply ask the straightforward question. (The real meaning, of course, would be still uncertain.) Areas of primary interest included CEO profile and attitude; the firm's orientation toward constituencies (executives, employees, stockholders, customers, society); the importance of company direction (growth, profits, financial condition); the importance of operational activities (products, new products, innovation, technology); the type of business structure (vertical integration, focus/relatedness of business, clarity and coherence of goals and strategies); the importance of company concern for the external environment (industrial economics, market sensitivity); a test for company distinctiveness (uniqueness, brand names, advertising, niche dominance); a sense of company attitude and commitment; and a host of other concepts. Several variables were used as corporate probes assessing the "company personality" (prominence of CEO picture, creativity of annual report, responsiveness in complying with request for information).

In tabulating the data, we opted for a simple positive (+), negative (−), or neutral (0) scoring. This was efficient, easy to analyze, and appropriate for the subjective nature of the inquiry. Every effort was made to generate unbiased results.[10]

REPORTING THE DATA

We present in Tables 9.4 and 9.5 the primary variables found to be most effective in distinguishing between the better and poorer

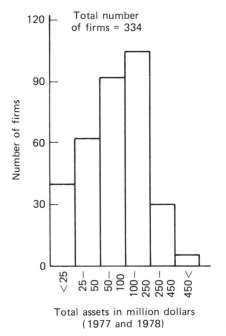

Total assets in million dollars
(1977 and 1978)

FIGURE 9.2. Distribution of mid-sized firms by total assets.

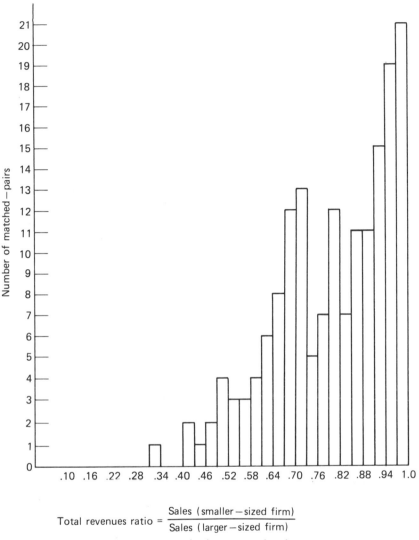

$$\text{Total revenues ratio} = \frac{\text{Sales (smaller–sized firm)}}{\text{Sales (larger–sized firm)}}$$

FIGURE 9.3. Matched-pair size distribution.

performing mid-sized firms. They are listed in order of differentiating power. The plus sign (+) means that the better performing of the mid-sized pair had the *higher* value/score for that variable; the minus sign (−) means that the better performing of the mid-sized pair had the *lower* value/score; and zero (0) means either that the firms were judged equal or that the question did not apply.[11]

TABLE 9.4. Characteristics of Better-Performing Mid-Sized Firms (Results of the Quantitative Variables[a])

	+/−/0/
The better-performing mid-sized firm has	
Higher ratio of after-tax profits to book equity	164/2/1
Higher ratio of after-tax profits to total sales	154/10/3
Higher 5-year mean after-tax return on sales	149/17/1
Higher ratio of sales in 1978 + 1977 divided by 1976 + 1975	132/31/4
Lower coefficient of variation for the 5-year return on sales	40/122/5
Lower ratio of total debt to total assets	41/121/5
Higher ratio of profits in 1978 + 1977 divided by 1976 + 1975	121/46/0
Higher ratio of net to gross plant and equipment	104/61/2
Higher ratio of largest business segment sales to total sales	84/46/37
Higher ratio of sales revenues to total inventory	102/64/1
Higher ratio of current assets to current liabilities	101/64/2
Higher ratio of total assets to employees	63/41/63
Higher ratio of total sales to employees	64/42/61
Lower ratio of gross plant and equipment to revenues	69/96/2

[a] Chosen by a higher average return on assets (earnings before interest and taxes divided by total assets, averaged for 1978 and 1977). Presented in order of statistical significance.

We advise caution in quick interpretation of the results. Several ambiguities are included. Differences among component industries may be radical (see below). Furthermore, we should expect a general biasing as a result of the experimental design. Better-performing firms, of any size, simply do more things—like plan for the long term, commit more funds, and produce fatter, more effusive, more colorful annual reports. Conversely, poorer-performing firms do fewer things—like plan only for the near term, commit less funds, and produce thinner, less effusive, less colorful annual reports. The more successful CEO should well be expected to be happier, more ebullient, more desirous of showing off his picture to an appreciative world. Thus, high significances, of themselves, are not so significant, and we are led, once again, back to the fundamental issue of causal direction.

We must ponder the classical impossibility of divining causation from correlation. Did the highly significant variable "cause" the

TABLE 9.5. Characteristics of Better-Performing Mid-Sized Firms (Results of the Qualitative Variables[a])

	/ / – /0/
The better-performing mid-sized firm has	
Dominance (or claims it) within its own corporate niche	98/7/62
Greater focus/relatedness for the entire company	105/17/45
Greater coherence in goals/objectives/strategies	103/17/47
Greater degree of corporate uniqueness/distinctiveness	86/13/68
Greater orientation toward sales volume/growth	77/10/80
Greater corporate commitment/dedication	95/20/52
Greater orientation toward the company's products	88/20/59
CEO letter evincing greater enthusiasm/excitement	91/22/54
Greater orientation toward customers	83/21/63
Greater clarity in stated goals/objectives/strategies	97/30/40
Greater market segmentation by product uniqueness	65/13/89
More aggressive/bullish risk-seeking approach	74/21/72
CEO letter evincing greater commitment/dedication	79/24/64
Higher CEO profile in annual report	79/24/64
Greater appreciation for own strengths and/or weaknesses	78/24/65
Greater stress on product quality	68/19/80
Better sense of industry/market environment	54/12/101
Greater orientation toward selling and marketing	80/27/60
Greater sense of importance for new products	80/27/60
Greater orientation toward innovation	72/23/72
Sent additional materials (e.g., a personal letter)	46/10/111
Brief specific business summary in annual report	59/17/91
Longer-term time horizon for corporate planning	69/23/75
CEO picture giving impression of better leadership	76/31/60
Greater stress on promotion/advertising in business	45/12/110
Annual report in which the CEO's picture is more prominent	77/34/56
Annual report more expensive (or better quality)	80/36/51
Annual report more creative	68/28/71
More family control of the business	54/19/94
Annual report more oriented toward stockholders	48/17/102
Greater market segmentation by geographic specificity	20/8/139
Annual report evincing greater enthusiasm/excitement	63/28/76
Active executives holding more stock	43/15/109
Greater market segmentation by customer/industry specificity	49/19/99

(Table continues on p. 260)

TABLE 9.5.   (continued).

	$+/-/0/$
Annual report that projects greater promotional intensity	75/38/54
More brand names	55/24/88
More shifts in corporate strategy	13/38/116
Annual report with more prominent executives	59/27/81
Greater orientation toward profits	56/25/86
Greater concern with production/manufacturing	60/28/79
Greater concern with issues of industrial economics	45/18/104
More backward integration	27/7/133
Sent more past annual reports in response to request	54/26/87
Annual report with more prominent directors	49/23/95
Greater emphasis on state-of-the-art technology	43/28/96
Greater sense of competitiveness in market	39/17/111
Fewer divestments/dislocations	20/43/104
Substituted form 10-K for annual report	0/9/158
Presented nonrequired financial data in annual report	41/20/106
Sent form 10-K in response to request	54/26/87
Annual report had a more detailed business description	49/31/87

[a] Chosen by a higher average return on assets (earnings before interest and taxes divided by total assets, averaged for 1978 and 1977). Presented in order of statistical significance.

better-performing firm to become better performing? Or did the better-performing firm generate the highly significant variable (or just discuss the variable in the annual report because it sounded good)? Notwithstanding this philosophical dilemma, the correlations that follow are real, distinguishing clearly between more and less successful mid-sized firms.

INTERPRETING THE QUANTITATIVE DATA

Following is a brief description of the most significant quantitative variables emerging from the data base.

1.   There is nothing surprising about the first three variables in Table 9.4: the returns on equity, sales, and sales over five years were expected to correlate highly with returns on assets. (The results confirm the consistency of the experimental design.)

2. The growth ratio (1978 + 1977 sales to 1976 + 1975 sales) suggests that successful mid-sized firms may be more growth-oriented than previously appreciated. The conventional wisdom that smaller companies should stress more efficiency and profitability than expansion and volume is contradicted here.

3. The lower coefficient of variation (for the five-year average return on sales) means that the better-performing firms have more stable profits as well as higher profits.

4. The lower ratio of debt to assets is indicative of greater financial strength and available debt capacity.

5. The higher ratio of net plant and equipment to gross plant and equipment suggests that the better mid-sized firms have newer assets. (Be careful, however, about cause and effect. The correlation is sure; yet the direction of causality must always be questioned. A "backwards causation," where the more profitable firms are more able to buy new equipment, certainly seems a reasonable if not enlightening likelihood.)

6. In a significant number of more successful mid-sized firms the largest business segment accounts for a higher proportion of the company's total sales. This fact is the first evidence of a fundamental idea: that better-performing mid-sized firms, on average, are more coherent in business strategies and more focused in business units. (See below for additional confirmation.)

7. The significance of higher inventory turn (sales/inventory) is what one might predict for opportunistic/efficient firms. (There may be some industry differences here. See below.)

8. The lower ratio of gross plant and equipment to sales suggests that capital intensity, on average, diminishes profit performance.

INTERPRETING THE QUALITATIVE DATA

The first twenty or so variables in Table 9.5 are all highly significant in the pragmatic as well as the statistical sense.

1. The number one variable was also the biggest surprise: The better-performing firms of the matched pairs have (or claim to

have) *dominance* (i.e., largest market share). Of course, each company defines its own corporate niche as it sees fit. What emerges so strongly is that these firms do not conceptualize their product/ markets in terms of traditional, broad industry categories. Their definitions are tight and tough. It's not "specialty chemicals" to Great Lakes; it's "bromine-based chemicals." It's not "writing utensils" to A.T. Cross; it's the "high-quality, high-priced" segment of the market.[12]

2.   The next two variables—focus/relatedness of the entire company, and coherence in strategy/goals/objectives—attained the highest number of "hits" (pluses), 63 and 62 percent respectively. The two concepts—focus and coherence—articulate well together, supporting a central idea of this work, a strategy we would have stressed more had not product dominance overshadowed it.

3.   Corporate uniqueness stands out as a strong predictor of mid-sized success, and its relationship with dominance seems clear. A dominant firm, almost by necessity, will be more unique than its paired mate; and conversely, uniqueness seems a necessary (but not sufficient) prerequisite for dominance.

4.   The fact that better-performing mid-sized firms show a greater orientation toward sales volume/growth contradicts conventional wisdom that smaller companies must subordinate growth for profits.

5.   Several variables work together under the general rubric of "product focus": product orientation, customer orientation, product uniqueness, product quality, new-product orientation, and innovation orientation. (This concept emerged strongly in the qualitative analysis of Chapter 6.)

6.   The profile and attitude of the chief executive officer are important.

7.   The role of long-term commitment is expressed by variables such as aggressive/bullish approach and the longer time horizons for corporate planning.

8.   Several variables confirm the relevance of perceptiveness in assessing both external environment and internal characteristics: a better sense of industry/market, awareness of issues in industrial

economics, a sense of market competitiveness, and a better appreciation of company strengths and weaknesses.

9. Profit orientation, while on the list, appears surprisingly low; its comparison with sales growth is unsettling. On average, these better-performing mid-sized firms are more concerned with effectiveness than efficiency.

10. Corporate coherence is demonstrated to be a strong predicter of mid-sized success. Table 9.6 summarizes four tests of coherence, derived from three independent methodologies and four nonrelated sources of data. All yield consistent results.

a) The largest business segment data showed that the majority of the better-performing mid-sized firms had a greater ratio of largest division sales to total company sales. This was calculated directly from each firm's annual report (from the required section on business segments), and means that the better-performing companies were more focused on one product/market.

b) The focus/relatedness of company businesses and the coherence of goals/objectives/strategies both showed that better-performing mid-sized firms are more focused in businesses and more coherent in goals and strategies. These were the collective judgments

---

TABLE 9.6. Corporate Coherence for Successful Mid-Sized Firms: Summary of Empirical Data

---

Largest Business Segment (ratio of largest segment sales to total sales):
  + = 84; − = 46; 0 = 37
  Success rate = 50 percent; error rate = 28 percent

Focus/Relatedness of Company Businesses:
  + = 101; − = 18; 0 = 48
  Success rate = 60 percent; error rate = 11 percent

Coherence of Goals/Objectives/Strategies:
  + = 103; − = 17; 0 = 47
  Success rate = 62 percent; error rate = 10 percent

Fewer Numbers of 4-Digit SIC Codes:
  + = 89; − = 46; 0 = 32
  Success rate = 53 percent; error rate = 28 percent

TABLE 9.7.   Test of Corporate Coherence: Matched-Pair Comparisons of SIC Codes

	SIC Code							
	Two-Digit			Three-Digit			Four-Digit		
	+	−	0	+	−	0	+	−	0
	69	37	61	84	45	38	89	46	32
Success rate	41%			50%			53%		
Error rate	22%			27%			28%		
Significance (zeros excluded)	.003			.001			.0005		
Significance (zeros included)	.02			.003			.002		

of the MIT research assistants who performed content analysis on the 167 pairs of annual reports.

   c)   The lesser number of SIC codes (Standard Industrial Code) that characterize better-performing mid-sized companies means that they have fewer distinct business segments and therefore have greater corporate coherence (see Table 9.7).[13]

BUILDING HIGHER-ORDER CONCEPTS

How to find more useful meaning? We need more comprehensive categories. We form higher-order "index variables" by combining several primary variables as building blocks. These broader, more general concepts are the simple linear sums of the component variables, each primary variable having equal weight. The definitions of the index variables are listed in Table 9.8, and are the same categories/concepts developed from the qualitative search in Chapter 6.

   How do the individual primary variables logically enhance the aggregate index variables? A good example is distinctiveness. Check these components: market segmentation by product uniqueness,

TABLE 9.8. Classification of Firms by Aggregate Index Variables: Definitions and Components of the Higher-Order Variables

Commitment: A composite measure of organizational determination and individual dedication on behalf of CEO, directors, executives, employees (6, 16, 32, 34, 36, 71, 72, 74, 79, 80, 82).

Fulfillment: A composite measure of the degree of personal satisfaction and job-related enthusiasm on behalf of the CEO, corporate executives, and all employees (20, 35, 37, 73, 81, 84).

Distinctiveness: A composite measure of corporate uniqueness, aspects of the firm's interaction with the environment that set it apart from competitors (57, 58, 59, 75, 76, 93).

Flexibility: A composite measure of the corporation's capacity/ability to change its current direction in order to take advantage of new opportunities and/or avoid new threats (4, 7, 9, 14, 44, 60, 83, 85).

Coherence: A composite measure of the corporation's focus/relatedness of business(es) and coherence of strategies/goals/objectives (15, 51, 52, 53, 68, SIC Code counts).

Clarity: A composite measure of the corporation's conception of its own operational activities and strategic goals/objectives (61, 62, 63, 67).

Progressiveness: A composite measure of the corporation's internal growth and development, its orientation toward new products and innovation, and its current expenditure for future progress (8, 10, 24, 27, 28, 46, 47, 50, 78, 92, 99).

Perceptiveness: A composite measure of the corporation's appreciation of the external market/industry environment, and its sense of internal strengths and weaknesses in relationship to that environment (19, 40, 64, 65, 69, 70, 88, 96, 98).

Dominance: A composite measure of the corporation's market share within its own tightly defined corporate niche, and the growth/selling/marketing orientation required to enhance that position (41, 42, 66).

Relevance: A composite measure of the corporation's (or the corporation's products') perceived need in the minds of customers (25, 39, 45, 55, 77, 94).

Consistency: A composite measure of the corporation's stability, in profits, production, organization, and strategy (30, 31, 38, 56, 89, 90, 91, 95).

(*Table continues on p. 266*)

TABLE 9.8. (*continued*).

Efficiency: A composite measure of the corporation's proficiency in producing the most output from a given quantity of input (2, 3, 12, 17,
26, 29, 43, 48, 97).

Notes: The numbers at the end of each definition refer to the component primary
variables as listed in Appendix I. A complete listing of the aggregate index variables with
their primary variable constituents appears in Appendix II (with success and error rates
for each). Of the 99 primary variables, 86 are included in the aggregate index variables.
Those excluded had a preponderance of zeros and/or could not fit into any of the strategic
categories.

market segmentation by geographic specificity, market segmentation by customer/industry specificity, evidence of corporate
uniqueness, dependence on brand names, and creativity of the
annual report. Each element fleshes out the concept of distinctiveness, adding substance and scope, imbuing it with more power,
making it more robust. (The internal structure of each index variable,
enumerating all component primary variables, is given in Appendix
II.)

Do these index variables have real import? How effective are
they in describing firm performance? The key issue is how well
can they discriminate between better and poorer-performing companies, how well can they tell the difference between good and
bad. To test the effectiveness of these index variables we simply
determine the algebraic sum of the pluses, minuses, and zeros
from each of the component primary variables. If this algebraic
sum is positive, the better-performing firm of the matched pair is
considered classified correctly; if the sum is negative, the firm is
considered classified incorrectly.

The results are shown in Table 9.9. On average, the composite
index variables have a classification success rate of 72 percent and
an error rate of 16 percent. The highest success rates are efficiency
and commitment (85 and 81 percent) and the lowest success rates
are fulfillment and clarity (64 percent each).[14]

The efficacy of index variables for predicting mid-sized financial
success is clear. These strategic concepts are the same ones emerging
in Chapter 6's qualitative search of top performers. The difference

here? We have defined them more precisely and tested them more rigorously, the latter across a large matched-pair data base.

The results are impressive. Every index variable has a success rate that exceeds the success rates of every primary qualitative variable and all but the most obvious quantitative variables (see Appendix II).

We can generate two still higher-order index variables by combining the first ones. These are shown in Table 9.10. Combining commitment, distinctiveness, coherence, and dominance, a classification success rate of 86 percent is attained with a 12.5 percent error rate. (If apparel companies are removed, the success rate climbs to 90.5 percent and the error rate falls to 9.5 percent.) When twelve index variables are combined together, the success rate is slightly higher, 87.5 percent, and the error rate remains at 12.5 percent. (Without apparel, the success rate is 92 percent and the error rate is 8 percent.)

The combined success rates for these higher-order index variables are superior to any of the first-order index variables. This supports

TABLE 9.9. Classification of Firms by Aggregate Index Variables (sample size: 72 matched pairs)

Index Variables	Percent Success Rate	Percent Error Rate
Commitment	81	14
Fulfillment	64	25
Distinctiveness	75	15
Flexibility	67	15
Coherence	81	11
Clarity	64	18
Progressiveness	78	14
Perceptiveness	67	22
Dominance	72	14
Relevance	69	22
Consistency	67	21
Efficiency	85	7
Totals	72	16

TABLE 9.10.   Classification of Firms by Aggregate Index Variables: Higher-Order Combination of Index Variables (sample size: 72 matched pairs)

Higher-Order Index Variable I: (commitment, distinctiveness, coherence, dominance)		
	Percent Success Rate	Percent Error Rate
72 matched pairs (6 industries)	86.1	12.5
63 matched pairs (without apparel)	90.5	9.5

Higher-Order Index Variable II: (commitment, fulfillment, distinctiveness, flexibility, coherence, clarity, progressiveness, perceptiveness, dominance, relevance, consistency, efficiency)		
	Percent Success Rate	Percent Error Rate
72 matched pairs (6 industries)	87.5	12.5
63 matched pairs (without apparel)	92.1	7.9

their legitimacy as elements of strategic importance. We use them in constructing the model for mid-sized firms.[15]

INDUSTRY DIFFERENCES

Different industries have different characteristics, and what may be a critical success strategy for firms in one may be a critical failure strategy for firms in another (or, more likely, just plain irrelevant). Criticism of management research has often focused on the confusing effects of mixing diverse industries within the same data base. The contingency of industry-specific variables is vital.[16]

Heretofore we have considered the entire mid-sized data base as an indivisible whole, lumping all industries into the same pot; we have had no regard for specific industry differences. This is a gap in our investigation, a gap of unsure import. It is more than mere irritance to suggest that what is true for the aggregate, no matter how large, may not be true for some of its components.

Table 9.11 shows the asset turn ratio (sales revenues divided by total assets) *dis*aggregated by industry. When assessed across the entire 167 matched-pair sample, 85 of the better-performing firms had a higher sales–assets ratio as did 76 of the poorer-performing firms—a result not significant. Disaggregating the data by industry provides interesting insight (though numbers within any given industry are too small for confidence). In apparel, where high turnover of inventory and assets is considered essential, the results show eight pluses and one minus.

TABLE 9.11. Disaggregation by Industry Groupings: Sales Revenues/Total Assets

Industry	+	−
Food and drink	7	7
Textiles	3	3
Apparel	8	1
Wood/paper/furniture	5	8[a]
Chemicals	2	6[a]
Soaps/cosmetics/drugs	6	2
Rubber/auto/aerospace	6	3
Building supplies	6	6
Metals	5	7[a]
Machinery/fabrication	10	7
Computers/copiers	7	1
Electrical/electronics	5	8[a]
Instruments/controls	5	6[a]
Medical equipment	4	2
Diversified	4	5[a]
Miscellaneous	2	4[a]
Total	85	76

[a] Industries where the majority of the sales–assets ratios are the reverse of the direction of the aggregate.

Yet in only six of the sixteen industries did more of the better-performing firms have a higher sales–assets ratio—the direction of the overall trend; in three of the sixteen the ratio was even, and in *seven* of the sixteen *fewer* of the better-performing firms had a higher ratio—*opposite* to the overall trend. This means that although the average of the sales–assets ratio across the entire aggregate sample was leaning in one direction, this condition was true in less than half the included industries.

Thus we confirm our suspicions. Meaningful information has been masked in the aggregate. The admixture of different industries has confounded and distorted the results. Consequently, individual industry analysis is essential for all but the most lopsided variables. With the sales–assets ratio, for example, it appears that the lack of significance across the entire sample may be caused by two significant trends, among two subsets of industry groupings, each pulling in opposite directions. (The two subsets appear to be characterized by different levels of capital intensity. Such results have been the basis for contingency theory.[17])

The same phenomenon is seen for each of the three inventory ratios (sales/inventory, inventory/assets, finished goods/inventory) presented in Table 9.12. All the footnoted numbers represent industries where the disaggregated results were the reverse of the aggregate average. This is especially important in the sales–inventory ratio, since in the aggregate a higher ratio correlated well with better-performing firms (confidence level at 0.01), whereas when the component industries were broken out, four leaned strongly in the negative or opposite direction (i.e., more of these better-performing firms had a lower sales–inventory ratio).[18]

In applying any of this data, we stress the importance of industry-specific analysis—not overall averages. Thus, pragmatically, we might speculate on underlying reasons for several trends (though small numbers command caution). In the food and drink and apparel industries, where inventory turnover is vital, twenty of the twenty-four better-performing firms have a higher sales–inventory ratio than their matched-pair mates. With respect to the finished goods–inventory ratio, food and drink and metal firms are sharply negative, with one possible explanation being perishability for the former and high cost for the latter. Indeed a lower finished goods–inventory ratio could give the better-performing metal companies greater

TABLE 9.12. Disaggregation by Industry Groupings: Inventory Ratios

Industry	Sales Inventory		Inventory Assets		Finished Goods Inventory	
	+	−	+	−	+	−
Food and drink	12	2	3	10	2	6
Textiles	4	2	3	3	1	3
Apparel	8	2	5	5	5[a]	3
Wood/paper/furniture	9	4	3	10	1	6
Chemicals	3	5[a]	5[a]	3	4[a]	2
Soaps/cosmetics/drugs	4	3	5[a]	3	4[a]	2
Rubber/auto/aerospace	6	3	5[a]	4	3[a]	1
Building supplies	5	7[a]	6	6	4[a]	3
Metals	8	4	5	7	0	10
Machinery/fabrication	11	6	6	11	5[a]	4
Computers/copiers	4	4	5[a]	3	4[a]	2
Electrical/electronics	5	8[a]	7[a]	6	7[a]	2
Instruments/controls	3	8[a]	7[a]	4	5[a]	3
Medical equipment	4	2	2	4	1	3
Diversified	12	2	7	7	3	4
Miscellaneous	4	2	2	4	1	4
Total	102	64	76	90	50	58

[a] Industries that run counter to the overall trends.

flexibility in competitive situations with larger firms. In other industries, where high inventories facilitate customer service, the reverse may be a more important strategy. (Such explanations are examples of contingency thinking; whether any are actually correct is another matter.)

What about the most significant variables, the primary conclusions of this work? Dominance is disaggregated by industry in Table 9.13. In every industry grouping, more of the better-performing firms are (or claim to be) dominant within their own corporate niche (although in some industries, such as textiles and apparel, the relationship seems less important). Similar results apply to uniqueness, coherence, focus, growth, debt–asset ratio, and net–gross plant and equipment. Most industries follow overall trends, although some less so than others.

TABLE 9.13. Disaggregation by Industry Groupings: Corporate Dominance

Industry	+	−	0
Food and drink	8	0	6
Textiles	2	0	4
Apparel	2	0	8
Wood/paper/books/furniture	7	0	6
Chemicals	5	1	2
Cosmetics/soaps/drugs	5	0	3
Tires/rubber/auto/aerospace	5	0	4
Building supplies	9	1	2
Metals	7	1	4
Machinery/fabrication	9	2	6
Computers/copiers	4	0	4
Electrical/electronics	10	0	3
Instruments/controls	8	0	3
Medical equipment	3	1	2
Diversified	9	1	4
Miscellaneous	5	0	1
Total	98	7	62

New-product importance and innovation evidenced positive significance across the data base. Yet when disaggregated by industry, some differences or refinements appear. For each variable in Table 9.14, compare the top three industries with the bottom three. The strongest relationship exists for the science-based industries.

Tables 9.15 and 9.16 present the higher-order index variable broken out by industry. Five of the six industries cluster around the impressive 72 percent success rate for predicting better performance in matched mid-sized firms. (The same applies to the combination of index variables. Five of the six cluster around a 90 percent success rate.)

CORPORATE CASES

The following companies are top-performing mid-sized firms. They are example "better halves" of the 167 matched pairs comprising the data base. For each company, we stress those primary variables deemed to be critical for long-term financial success.

Neutrogena. Sales in 1983 were $45.5 million; profits, $3.2 million; return on average equity, 35 percent. (First half revenues for 1984 were up 34 percent, earnings up 49 percent.) Neutrogena (Los Angeles) manufactures and markets high-quality soaps and other specialty skin-care products. The company is a market leader in the sale of premium-priced soaps specifically formulated to be mild and suitable for normal, sensitive, and problem skin. The orange-translucent color of its soap is distinctive and the "Neutrogena" name has come to represent the company's unique image

TABLE 9.14. Disaggregation by Industry Groupings: New Product Importance and Innovation

Industry[a]	+	−	0
	New Product Importance		
Apparel	5	4	1
Wood/paper/furniture	2	5	6
Metals	5	3	4
Computers/copiers	6	0	2
Electrical/electronics	8	0	6
Instruments/controls	7	1	2
. . .	. . .	. . .	. . .
Totals	80	28	59
	Innovation Orientation		
Apparel	1	5	4
Metals	4	3	5
Building supplies	4	4	4
Computers/copiers	5	0	3
Electrical/electronics	9	1	3
Instruments/controls	6	1	4
. . .	. . .	. . .	. . .
Totals	69	24	74

[a] Note differences between the top three and the bottom three industries for each variable. Industries given are only examples. Total number includes entire data base.

TABLE 9.15. Classification of Firms by Aggregate Index Variables: Success and Error Rate (sample size: 72 matched pairs)

Industry Group	Percent Success Rate	Percent Error Rate
Instruments/controls	74	14
Cosmetics/soap/drugs	84	8
Apparel (men's and women's)	60	31
Diversified	71	16
Electrical/electronic	78	11
Machinery/metal fabrication	68	18
Totals	72	16

Note: All twelve aggregate index variables are combined and the total results are tabulated for each specific industry in the sample.

and style. All company products are coherent—shampoos, creams, oils, gels—and all relate to this same primary competency and competitive advantage. Company goals are well articulated and clear; the stress is on product; and the CEO plays a prominent role.

Goulds Pumps.   Sales in 1983 were $275 million; profits, $14 million; ten-year average return on stockholders' equity, 24 percent. Goulds Pumps (Seneca Falls, New York, near Rochester) designs, manufactures, and services centrifugal pumps for industrial, agricultural, commercial, and consumer markets. (Industrial markets account for about two-thirds revenues.) The company is an acknowledged leader in its industry and the world's largest manufacturer dealing exclusively with centrifugal pumps. Focus and coherence are clear. "Providing the best customer service at the lowest possible cost" is the heart of Goulds' philosophy; quality is their stated "corporate commitment." ("Dimensions in Quality" is the theme of the 1983 annual report.) The company is sensitive to the external environment and prepared for the economic slump early ("we are not a Company that permits our destiny to be controlled by external forces which we cannot control"). Expenditures in 1983 for plant and equipment exceeded depreciation by 25 percent. CEO Vincent Napolitano received *Industry Week's* Excellence in Management Award in 1982 for his "outstanding efforts in im-

plementing and maintaining sound labor–management relations."
A 1980 strike prompted "Vince" to search for the real cause of the
unrest; he sought to erase the "us versus them" mentality. He
established several new concepts: a series of "jobholders'" meetings
patterned after stockholders' meetings; a Labor–Management
Committee to deal with unusual issues; an "open-door policy"
under which employees have the right to escalate problems up
the corporate ladder until a mutually satisfactory solution is found;
a $1 million, 21-acre recreational area open to employees and fam-
ilies. "What we're trying to say," Vince stresses, "is that we care
about the employees and that we understand how important it is
for people to feel good about their company. But they can't feel
good about their company unless we feel good about them."

Russell Corporation. Sales in 1983 were $319 million; profits $27
million; ten-year sales growth, 13.9 percent; ten-year earnings
growth, 22.4 percent. Russell (Alexander City, Alabama) is one of
the most profitable and technologically advanced companies in
textile or apparel. It is a vertically integrated designer, manufacturer,

**TABLE 9.16. Classification of Firms by Aggregate Index Variables:
Higher-Order Combination of Index Variables**

Industry Group	Four Index Variables[a]		Twelve Index Variables[b]	
	Percent Success Rate	Percent Error Rate	Percent Success Rate	Percent Error Rate
Instruments/controls	91	9	100	0
Cosmetics/soap/drugs	100	0	88	12
Apparel (men's and women's)	56	33	56	44
Diversified	93	7	100	0
Electrical/electronic	92	8	92	8
Machinery/metal fabrication	82	18	82	18
Totals	86	12.5	87.5	12.5

[a] Four index variables: commitment, distinctiveness, coherence, dominance.
[b] Twelve index variables: commitment, fulfillment, distinctiveness, flexibility, coherence, clarity, progressiveness, perceptiveness, dominance, relevance, consistency, efficiency.

Note: Index variables are combined together—whether four or twelve—to form higher-order index variables, which are then analyzed in the same manner for each specific industry.

and marketer of leisure apparel, athletic uniforms, and a comprehensive line of lightweight woven fabrics. The company's manufacturing operations include the entire process of converting raw fibers into finished apparel and fabrics. Russell belives it is the largest manufacturer of athletic uniforms in the United States. Excellent profit margins (for this industry) are partially a result of increased sales volume, but also reflect the productivity of manufacturing facilities. "Our commitment to investment in modernization of our plants is paying off," states the president. Russell's ultramodern equipment combined with the start-to-finish control (which vertical integration allows) makes the company one of the industry's low-cost producers. "We start it—We finish it" is Russell's slogan. They do it all: spinning, dyeing, fabric formation, designing, cutting, sewing, finishing, inspection, packing, marketing, and distribution. (Capital expenditures have averaged 287 percent of depreciation and 84 percent of total cash flow for the five years 1978–1982.) Historically the company has sold its functional sportswear under private label to mass merchandisers, discount stores, and in recent years, to other apparel makers such as Levi Strauss and Nike. The company is now venturing into a line of branded sportswear that is being marketed to upscale department stores and specialty shops.

Binney & Smith.   Sales in 1983 were $125 million; profits, $11 million. The company (Easton, Pennsylvania) manufactures and markets the Crayola brand crayons (some 2 billion per year) and other art supplies—"a line of products that stimulates creativity in children and adults alike." "Our toys run on imagination," proclaims a typical advertisement. "Our products work on imagination," states the company's 1983 annual report, which is dedicated to "our consumers and our employees, and to all those who value the creative spirit." (The strength of Binney & Smith's competitive position is underscored by the fact that it recently settled an antitrust suit for $5 million.) With major physical expansions completed, the company seeks to keep capital expenditures to a level no greater than depreciation in order to generate the net cash needed for funding acquisitions or other product line additions. Clearly, Binney & Smith seeks to capitalize on its most important asset—the Crayola brand name. Research and development of new products began in 1980 and 1981. The first success is Crayola Drawing Markers—a fine-tipped version of Crayola Coloring Markers, already the market leader in the broad-tipped marker field. Also well received is the Crayola Designer Kit for interiors, an activity set providing the tools for home decoration and interior design. A third is DabberDoo, a kit that encourages creative self-expression through stenciling and decorating. Contemplated for the future are concepts for video software cartridges in joint venture with a major toy company. Dominance, relatedness, coherence, distinctiveness, clarity, and surely product emphasis are all at work here. (In June 1984, Hallmark Cards, the world's largest manufacturer of greeting cards and a private company, agreed to purchase Binney & Smith for $203.5 million. Though we always lament the passing of a top-performing mid-sized firm, it does seem a nice fit.)

CHAPTER 10

BUILDING THE MODEL

Why It Works,
What It Means

We now put it together. Thus far we have described, defined, organized, categorized, and predicted the behavior of successful mid-sized firms. We sought "cause" by seeking "correlation"; the former more an art, the latter more a science. We used two independent yet complementary methodologies—one qualitative (Chapter 6) and one quantitative (Chapter 9)—to develop twelve strategic categories (Table 9.8). Here we meld the methodologies and combine the categories.

Linkages and junctions are what we seek. Can we connect the strategic categories? Is union possible? Can we discern "causative pathways" among the twelve? Which of the categories are more important, more determinant of mid-sized success? What are the relationships, what are the bonds, among the categories? What we want is a *model*.

MODELS AND WHY USE THEM

Models are the talk of our times. They appear everywhere; they are used on personal computer spread sheets and for portraying biochemical molecules. Aeronautical engineers test new aircraft designs with numerical models on supercomputers just as automotive engineers test new car designs with clay models in wind tunnels. Models, however, for all their sophistication, are but shadows of what really exists. Models, in short, *represent* reality— which means, of course, that they are *not* reality.

Models are both useful and dangerous—curiously for the same reason: They simplify the world. As such, they make complex systems accessible to study; but they also make assumptions difficult to assess—the former gives understanding, the latter caution.

Models are necessary to reduce unmanageable and unintelligible data to manageable and intelligible proportions. Models can capture insight by highlighting essential signal and ignoring masking noise. Yet models must be kept honest by tests in the real world. Just as models are needed to ascertain the relevance of data and events, data and events are needed to enhance the confidence of models. The feedback is positive, with each pass improving the process.

An analogy may help. Models can be compared to nets that are dragged through oceans of fish. Only the fish that have a certain size or shape are caught; the vast majority pass right through untouched and perhaps unnoticed. The nets, in the analogy, are the models, and the fish are the data. These data, for their part, are not passive in the process. Imagine—and here the analogy strains—the fish (data) modifying the nets as they pass through, so that on subsequent passes the nets (models) become structurally improved and will thereby catch even more relevant fish-data.

The ultimate test of a model is its applicability, its capacity to describe and predict. How completely is reality portrayed? How accurately are future events projected? There is a tradeoff here, and a test. A model must produce more explanatory elegance and predictive power than it gives up in lost detail and ignored data.

Although analytical numbers are used in building the model, cases control its design. Corporate reality, we insist, is the touchstone.

GATHERING THE PIECES

First, some of the strongest primary variables are linked to the strategy categories (see Table 10.1). Next, the top-performing firms

TABLE 10.1   The Better-Performing Mid-Sized Firm, Categorized by Qualitative Variables

Primary Variable (Qualitative)	Strategy-Category
The Better-Performing Mid-Sized Firm Has:	
Dominance (large market share) within its own corporate niche (or claims to have it)	Dominance
Greater focus/relatedness for the entire company	Coherence
Greater coherence in goals/objectives/ strategies	Coherence
Greater degree of corporate uniqueness/ distinctiveness	Distinctiveness
Greater orientation toward sales volume/ growth	Progressiveness
Greater corporate commitment/dedication	Commitment
Greater orientation toward the company's products	Relevance
CEO letter (in annual report) evincing greater enthusiasm/excitement	Fulfillment
Greater orientation toward customers	Relevance
Greater clarity in stated goals/objectives/ strategies	Clarity
Greater market segmentation by product uniqueness	Distinctiveness
More aggressive/bullish risk-seeking approach	Commitment
CEO letter (in annual report) evincing greater commitment/dedication	Commitment
Higher CEO profile in its annual report	Fulfillment
Greater appreciation for its own strengths and/or weaknesses	Perceptiveness
Greater stress on product quality	Relevance
Better sense of its industry/market environment	Perceptiveness

are scanned to discern linkages among these categories, to get a first feel of directional flow. What are the mechanisms of cause and effect? Which strategic categories are active in top-performing mid-sized firms and which ones trigger the others?

The qualitative approach (Chapter 6) suggested the preeminence of coherence, commitment, dominance, and distinctiveness—with coherence being almost ubiquitous, and dominance a surprise.

The quantitative approach (Chapter 9) stressed the power and persistence of dominance, focus/relatedness, coherence, uniqueness/distinctiveness, commitment, progressiveness (sales revenues growth, new products, innovation), and several other strategic categories.

The task here, more sense than science, is to *link* these categories in rational and realistic fashion. The object is to generate a model for top-performing mid-sized firms.

We developed the model by trial and error. There was neither mathematical formula nor magical method to deduce or divine the "perfect pattern." There was no "archetype" of mid-sized firms awaiting discovery. We sought a framework of organization, a "map" that could portray an intricate landscape, a mechanism that could simplify a complex system.

Such model-making must take place in an environment of real cases, a working atmosphere where functioning firms drive the model-formulating process. This we have watched for nine chapters; we have seen the input and impact. In examining more than three dozen company cases we have been building the foundation. Corporate reality must be bedrock.

We start with a holistic search of the 128 top-performing firms (Chapter 6). What are the "links" and "causative pathways" among the categories of critical success strategies? What impressions surface, what sense of link or cause comes? The results are intuitive. What follows is more insight than analysis.

Seven such linkages are noted, two of which are "strong": from distinctiveness to coherence (strong), from commitment to distinctiveness (strong), from progressiveness to dominance, from perceptiveness to progressiveness, from clarity to coherence, from dominance to consistency, from fulfillment to commitment.

TABLE 10.2   The Better-Performing Mid-Sized Firm: Categorized by Quantitative Variables

Primary Variable (Quantitative)	Strategy–Category
The Better-Performing Mid-Sized Firm Has:	
Higher ratio of after-tax profits to book equity	Efficiency
Higher ratio of after-tax profits to total sales	Efficiency
Higher five-year mean after-tax return on sales	Efficiency/ Consistency
Higher ratio of sales in 1978 + 1977 divided by sales in 1976 + 1975	Progressiveness
Lower coefficient of variation for the five-year return on sales	Consistency
Lower ratio of total debt to total assets	Flexibility
Higher ratio of profits in 1978 + 1977 divided by profits in 1976 + 1975	Progressiveness
Higher ratio of net plant and equipment to gross plant and equipment	Progressiveness
Higher ratio of its largest business segment sales divided by total company sales	Coherence

Next we consider the most significant primary variables correlated with mid-sized success (Chapter 9). All can be embedded within one of the categories of critical success strategies. The listing of rank-ordered qualitative variables (Table 9.5) can be so transformed (Table 10.1). A similar transformation of quantitative variables is also made (Table 10.2).

PUTTING THE PIECES TOGETHER

The diagram in Figure 10.1 is the product of trial and error, the repetitive interaction between theory and practice. The model is based on empirical data, sure; but it is also based on gut feel. Numerical results are important, but case studies are critical. Operational reality more than statistical significance is the cohesive bond for modeling top-performing mid-sized firms.[1]

The model will fulfill its intended (and limited) potential if it helps organize and/or clarify what seems like an unkempt collection of unrelated concepts. We seek both description and prescription, the former to explain, the latter to recommend. What we propose, therefore, is not to justify the model, but to explain it; not to refute alternative arrangements, but to elucidate this one.

Six of the twelve critical success strategy categories form the "inner circle": commitment, distinctiveness, coherence, progressiveness, dominance, and consistency. Each of the other six categories articulates with one member of the inner circle: fulfillment–commitment, flexibility–distinctiveness, clarity–coherence, perceptiveness–progressiveness, relevance–dominance, and efficiency–consistency.

How did we determine the direction of causal flow? The process was more intuitive than analytical, more holistic than deductive, more affective than cognitive. Yet the intuition, the holism, and the affection were derived directly from hundreds of hours with hundreds of firms, from overt observations and subliminal impressions, from the facts and from the feelings.

How do critical success strategies function? The model represents strategic mechanisms arising from our clumping of companies. As such it should suggest potential modes of action.

Of the 334 mid-sized companies that comprise the data base, some are good and some are bad; but only a very few of the good ones evince all elements of the model, and only a very few of the bad ones evince none of them.

The model is a composite, a structured pattern of strategic categories. One should not expect to find all of its components in any one mid-sized firm, no matter how top-performing it may be. But one should use the model as a guide, as a map, in a "new kind of 'case study' done with theoretical alertness."[2]

How can the model be used in running real companies? How to trace the mechanisms of strategic success? First, determine which categories are strongest in a better-performing firm, and then project their dynamic effect on the corporate system by following the pathways in the model. Similarly, one can intervene in a poorer-performing firm by stimulating several strategic categories in order to activate all. Any of the strategic categories can drive the model.

STRUCTURING THE MODEL

The model is composed of twelve elements, twelve higher-order categories of critical success strategies. As they are linked in Figure 10.1, there are thirteen pairs of pathways between the strategic categories. These connections were chosen on the basis of "impressions" gleaned from qualitative case studies. We now subject them to quantitative analysis.

The strategic linkages are not equal in either power or practice. On almost every corporate test, commitment, distinctiveness, coherence, and dominance evince greater strength than consistency and progressiveness, the other two members of the model's inner circle. Consequently, we emphasize the central presence of the "Big Four": commitment, distinctiveness, coherence, and dominance. This is core. A modified scheme of the model, reflecting the relative importance of strategic categories, is presented in Figure 10.2. A further modification, reflecting the relative strength of association among strategic categories, is presented in Figure 10.3.[3]

COMPANIES AND CAUSE

Statistical significance is one thing; practical significance quite another. Having demonstrated the numbers, we must still establish the meaning.

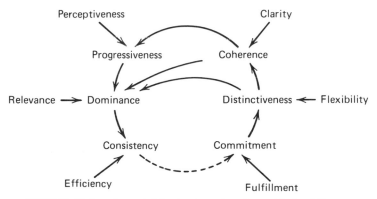

FIGURE 10.1. A model for best-performing mid-sized firms.

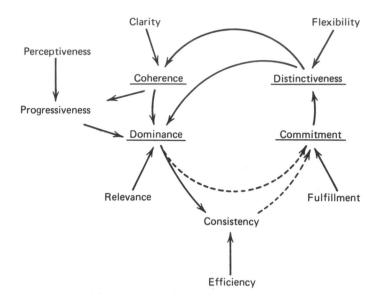

FIGURE 10.2. A model for best-performing mid-sized firms, by importance of strategic categories.

How to ascertain effectiveness of the thirteen strategic category pathways? How to use the model for explaining real-world situations? We return to the 128 top performers. We look for evidence of linkages or causative pathways as specified by the model. (The process is judgmental; its bias cannot be denied. Yet what is a defect of methodology may bring benefit in application.)

The construction of models alters one's views. The process itself shifts appreciation of relevant data. This is always true, whether models are created consciously and overtly or unconsciously and covertly. Human perceptions are not omniscient, and it is the existence of models—or mental sets—that focuses interest and directs attention.

Having the model in mind affected the search. It could not be otherwise: Models reorient cognitive systems. Information that would have been ignored without the model becomes relevant and recorded with the model; information that would have been noted without becomes irrelevant and discarded with. The bias is real. It is always there, humming and working. (One is never without models; we constantly employ simplifying views of reality. The only issue is which model at which moment.)

Table 10.3 lists the results of our search for linkages/causative pathways among the 128 top-performing mid-sized firms. Each company was allowed multiple representations in as many strategic categories as seemed appropriate. The number of firms ascribed ranges from a low of 15 (from flexibility to distinctiveness) to a high of 81 (from distinctiveness to coherence). Note that the four pathways flowing into dominance all record high numbers.

To get operational feel for the linkages/pathways, we give some example companies (many are old friends).

1. *Plenum Publishing* specializes in scientific publishing where it has great comparative strength and substantial market share, especially in the translation of Russian esoteria. (From distinctiveness to coherence, from clarity to coherence, from coherence to progressiveness, from progressiveness to dominance.)

2. *Shaklee Corporation's* success is derived from its highly motivated part-time field force as much as from its concentration in

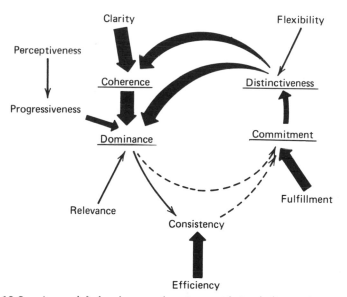

FIGURE 10.3. A model for best-performing mid-sized firms, by strength of association between strategic categories.

TABLE 10.3.   Testing the Model-Map: Coding the Causative
Pathways (sample: 128 top-performing mid-sized firms)

Causative Pathway Category	Firms	Percent
From fulfillment to commitment	25	20
From commitment to distinctiveness	57	45
From flexibility to distinctiveness	15	12
From distinctiveness to coherence	81	63
From clarity to coherence	41	32
From coherence to progressiveness	39	30
From perceptiveness to progressiveness	35	27
From progressiveness to dominance	39	30
From relevance to dominance	41	32
From distinctiveness to dominance	31	24
From coherence to dominance	27	21
From dominance to consistency	33	26
From efficiency to consistency	17	13
Total	481	
Average percentage		29

health and nutrition. (From commitment to distinctiveness; from
distinctiveness to coherence; from perceptiveness to progressiveness; from distinctiveness, coherence, progressiveness, and relevance to dominance.)

   3.   *Marion Laboratories* has a unique approach to R&D, seeking
to exploit the basic research of foreign pharmaceutical companies.
(From perceptiveness to progressiveness, from efficiency to consistency.)

   4.   *Noxell's* continued success within the fiercely competitive
cosmetics/consumer products industry is attributable to its high
organizational commitment and strongly branded products. (From
commitment to distinctiveness, from distinctiveness and relevance
to dominance.)

   5.   *A.T. Cross* controls the high end of the mechanical writing
market by personifying quality and elegance. (From distinctiveness
to coherence and dominance, from clarity to coherence, from perceptiveness to progressiveness, from relevance to dominance.)

   6.   *Nucor* is a steel-industry leader in revolutionary minimills
and is a national leader in incentive-based compensation systems.

(From fulfillment to commitment, from efficiency to consistency, from flexibility to distinctiveness, from distinctiveness to coherence.)

7. *Dynatech* parlayed competency in research and development into a diversified technology company. (From perceptiveness to progressiveness, from fulfillment to commitment, from flexibility to distinctiveness.)

8. *La Quinta Motor Inns* offers high value to guests, with fine facilities at reasonable prices. (From perceptiveness to progressiveness, from progressiveness to dominance, from fulfillment to commitment, from relevance to dominance.)

9. *Texas Business* is the leading business magazine in Texas, energized by a high-profile chief executive. (From fulfillment to commitment, from relevance to dominance, from clarity to coherence.)

10. *Guilford Mills* is a highly efficient textile company, the largest warp knitter in the world. (From efficiency to consistency, from coherence to dominance.)

11. *Keystone International* is a world leader in flow-control technology. (From coherence to dominance, from efficiency to consistency, from relevance to dominance.)

12. *Great Lakes Chemical* is the world's largest producer of brominated specialty chemicals. (From coherence to dominance, from clarity to coherence, from progressiveness to dominance, from perceptiveness to progressiveness.)

13. *Hillenbrand Industries*, with strong family control, is committed to achieve and sustain market dominance in four industries —caskets, electric hospital beds, luggage, security locks. (From commitment to distinctiveness, from progressiveness and relevance to dominance.)

14. *Bacardi Corporation's* success is derived from its "reputation for producing the world's finest rum." (From distinctiveness to coherence, from coherence to dominance, from distinctiveness to dominance.) (See page 344.)

15. *La-Z-Boy Chair* is founded on the twin pillars of personal commitment to family pride and corporate uniqueness of product distinction. (From commitment to distinctiveness, from distinctiveness to coherence; from distinctiveness, coherence, progressiveness, and relevance to dominance; from dominance to consistency.) (See page 345.)

16. *Fort Howard Paper* concentrates on a narrow range of industrial tissue products and stresses the efficiency of its production processes and facilities. (From efficiency to consistency, from distinctiveness to coherence, from dominance to consistency.) (See page 433.)

17. *Commerce Clearing House* serves its focused market of accountants and attorneys with a variety of critical current information. (From distinctiveness to coherence; from distinctiveness, coherence, progressiveness, and relevance to dominance.) (See page 346.)

18. *International Flavors & Fragrances* is the leading creator and manufacturer in its field. "Our business is serving two of the five senses—taste and smell." (From clarity to coherence; from distinctiveness to coherence; from coherence to progressiveness; from distinctiveness, coherence, progressiveness, and relevance to dominance.) (See page 354.)

19. *Maytag* established itself as the industry's product leader, thereby obtaining premium prices for its appliances from customers desiring the best quality, performance, and reliability. Maytag's high-road philosophy extends from higher wages for employees to the best network of dealers. (Most of the strategic pathways are represented here.) (See page 344.)

20. *Everest & Jennings*, family controlled and dedicated, focuses on the production of wheelchairs and other rehabilitation products. (From commitment to distinctiveness; from distinctiveness to coherence; from coherence to dominance.) (See page 334.)

Most of the preceding descriptions were taken from the companies' annual reports. Having poured through hundreds of these documents at several stages of the study, one gets a sharp sense of the importance of models. Information that slipped by unnoticed on the first or second pass jumped out abruptly on the third. A specific model (or formal framework) is, in effect, a "conceptual lens"; it is a cognitive construct that magnifies, highlights, and reveals as well as shrinks, blurs, and obscures. One experiences the rush of model-specific information; previously ignored or unseen, it suddenly leaps to life, grabbing attention and redirecting vision.

TO FLOURISH AND FLOUNDER

The Dr. Pepper Company exemplifies the best characteristics of leading mid-sized firms, and what happens when a winning game is changed. The story is about segment strength and industry weakness. It is a tale interesting and instructive, and we explore it in depth.

A heralded success story in a brutal industry, having flourished quietly among warring giants, Dr. Pepper confronted the classic conundrum: Remain regional? Or go national? Staying small could invite competitive crush; becoming large could provoke monster retaliation. The choice was clear and the decision was made.

For a glorious decade the Dr. Pepper Company enjoyed unparalleled progress as a Southwest-based soft-drink producer. Between 1973 and 1981 sales grew from $121 million to $370 million; return on sales averaged 8 percent; return on stockholder equity averaged 25 percent. The company was considered one of the best managed in the country; it was a classic case of corporate strategy,[4] and we had highlighted it as a top-performing mid-sized firm in *Texas Business* magazine.

Everything seemed right. Dr. Pepper dominated its own market, well segmented by flavor and geography. It appeared immune from the titanic struggles between the cola supergiants thundering in soda stratosphere. Its crusty chief executive and spirited corporate culture maintained strategic coherence and employee enthusiasm.

But choice brought change. Ironically, it was Dr. Pepper's success that afforded dangerous options: Stay small or expand? Keep in place or challenge the mammoths? The opportunity was there and the temptation was great.

Dr. Pepper began an aggressive national campaign in the late 1970s. It acquired Canada Dry in early 1982. It entered the ring with thoughts of a championship. But then the heavyweights took notice.

One of the most difficult years in Dr. Pepper's 98-year history, and clearly the worst in recent memory, was 1982. Net earnings, $12.5 million, were *down* 58 percent on a sales increase of 39 percent, to $516 million (reflecting the Canada Dry acquisition). Returns on sales and equity plummeted, to 2 and 9 percent, respectively. Fourth-quarter sales were up 47 percent, but the bottom line— where it counts—was cherry red: The company incurred its first loss, $4 million. Debt to total capital, largely as a result of the Canada Dry acquisition, leaped to 44.7 percent from 7.5 percent. Cash requirements skyrocketed. Capital expenditures totaled $64.8 million in 1982 versus $23.3 milion in 1981. The Big Leagues require a Fat Checkbook.

Reasons for the dramatic decline? According to Dr. Pepper, there were three, all derived from competition and overgrowth.

1.   *Price Wars.*   High levels of competitive discounting eroded operating profits. (This was especially true in the Southwest, Dr. Pepper's home court and "the scene of some of the heaviest discounting in history.")

2.   *Overbuilding.*   Several divisions were "simply too large to support either current or long-term business needs." Overheads and operations could not be sustained.

3.   *Spreading Too Thin.*   In an attempt "to be as supportive of our markets on as broad a scale as possible, there may have been a dilution of marketing effort in key areas that was heightened by the major brands' competitive activities." The overall market share for the Dr. Pepper brand (including Diet) slipped from 6.5 to 6.0 percent—a point of serious management concern. The new diet drinks from Coke and Pepsi were muscling Dr. Pepper off the shelves, and the company fell from third to fourth place behind a resurging Seven-Up.

In September 1983, with profit recovery clear but long-term prospects shaky, Dr. Pepper announced that it was retaining an investment banking house to seek a merger or sale of assets. (In 1983, Dr. Pepper earned $21.6 million on $560 million in revenues, better than 1982 but still below industry norms and well below historical averages.)

"Simply stated," wrote Chairman W. W. "Foots" Clements to bottlers, "management of this company and its directors are committed to insuring that we explore every conceivable opportunity to remain competitive"—which meant, of course, that there was

Trouble in River City. (Whispered one wag: "With a $2.5 million fee on the line, you can be sure Lazard Freres will find a buyer.")

When the dust settled, none of the hypothesized corporate suitors showed up. Castle & Cook, the diversified food and real estate company, made a run, but lost to a small investment firm, Forstmann Little, who pulled off "a leveraged buyout," in a prime example of Wall Street's Magic Brew.[5] Dr. Pepper was taken private in a transaction valued at $648 million.

As the *Wall Street Journal* reported it, Clements knows how to say goodbye with class. At Dr. Pepper's last shareholders' meeting as a public corporation, all were seized by nostalgia and some began to cry. But then Clements added: "We all know the show's not over until the fat lady sings." That was the cue for Melody Jones, a rotund Texas singer, to waddle on stage. Dressed in a toga and armed with a spear and breastplates embossed with lions' heads, she belted out "Auld Lang Syne." Rather unconventional, but pure-bred Foots.

It was a strange twist to a long story. But the Dr. Pepper saga extends both ways, and although we discuss its recent decline, we should not overlook its prior advance. There are two stories here, the rise as well as the fall, and both are worth telling. For a decade Dr. Pepper had been one of the finest examples of mid-sized success.

Dr. Pepper, Giantbeater

"I've been selling the greatest product in the soft drink industry for forty-two years. If everyone knew what I did about Dr. Pepper, and the people who contributed to its success, there could be no doubt about the future. Dr. Pepper has the potential to become the number one selling soft drink." So stated Woodrow Wilson Clements, the frank-talking, cigar-smoking CEO, the man called one of the best instinctive marketers in the United States. If Dr. Pepper's unique flavor is the company heart, Foots is the company soul.

Starting as a route salesman in Tuscaloosa, Alabama, in 1935, Foots became vice-president of marketing in 1957, executive vice-president in 1967, and president and CEO in 1970, adding the chairman title in 1974. His tenure of leadership, not coincidentally, paralleled Dr. Pepper's period of growth—explosive growth—when "that Texas drink," previously ignored by the cola megaliths, broke loose on the national scene.

Market Segmentation

The history of Dr. Pepper was a premier success story in strategic management. Conventional wisdom says that profitability is directly related to market share. How then did this small-share company so persistently outperform the vastly larger-sized Coke and Pepsi with their imposing national dominance?

There's no mystery here. The theory's right; it's the market *segmentation* that's key. Dr. Pepper has never been, in a very real sense, a "small-share company." It in fact has been the market leader, the dominant one—but not for all soft drinks and not nationally. Dr. Pepper's segmentation has been by flavor class and by geography. First, it is *the* "Dr. Pepper" flavor; of those who want this unique taste, 90 percent will buy Dr. Pepper specifically, not its imitations. Second, Dr. Pepper has always been exceptionally strong in Texas, where its 24 percent share has long competed equally with Coke and Pepsi. Of the top 20 Dr. Pepper markets on a per capita basis, 17 are clustered in the Lone Star State.

The vast dispersion of Dr. Pepper's market share from region to region has been an *asset*, not a liability, in the company's fight for profits and return on investment. In Waco, for example, Dr. Pepper outsells Coke and Pepsi combined, averaging 250 bottles per person per year; its 100,000 citizens outguzzle Detroit's 1,500,000. In New England, on the other hand, Dr. Pepper's 2 percent is minuscule. Finding the drink is hard in some areas of the country—a condition that has changed over the past several years. (But maybe that wasn't so good. The same strategic theory that predicted regional success predicted national distress.)

History of a Winner

It's the stuff of which soap operas are made. Small-town soda jerk mixes twenty-three flavors and secret ingredients, and names it after his girl friend's father, attempting to woo her. A chemist, R. L. Lazarus, discovers it, and the new bubbly beverage is dispensed at the Old Corner Drug Store in Waco, Texas. The year is 1885, about when Coca-Cola appears in nearby Georgia.[4]

Family managed, Dr. Pepper grew slowly, expanding cautiously into surrounding towns, its bottles shipped via Wells-Fargo Express—with a reputation built on the curious combination of sparkling refreshment and medicinal mission. For more than half a century the company insignia was an iron anvil, surrounded by entwined grain and sporting the headline, "DR. PEPPER'S PHOS-FERRATES—Wheat and Iron."

From the 1920s through the middle 1950s, Dr. Pepper was run by J. B. O'Hara, who transferred the headquarters from Waco to Dallas and introduced the bottlers' franchise program in 1926. The year 1956 marked the beginning of the modern era of the company. W. R. Parker, coming out of General Foods, brought to the leadership of Dr. Pepper a fistful of modern marketing and promotion techniques. His chief assistant in the effort to expand Dr. Pepper from its Southwest spawning grounds was a hungry W. W. Clements.

In 1962 Dr. Pepper lost a battle and won a war. Pepsi-Cola, claiming trademark infringement over the "pep" similarity, pressed a legal suit. Dr. Pepper countersued, and when the dust settled, the courts (and then the Food and Drug Administration as well) ruled that Dr. Pepper was not a cola but a separate and distinctive flavor. This decision cleared the way, ironically, for Coke and Pepsi's independent bottlers to begin carrying Dr. Pepper without violating their cola franchises. The period of rapid sales expansion—from $17 million in 1962 to $138 million in 1975—was highlighted by the dramatic introduction of Dr. Pepper into New York City in 1970. (But early success made the eyes grow big.)

One Tough Competitor

For almost twenty years since the early 1960s, Dr. Pepper grew at two to three times the industry average, while maintaining an impressive return on equity—hitting 28–29 percent in 1976–1978 (the national average is about 14–15 percent). Such bottom-line sparkle put Dr. Pepper first among soft-drink firms and 79th among the top 1000 corporations on *Fortune's* famous list. (This compared with Dr. Pepper's position of 598th in size. A company always wants to be higher in profit comparisons.)

During this period, Dr. Pepper climbed past Canada Dry Ginger Ale, surpassed Royal Crown Cola, and finally overran Seven-Up, moving from the sixth to the third largest selling soft drink in the country. Diet Dr. Pepper, introduced in 1962, grew to tenth, advancing even faster than its big brother. Together, the two drinks had 7 percent of the total market, grossing some $360 million in 1981. (But, as the world learned in the 1970s, there are limits to growth.)

Dr. Pepper's sales, large in comparison with ordinary firms, must be viewed relatively, against its competition, pitted head-to-head with the soft-drink mastodons. Coca-Cola's *net profits* are greater than Dr. Pepper's sales, and Pepsi-Cola has revenues thirteen times as much. That's enough firepower to make most mortals blink; but it seemed more opportunity than threat to the aggressive managers at Dr. Pepper's magnificent Dallas headquarters, surrounded by nine acres of beautiful park land. "We've just started," Clements boasted in 1981. "Our potential is tremendous." (It is said by gambling professionals that the worst thing to have is a long winning streak—you think you're infallible.)

The chairman's personality seems to radiate from every product, peer out from every ad, reflect from every face. "Our number one objective," he expounded, "is not to be the biggest company in the soft drink industry, but the best."

"Some observers have questioned our ability to compete with Coke and Pepsi. I can assure you that we are in a better position today [1981] than we've ever been. Competition in this industry has always been keen. That's one of the reasons we've grown to a $17 billion-plus industry. Competition brings out your best. Forces it out. We've always had it; we still have it; and we'll continue to have it."

The spin-off is strong. Foots is everywhere. The corporate camaraderie is infectious, the atmosphere familylike. There is genuine identification with their company, an almost theological belief in the "goodness" of the product and a virtually evangelical verve in its promulgation. "We're pure-bred Texas," purred one middle manager, "born in Waco, reared in Dallas."

But don't let the homespun hospitality fool you. These boys are all business. Territory takers. Guerrilla fighters.

Dr. Pepper's management lives marketing. They compete for time in the consumer's eyes and for space in his stomach; for the promotional attention of its bottlers and for the shelf space of its retailers. Keys to success—supporting their drink's gustatory appeal—are the integrated approach to media and point-of-purchase advertising, attractive packaging, controlled distribution, and competitive pricing.

Some years ago the company informed the world that they intended making Dr. Pepper the country's number one soft drink with a 10 percent market share in 1980 and 15 percent in 1985. A little ambitious? A lot dangerous! Every increased point for Dr. Pepper would mean a point gouged out of someone else's hide. And with the principal players most formidable, the leather has been tough. Coke and Pepsi are food and beverage behemoths, and in the eternal war between the two clashing titans, wanderers on the battlefield can be crushed.

A harbinger of things to come, 1979 was a tough year. Dr. Pepper's sales grew only 4 percent, barely more than the industry's meagre 3.6 percent average. Although competition was fierce, Clements still predicted growth rates about 1½ times the industry's through the 1980s. (But then came 1982, and the bubble burst.)

Kingpin Bottlers

One key factor is the independent bottler. Herein lies the unique structure of the soft-drink industry. Dr. Pepper manufactures and markets the concentrates and fountain syrups of its drinks to some 475 independent bottlers in the United States. Although Dr. Pepper does some canning and owns several bottlers, the vast majority of its sales is conducted through these independent licensees. (Coke and Pepsi are similarly organized. They, however, work with bottlers whose primary loyalty is to them.) These regional companies add sweeteners and carbonation, bottle the product, and distribute it to hundreds of retail stores, soda fountains, and dispensing machines in their areas. Although ostensibly a "Coke" or "Pepsi" bottler, many add other flavors—even competing ones—to round out their product line. Since Dr. Pepper is not considered a "cola"— according to that landmark 1962 Supreme Court decision—the independent bottlers can carry it. "We're getting our sales organization off their cans," Clements asserted, "and working with our bottlers."

Most of the Dr. Pepper bottlers sell either Coke or Pepsi as their primary product. They spend substantial sums discounting their flagship drink—whether Coke or Pepsi—in the nonstop wars of price and promotion. Such battles often cause Dr. Pepper to be the highest priced soft drink in the local market. The bottler believes that since 70 percent of sales comes from a major cola, he must protect it. Dr. Pepper people maintain that the bottlers' real growth is their drink, distinctively flavored and uniquely positioned.

The relationship between Dr. Pepper and the independent bottlers is called friendly by observers. Some say it's the best in the industry. Pepper people aren't big enough to bludgeon, confided one insider, so they're smart enough not to try. At least not until recently. At an annual meeting of its franchised bottlers some years ago, the assembled multitudes were berated for "sitting on the brand" and accused of using Dr. Pepper profits to subsidize other flavors—the industry's version of the unpardonable sin.

Speaking to financial analysts at the World Trade Center in New York in February 1982, Clements campaigned, "a strong bottler organization, probably in total stronger than Coke or Pepsi." He asserted that "we have the strongest bottlers of Coke and the strongest bottlers of Pepsi," and that being the second brand to a bottler is not a disadvantage. With the cola demand flat for twenty years, Clements campaigned, the uniqueness of Dr. Pepper offers the bottlers their best potential for plant growth.

Shifting Strategies and Breaking Barriers

To assess the strategic management of a company, one must understand the product–market environment in which the firm functions. (In academic business circles this discipline is called "industrial economics" or "industrial organization.") The soft-drink industry, with its special relationships between concentrate manufacturers and independent bottlers, is often used as a prototype for such analyses.

Professor Michael Porter of the Harvard Business School advocates the structural analysis of industries for strategic management. (See his book, *Competitive Strategy*.) Grouping firms by broad strategies, Porter asserts, can be a useful tool because it helps highlight competitor similarities and differences without coping with the inexhaustible detail of each firm. Different strategic groups have different structural positions. Much depends on a company's industry location: the height of entry barriers, the power of customers and suppliers, the threat of substitutes, and the rivalry of competition. (Entry barriers are called "mobility barriers" because they deter the shift in firm strategic position from group to group within an industry just as they impede the entry of new firms into the industry.) Thus Dr. Pepper, the regional firm, was long in a different "strategic group" from Coke and Pepsi and Seven-Up, the national firms. Though appearing the same, Dr. Pepper was in fact quite different, as if in an entirely different industry.

No more. Like a whirlwind, Dr. Pepper shifted strategies, broke the barriers, and moved up into a new strategic group—the big leagues—defying economies of scale, channels of distribution, brand loyalty, advertising power, and in retrospect, plain common sense. If ever one wanted proof that regional and national markets can behave like entirely different industries, look no further than Dr. Pepper.

Dr. Pepper's Critical Success Strategies

Why had Dr. Pepper been so successful, outperforming its larger rivals, breaking barriers, and building share? Following were its critical success strategies.

☐ Strong market position in a focused segment of the industry; segmentation by flavor (92 percent of the "Pepper" category) and segmentation by geography (concentration in Texas and the Southwest).

☐ A growing industry is the best time to build market share (since one's rivals are still increasing in absolute size even though they are losing percentage share).

☐ Dr. Pepper offers a unique flavor. This reduces price competition and aids market penetration.

☐ The narrow product line facilitated focus. (A lost advantage once Dr. Pepper arrayed thirty flavors through Canada Dry.)

☐ Dr. Pepper could pick and choose the best bottlers in each area. (What did these bottlers gain? Incremental profit with little risk, bargaining strength with Coke or Pepsi, and significant growth potential.)

☐ Diet Dr. Pepper had some taste superiority over the diet colas, an advantage that was dulled by the introduction of the new artificial sweetener, aspartame (Nutrasweet).

☐ Dr. Pepper had a stellar record in advertising, marketing, and bottler relations.

☐ The internal corporate culture was unified with commitment and belief. The organizational structure could be characterized as "ideological" more than bureaucratic, almost "religious" or "evangelical" in its fervency.

☐ The catalyst for much of the above was the boss, W. W. "Foots" Clements. (The current transition under way, from internal charismatic leadership to external professional management, augurs change, for better and for worse.)

There are profound differences between regional and national firms, and the leap from "number one regional" to "number three national" was long and shaky. Changing organization and additional overhead are only two of the subtle structural shifts not immediately apparent.

Playing Big League Ball

Crowding the high-rolling game, some fresh money has upped the ante, hurling dollars right into the megabuck stratosphere. The stakes are enormous—some of the best profits in American business are made in soft drinks. Procter & Gamble, a consumer products steamroller, bought the non-Canadian operations of Crush International Ltd., snatching it from Dr. Pepper, which had been courting Crush for two years.

Then there's Phillip Morris. Fresh from victory with Miller Beer (where it spent enormous sums to increase plant capacity and market share), the massive tobacco company bought Seven-Up, infusing it with millions to build new facilities and support vigorous advertising. Their aggressive "UnCola" campaign, not having made much inroad, was transformed into the combative anticaffeine campaign. Swiping at Coke, Pepsi, and Dr. Pepper in one shot, Seven-Up bared both fists for an all-out fight. (A Dr. Pepper spokesman called the ads "disappointing," not equaling Pepsi's outrage and threat against bottlers. The irony of Phillip Morris, one of the country's largest cigarette companies, pounding the health podium must raise some eyebrows — even in the pragmatic world of hard-ball advertising.)

Foots seemed unafraid. Had he not changed the structure of the industry? Had he not bearded the lion in its own den by getting the Coca-Cola Bottling Company of New York—not owned by Coca-Cola—to bottle Dr. Pepper, pile cases of it on Coke trucks, and market "that Texas drink" to millions of New Yorkers? Had he not been willing, even desirous, of waging war with "Mother?" (Coke, of course, counterattacked; it marketed remarkably similar flavors with remarkably similar names—"Texas Stepper" and "Mr. PiBB"—in Dr. Pepper's home territory, though without notable success. With his wry bluntness, Clements suggested that if Coke realized how hard it was to sell Dr. Pepper they would stop trying to imitate it. Supposedly it takes an average new customer some eight bottles to develop a "Dr. Pepper taste." Foots, by the way, credits Mr. PiBB with expanding the "Dr. Pepper market," taking sales away from the colas.)

Dr. Pepper has some serious competitive weaknesses; there's no denying the economic muscle of massive size. Yet Clements focused on the mystique. "If I had seen Dr. Pepper like everyone else does when I took over in 1967, we'd still be in fifth or sixth place," he informed the *Wall Street Journal* without pretense or false humility. "I knew the product better than any of my predecessors, and I had higher expectations of what the product could do."

Commenting on the loss of Crush, one analyst characterized Dr. Pepper as being in a race. If they don't expand through acquisitions, he predicted, they'll be submerged by the competition or swallowed by a predator. (A prophet, that fellow, but maybe a false one.) Clements conceded that he needed a larger dollar base, desirably with strong international position. The "solution" came, in two parts, late in 1981—but with that solution came new problems, and a future that would corkscrew.

First, Dr. Pepper acquired U.S. marketing rights to the Welch's line of carbonated soft drinks, the leading product in grape sodas. Then came the big hit, Canada Dry. (Big is right: By paying $143 million to Norton Simon for its well-known soft-drink business, Dr. Pepper made a "bet the company" move. Dr. Pepper's total net worth at the end of 1981 was *less*, $124 million.)

A classic beverage company, Canada Dry has the dominant product in each class of mixers: club soda, tonic water, bitter lemon, and its most famous product, Ginger Ale. (Barrelhead Root Beer is the second largest in its category. Also included in the Canada Dry constellation are the NoCal and Cott lines.) The successful repositioning of Canada Dry's Club Soda as America's number one sparkling water was spear-pointed by French actor Louis Jourdan, the spokesman in national advertising—a direct shot at Perrier, the wildly more expensive French import.

Thus, the Dr. Pepper company became a major player, with twenty-seven different flavors (rather than two), many of which enjoyed primary or secondary position in their flavor class, all sold with recognized brand identification. With Canada Dry's 3.0 percent market share, the Dr. Pepper company attained a full 10 percent of the U.S. market, with gross sales over $500 million. Not bad, from Waco. (But not good enough: Bigger was not better.)

Consumer Recognition

By all accounts Dr. Pepper, the bubbly-fruity amalgam, cannot be described. How then to link the product of the company with the consumers of the drink? "One of our major challenges," Clements reflected, "was to establish consumer taste habits for a unique and indescribable drink. Milk tastes like milk, coffee like coffee, and

Dr. Pepper like Dr. Pepper. You don't know what it is until you've tasted it."

One of his first decisions as executive vice-president was to hire a new advertising agency. Young and Rubicam won the account and produced the slogan, "America's Most Misunderstood Soft Drink." The appeal was to young people, the largest consumers of soft drinks. Teenagers consider themselves "misunderstood." But more than ad hype was embedded here: Dr. Pepper was in fact misunderstood. Foots puts it straight: "People never knew whether to drink it or rub it on."

Clements described his marketing problem in a 1975 speech to bottlers. "The difference is in building a business on an original flavor with a distinctive taste, and a name that is a misnomer, from doing business with a flavor that is well known and a name that identifies that flavor." The solution set, according to Foots, had five elements: perfect product (it must taste right); distribution and availability (people must be able to find it); sampling (the single-drink outlet must be increased); point-of-purchase advertising (the obvious reason); media advertising (the obvious impact).

The content of Dr. Pepper's advertising differed sharply from the cola giants. Whereas Coke and Pepsi used fresh scenes of attractive people and catchy jingles of upbeat music to trigger positive emotions, Dr. Pepper had more direct objectives. The drink from Texas had to establish its brand awareness in the national consciousness; it had to position its original flavor as distinctively non-cola. One early theme was "The Most Original Soft Drink Ever." Certainly the most successful was the "Be A Pepper" campaign.

Begun in 1977 and evolving through several stages, "Be A Pepper" has ranked among the top ten commercials according to consumer surveys. In 1981 it was rated ahead of every other soft drink and second only to Miller Lite Beer in response to the question, "What is your favorite TV commercial?" The magnificent Mickey Rooney commercial—where the Be A Pepper theme was whistled and no words were spoken—was an artistic masterpiece for the hardsell medium. Dr. Pepper's recent advertising strategy focuses on taste, the sugar-free drink, and increasing sponsorship of events such as rock music shows.

The Classic Conundrum

No one-man band, Clements brought in a food-marketing executive, a seasoned professional near the top of Procter & Gamble (the $12 billion behemoth that dominates almost every product class it enters). The chairman described his new protégé as "brilliant and innovative, especially in marketing. He doesn't have a watch. He works with the calendar and so sets a tough pace for those who work for him." In typical self-deprecating style—which everyone enjoys and no one believes—Clements noted that "Chuck [Charles L. Jarvie, 49] and I complement each other completely. I'm lazy and slow; he's smart and fast, and I'm willing to let him do all the work."

But not for long. Less than two years after Foots brought him in, Foots put him out. The wrong man at the wrong time? Or does the chairman have itchy feelings with those reins?

One great question at Dr. Pepper has been succession. What happens after Clements, now near 70? It's a difficult issue for a company run by a long-term and well-loved leader. Jarvie, the ex-heir-apparent, was an ambitious outsider who, it is said, had pushed people around in the in-bred Dr. Pepper family. He had appointed former colleagues, shifting positions in the sales and marketing hierarchy. A clash of management styles between Clements and Jarvie was, according to company insiders, more the fact that the P & G alumnus never came to understand how to run a franchise soft-drink business. He had overstaffed Dr. Pepper's sales force and was unable to transpose a power marketing strategy to Dr. Pepper. There was respect for Jarvie, but little affection. Foots is one tough act to follow. For "regional Dr. Pepper," professional succession would have been important; for "international Dr. Pepper," it's critical.

Repositioning

In March 1984, just after its board approved the Forstmann Little leveraged buyout, Dr. Pepper sold its Canada Dry division to the Del Monte unit of R.J. Reynolds Industries for about $150 million, only marginally more than it had paid to Norton Simon two years before.

The deal makes sense on both sides. The giant tobacco company, seeking to diversify into foods and beverages, is acquiring a strong, quality entry in the growing worldwide soft-drink business. Dr. Pepper is once again able to concentrate its limited resources on its primary product (resources that are even more limited after loading the balance sheet with the huge debt of a leveraged buyout[4]).

"With the sale of Canada Dry, we will be more single-focused on Dr. Pepper," said Joe Hughes, who was named president and chief operating officer following the resignation of Richard Armstrong, the former president of Canada Dry who took over from Jarvie. Hughes knows the company well. His association began back in 1954 when he handled Dr. Pepper's public relations for an outside agency. He joined Dr. Pepper in 1968 as vice-president of franchising. "We have some shoring up to do in our marketing and bottling," he says, "but we have a product capable of competing." Not quite the hubris of five years ago, but realistic and probably right.

Crusty and proud outside, Woodrow Wilson Clements is devoted and humble inside. His unabashed belief in God emerges by design in every speech. He has given away thousands of marbles with the Golden Rule written on them. "Can you build a competitive business on the Golden Rule?," people often ask him? His answer

---

HOW "FOOTS" GOT HIS NICKNAME

" . . . I'll be glad to tell you. My feet grew up before I did. I had rather small legs and I played football. Well, with the football pants just reaching my knees, and my big feet none too graceful, why that's where I picked up the nickname . . . I've always used it. My Christmas cards go out in footprint form, and everybody calls me Foots. When I became President, an executive suggested that I might want to use my real name— it was a little more sophisticated (named after a President and all that—my mother wanted me to be President). I said no— I *got* here using the nickname Foots and I'm going to continue using it. Now of course I sign my checks differently—but everything else is Foots."[4]

is solemn, "You cannot build a business that will last except by practicing the Golden Rule. Our people are taught this. It is our foundation." One can almost envision our Heavenly Father, looking a touch like the kindly, grandfatherly Foots, having just created the heavens and the earth, resting on the seventh day with a burning sceptre in one hand and a cold Dr. Pepper in the other.

WHERE WE HAVE COME

We take a quick review, in preparation for conclusion.

Two different methodologies, one qualitative (Chapter 6) and one quantitative (Chapter 9), supported twelve categories of critical success strategies for top-performing mid-sized firms: commitment, fulfillment, distinctiveness, flexibility, coherence, clarity, progressiveness, perceptiveness, dominance, relevance, consistency, and efficiency. Of the twelve, four had superior strength: dominance, coherence, distinctiveness, and commitment.

Seven groups of primary variables, all underlying the above categories, could describe better-performing mid-sized firms and differentiate them from their poorer-performing matched-pair mates. In approximate order of discriminating strength, the seven are product dominance (large market share within a tightly defined niche); corporate focus/relatedness of products; corporate uniqueness of products; corporate/CEO commitment/dedication/enthusiasm and CEO personal profile; product relevance (product quality, product/brand name, customer orientation); sales volume growth; and corporate progressiveness (new products, innovation orientation).

Dominance and sales growth were surprises, the former because it contradicted mid-sized definition, the latter because it challenged prevailing wisdom. The recurring theme embedded within all seven variables, a leit motif of the entire study, is the ubiquitous importance of company products (especially their proprietary distinctions).

How do these results articulate with the limited literature about mid-sized firms? How do published suggestions compare with our current conclusions? First of all, they are not the same. Although we include traditional strategies for mid-sized firms in our collection, several are more weak than strong. Efficiency, flexibility, relevance (customer service), and progressiveness (new products) are generally touted as keys for mid-sized success. We record and report all four, but the two usually stressed—efficiency and flexibility—were less important in almost every one of our tests.

Our foremost strategic categories—dominance, coherence, distinctiveness, commitment—are judged unevenly by the literature. Distinctiveness is mentioned often in one fashion or another; commitment and coherence are found on occasion; dominance is hardly thought relevant at all. Furthermore, in seeming contradiction to the literature, the importance of sales volume/revenue growth, which emerges so distinctly from our data, is the very element most often condemned by authors advising medium-sized companies.

Simply stated, we say "dominance, distinctiveness, coherence, commitment, growth"; others say "efficiency, flexibility, opportunism." (There is general agreement on product orientation, customer orientation, and new products/innovation.)

Why the discrepancy? Why the sharp difference between our results and what conventional wisdom would have expected?[6]

The solution, we propose, is that the inconsistency is more apparent than real: We are answering different questions.

Most literature deals theoretically with the ideal, answering the *prescriptive* question, "How *should* mid-sized firms behave in an environment populated by larger competitors?"

Our research was designed to deal practically with the real, answering the *descriptive* question, "How *do* mid-sized firms behave in an environment populated by larger competitors?"

In addition, most authors concern themselves with *average* firms, whereas our work centers around leading firms. Combining these two conceptual differences, we reformulate the questions asked. The literature asks, *How should average mid-sized firms behave?* We ask, *How do leading mid-sized firms behave?* There is no contradiction. Both questions are relevant.

To conclude this section, we stress once again the great chasm between correlation, which we have shown, and cause, which we have sought. Battles have been waged over which of the two highly related variables "caused" the other.

Though almost impossible to answer with confidence, the challenge of the question is essential for good science. Sloppy causal associations, especially those based on common sense, are counterproductive and self-defeating. In this regard we pose the findings of our work not as definitive conclusions but as alternative postulates. Two examples follow:

1. Does dominance "cause" high profitability or do highly profitable firms become dominant (the result of other, even random reasons)?
2. Do distinctiveness, coherence, commitment, and the other key variables "cause" better performance or do better-performing firms merely exhibit these traits (or worse yet, just talk about them)?

Arguments from logic cut both ways. It may seem satisfying to direct the causal flow from these variables toward better performance. It may seem logical to tie high returns to dominance, distinctiveness, coherence, and commitment. However, it may be just as logical to explain why a high-flying firm would be committed, would be naturally distinctive, would stress sales growth (profits taking care of themselves), would not diversify (therefore remaining more coherent), and so on. Correlation is a necessary but not sufficient condition of causality. In other words, you cannot have cause without correlation; but you can well have correlation without cause. The dilemma of causation cannot be lightly dismissed.

Our results are results—remember that—we make no authoritative association between demonstrated correlation and desired causation. Taking another example, coherence of company goals/strategies correlates highly with the better of the matched pairs. That is fact. To make the leap, however, and conclude that coherence *caused* better performance is to jump out of science and fall into divination.

On the other hand, such caution should not inhibit us. We should make logical suggestions; we should set forth helpful recommendations. But when such proposals are made, we should distinguish fact from opinion—we should specify what the data showed, what the correlations are, and where the "leaps" are taking place. We all, without doubt, like to leap.

RECENT RESEARCH

How do our results compare with others? Following are some relevant reports.[7]

A survey of 186 CEOs from small, medium, and large companies indicated that "CEOs in medium-sized firms turn out to be more *entity-oriented* than CEOs in small and large firms."[8] ("Entity orientation" is contrasted with "stockholder orientation"; thus the entity-oriented executive will trade off stockholder financial returns in order to augment company size and scope.) The author states that "it is obvious that CEOs from medium-sized firms stressed growth more than did their counterparts in small and large firms. Growth will perpetuate the business entity and is an integral part of the arguments of the entity theory of the firm." (Another author propounds a "life cycle theory of the firm," postulating that as a firm ages and matures, the tendency increases for managers to pursue enterprise growth, rather than stockholder return.[9])

Ambition for expansion also emerges from the above survey: "Because of opportunities and psychological and potential financial rewards, CEOs in medium-sized firms are more ambitious in expansion than are those in large firms. Growth-minded executives may be more likely to slight short-term return on shareholders' investment."[8] (This confirms our findings of growth orientation. Certainly the presence of CEO ambition—as measured by CEO profile, commitment, enthusiasm/excitement—was evident in our better-performing mid-sized firms.)

A 1972 survey combined large- and small-company presidents ($80–$600 million and $2–$10 million in annual gross sales, respectively).[10] The large-company presidents were asked to give the most important limitations imposed by large size. The top three were "limits flexibility, ability to change course quickly"; "reduces ability to attract entrepreneurial personnel"; and "limits capacity to take risks." Inverting questions and answers, the comparative advantages of smaller firms become flexibility, entrepreneurial personnel, and risk-taking capacity—all of which emerged from our data base. The small-company presidents were asked to suggest areas in which small businesses have greater flexibility than larger businesses. Topping their list were "customer service" and "product changes"—again consistent with our findings.

An ingenious study of the *Fortune* 500 confirms the importance of focus, relatedness, and coherence.[11] Firms that diversified with newer activities centered around older skills were compared to firms that diversified without concern for current competencies. The "concentrics" beat the "unrelateds" in levels of profitability and rates of growth.

Innovation appears to be governed by a "threshold effect," augmented by medium size and inhibited by excessive size. This also seems true in the Soviet Union.[12]

With respect to the four characteristics underlying the success of three low-market-share companies (Chapter 4), our data strongly confirm two, support a third, and seem to contradict the fourth.[13] The two strongly confirmed are "segmentation," and "ubiquitous CEO." Hammermesh et al. state that "most businesses must compete in a limited number of segments within their industry [compare focus/coherence], and they must choose these segments carefully . . . most successful companies define market segments in unique and creative ways [compare distinctiveness]. . . . To be successful, a low market share company must compete in the segments where its own strengths will be most highly valued and where its larger competitors will be most unlikely to compete. . . . The important thing is that management spend its time identifying and exploiting unique segments rather than making broad assaults on entire industries."

Does the fact that dominance was a prime result of our study contradict this low-market-share orientation? Not at all. Dominance in our data base was entirely self-defined. Our mid-sized firms conceived their product/markets to be so bounded that their dominance developed almost from the definition itself. The above concept of market segmentation says essentially the same thing, though in different form. By "identifying and exploiting unique segments," low-market-share firms indeed achieve the same dominance (which, though sounding somewhat incongruous, is quite logical).

The "ubiquitous CEO" seen in successful low-market-share firms is a characteristic called "striking" by the above authors; the CEO's influence was "pervasive" (compare high personal profile); his personality was "dynamic, tough, strong-willed" (compare CEO commitment).

"Efficient R&D," one of the four keys, did appear in our study (recall Marion Laboratories), but not as often as other concepts not mentioned in the Hammermesh paper.

The one apparent contradiction between their case-oriented study and our combined methodology has already been highlighted: "eschew growth for growth's sake" and concentrate on profits. As suggested, this prescriptive call is no doubt appropriate for the great majority of mid-sized firms but probably not as appropriate for the best of the bunch (many of which will become tomorrow's large-sized firms).

Our results must be read as consistent with the fundamental PIMS conclusion that "businesses with a high share of their served markets are generally, and often considerably, more profitable than those with a low share."[14,15]

The PIMS group measures market share "relative to the 'served market,' i.e., the specific segment of the total potential market in which the business is making a serious competitive attempt, by offering a product or service that is suitable for that segment and by addressing its marketing effort to that segment."

Sidney Schoeffler, PIMS director, emphasizes that "this result is *not* a simple matter of large businesses earning greater profits than small businesses. Large businesses which have a small share of a large served market are generally *less* profitable than small businesses which have a large share of a much smaller served market. . . . What matters is not how large a frog you are, but how you rank in your particular pond."

There are two basic ways to achieve strong market position: Become large or segment your market. Whereas the former is the common stereotype, the latter is the most critical—a fact we found striking.

The importance of product dominance within company-defined market segments is established. Now we push further: How did these firms become dominant? Why does dominance lead to higher and more stable profits?

The first question—How dominance?—we address with our conceptual model, stressing four pathways that lead to dominance (Figures 10.1 to 10.3): From commitment to distinctiveness to coherence to dominance; from coherence and perceptiveness to progressiveness to dominance; from distinctiveness to dominance; and from relevance to dominance.

The second question—Why is dominance profitable?—has at least three answers.

1. *Economies of scale*, the power of high numbers, repetitive runs, and mass movement—in purchasing, production, distribution, financing, marketing, and a host of other business functions.
2. *The experience curve*, in which lower costs are achieved as a function of cumulative products produced (see note 4, Chapter 2).
3. *Bargaining power*, through which the high-share firm is not intimidated by competitors, suppliers, or customers, and thereby keeps more benefits from its higher efficiency, quality, or competence.[15]

The net result of dominance? Higher and more stable profits.

Writing in the early 1970s, Peter Drucker noted that "size by itself has major impact on strategy. And strategy, in turn, has major impact on size. The small organization can do things the large ones cannot do. Its simplicity and its small size should give it fast response, agility, and *the ability to focus its resources* [emphasis added]. But the large organization, in turn, also can do things the smaller organization cannot do. It can commit resources for a much longer time, for instance, to long-term research projects which are beyond the staying power of the small business. The question 'What strategies befit different sizes?' is thus of crucial importance to top management."[17]

So Drucker brings us back full circle to his original questions, "What is our business? And what should it be?" Only now the essence of the issue has become richer, more subtle and more profound, embedding contingencies of size, structure, industry, company focus, market position, corporate personality, and so on.

Understanding these factors, and exploiting them for organizational progress, is the core of creative management.

PRESCRIPTIONS

Having completed the journey and sporting some sense of how mid-sized firms travel, one braces for the inevitable questions set in the subjunctive mood: "If you were the CEO of XYZ medium-sized company, what would you recommend regarding . . . ?" "If you were chairman of ABC mid-sized firm, what strategies would you establish for . . . ?"

The questions are legitimate; after all, no one does strategy research solely for its own reward or beauty, the way one might, say, climb a mountain or paint a portrait. Strategic management research, to be worthy of its calling, ought to facilitate on-line corporate intervention.

Yet to the researcher, the aphorism often applies: "The More One Learns, the Less One is Sure." A little knowledge about a given subject can make one able, even confident, to proffer flip advice to all within earshot. A little more knowledge and one grows strangely silent.

They are a mixed bag, the firms of our study, a diverse lot. Few conclusions apply to all. Blithely constructing categories and classifying companies is to operate on thin margin indeed. One must keep ever mindful of "contingency theory," that branch of strategic management fated to falsify every generality.

CONTINGENT RECOMMENDATIONS

Following are some examples of contingency theory in action:

☐ Guerrillalike opportunism may be more efficient for weaker mid-sized firms and more effective in low-capital-intense industries.

☐ Customer orientation may be more effective in high-capital-intense industries and when quality, not price, is the prime strategy.

☐ High executive and employee satisfaction and fulfillment may be more important in low-capital-intense industries.

☐ High CEO profile may be more important in industries with one or more of the following characteristics: low technology, low capital intensity, soft goods, family controlled.

☐ Efficiency in research and development may be more important in high-technology industries.

☐ Consistency and focus may be more critical than flexibility and opportunism in a mature industry and vice versa in a rapid-growth industry.

☐ Vertical integration and high segmentation may each be more critical in a mature industry than in a rapid-growth industry.

☐ The "profits more important than growth" recommendation may be more applicable when the industry is mature and when the firm is not a top performer.

INDUSTRY CHARACTERISTICS

The most critical contingencies are often industry related. The economic nature of products and the industrial organization of markets are usually prime determinants of firm strategy and structure. Differences among industries, whether recognized or not, can swamp more subtle factors in strategic management.

Following are four kinds of industries in which small and medium-sized firms can more easily maintain competitive parity with their larger-sized rivals:

1. Industries that are regionally focused in either sales or production. Examples: contract construction, engineering design (low to medium technology), short-distance transportation, fast-service businesses (such as printing), high weight-to-price products (such as concrete and bottles), time-dependent products (such as fresh bread and milk).

2. Industries in which companies frequently change their models or products due to fashion or style shifts. Here small size can be an operational advantage, and larger firms must organize themselves into tight functioning units to compete efficiently. Examples: fashion apparel, ready-to-wear soft goods, spectacle frames, interior design products (such as furniture), other products susceptible to quick design change without advertising inducement.

3. Industries in which products are mass produced in quantities too small for large firms. Examples: specialized machine tools, high-tolerance parts, low-use specialty chemicals.

4. Industries in which firms manufacture products to meet custom specifications of individual buyers. Examples: job-shop operations in low technology (such as wood fabrication), medium technology (such as plastic fabrication) or high technology (such as electronic design); engineering draftsmanship; customized machine tools; repair and alteration shops.

STRATEGIC OPTIONS

Thus, the strategic manager is beset with a bewildering array of descriptive analysis and prescriptive advice. One can begin more confused than clear. The first steps in a simplifying process often proliferate more options and spin more convolutions than had existed before. Yet there is more "grouping" than "splitting" here, more convergence than divergence. Even with its complex and qualified conclusions, strategic management is an open window on a new world. Its directives offer clarity of thinking and focus of direction, especially when compared with the limitless possibilities engulfing the practicing executive of a modern company.[18]

Even the process of uncovering and enumerating strategic alternatives can catalyze cognitive breakthroughs for senior management. Such formalisms must not, to be sure, detract from executive experience and personal intuition; rather, the strategic insights should augment experience and enhance intuition. (For example, a CEO might balance the prescription to maintain company coherence with the imperative to innovate and create new products. For another, he might strive to achieve distinctiveness by segmenting his market through aggressive product differentiation, whether real or imagined, always keeping in mind that his own presence is a vital part of the picture.)

Let's get specific. We have made no small effort to describe and dissect critical success strategies of top-performing mid-sized firms. Can these creative concepts be applied practically, by real managers in real companies? Take a chief executive running a mediocre mid-sized firm—what value can he make of all this? The following are some models such a CEO might consider.

- ☐ Emphasize one particular technology, like Molex in electronic connectors or Keystone in flow controls, in order to dominate a market.

- ☐ Work intimately with end users, like Shaklee with vitamin buyers in their homes or Marion Laboratories with doctors in their offices, in order to cement long-term commitments.

- ☐ Limit the geographic borders of the marketing attack, like Dr. Pepper (used to) in the Southwest or Coors Beer (used to) in the West, in order to build and protect share.

- ☐ Develop a manufacturing strategy, like Tandon in disk drives or the Martinsville three in textiles (sweat shirts), in order to produce high quality at lowest cost.

- ☐ Focus on a particular customer, like Russell making active apparel for athletes or Plenum publishing technical books for scientists, in order to establish market reputation.

- ☐ Establish a distinct quality position, like A.T. Cross in pens or Neutrogena in soap, in order to maximize margins.

- ☐ Offer value to end users, good quality at reasonable prices— like La Quinta in motel rooms or Eagle Clothes in men's suits, in order to attract and maintain new customers.

- ☐ Have the dynamic leadership of an all-pervasive chief executive, like Charles Hurwitz in finance or Stephen Cannell in television, in order to achieve spectacular growth.

- ☐ Expand the product offerings of a well-respected brand name, like Noxell with Noxzema or Binney & Smith with Crayola.

- ☐ Develop public awareness in the local community, like MCO Holdings in real estate development or *Texas Business* as the state's only business monthly magazine, in order to take advantage of the unique franchise.

- ☐ Pound one strong product, like Goulds in pumps or Deluxe Check Printers in bank checks, in order to build market dominance.

☐ Develop a new product concept, like Trus-Joist in construction components or PharmaControl in drug delivery systems, in order to create a new market.

☐ Develop high brand recognition, like Maytag in washing machines or Bacardi in rum, in order to control the market.

☐ Produce numerous products serving the same audience, like Commerce Clearing House's publications for attorneys or Everest & Jennings' products for the handicapped, in order to expand business while keeping coherence.

☐ Zero in on one sector of a large industry, like Fort Howard in the industrial use of paper products or Tokheim in control equipment for gasoline service stations, in order to maintain focus on company competencies.

☐ Stress efficiency in areas where others spend lavishly, like Marion Laboratories in pharmaceutical licensing or J. L. Clark in metal can production, in order to cut costs and boost profits.

☐ Market one product for a variety of separate functions, like Great Lakes Chemical with brominated chemicals or Guilford Mills with warp knitting, in order to maintain coherence.

☐ Concentrate on market share for all products, like Hillenbrand in caskets, electric hospital beds, luggage, and locks or Simplicity Pattern in sewing patterns, in order to maximize profits.

☐ Encourage employee commitment, like Nucor in steel or Molex in electronics, in order to generate enthusiasm and maintain consistency.

☐ Develop new technologies for older industries, like Kennametal in industrial tools or Loctite in chemical adhesives, in order to refresh competitive advantage.

☐ Seek new opportunities aggressively, like MacDermid in chemicals or Ametek in solar energy, in order to generate new products and markets.

☐ Emphasize research and development, like Dynatech in high technology or Tyco in diversified products, in order to take advantage of strong central skills.

☐ Build dedicated, hard-working employees, like Nucor in steel and Goulds in pumps, in order to increase productivity.

With the generalized model available, and with specific examples given, the chief executive can choose to move his firm in multiple ways. He can enter the system with discretion and control, intervening actively and knowledgeably to bring about positive change. The model, of course, is only the vehicle; the executive, of necessity, must be the driver.

NEW VENTURE MODELING

Try something different. Can the strategic categories help structure a *new* company as well as improve an existing one? When the venture begins medium sized the application can be interesting.

Galram Technologies Industries Ltd. was formed by the Government of Israel to develop, produce, and market commercial applications of its military technology.[19] The company has access to the capabilities of "Rafael," Israel's largest research and engineering organization for sophisticated weapons development, as well as to existing Rafael technologies and products. No other company has such access.[20]

Rafael operates at the state-of-the-art in producing guided missiles, electronic warfare systems, and advanced armor. It has almost 7000 employees, one-third of whom are scientists and engineers. Its sales total several hundred million dollars a year. While Rafael's work remains largely secret, its technological excellence has been publicly evident in Israeli air-combat successes such as the destruction in Lebanon of a significant portion of the Soviet-built Syrian air force and missile defense system without the loss of one Israeli aircraft (1982).

Galram is located in the middle Galilee, near Haifa in northern Israel. It is intended that Galram become a private company, with outside investors owning 50 percent and the government owning 50 percent.[21] Its mission is the commercialization of defense-related technology, adapting military technologies and products for the civilian marketplace. Galram is designed to become a real business; as such the private structure is essential.

In operation since late 1982, Galram has set up divisions in electronics and electro-optics. It is establishing divisions in industrial automation and robotic systems, microelectronic components, and biomedical engineering. Galram has identified an extensive number of advanced projects, based on proprietary Rafael technology, that show promise of commercial success in the near-to-mid term.

Galram's electronics division has about 50 employees and will generate about $1.8 million in sales in 1984. The electro-optical division also has about 50 employees with a backorder of several million dollars. All orders are currently for the Israeli Defense Forces. Some products have fascinating potential, though not yet developed. For example, the electro-optical division produces a thermal imaging system that televises distant objects without the need for *any* external illumination. It is the ultimate for seeing in the dark. While the military applications are obvious (such as night vision and fire control systems), the civilian applications could be significant—such as naval navigation (coast guard); rescue missions (lost humans and animals); medical imaging; industrial (heat leakage detection, energy loss monitoring, diagnostics of electronic assemblies); and agriculture (crop disease detection, forest fire control).

Galram is traveling a new road. Marketing civilian buyers cannot be equated with supplying military services. The psychology of operations as well as the needs of customers differ radically.

Following are the strategic categories, and how each might help this innovative medium-sized firm to flourish.

Commitment.   All Galram and Rafael employees begin with extraordinarily high motivation. Their dedication is special. Once moving to the private sector, however, new forces are engaged. For example, appropriate mechanisms of compensation and reward must be considered.

Fulfillment.   Opportunities to develop leading edge technology are their own reward, amplifying dedication to defense of country. New necessities to promote commercial exports offer additional satisfaction.

Distinctiveness.   The Rafael relationship produces a unique company without close comparison. The mystique as well as the technology can produce business benefit.

Flexibility.   Rafael's extensive "knowledge centers" (several hundred) supply expertise in virtually every area of modern technology. Its scientists and engineers are used to rapid shifts in projects and priorities, and intense pressures to produce and provide are nothing new.

Coherence.   The focus on commercializing military technology creates strong cohesiveness. For example, biomedical engineering takes advantage of distinctive competencies in electronics, signal processing, tracking, communications, and so on (whereas genetic engineering—biochemistry—would not).

Clarity.   Galram has a precise purpose that must be followed. The danger of allowing exciting technology to outrun market needs must be recognized and resisted.

Dominance.   Every product should be defined by both technology and market to be foremost in its class (stressing the latter). Anything else, no matter how intriguing, should be avoided. Tight targeting is critical. Galram must only go where its comparative advantages generate competitive edge—and those advantages give real opportunity.

Perceptiveness.   Awareness of international market needs, current and future, is the key here. The temptation to equate technological capability with commercial necessity must be fought.

Progressiveness.   This is easy. Rafael provides world-class leadership in technology, driven by the most powerful possible motivation. Furthermore, there is strong impetus to build a substantial commercial company—for all the usual reasons and then others.

Relevance.   This is harder. Market demand must always come first. Distribution and service are critical. Galram should structure joint ventures with experienced marketing organizations in different products and in different countries.

Consistency.   Rafael provides stability, in technological capability and end-user requirements. It is a captive customer. By supplying some of Rafael's continuous manufacturing needs, Galram can amortize overheads, thereby offering similar products for civilian markets at competitive prices.

Efficiency.   This is a potential problem since quality control for military systems is far more critical and far more costly than for civilian products. Galram must articulate efficient manufacturing with financial optimization.

Galram is important for Israel. It is an interesting experiment in the design of medium-sized companies.

FROM STRATEGIC CATEGORIES TO CREATIVE STRATEGIES

We began the book by offering ten "Creative Strategies" for mid-sized success, principles we then used in describing corporate cases. Though presented at the outset, these pragmatic prescriptions are the work product of the entire effort. Each Creative Strategy was derived directly from the information considered throughout every chapter. The order of Creative Strategies is the order of importance, as determined by both numerical tests and perceptive impressions.[22]

Structured for managerial application, each Creative Strategy from Chapter 1 developed as the product of one (or more) specific strategic category(ies) from Chapters 6, 9, and 10. Tying together Creative Strategies and strategic categories ties together the entirety of the book. The lineup is presented in Table 10.4.

TABLE 10.4   Matching Creative Strategies and Strategic Categories[a]

Creative Strategy	Strategic Category
Dominance ⟷	Dominance
Product Emphasis ⟷	Coherence, Relevance
Distinctiveness/Uniqueness ⟷	Distinctiveness
Focus/Coherence ⟷	Coherence, Clarity
High-Profile CEO ⟷	Commitment
Employee Opportunity ⟷	Fulfillment
Efficient Innovation ⟷	Progressiveness, Efficiency
External Perception ⟷	Perceptiveness
Growth–Profits Tradeoff ⟷	Consistency
Flexibility/Opportunism ⟷	Flexibility

[a] Creative strategies are from Chapter 1 and are used to analyze corporate cases. Strategic categories are from Chapters 6, 9, and 10 and are the product of data and analysis.

CONCLUSION OF THE MATTER

This work had three objectives, one practical, one social, one methodological—all interweaving with exquisite richness. The *practical* objective was to understand why some medium-sized companies are successful, outperforming their industries' leaders. The *social* objective was to strengthen the collective position of medium-sized companies within the American economic system. The *methodological* objective was to develop the science and advance the art of strategic and creative management, combining case studies, analytical techniques, and conceptual models.

The broader bearing of the work, if one may be so bold, embraces the same three levels. First, at the microlevel of the firm, an individual medium-sized company can maximize strengths and minimize weaknesses by applying the appropriate strategies. Top management can engage the mechanisms of success by using the Creative Strategies, thereby activating the strategic categories. Such a formal framework, however, must only be used as a guide; there is no substitute for executive sense and managerial judgment.

Second, at the macro level of the socioeconomic system, improving mid-sized performance strengthens sector vitality and industrial robustness. Financial economics and organizational psychology bolster each other: Successful medium-sized companies augment executive commitment, enhance worker content, encourage entrepreneurial innovation, and stimulate marketplace competition. Vigorous medium-sized companies support functional pluralism and dynamic diversity, reinforcing our political philosophy; thus the concentration of corporate power can be resisted without the artificial intervention of legislative regulation and agency edict.

The third level on which we operate is the methodological, the design and structure of ways and means to discover concepts and confirm import. Truth is power. The elegant articulation between practice and theory is the cornerstone of both business triumph and research relevance. Strategic management, and creative and innovative management, are the new tools of a new world; they are the critical link between executive direction and corporate achievement, the functional bond between individual action and organizational success. When companies prosper everyone gains.[23]

We see high history here, the irresistible impetus of group dynamics expressing personal desire. No longer must we fear giants gobbling up dwarfs, with the inevitable demise of medium-sized firms. Though economies of scale favor industry mammoths, human factors are undermining the trend and turning it around.

Many creative and innovative people now seek smaller businesses, enterprises where they can feel the tangible results of their own handiwork. They want to touch closer to action, participate more intimately, work nearer the top. They demand meaning, relevance, impact—qualities more accessible in small and medium-sized companies.

We are witnessing a migration of human skill, a social shift of profound consequence. The pressure is inexorable, the direction clear. The power of larger firms will ebb, and the vitality of smaller firms flow. The natural force that builds organizations must also limit them. For the flourishing of human beings this is good.

PART TWO

CREATIVE STRATEGIES IN ACTION

Devising Creative Strategies

What to Do, How to Do It

Part Two is organized by Creative Strategy, one minichapter for each of the ten. The structure differs from Part One; the presentation here is not linear, the access is random—the reader can enter and exit at any point. The objective is exposure. We meet a large number of interesting medium-sized companies, situations set for strategic assessment and problems poised for creative solution. Although discussion of each firm is limited, we go right for the critical cause of success.

Each Creative Strategy minichapter is divided into two sections: the first presents problem companies needing strategic change and offers some possible solutions—we call this section "Issues and Ideas"; the second describes active companies exemplifying the creative strategy—we call this section "Current Cases." (Note that the problem companies in the first section are all constructed situations, they are not real; the active companies in the second section are actual cases, they are real.)

The reader is encouraged to devise alternative scenarios for each problem (the "Issue") before reading the suggested solution (the "Idea"). The prime point is to expand options, extend boundaries, break tradition. Experiment; be different; try the unusual. There are no "right" and "wrong" answers here; there are innumerable ideas (only one is given) and the reader's may well be better than the author's—if so, I am pleased.

Deciding where to classify firms was not an easy task. It's a rare business that depends on one Creative Strategy at the exclusion of others. Often the decision was made to include an interesting company, and then the best Creative Strategy was chosen in which to place it. (Problem companies are based on actual business situations, though all are disguised and some are composites.)

The reader, remember, can wander and wonder through the Creative Strategies. Skipping and scanning are permitted. Part Two is designed for browsing.

Many of the corporate cases to follow are derived from stories in *Forbes* and *Inc.* magazines; wherever one of these publications is cited, all quotes are taken from that source. If no reference is given, most of the information and quotes are taken directly from the companies' annual reports or derived through personal contact.

CREATIVE STRATEGY 1

DOMINANCE

Dominate Your Corporate Niche

ISSUES AND IDEAS*

Problems

The Wheeling Machinery Company had a strong share position (40%) in a small industrial product whose market had remained flat for five years. Company sales had drifted down to about $50 million, and profits had slid (1983 earnings, a scant $1 million, off from $7.5 million on $80 million in 1977)—the result of fierce competition among companies seeking to fill their partially empty plants. Wheeling now had excess facilities not being utilized. The company had not paid dividends in four years and had thus accumulated a cash position of $25 million, which it was keeping in short-term investments. Wheeling's board was asked to consider four alternatives: (1) a large dividend; (2) partial liquidation; (3) acquisition

* All cases in "Issues and Ideas," remember, are composed and composites; they are not actual companies.

of its second strongest competitor (a $30 million company with about 22% share); and (4) acquisition of a much larger distributor of machine parts ($110 million in sales). The competitor was earning $1 million per year and asking $17 million. The distributor was earning $3 million per year and asking $20 million.

State Monthly was a general-interest magazine located in a midwestern industrial state. The publication was struggling with low visibility and intense competition from two city magazines in the state's largest cities. *State Monthly* was trying to attract all readers by combining business, home, and entertainment oriented articles. Revenue falloff had prompted the owners to beef up the advertising department and cut back editorial. The state itself, with high unemployment, was prototypical of the American "Rust Belt" and had a low self-image. The new governor, however, had just begun a major initiative to attract contemporary industry.

Plum Semiconductor could not compete against industry leaders. Though at the leading edge of technology during the late 1970s, the company fell steadily behind thereafter due to the tremendous financial resources of competitors (many of whom were bought by large corporations). Sales kept constant at about $60 million for the past four years—a death knell in high tech. Profits plummeted and a first loss was sustained. With the stock price low, the huge amount of equity needed to remain in the game was out of reach. Only Plum's first-rate distribution system for its products was keeping them afloat. Management had been approached to handle the products of other companies, but had to put all discretionary resources into supporting the enormously expensive semiconductor operations.

The Westbrook Times was one of three daily newspapers in a city of less than 500,000; two were published in the morning and one in the afternoon (*The Times*). The three papers had about equal circulation—and all were losing money and sinking slowly. The three, however, were fiercely independent and highly competitive, and there was little chance of one buying another or any of the three leaving the market soon or gracefully.

Major Appliance Distributors was a wholesaler of household appliances and handled many leading brands. Its volume of $65 million was coupled with the low margins of the middleman in an industry characterized by severe price competition. There were constant threats of suppliers going directly to retailers, or retailers going to very large, out-of-state wholesalers.

Solutions

The Wheeling Machinery Company should consider purchasing its competitor even though the price is much higher in relationship to profits. Assuming no antitrust problems, the company would control almost two-thirds of the market and be in a position to exert market power—and attentuate the severe price competition. Furthermore, if facilities could be combined, the profit potential of the combination could be substantial. (Estimates could be as high as $6–$8 million per year.)

State Monthly should redirect its editorial thrust. It should shift away from general readership and establish a niche that it can dominate. By changing its focus to "State *Business*," the magazine can establish itself in the vanguard of the state's industrial resurgence. Indeed, it should take a leadership role in the revitalization process. The editorial thrust should show how business in the state can take advantage of the coming changes. The publication should make maximum effort to upgrade its editorial product before going after additional advertising.

Plum Semiconductor might consider a radical restructure of its business. It cannot compete in semiconductor design and manufacture, so why put effort into a losing cause? It should sell off the semiconductor business, getting a good price. (Best targets would be companies that either have a current semiconductor operation or want to buy their way into the industry quickly.) Plum should then concentrate resources and talents on its distribution business. An appropriate goal might be becoming the leading independent distributor for small companies at the forefront of their specialized technologies. Achieving strong market position in distribution is realistic; in semiconductors, hopeless. (In selling the semiconductor division, Plum should negotiate for a continuing—and guaranteed—distribution contract for a number of years, thus maintaining the base for building the new business.)

The Westbrook Times should consider merging with one of the morning papers. Neither would give up editorial independence, but overheads could be amortized and eliminated. The combination would then dominate the market (two-thirds), and thereby be able to offer special advertising and circulation advantages.

Major Appliance Distributors must take as strong a position in its region as possible; large volume is critical to compete against the national distributors. The company must add value to its products. It should stress local service and reliability. It could, for example, add an extra ninety days to the warranties; it could provide service contracts at low fees to help retailers move their products with end users. It could guarantee 48-hour delivery, giving an additional 5 percent off the price if they miss. The company must strengthen its business in the short run and build up a prominent position in the market—it can raise prices back up (e.g., for service) after establishing itself as the reliable resource and low-cost source.

CURRENT CASES*

Tokheim Corporation (Fort Wayne, Indiana) is America's largest domestic manufacturer of gasoline pumps/dispensers with a 34 percent market share (1983 revenues, $118 million; profits, $7.3 million). Tokheim is also the market leader in the next generation of highly automated electronic pumps and has established a joint venture to produce the subsequent (third) generation of credit card (or debit card) systems that works like automatic teller machines at banks. Thus the company is well positioned to take advantage of the increasing productivity push of major oil companies. In addition, the company makes other devices and systems for the movement and measurement of liquids—for example, the monitoring of self-service pumps, industrial fluid meters, and fuel pumps of multiple varieties. Tokheim is distinctive and coherent, both of which lead to dominance. Its sensitivity to future market needs keeps it out front.

* Current Cases, remember, are real; they are actual companies.

J. M. Smuckers Company (Orville, Ohio) is the nation's largest producer of jams, jellies, and preserves (1983 revenues, $200 million; profits, $12 million; return on equity, a consistent 15 percent). The company has a marvelous motto—"With a name like Smuckers, it has to be good." With little growth in its market, Smuckers needs an acquisition. (The industry is virtually flat, growing maybe 2 percent a year, and national competitors—Welch's and Borden's—and regional competitors—private labels—give hard fight.) "You know, we are having the hardest time finding a company to join us," admits Chairman Paul Smuckers, grandson of founder Jerome and father of President Tim (a family-controlled business, this; they own 30 percent of the stock and you can feel their commitment). Not finding that acquisition may not be all that bad. Smuckers has had some real bombs: forays into gourmet gifts, packaging, and pickles all had to be sold off. (Anything not in line with company coherence has not stuck, if you will, to the jams.) In its basic business Smuckers is strong. They run a tight ship—though sales have doubled over the last ten years, employees now number 15 percent less than a decade ago. On the marketing front the company is developing weak areas (such as the South where its share hovers at about 15 percent) and expanding strong areas (such as San Francisco where its 65+ percent share is encouraging the introduction of more exotic, higher-priced products). A recent acquisition of a line of gourmet jams and jellies, Dickinson Family, Inc., was a good fit—but hardly a ripple on top or bottom lines. How to diversify and expand without compromising the basic business? That's the issue here. Let's hope the emphasis remains on the latter. (*Forbes*, January 30, 1984.)

Computer Language Research, Inc. (Carrolton, Texas) processes income tax returns for high-bracket persons, 300,000 of them to be precise, an incredible 70 percent of the individual returns prepared by the nation's Big Eight accounting firms (1983 revenues, $85 million; profits, $8.5 million). With massive Amdahl and IBM mainframe computers, CLR provides the number-crunching service for an enormous share of the elite accountants in America. "We do 80 percent of our individual income tax work with CLR," said a tax and computer specialist at Arthur Young & Co. "We concluded that dollar for dollar, we get more and better service from CLR

than from its competitors. CLR is the Cadillac of the industry."
The stock market likes the company as well. At last glance it valued
the stock of the founding Winn family (85% of the company) some-
where in the quarter-billion-dollar range. The company is looking
ahead into electronic publishing (providing automatic text for-
matting), but it is hard to imagine ever equaling their superb market
position in tax processing. (*Forbes*, January 30, 1984.)

Angelica Corporation (St. Louis, Missouri) provides uniforms
to service industries and rents linens to health care operations
(1983 revenues, $220 million; profits, $15 million). When Les Loewe
became chief executive in 1980, the company had many years of
lukewarm performance (returns on equity of 11 percent, and returns
on sales of 4 percent). He knew what to do. He shut down every
division where Angelica didn't lead the market, such as disposable
products, unlabeled commodity textiles, and 160 retail stores. He
did the job. Angelica today has strong market position in two
growth industries. As services expand in the economy—hotels,
fast-foods, airlines, and so on—the need for uniforms follows suit.
On the linens side, Angelica markets laundered sheets, pillowcases,
and other such stuff to hospitals and health-oriented institutions.,
This is big business. (Health care is 61 percent of company business.)
Since Angelica can cut customer costs by 25 percent, expense-
conscious hospitals are ready buyers. Loewe credits a decentralized
management system for Angelica's profitability: "I might be able
to make a better decision than the guy in charge. But in 99 percent
of the time that won't be the case." Decentralization, he stresses,
has a critical spin-off—it frees senior management to plan and
strategize. As for future expansion, Loewe is considering using
his $26 million in cash to buy existing laundries or start new ones.
He's found a winning niche, and he's going for dominance. (*Forbes*,
February 13, 1984.)

Everest & Jennings (Los Angeles, California), family controlled,
manufactures medical rehabilitation products—wheelchairs,
stretchers, convalescent lounges, fracture equipment, and the like.
(Revenues in 1983 were $158 million; profits, $.3 million; 1982
revenues, $146 million; profits, $3.5 million—long prior history of
excellent returns.) The products are synergistic, the line coherent;
the mechanisms and markets consistent (low-to-moderate tech-

nology, mechanical devices, hospital oriented). The company pioneered (in the 1930s) simple, folding wheelchairs—and was so successful, and became so dominant, that antitrust action was initiated. More recent diversification efforts exploit central skills. With the strategic objective to "improve the quality of life for the handicapped," Everest & Jennings is currently developing innovative systems for various forms of disability (such as sophisticated, electronics-controlled prosthetic devices to aid paraplegics).

Chyron Corporation (Plainview, New York) is the leading manufacturer of digital titling and graphics equipment for television broadcasting stations and video production companies (1983 revenues, $16.9 million; profits, 4.3 million). The company's electronics graphics generators create graphic symbols which are stored and assembled by computers and displayed through home television sets and other video broadcasting equipment. The company's equipment is recognized as state-of-the-art, and the Chyron name is virtually a generic word in the industry. Note the primary lesson: You do not have to be large to dominate. The company also makes video cassette cleaners and evaluators.

Deluxe Check Printers (St. Paul, Minnesota) dominates the market for producing and marketing checks, deposit tickets, and related forms for financial institutions and their customers. The company has outgrown its prior classification as a top-performing mid-sized firm (1983 revenues, $620 million; profits, $77 million; ten-year average return on sales, 10.6 percent; return on equity, 25.8 percent—1974 revenues, $178 million). Deluxe is noted for its prompt, accurate, and dependable service, made possible by over sixty production plants throughout the United States. Yet there may be some problems brewing at this mid-sized graduate. Since 1977, the growth rate of orders for Deluxe checks has fallen from 9 percent to almost zero, while the national average has maintained a steady 6 percent increase. Has life as a giant become more cumbersome? Indications are that Deluxe has been losing market share to smaller, more aggressive competitors—truly mid-sized companies such as John H. Harland Company (which has maintained a 12 percent annual growth in units for the past five years), Rudco, and Rocky Mountain Bank Note. (Deluxe's share declined from 61 percent in 1979 to 54 percent in 1982; *Forbes*, May 23, 1983).

Clearly, the check printing industry is becoming more concentrated—from about fifty firms in 1972 to thirty-five in 1982, with experts expecting the number to drop further (perhaps to as low as five in five years). There are additional problems on the horizon, ones that will affect the entire industry. Forecasts of electronic transfer replacing checks are called "superficial" by the company, which believes "checks will continue to be the primary method of making payments for many years to come." Nonetheless, experts expect that automated teller machines will reduce the number of checks written for cash (this, however, is only 4 percent of the market). The big hit will come when debit cards replace checks for point-of-sale purchases, since 32 percent of personal checks are written directly to merchants. Deluxe must remain alert and aware. It is now committing itself to "expanding our business both within the context of checking account services as well as in new related areas"—for example, computer forms and direct-response products.

Applied Magnetics (Goleta, California) claims to be the world's largest manufacturer of magnetic heads for the computer industry (1983 revenues, $102 million, profits, $6.9 million; 1981 revenues, $67.6 million; profits, $16 million—a whopping 23.8 percent after-tax return on sales). The company designs, manufactures, and markets magnetic heads—the electromechanical interface used for reading and writing electronic data in tape, rigid-disk, and floppy disk drives. Its products are sold to original-equipment manufacturers in the peripheral memory segment of the computer industry. The growth of microcomputers puts Applied Magnetics in excellent strategic position. While there are over thirty companies in disk drive manufacturing (such as Tandon and Seagate), there are only three domestic independent volume manufacturers of recording heads—one of the most critical and expensive components in the disk drive. Extensive in-house manufacturing of recording heads is not anticipated among the disk drive makers due to difficulty in developing the recording head technology. Higher density and faster retrieval of stored information—the critical specifications—relate to the recording technology, and Applied Magnetics was the first independent to introduce the new-generation (thin-film) heads. The company is the second largest buyer of ferrite cores behind IBM and thus obtains the benefits of high-volume purchasing from low-cost Japanese suppliers. Its dominant market position gives it the power to maintain technological lead and high profits, while making it inefficient for customers to integrate backwards and "make" instead of "buy."

Tennant (Minneapolis, Minnesota) is the world's leading manufacturer of industrial floor maintenance equipment (recession-battered 1983 revenues, $107 million; profits, $6.4 million; ten-year 1972–1981 return on sales, 9.4 percent, return on equity, 21 percent). The company provides one specific product and markets it widely to diverse institutions and organizations—"Wherever work, play, travel, or public areas present a floor or other horizontal surface that needs cleaning or wear protection, Tennant Company products can be found." Tennant believes that the reason for its success lies in its "ability to exploit an attractive strategic position by expanding markets through new and improved products and increased marketing resources."

Warner Electric Brake & Clutch Company (South Beloit, Illinois) claims to be the largest supplier of industrial electric brakes and clutches, and the largest manufacturer of precision ball bearing screws for numerically controlled machines (1983 revenues, $165 million; profits, $7 million; ten-year return on sales, better than 6 percent). Its products coherent, its market diverse, Warner sells "to original equipment manufacturers, as well as manufacturing companies in many different industries for machinery updating and automation." Most important industries served include automobile air conditioning (21 percent), plant modernization (19 percent), machine tools (14 percent), and information processing (11 percent). Warner's step motors and electric clutches and brakes are critical components of such diverse products as air-conditioning compressors for Chrysler, floppy disk drives for Digital Equipment and Shugart Associates, and copiers for Xerox (Warner has some two-thirds of Xerox's business). The company has an excellent record of matching performance to plan, and despite the fact that the automobile business is a large part of sales, efficiency has led to consistency.

Carlisle Corporation (Cincinnatti, Ohio) is highly diversified—construction materials (rubber and plastics), recreational tires, aerospace, automotive, data communications, and general industry—and seeks predominance in each of its primary product areas (1983 revenues, $412 million; profits, $23 million; 1980–1982 return on sales, 7.5 percent). The company claims that it "has become the leader or has attained a major market position in sales in many of its products." The company emphasizes decentralized management: each division or subsidiary has full responsibility for its engineering, product development, manufacturing, marketing, and administration. One Carlisle objective is to "balance sales of aftermarket products with original equipment products." Carlisle, as a conglomerate, articulates a threefold financial goal: 20 percent annual earnings growth; 7 percent return on net sales; 20 percent return on invested capital. "Short- and long-term planning with heavy emphasis on objectives, strategy and implementation, is an integral part of the management philosophy. Planning is interwoven with day-to-day decision making; it is not a separate activity. Extensive planning coupled with timely reporting of results is one of the key means of maintaining control in the Company's decentralized organization."

Econolite Control Products (Anaheim, California) is the largest American manufacturer of traffic lights and controllers, marketing its products and systems to electrical contractors and state and local governments (1984 revenues, about $18 million; pretax profits, about 7-10 percent). Prior to 1978, the company was operated as a money-losing division of a larger corporation (Altec). When entrepreneur Steve Onderdonk and partner Michael Doyle bought Econolite (signing personally for all debts of the highly leveraged acquisition), major changes were made to this 50-year old sleeper: Employees were cut back from 225 to 170 (now built back to 200); intracompany mail, messages and messengers were drastically slashed ("in and out" baskets were eliminated, purchasers and schedulers were positioned with desks abutting); manufacturing space was consolidated (excess space was subleased at 50 percent more rent than the master lease); regional offices were established to provide local servicing; regional subassembly plants were set up to reduce transportation costs. Today the company is one of the few profitable firms in the industry. Econolite now controls some 75 percent of the business in the eleven Western states, with dominant positions claimed for other key regions such as Chicago and Baltimore. Concentrating in areas of strong market share is a central strategy. Tempting contracts from foreign countries are scrutinized. "My concern is not getting orders," says Onderdonk. "It's getting paid." Such commitment and concern, while present in firms in all sizes, comes a bit easier in small and medium-sized companies.

CREATIVE STRATEGY 2

PRODUCT EMPHASIS

Be Product Oriented

ISSUES AND IDEAS

Problems

Trylon Corporation was a diversified distributor of industrial components and had maintained an enviable record of 25 percent compound growth for almost a decade. Sales were over $230 million, but profits had fallen below 1 percent. Growth had been maintained through acquisition of smaller, almost entrepreneurial shops, and there were now twelve operating divisions—the organizational structure based largely on geography, not product. The company president used to boast that his company was so good "all we have to do is 'take orders.' " But competition had become tough; margins had to be cut drastically to prevent manufacturers from doing their own distribution—and the president no longer talked about "taking orders."

Friendly Software, Inc., hit it big with one best-selling program for the IBM personal computer. Sales went from $0 to $23 million in two years. Several other products were then introduced, but none ever approached the success of the initial program—which, with some updates, continued to sell well.

Sturgis and Wellon was a class publisher of general books with a scholarly skew. Sales oscillated between $4 million and $6 million for a decade, but profitability was dwindling (since real revenues, adjusted for inflation, were declining). Earnings from their superb engineering handbook series were growing, though dissipated by lengthy treatises on literary criticism (which always received critical acclaim). The company was public and some large stockholders were not pleased.

The Massachusetts Surgical Supply Company had an exceptionally strong balance sheet for a small company, and the firm used its financial strength to offer attractive terms to prospective customers. These sales incentives stressed payment ease and reliability of shipment, and Mass Surgical grew nicely from its founding in the early sixties. With a volume hovering at $30 million in the late seventies—its product line was old and stable—the company began to lose pace with the industry as competition in the medical supply business heated up. A heavy commitment to marketing—space advertising and new salesmen—made brief impact increasing sales but long impact decreasing profits.

Pure Sound, Inc., was a small American manufacturer of high-end stereo equipment, competing against the major Japanese companies that dominated the market. For years it produced good but not outstanding components, and had a small but loyal group of customers. Then, almost unexpectedly, came a design breakthrough. The sound quality of their new line was distinctly superior to anything in its price class, though the specifications somehow didn't reflect it. The reviews were great but sales were slow—the market, apparently, was skeptical.

Solutions

Trylon Corporation must add value to its products, not just distribute them. Only by creating added value can the company justify higher margins. Trylon should restructure itself by divisions along basic product lines. Proprietary elements or expertise should be developed for each area. For example, the company can offer extended service. Or it can upgrade its salesmen's technical and business knowledge so that they can work with customers in the use and planning of their products. Or it can expand its product line in specific targeted areas in order to offer customers the most comprehensive selection.

Friendly Software, Inc., began a book publishing division. The first books were all centered around the firm's popular software program for the IBM PC. Soft-covered and published rapidly, they taught users about the program and gave example applications. With the initial success, Friendly developed a strong reputation for publishing software-support books; they began receiving numerous proposals from outside authors that resulted in a broadening of the product line.

Sturgis and Wellon should stress its profit-making strengths. (By accepting public money, a company has this obligation—any intellectual or social goals, however laudatory, should be pursued through other organizations.) The company should focus its efforts on its best products—engineering and technology. It should invest in engineering and technological publications—monographs, series, handbooks. It should develop international markets for these same products (where American expertise is recognized). Even a name change (e.g., Technology Reference International) should be considered.

The Massachusetts Surgical Supply Company must use its financial resources to develop its product base. The medical support industry is relatively price inelastic; product performance is what counts here. The company must expand technological awareness in order to create new product demand. Its current offerings are simply outdated and tired—a terrible image in health care. The company must reshape customer perception of its products. Even the aesthetic design of products is critical, giving the form of leading-edge technology, if not the substance.

Pure Sound, Inc., had to find a way to get customers to listen to its components. Quality and reliability were characteristics the market understood. A warranty of ten years was established—longest in its class. The fact of the warranty itself bolstered confidence, inducing people to at least give a listen. The sound sold itself. People bought the equipment and the company's reputation spread.

CURRENT CASES

Bacardi Corporation (San Juan, Puerto Rico) is a one-product company founded on the branded reputation of its famous rum (1983 revenues, $175 million, not including excise taxes; profits, $59 million; five-year average return on sales, an incredible 32%). "Behind the Bacardi name is a reputation for producing the world's finest rum, a great rum carefully nurtured and mellowed with age." In less than ten years Bacardi has grown from Number 10 on the list of Best Selling Brands of distilled spirits to Number 1—a prediction made by the company some years ago and recently fulfilled. Bacardi is the purest form of product emphasis, and its dominance is derived directly from this coherence.

The Maytag Company (Newton, Iowa) has established powerful strategic position by manufacturing and marketing household appliances with the highest perceived quality in its categories—primarily washing machines, dryers, and dishwashers (1983 revenues, $597 million; profits, $61 million; return on sales 1978–1980, 11.3 percent; return on equity 1978–1980, 23.7 percent). Product perception is all-important. Maytag sells its appliances at premium prices to customers willing to pay extra for quality, reliability, performance, dependability, and service. Supporting this strategy is the entire company effort, internally consistent from R&D to advertising. Maytag does not introduce a new product unless it is demonstrably superior to competition and previous products. Maytag's marketing strategy is matched to its product strategy. The company has worked to establish a network of independent dealers who are offered high profit margins to establish long-lasting relationships—relationships critical to support Maytag's ultimate household customers. Located in a small Iowa town and paying its workers highest compensation in the appliance industry, Maytag's strategy is coherent through all phases. Recently Maytag made some major moves: the acquisition of the Hardwick Stove Company, which has begun manufacturing a complete line of Maytag brand cooking products such as ranges and microwave ovens; the acquisition of the Jenn-Air Corporation, which sells appliances to the home construction and remodeling industries; and the agreement with Montgomery Ward to sell Maytag appliances in their major-market stores. While the moves seem appropriate, Maytag will have to take special care to protect its essential character. As product lines broaden, as appliances are manufactured at remote locations, subtle shifts can creep in—basic image can suffer and a winning game can change.

Spiegel, Inc. (Oak Brook, Illinois) is the nation's fourth largest catalog company (1983 revenues, $612 million; profits, $12.3 million). When CEO Henry Johnson took over in 1977, Spiegel was losing price-conscious customers to discounters like K Mart. A repositioning was what the doctor ordered. Out went the cheap polyesters and give-aways on daytime TV game shows. In came a glossy, high-fashion catalog packed with clothing and home furnishings designed by well-known names such as Liz Claiborne and Pierre Cardin. Specialty catalogs were also begun, twelve per year, featuring upscale items such as lingerie, gourmet cooking, and furs. The mail-order business has grown dramatically, twice as fast as retailing, and Spiegel will have to continue segmenting the market to compete. The trend is encouraging. (*Forbes*, July 4, 1984.)

La-Z-Boy Chair Company (Monroe, Michigan) is the leading producer of reclining chairs in the United States (1984 revenues, $255 million; profits, $23 million; average nine-year profit growth, 21 percent). In addition to its 10,000 accounts, La-Z-Boy supplies its full line to 200 independently owned La-Z-Boy Showcase Shoppes—sleep sofas, swivel rockers, stationary sofas. The company is founded on the twin pillars of personal commitment and product emphasis. Family controlled and managed, La-Z-Boy radiates pride: "Born in the year of the Great Depression of 1929, La-Z-Boy has come to epitomize one of the most unique success stories of the American free enterprise system. We pledge to maintain that tradition." Great individual fulfillment is evinced by senior management. The distinctiveness of the "world-famous Reclina-Rocker chair set the pace for the development of the motion chair, challenging all other facets of the furniture industry." La-Z-Boy boasts that "our sales force is the most formidable in the furniture market place" and that "year after year new products have been introduced and our sphere of influence continues to expand." The company enjoys relative isolation from recession—when customers cannot afford to decorate an entire room, they often settle for a comfortable chair. La-Z-Boy does not sell on price; the company cuts its own swath. Although there are many cheaper recliners on the market—a Reclina-Rocker can top $800—La-Z-Boy offers customers an incredible 50,000 style and fabric combinations.

Commerce Clearing House (Chicago, Illinois) is a leading publisher of current information primarily in the fields of tax and business law (1983 revenues, $379 million; profits, $25 million). Its principal publications are in the form of loose-leaf news reports, which are offered on an annual subscription basis. Each series of reports, available selectively, is devoted to subject matter within a special class; for example, federal income taxes, federal estate and gift taxes, state taxes, trade regulation, labor law, securities law, and so on. The company's coherence is "market pulled" rather than "product pushed," serving the changing needs of attorneys and accountants. Other businesses serving this same market include Corporate Services (from statutory representation to clerical assistance) and Computer Processing Services (income tax returns). Considering the high professional level of its customer base, product output is far more important than company image: CCH must maintain a dignified, even staid public posture.

Worthington Industries, Inc. (Columbus, Ohio) is a leading manufacturer of metal and plastic products, using its longtime position as one of the country's top-performing mid-sized firms to elevate it into the *Fortune* 500 (1983 revenues, $450 million; profits, $20 million; 1975 revenues, $91 million; five-year return on equity, 1975–1979, 30.4 percent; Worthington's ten-year, 1972–1982, total return to investors—share price appreciation plus dividends— was fifth highest on the *Fortune* 500). The company claims to have become the largest in "intermediate steel processing" by filling a distinct "gap" in the market, stressing flat-rolled steel and short lead times. Worthington built its reputation for quality and service leadership in its original and largest operation, close-tolerance processed steel. Customer acceptance rate is over 99 percent, unmatched in an industry where the average rejection rate is about 4 percent. Worthington is also the recognized leader in low-pressure cylinders, manufactured to strict standards. Its pipe fittings division offers a unique quantity unit buying program that simplifies ordering procedures and allows a customer to combine orders for a variety of products and receive quantity pricing. Salespeople receive up to six months of in-plant work experience in all phases of operations, including production, scheduling, shipping, and technical services. This rigorous training enables sales personnel to fix accurate delivery schedules and to assist customers in determining their material needs for new products and services. Worthington claims to be carrying its reputation into other fields as diversification brings entry into new businesses (customized plastics and coated glass). Worthington, however, is now playing a new game, whether the same strategies apply remains to be seen (and first results, though the economy was weak, show financial returns sliding).

Dryer's Grand Ice Cream (Oakland, California) manufactures high-quality ice cream and markets it in nineteen Western and Midwestern states. Dryer's uses a high-price strategy, selling its ice cream about 25 percent above the rest of the brand names found in supermarkets. Chairman T. Gary Rodgers explains: "It is frightening to take this to its logical conclusion but, up until this point, a price hike has never hurt us and often sales have picked up as a result." Nothing like customer perceptions to turn miracles. (*Forbes*, November 7, 1984.)

Hogan Systems, Inc., (Dallas, Texas) designs and markets complete software systems for banks (1983 revenues, $17.1 million; profits, $3.7 million; earnings increasing 43 percent per year; stock market multiples well exceed industry averages). Its greatest strength is its product, which is well matched to the current needs of banks beset by changing technologies and having new business opportunities for enhanced computer services. Hogan's off-the-shelf software packages are both comprehensive and flexible, the former to take care of standard financial procedures, the latter to allow individual banks to satisfy special needs. Hogan's software may cost 50 percent less than a customized system. Comprehensive programs handle all critical bank functions: deposit processing, from simple cash transactions to the opening of IRA accounts; loan processing, from commercial to consumer to mortgage; electronic teller control; bank record preparation, enabling a complete customer history to be compiled (useful for offering new services to current or past customers). "Hogan has no real competition, its management is talented and its product is top-flight," commented a Prudential-Bache analyst. "What more could you want?" Some eighty-five banks had laid out between $100,000 and $350,000 for some 220 systems by the middle of 1983. Hogan's objective is to market its entire five-part package, at a cool $1.6 million. About 25 percent of customers have bought the whole hog (while many of the rest are trying a bite to see how it tastes). Hogan sees its market as financial institutions with more than $750 million in assets. That means about 400 potential customers in the United States, and another 400 abroad. (Hogan has sold systems in Australia and has opened an office in London.) As to the threat of market saturation, Richard Streller, Hogan's conservative-sounding president, believes that "changing technology alone will keep us in business. And don't forget, we have no direct competition." (Distinctiveness, progressiveness, and relevance here; each leads to dominance.) Streller is quick to react to potential problems, solving them before they become serious. He acts fast to support staff, adding personnel to overburdened areas—especially sales and customer support. He is giving his people excellent opportunity— he must be, since his turnover is abnormally low in an industry where it is normally high. ("We've lost no one we didn't want to lose.") Instilling confidence is critical, and having the right image is important. "The look is intentional," states Streller. "Our customers are the biggest banks and thrifts in the country. We can't afford to look like a bunch of guys working out of a garage in Silicon Valley." (*Forbes*, August 29, 1983.)

Leslie Fay (New York City) produces fashion-oriented women's apparel at popular prices (taken private in a highly successful leveraged buyout—revenues, several hundred million dollars; highly profitable.). The company's marketing efforts focus on the retail level with the use of special events, such as in-store fashion shows. Leslie Fay's strategy is to become a "prime resource in virtually every major department and specialty store across the country" and "a major resource in virtually every merchandising category in which we are now represented."

Pacific Lumber (San Francisco, California) manufactures forest products and cutting and welding equipment (1983 revenues, $240 million; profits, $28.4 million; 1979–1981 return on sales, 16.6 percent). This San Francisco-based company derives 26 percent of its revenues from timber—redwoods, fir lumber, and logs—and more important, 51 percent of its profits. Cutting and welding equipment generate 67 percent of revenues and 39 percent of profits. Pacific Lumber combines focused geography, customer sensitivity, and product quality to outperform larger rivals.

Ultralight Products (Temecula, California) is the leading producer of hang gliders in the United States and is developing a state-of-the-art ultralight aircraft (1983 revenues, $1 million; losses caused by R&D funding). Ultralight ("UP") was founded over a decade ago by Peter Brock, an internationally known automotive designer and racer who has numerous innovations to his credit. Product performance is virtually an obsession, and he attracts other inventive types to help share (and create) his dreams. Brock's business partner is Stan Polley, an investor-entrepreneur from the entertainment industry. UP pioneered the hang gliding industry, with sales topping $2 million at its peak. Today the company believes that its ultralight aircraft (weighing less than 250 pounds) has major commercial potential. The plane (the "Arrow", costing about $7500-$8000 in kit form) was designed by top aeronautical engineers and is at the leading edge of technology. UP claims that the Arrow can outclimb, outhandle and outfly every other ultralight and many general aviation planes (costing ten times as much). Polley-Brock envisions a large market for this pathbreaking aircraft, both recreational and commercial in the U.S. (such as agricultural spraying and utility line inspection), and commercial in foreign countries (oil pipeline inspection); military applications (such as anti-guerrilla defense and clandestine activities) are also being considered.

CREATIVE STRATEGY 3

DISTINCTIVENESS/UNIQUENESS

Be Different

ISSUES AND IDEAS

Problems

The United Commodity Company was a medium-sized trader of two important commodities, maintaining 5–8 percent of the world market estimated at $6 billion annually. Its three major competitors controlled 55 percent of the market, the remainder being split among dozens of smaller trading houses and individual entrepreneurs. The company bought its commodities in the United States and South America and served Europe, Africa, and the Middle East. United's expertise stressed the bagging and loading of the two commodities, and its special facilities in Europe were the most efficient in the world. But when a major market opened in the Far East, it seemed as though United couldn't compete. The president noted that "although we can buy our commodities almost as cheaply as our American competitors, we cannot compete on shipping costs. There is no way we can buy in America, ship to Europe for bagging, and then reship to Asia. I guess we'll have to pass."

EuroDesign Fashions had annual sales over $200 million in women's wear, largely derived through its catalog sales, which were published regularly (bimonthly) in magnificent magazine format. The company was extremely profitable in its early years, but growth and profits had slowed recently. The company had a large cash position and was seeking new areas for entry. The EuroDesign name was well respected in the middle price ranges.

The High Fashion Dress Company had a long history of profitable sales between $120 and $160 million. It had a well-known name in the upper price range with a reputation for consistent quality and good value. Though the company was merchandising in all areas of women's wear—not just dresses—the business was stagnating. The High Fashion name was magic, though the upper price ranges seemed to have been saturated. After much study it was decided not to introduce a lower-priced line of "High Fashion" merchandise—"trading down" was not advised. The company brought out another name for its more popular priced products, but the line received a lukewarm reception.

Organic Health was the largest regional producer of health foods in the south central states. It generated volume over $30 million per year and its profitability was good. Customers were loyal, but growth had slowed after several years of increase. Management decided to "go national," projecting some $100 million within four years.

Solutions

The United Commodity Company should take advantage of its distinctiveness—most efficient bagging facilities and European location. Some large ships delivering manufactured goods to Europe from Asia (Japan, China, Korea) were returning to home ports partially empty. A marginal cost analysis showed that by filling those ships with their commodities, United could become competitive—but only in a complex three-way transaction among the shipping companies, the potential purchasers, and themselves. Their efficient facilities could fill those ships much faster than anywhere else, thus saving substantial costs in ship downtime.

EuroDesign Fashions has two interesting options, in addition to a general acquisition program. It can consider turning its magazine into a specialty publishing business—advertising other manufacturers' products and even charging a subscription/cover price. (There are difficulties here—large circulation "freebees" do not a magazine make.) More likely, the company should look for acquisitions whose products could comfortably come under the EuroDesign umbrella—using the name and being featured in the catalogs. For such products the company could even afford to outbid other potential buyers, since it would be able to generate greater operating leverage.

The High Fashion Dress Company might consider capitalizing on its superb name by opening up retail stores. The product lines to be carried—from all top-level designers and manufacturers—would have to maintain the high standards demanded by the brand name. Stores could be opened in key areas—New York, Beverly Hills, Boca Raton, Las Vegas, Palm Springs, Paris, and so on—building the image and cachet. Structured right and promoted properly, the retail business would provide excellent support for High Fashion's manufactured products.

Organic Health's first season "going national" was an unmitigated disaster. The losses incurred wiped out two years of prior profits. The company learned that there is a substantial difference between regional and national companies. Success in one strategic group is no guarantee for success in another, even though the industry may, at first glance, seem the same. Organic Health should rather capitalize on its excellent name in its own area by expanding its product line locally. The company's loyal customers would be a ready market. Some extensions beyond the traditional health foods should be tried—perhaps dairy products, poultry, frozen foods, and so on—but each must maintain the distinctiveness of "Organic Health."

CURRENT CASES

GTS Corporation (Houston, Texas) collects and processes old data for seismic analysis (1983 revenues, $12.4 million; profits, $1.9 million; return on equity, averaging 28 percent). How has GTS been so successful? Before we tell you, consider its liabilities: first, its $12 million in revenues aren't a tenth of a percent of the $19 billion oil exploration business; second, the whole industry has been depressed. How then the success? A very tight market segment, distinctive and relevant—producing a near monopoly (i.e., dominance). Seismic analysis is the process of sending shock waves into the ground and recording the response, the assessment of which yields clues as to the location of oil and gas deposits. Today, all seismic data is recorded on magnetic tape, so it can be stored and processed easily. But it wasn't always that way, and here's where GTS gets busy. GTS collects the back *paper* records of seismic readings. There is an enormous amount of these records around, stuffed in dank drawers and lying on dusty shelves—data representing some 4 million linear miles of earth. GTS has been cornering the market for this paper tape. It already owns or has rights to half, and is adding paper for 800,000 miles every year. Though some of the seismic responses may be as old as fifty years, in the words of Chairman Phillip Work, "Rocks don't move." For an oil company to prepare a new seismic analysis, it can cost $5000 a mile. To buy GTS's reprocessed geophysical readings, the company can save $4900. (Cost is as little as $100 a mile.) GTS's proprietary technology converts lines on paper to bits in a computer, and with software alchemy turns old graphs into seismic gold—modern analytical cross sections of oil and gas ground. CEO Work had come to GTS to save it from another brainstorm of the original inventors, a process that worked but wasn't wanted. GTS was languishing. But Work is a big thinker ("It takes the same effort to sell something for $5,000 as it does for $500,000."), and when informed one bright day that the company was about ready to burn thousands of miles of useless paper tapes abandoned in a warehouse, he said, "Stop!" (*Forbes*, February 13, 1984.)

International Flavors & Fragrances (New York City) is a leading creator and manufacturer of essences used by other manufacturers to impart or improve flavor or fragrances of a wide variety of consumer products (1983 revenues, $461 million; profits, $68 million; five-year average return on equity, 21 percent; return on sales, about 14 percent). "Our business," proclaims IFF, "is serving two of the five senses—taste and smell." Stress is placed on constant improvements of the "stability, quality, safety, shelf life and performance of our products." R&D expenditures are very high, and the realization is clear that these investments "take a long time to pay off." Long-term thinking is of paramount importance: "Apart from other benefits, our R&D program helps to insure our access to an adequate supply of flavor and fragrance materials at a time when supplies of traditional natural materials are becoming more expensive, and in some cases, more limited, because of weather changes, rising labor costs and ecological concerns." Leadership in the field is also said to result from "our worldwide investment in production facilities and in trained people." IFF's CEO chides the competition, "There are too many chickens out there, too many 'me-toos.' " Corporate emphasis on quality and learning is exemplified by their sponsorship of public television programs on art and knowledge.

Spectrum Control, Inc. (Erie, Pennsylvania) designs and manufactures filters for controlling the electronic noise emitted by microprocessors (1983 revenues, $16 million; profits, $1.7 million; five-year return on equity, 29 percent). With the explosion of microprocessors—found not only in personal computer and video games but increasingly in appliances and electric devices of all kinds—background emissions are becoming a problem. (The inadvertent emission of random radio frequencies can cause unexpected interference of electronic communications.) The potential problem has become so serious that the Federal Communications Commission has ruled recently that machines using microprocessors must comply with an emission standard for radio frequencies in order to contain this new kind of pollution. This environmental "threat" to most electronic manufacturers is an environmental "opportunity" to Spectrum Control (see Chapter 7 for a discussion of opportunities and threats). The company has become a pioneer in making filters for controlling electronic pollution; it is also in the business of testing products with microprocessors to determine radiofrequency emission levels for manufacturers. (*Forbes*, November 7, 1983.)

Crown Books (Landoor, Maryland) operates 150 discount bookstores (1984 revenues, $91 million; profits, $4.9 million—an increase of 49 percent and 113 percent respectively over fiscal 1983). Its slogan tells book lovers they will "never have to pay full price again," and the company is eagerly taking market share from the two giants of the business, B. Dalton Bookseller and Waldenbooks (not to mention the small independents). While most bookstores are always running some sort of sales, rarely can you buy a current bestseller at anything other than list price. At Crown, bestsellers are discounted 35 percent, and the entire stock from 10 to 50 percent. How can they afford to take lower markups? Rent, for one thing. You'll never find a Crown bookstore in a glittering mall, hardly ever near a B. Dalton or Waldenbooks. Want a discount Crown book? Check out their low-cost strip center units, near supermarkets and drugstores. Store designs are standardized and clustered for efficiency in distribution and advertising (e.g., fifty-five outlets in Los Angeles, thirty-five in the D.C. area, twenty-five in Chicago). [Compare Eagle/April-Marcus stores for off-price menswear; the similarities are strong—see Chapter 5.] One critic claims that Crown "isn't interested in important books that last. It's interested in the bottom line." (Though one must respect the importance of "books that last," interest in the bottom line is the only way to make sure that the bookstore itself "lasts.") Crown recently raised $60 million in a public offering with which it intends doubling in two years. One competitive advantage that must be mentioned: Crown's CEO, Robert Haft, is the son of the founder of Dart Drugs, which, together with Thrifty Drugs (both West Coast based), owns about two-thirds of the company. Though the drug chains have provided help in financing and location selection, Haft insists that it's Crown's strategic position that makes the difference. (And don't forget commitment, distinctiveness, and coherence). (*Forbes*, January 16, 1984.)

LyphoMed (Chicago, Illinois) is a highly specialized, highly successful drug company that manufactures and markets supplemental nutrients for intravenous feeding of hospital patients (1983 revenues, $19 million; profits, $2 million). Patients being fed intravenously for long periods of time require more than sugar-and-water solutions. They need proteins, carbohydrates and fats—these primary elements constitute a large market and generate big bucks, and the major pharmaceutical houses compete to provide them. No mid-sized terrain here. LyphoMed, on the other hand, attacked where the enemy retreated (or ignored); they went after the supplementary nutrients—the abandoned territory—the electrolytes, vitamins, and trace elements (e.g., zinc). In the beginning not all hospitals saw the need for these supplements, and there was no prime source of their supply. That's the niche that LyphoMed went after, hitting it with full power. In a brilliant marketing move, they gave their supplements the clever name "micronutrients"—creating, in essence, a generic name for their proprietary product. Sales, today, are made both through medical distributors and directly to hospitals. LyphoMed's chief executive is Bombay-born John Kapoor, a Ph.D. in medicinal chemistry. He purchased LyphoMed from the Stone Container Corporation, which had sought diversification in the company (its original business was freeze-dried drugs). The $75,000 they were losing every month, however, was not the kind of diversification Stone needed. (Kapoor comments in retrospect that it was a case of "a big company getting into a business it didn't know anything about.") LyphoMed's remarkable turnaround was entirely the result of targeting a market considered too small for the major drug companies to bother with. (On analysis with the model, several paths lead to dominance: Perceptiveness to progressiveness to dominance; relevance to dominance; distinctiveness to coherence to dominance.) As more hospitals recognize the need for micronutrients, the market will grow—estimated at 25 percent annually (Kapoor estimates worldwide sales at $85 million in 1984, swelling to $220 million in 1990). Might such growth attract The Majors? "We don't think those numbers are big enough for any of those companies to make a commitment," says Kapoor, possibly with more hope than confidence. His perceptions may be somewhat affected by the $25 million worth of LyphoMed stock he holds, the result of a recent public offering—not a bad return for the $24,000 he scraped together to seed the purchase ("as much cash as I could raise without taking out a second mortgage on my house"). LyphoMed's strategy of niche identification and dominance is somewhat contradicted by a recent acquisition of a home nursing service for the critically ill. In going after home health care, Kapoor is now seeking a minuscule piece of what will become a huge market. He hopes to identify an isolated segment. He'd better. (*Forbes*, February 27, 1984.)

Scan-Tron Corporation (Long Beach, California) manufactures preprinted test forms and the machines to read and score the answers (1983 revenues, $11 million; profits, $1.4 million; fiscal

1984 should generate higher revenues and a return on sales approaching 15 percent). In 1983 Scan-Tron machines processed over 175 million tests. (The machine is an optical mark reader, and it uses fiber optics technology to scan pencil marks; it then tabulates right and wrong answers and prints the score—at forty a minute.) The key to success, however, is not blazing high tech—just common sense marketing. Give away the razor, is the familiar marketing aphorism, if you keep selling those razor blades. Scan-Tron's got the technique down pat. It will place its machines in schools at no cost, provided that the institution is large enough to consume huge numbers of tests. A high markup is maintained on the forms in order to cover the cost of initial equipment and continuing maintenance. It is an interesting strategy on several levels (as distinctiveness, coherence, and relevance lead to dominance). It is difficult for local schools to spend big bucks on capital purchases; furthermore, the buy decisions are often at the district level. But procuring the test forms is much easier (even if the eventual dollars are more, the allocation is spread out). "Test forms can be bought from funds that come right to the local school," notes William Sanders, Scan-Tron's chairman and founder. "It's like a big petty cash fund." Timing is also good. As school boards look for ways to reduce budgets, the pupil–teacher ratio usually goes up—which increases the need for higher productivity, hence internal pressure for automation of test grading. "Counting marks on a piece of paper comes close to idiot work," begins Sanders' dollars-and-sense pitch. "Paying professional people to do that is a waste of money." Who does the best selling? Who else but teachers? Scan-Tron hires ex-teachers who want to maintain relationships with education—but who also want to double or triple their salaries. (Nothing wrong with that.) Any worry about major firm competition? Scan-Tron, according to Sanders, controls a nice niche, but not "really sexy enough for the big boys." Sanders stresses his primary market (82 percent in education), but sees broader vistas— hospitals, governmental agencies, major companies. "As computers proliferate, the way in which you enter the data into those computers becomes tremendously important. We're only limited by our imagination." Just so long as that imagination doesn't forget home base. (*Forbes*, January 16, 1984.)

Heaven Hill Distilleries (Bardstown, Kentucky) manufactures and markets some 200 local and private brands of bourbon (1983 revenues, $85 million; profits, healthy—family controlled). Primary brands are Evan Williams (growing at 20 percent per year and accounting for 40% of the company's bourbon volume); Heaven Hill (strong in Kentucky and surroundings); and a host of other private-label brands for diverse customers from Safeway (Old Calhoun) to Harvard (Harvard Gentlemen). In an industry down more than 10 percent from its 1972 peak, Heaven Hill is growing at a "double-digit" rate, according to CEO Max Shapira, the Harvard MBA son of one of the five brothers who founded the firm after Prohibition ended. The prime reason for Heaven Hill's success? The company's innovative distribution system. Heaven Hill sells its bourbon whisky in bulk to over 200 distributors across the country, then bottles and ages it for them *prior* to shipping. The cost to the distributors averages about $1 million; and remember, they are paying the hard cash long before they receive the hard whisky. What a way to finance inventories, or more to the point, what a way to *minimize* inventories! The distributors, for their part of the tradeoff, can control more of the process—determining proof, length of time for aging, and method of marketing (some stress radio, others newspapers, still others point-of-sale). The distributors, then, are virtual partners with Heaven Hill, each one an entrepreneur, each one expert in his given geographic area. "The key to this business," states Shapira, "is knowing what's going on, not nationwide, but in individual states and even cities." (*Forbes*, July 4, 1983.)

Timberland (Newmarket, New Hampshire) manufactures durable work boots (1983 revenues, about $70 million; pretax profits, $9–$10 million). Beginning corporate life as struggling makers of men's shoes (Abington Shoe), the Swartz brothers (sons of founder Nathan) came upon an insulated and waterproof boot made in Canada. They improved it by injection molding (chemical bonding instead of stitching), using high-quality materials developed by Goodyear to create exceptional durability. The first Timberland boots, all 5000 of them, were sold in 1974. Chic stores such as Bloomingdale's, Bergdorf Goodman, and Saks put in their orders. In 1983, 1.8 million pairs retailed at $70–$80 a pop. The company has moved to take advantage of its brand identification by bringing out lines of boat shoes and hand-sewn moccasins. (Unit sales of both will match Timberland's Big Boot.) The Swartz brothers credit Len Kanzer, a Boston ad man, for convincing them to make the boot a fashion item—stressing its distinctiveness. So the company that used to sell unlabeled shoes to Army and Navy stores was suddenly advertising in the *New Yorker* magazine—betting the company and winning the pot. No denying that distinctiveness, clearly causative of niche dominance. (*Forbes*, April 25, 1984.)

Analog Devices (Norwood, Massachusetts) manufactures interface equipment straddling the fence between analog and digital equipment (1983 revenues, $214 million; profits, $18 million). There is continued need for analog (or continuous scale) devices in a world gone digital (data in discrete bits). It is easier for the brain to sense movement in a needle progressing along a scale (analog) than in numbers changing on a LED readout (digital). Airplane pilots, as an example, have dozens of instruments they must keep track of constantly. Change is critical and reaction time even more so; the eye catches movement of a needle faster than the shift of a number—hence the need for analog scales. Communication between analog machine sensors and digital computers also requires company interfaces. Specialization is efficient, states Analog's CEO, in a period of rapid technology advance. But as pace slows, vertical integration becomes important. Analog has big ideas; plans call for $800 million in revenues in the not-too-distant future, encompassing the manufacturing of complete systems— robotic controllers, vision systems, and perhaps entire robots. "If we don't do it now," reasons the CEO, "the large systems house will pull the stuff we produce for them in-house." The best defense, as they say, is the best offense.

Kaufman/Astoria Studios (Astoria, New York—in Queens, just across the 59th street bridge from Manhattan) operates the largest motion picture studio in the U.S. outside California. The company owns or operates 13 acres encompassing numerous stages and facilities for producing everything from major motion pictures to television commercials, from video cassettes to music recording. The studio is the brainchild of George Kaufman, a major real estate developer, who has a vision still grander. He foresees an ultra-sophisticated complex of production companies, electronic tele-communications capabilities, satellite linkages, and studio tours — all maximizing the growing media importance and entertainment opportunity in New York. Competing with the Hollywood majors is difficult, but the New York geography cuts a clear difference. There are many major studios in Southern California, but Kaufman/Astoria can dominate the Northeast. Kaufman's corporate strategy is also distinctive/unique: Astoria Studios does not intend to own everything as does a traditional studio megalith; rather the strategy is to participate with creative professionals and investment partners, thereby attaining greater operational and financial leverage. Such an approach is resonant with the entrepreneurial penchant of many entertainment and telecommunication executives, especially the innovative ones; they want to run their own show, control their own company—they would rather struggle on their own than be swallowed by a Major. Kaufman/Astoria can give the best of both worlds, entrepreneurial independence combined with large or-ganization clout. Furthermore, Kaufman has gathered together a high-powered group of partners/associates, including Robert Sar-noff, the former president of RCA, and motion picture professionals such as publicist Harold Rand. (Investment banker Roy Ashton and the author are financial advisors to Kaufman/Astoria Studios.)

CREATIVE STRATEGY 4

FOCUS/COHERENCE

Strive for
Strategic Tightness

ISSUES AND IDEAS

Problems

The Western Engine Company was an old line manufacturer of machine parts for engines of all kinds. It prided itself on having one of the country's most comprehensive lines of parts, and on serving the broadest cross section of industries. Western was able to supply thousands of production and custom parts for numerous industries—automotive, farm machinery, aircraft, railroads, and so on. The problem was profits, a loss of $1 million last year, widening this year. Sales had declined some 35 percent with the general recession (down to $27 million), and the business was being attacked on two fronts. On the one hand, their larger customers were bringing more subassemblies in-house; and on the other hand, smaller, more specialized firms were eating away at their traditional markets.

The Gauge & Meter Company began as a manufacturer of monitoring devices for industrial markets. With early success came expansion and diversified acquisition of several small machine tool companies. Volume had peaked at $145 million in 1980, but slid back to $120 million by 1982, turning the bottom line bright red. G & M was making many products for many markets—but making no money.

The Missouri Group was a diversified conglomerate with sales of $300 million. It operated through seventeen divisions, with 50 percent of volume generated in food supplies, recreation, piping, and machine tool distribution. (The piping division was the second largest in the South—and did $60 million.) Each division was wholly independent and reported directly to the president, although several staff vice-presidents took an active part in overseeing budgets. The company had been barely breaking even for five years.

First City Financial was a privately held, medium-sized bank in a large Eastern city where competition in financial service had become white-hot. Projections showed dismal profitability. Spreads between deposits and loans were too thin to support the advertising and overheads required, especially in the new, capital-intense technologies of retail banking. A national financial institution had just approached First City with a low offer of acquisition, yet the founding family did not want to give control to an out-of-state entity.

Solutions

The Western Engine Company should reduce its overheads and breakeven point and focus its energies. To hope to return to the bounteous days of the fifties and sixties would be foolish. The company should tighten its target. It might select one industry, for example, and serve it with its comprehensive line of specialized products. Since the major farm machinery corporations were having difficulty and many of the supporting firms were leaving the industry, competition was reduced and profit potential would be enhanced. This might be an appropriate market to attack.

The Gauge & Meter Company should divest itself of those smaller divisions in which it is not a market leader. It should select the one product area—gauges and meters—in which it maintains good market share, and seek to sell those products to as many industries as possible.

The Missouri Group must focus its businesses. Only those areas where the company is (or can become) a major player should be kept. Since the company has the second largest piping company in the South, that division should be emphasized. Perhaps the company could expand piping (or buy a competitor) with the cash generated from the sale of other divisions.

First City Financial should close down its retail locations. Competing against the giants—who are willing to sustain large losses for years to build market share—is suicidal. First City should concentrate instead on the commercial middle market, medium-sized companies whose headquarters are local. If strength of national association is needed, First City might consider allowing a major institution to buy a minority position.

CURRENT CASES

Loctite Corporation (Newington, Connecticut) is a highly coherent company, producing and marketing engineering adhesives, sealants, and other specialty chemicals (1983 revenues, $216 million; profits, $17 million; five-year return on sales, 1976–1980, was 14%). Coherence is based on families of "sticky" chemical products that join things and seal things. Distribution is worldwide and principal markets are industrial manufacturing and repair, automotive maintenance, and the home and car do-it-yourself repair field. Loctite claims it "has always been, and intends to remain, a company focused on its mission." The company's initial objective was "to augment with sealants and adhesives a wide variety of mechanical methods of assembling fitted parts." With its expanding technology, with its entry into the consumer and auto repair markets, the company's mission has been restated: "We will be the number one market-share seller of high value, branded, chemical products that help our customers assemble, seal, repair and maintain the things they own or make." The company is already the world's leading manufacturer of two classes of industrial adhesives. Great awareness of corporate strengths and weaknesses is sensed. Loctite's marketing strategy has been defined as a "think small" chemical specialty approach combined with a program of increasing public awareness (promoting the message, "Some parts just have to be Loctite safe"). Ability to see long-time horizons is explicit: "One of our deliberate strategies over the last twelve months was to fund future growth rather than to squeeze the bottom line for the last few cents in earnings per share." Loctite has invested in its sales force and increasing R&D as well as making fixed plant and equipment purchases.

Echlin Manufacturing Company (Branford, Connecticut) is a worldwide producer of parts and supplies used to maintain or improve the efficiency and safety of motor vehicles (1983 revenues, $565 million; profits, $31 million). Products include electronic and electromechanical parts, fuel system parts and test equipment, and a variety of brake parts and controllers. Markets include all types of motorized vehicles from automobiles to tractors, trucks to boats, industrial motors to recreational vehicles. Family controlled (though no longer family operated), Echlin is both aggressive and progressive in an industry where Dana and Eaton are each more than four times larger. (In 1977, the company ranked high among the *Fortune* 1000: 157 in returns on equity; 89 in earnings per share growth; and 7 in total returns to investors over ten years. For comparison, Echlin's sales and assets ranked 629 and 626, respectively.) The company highlights the "Reasons for Echlin's Superior Performance": Concentrated efforts ("While the Company has many product lines, it is in one business"); its specific industry segment is growing (engine efficiency and highway safety); customer service and response (maintaining inventories high enough to meet immediate and often urgent needs without incurring huge costs); optimizing R&D (supplementing internal R&D programs with outstanding external professionals in the academic and business worlds working on an official Scientific Advisory Committee). Other reasons for corporate success stress finance, organizational structure, and the high standards, performances, and momentum of its people. (Other Creative Strategies at Echlin in addition to Focus/ Coherence are: External Perception, Efficient R&D, and Product Emphasis.)

Kennametal, Inc. (Latrobe, Pennsylvania) has maintained a leadership position in tooling systems technology and metal-working markets by combining its advanced product line with a direct sales approach. (Five-year return on sales, 1978–1982, was 10 percent. In fiscal 1983 Kennametal suffered its first loss year since 1947, $11.2 million, reflecting severe depression in product demand. Costs were reduced, recovery has begun, and analysts expect a return to solid profitability. In fiscal 1984, Kennametal earned $12.0 million on revenues of $319 million.) Kennametal is an integrated tool company specializing in the manufacture and application of cemented carbide alloys through powder metallurgy. Tungsten carbide is the hardest metal made by man. Kennametal tungsten carbide compositions are used to machine, cut, shape, and form steel, aluminum, wood, plastics, coal, rock, and other materials. The company is coherent in technology and products and widely diversified in industry applications — providing complete tooling systems for metal cutting and forming (70% of sales); mining and construction tools; and components subjected to extremes of abrasion and corrosion wear, temperature, and pressure. A family-controlled and operated company, Kennametal has been one of the industry's most consistent performers. (The commitment of the founder yields distinctiveness and coherence.) Kennametal articulates five corporate objectives, each of them working to maintain strong technological leadership in product performance, product quality, and timely service to customers: (1) To add new and improved products and services that are logical extensions of the present business (i.e., focus/coherence); (2) to assure adequate inventories of essential raw materials; (3) to practice conservative accounting and to keep a strong balance sheet and sound capital structure; (4) to achieve, long term, a 20 percent return on stockholders' equity; and (5) to attract, develop, and maintain a strong management team capable of achieving stated business goals.

Thomas Nelson, Inc. (Nashville, Tennessee) is the world's largest publisher of bibles (1983 revenues, $47 million; profits, $3 million). Bibles comprise three-quarters of Nelson's sales, and although the market may seem saturated, it is most assuredly not. Nelson publishes an incredible 550 different types and styles of bibles, some with different translations, some with special references, some with notes, some with pictures—it's a long list. Not included are the "private-label Bibles" (how's that one, marketing students?) sold to television evangelists (Jerry Falwell, for example, purchased 200,000 "Bicentennial Bibles"). Nelson recently spent $4.5 million on creating a new version, the *New King James Version* (cleaning up some archaic words, changing "thou" to "you" and the like), and another million advertising it. In less than a year, more than 1 million were sold. The Bible costs Nelson $4 to print; they whole-sale it, say to K Mart, for $8; and it retails for $16. A nice price, and a nice profit—giving Nelson their investment back within a year. Fidelity to the orginal is the critical element here. Nothing is more important for Nelson's fundamentalist market. (Zondervan's competing *New International Version* is critiqued chapter-and-verse for departing, however so slightly, from a literal translation. But it is *Reader's Digest Condensed Bible* that gets the broadside. The *Reader's Digest* version, comments a Nelson editor whenever he can—trade shows, television interviews—leaves out more than just the repetitions and genealogies as they claim; they also leave out that passage in the book of Revelation condemning anybody who would subtract words from the Book!) Founder and CEO of Thomas Nelson is a rather remarkable Lebanese immigrant, Sam Moore, himself a born-again Christian. He's also a "born-before" salesman. "Winning," he confides, "is a habit." Nelson publishes other books for the religious market, inspirational and evangelistic works; but it was a recent acquisition that raised some eyebrows. As part of his grandiose vision to become a "$500 million avant-garde publisher" within a decade, Moore bought Dodd, Mead & Co., an old-line New York publishing house, whose sales had fallen on hard times. Given the job of resurrecting the firm, so to speak, was a wily, sensitive publisher (Lew Gillenson) fresh from the wars of running another Church-backed publishing house (Everest House) with secular subjects founded on religous intent. Imposed restrictions on certain kinds of books—immorality or Satanic-stuff, for example—does not go down too well with the elite New York publishing establishment. Whatever his success in secular publishing, Moore radiates commitment in religious publishing and that leads to the distinctiveness and coherence that produces dominance. (*Forbes*, May 9, 1983.)

Discount Corporation of New York (New York City) buys securities from the government and sells them to big buyers, such as pension funds and commercial banks (1983 revenues, $97.5 million; profits, $6.3 million. 1982 revenues, $230 million; profits, $26 million; return on equity has ranged from 22 to 97 percent between 1979 and 1982.) The company deals only in large quantities. ("Anything less than a million dollars," says CEO Ralph Peters, "is an odd lot.") Discount is called the "Tiffany" of the bonds business (the "Discount" name is meaningful only in the technical sense—the company, you can be sure, does not "discount" anything, especially commissions). Commissions, one should understand, are not the generator of revenues. "The big money comes from correctly predicting interest rates and buying and selling accordingly," asserts Peters. Discount is often forecasting rates only a few *hours* at a time. (In the bond business, a day is considered long term.) The secret of Discount's success? Said a customer, "When all of their information comes together, they are right more often than they are wrong." The Treasury Department and Federal Reserve have been known to call on Discount for advice on debt management and monetary policy. With most companies in brokerage and financial services diversifying and expanding, Discount is sitting tight—and pretty. (Two small business extensions are not yet profitable). Concentration on expertise is their secret. Clarity of purpose leads to coherence in business which generates dominance of selected segment. (*Forbes*, March 14, 1983.)

ASK Computer Systems (Los Altos, California) designs turnkey computer systems for manufacturing plants and markets them to medium-sized companies (1983 revenues, $39 million; profits, $3.9 million; annual average compound growth rate, 1978–1983, is 93 percent, making ASK the eleventh fastest-growing company over that time). Sandra Kurtzig founded the company with $2,000 in 1972; she was worth at last look, still with 28 percent of the company (no venture capital was ever cut in before the public offering), some $65 million. What was her starting strategy? With degrees in math, chemistry, and engineering, augmented by marketing experience at General Electric, she knew what manufacturers wanted "and I could translate those needs into easy-to-use software." In 1978, after hiring a few young engineers, some of her standardized packages hit paydirt—programs that improved inventory control, and facilitated financial and production management. An early deal with Hewlett-Packard enabled Kurtzig to market a turnkey system—that is, a complete, ready-to-use system of hardware and software—to plant managers several years ahead of the pack. ASK is now Hewlett-Packard's largest wholesaler buyer of minicomputers. James Mendelson, a Morgan Stanley analyst, explains her advantages, "ASK's competitors were mainly selling technology. ASK packaged well and was able to push economic benefits to its customers. That's how they've built sales." A typical customer is a manufacturer with revenues between $10 million and $20 million, who may pay $250,000 for the six main programs. (Just the software costs $190,000—about 20 percent of customers go this route.) Concerned about how big these numbers look, ASK asserts quickly that customers recover their costs within a year. (Initial cost, or total costs, is not specified.) A new marketing device is ASKNET, through which customers can rent software for $4000 to $8000 a month. During the recession, even larger companies opted for this route, and it became the company's fastest growing segment (but probably cannibalized outright sales). Since many companies strong enough to buy are now happily content in the rent mode, ASK is raising its rates, hoping to nudge customers into purchases. (But be careful about alienation.) ASK is adapting its programs to Digital Equipment's computers, planning to capitalize on DEC's huge embedded base, some six times the size of Hewlett-Packard's. A recent diversification into microcomputer software addresses a radically different audience—individual consumers—and will require new skills in marketing not compatible with current competencies (ASKing for trouble?). But ASK is planning for the future, as the mini and micro markets collide over the next few years. "When I first started," laughs Kurtzig, "I'd go to cocktail parties and tell people I was in software. They usually thought I made women's underwear." (*Forbes*, Fall 1983/Special Issue.)[ASK's microcomputer division was closed recently at a reputed loss of $850,000.]

Oak Hill Sportswear (New York City) manufactures middle-market women's clothes, mannishly tailored shirts, and moderate-priced sweaters (1983 revenues, $85 million; profits, $3.5 million;

with an average return on equity of 141 percent between 1978 and 1982—generated, however, on a very low base; Oak Hill placed second on *Forbes* 1983 list of the best small public companies in the country). Defying conventional apparel wisdom that a company must go low end or high end, but avoid the middle, Oak Hill's retail price points are $16–$20 for shirts, and $22–$28 for sweaters. "We don't know the field of high-priced designer items," stated Chairman Arthur L. Asch, "and I think it would be foolish of us to enter it right now." Looking in the other direction, Asch says, "There is no reason for us to go low end. We manufacture quality products, and if you do, you don't have to sell cheap." There is an interesting story here, quite apart from the success of Oak Hill products. The name of the corporation until recently was, of all things, "Bio-Medical Sciences, Inc."—and the name naturally caused confusion. The reason is logical when one understands the complex laws governing the use of net operating loss (NOL) carryforwards. The original company had run up multiple millions of dollars of losses in their unsuccessful disposable instruments business, but without profits or the hope of profits, there was no way to utilize the tax shelter. Enter one Wilmer Thomas, a financier skilled in such matters. He took Oak Hill, an unrelated profitable company, and leveraged it into Bio-Medical Sciences, being careful to watch all the rules and regulations so as to not jeopardize the NOL. It was a sweet deal, for everyone concerned, including, of course, Wilmer. Only when the tax loss has been used up, and the equity returned to its preleveraged position, can the traditional ratios of financial performance have real meaning. Asch predicts pretax margins of 12 percent, exceptionally good for a tough industry. (*Forbes*, January 30, 1984.)

Cellu-Craft (New Hyde Park, New York) makes flexible packaging for the food and drink industries (1982 revenues, $46 million; profits, $2.4 million; return on equity about 30 percent—taken private in March 1983). When attorney Selig Burrows took over the company, it was bankrupt in all but name. How the turnaround? Of the company's 600 or so customers, most were too small to produce profits. The company had been trying to become a diversified packaging enterprise through acquisitions, but old management kept leaving (the perennial problem with acquisitions of small private companies). Burrows planned the business strategy. "We concentrated on our strengths, the areas where we have good market penetration and where the product has the most value added, so we're not being undercut by smaller competitors all the time." (Areas of market leadership include cheese, snack, and confectionary packaging and labels for plastic soft-drink bottles.) A bag company was divested. "I don't want to be in that business," states Burrows (supporting the theory that CEO desire is a good predicter of strategy). "Anybody with a garage and a few bucks to buy a machine can get into it." Cellu-Craft targets the top fifty food companies, those that will control 90 percent of the market by 1990. "We won't take a customer unless he's got the potential of giving us at least $100,000 worth of business a year," says the company's operations chief. "Larger companies don't buy on price alone, which smaller companies tend to do." Cellu-Craft is a classic medium-sized manufacturing company. It competes in a $5 billion industry against companies on both ends of the scale—on the upper end with billion-dollar giants who can muster economies of scale for high-volume commodity items, and on the lower end with job-shop opportunists who can undercut price on low-volume, easy-to-make products. Mid-sized positioning, therefore, must be carefully planned, focusing on product lines more difficult to manufacture, with large but not too large required volumes. (Example: laminate labels for plastic soft-drink bottles composed of several materials and with complex graphics.) Cellu-Craft's pretax returns on sales are about 8.5 percent, better than the 5.5 percent average of the industry. Reasons cited by management for fine performance include watching overheads; productivity (sales per employee is double the industry's); keeping plants at a size where one man can run them; and sticking with larger customers ("tying our wagon to their star"). The strategies are clear and coherent. (*Forbes*, August 29, 1983.)

After Six (Philadelphia, Pennsylvania) began corporate life as a retailer and renter of men's formal wear (1983 revenues, $42 million; profits, $3.6 million—8.6% return on sales, up from an average of 1.4 percent in the five prior years; return on equity, 27 percent, up from 4 percent). From 1966 to 1979 the company diversified into many areas (manufacturing and retailing men's suits, uniforms, shirts, women's tailored clothing)—but only succeeded in adding to its debt, not profits. By 1981 After Six's debt was double its equity, and its bankers pulled the string. A new president came in (we'll ignore the family fights) and began shedding all those acquisitions. (One division, Morvilles, with several high-class menswear stores in Philadelphia, was "liquidated" and turned around by April-Marcus—see Chapter 5.) Performance improved—the simple power of clarity and coherence again. New diversification moves are being considered, though now related to central competencies. Licensing out the After Six name is one, like for formal jewelry. Licensing in some designer names is another, like Bill Blass and Yves Saint Laurent for tuxes. A third may be bridal wear. "Since 70 percent of our business is already due to weddings," explained the After Six CEO, "it would be a natural extension." Well, maybe. (*Forbes*, January 16, 1984.) [Taken private by management in a September 1984 leveraged buyout.]

Broadview Associates (Fort Lee, New Jersey) is in the business of arranging mergers and acquisitions, specifically for computer service companies (Broadview is a private firm). The company competes successfully in the violent jungle where major investment banking firms prowl. How? In two ways: first, by specializing in a tightly defined segment (more limited than even computer companies; not hardware, not software—just service); and second, by sticking to the small stuff (typically between $1 to $3 million per deal, as compared to the average $23 million for the 2346 deals of all kinds in 1982—a statistic skewed by the mega-billion-dollar transactions). Between 1979 and the middle of 1983, Broadview husbanded about 100 deals through the laborious and often frustrating process, a remarkable 30 percent of the mergers and acquisitions in the industry. The two Broadview partners certainly lead from personal strength: Gerald Mintz used to head up ADP's acquisition program; Bernard Goldstein was an entrepreneur who started and sold two computer service companies. (The two are complementary, Mintz cavalier and frenetic, Goldberg thoughtful and considered.) Both are fulfilled in their work and committed to their companies. (Commitment, distinctiveness, clarity, and coherence all lead to dominance.) Mintz began Broadview with, well, a broad view of mergers and acquisitions. Though the name remains, the strategy focused quickly. "I had a manufacturer of steel pails, a hotel and a maker of extruded aluminum parts for the aerospace industry," he remembers. "Who the hell knows who to sell that to? I decided I should specialize in the industry I knew." (*Forbes*, July 4, 1984.)

Advest (Hartford, Connecticut) is a brokerage house whose target customers are independent businessmen and professionals (1983 revenues, $125 million; profits, more than double 1982; return on equity, 30 percent—spurred by the surge in stock market trading). In an attempt to remain independent—and not go the way of other proud regional houses such as Robinson Humphreys (into American Express) or Rotan Mosle (into Paine Webber)—Advest has snapped up seven small brokerage companies in under two years (contributing 25 percent of sales and 22 percent of earnings). The key, however, is marketing. What can Advest do that the giants cannot? Tight targeting. "Unselective, mass marketing," says senior vice-president for marketing Judith Johnson, "doesn't work anymore." No longer content to follow the Merrill Lynches of the world, Advest is going after big brokerage customers—especially principals of private companies (sales between $1 million and $20 million) and independent East Coast lawyers and accountants. But what can Advest offer? Anthony LaCroix, Advest's chairman, has the answer. Target customers are competing constantly against giants in their own businesses and professions. They are out there pitching the concept that smaller firms provide more personalized service. So, goes the theory, they should be more receptive to the same pitch from Advest. The company is investing heavily in advertising ($1.5 million over two years), a new corporate symbol (a fox—cleverer than the Merrill Lynch bull?), and a series of in-depth seminars teaching brokers about tax, estate, and retirement problems (important to independent businessmen and professionals). Advest's strategy is clear, leading to coherence. Whether it can generate sufficient distinctiveness, however, is another issue. With the jury still out on the new thrust, Advest is not dismissing its current customer base—60 percent of whom earn under $40,000 per year. Also under consideration is the banking business, should brokerage befall hard times. The company is a good one; the only question is whether they can remain independent. Check back in a couple of years. (*Forbes*, September 23, 1983.)

The Home Depot, Inc. (Atlanta, Georgia) are supermarket-sized home-improvement centers, with high inventories and nationally advertised brands (fiscal 1984 revenues, $256 million; profits, $10.3 million). The company's nineteen retail outlets have huge floor plans (averaging 80,000 square feet), massive displays of products ($4–$5 million in retail value), and expert sales help (125–150 personnel per store to assist customers with their do-it-yourself project needs). "We are not a recession baby," explains CEO Bernard Marcus, who helped found the company in 1978. "When new housing starts are down, people remodel. When they're up, more old homes come on the market that need repair. In either case, people want to save money. There's nothing more frustrating than calling in a plumber and spending $75 on what it would cost you $1.95 to do yourself." With confidence in his market positioning, Marcus plans to open eleven stores in 1984 (projected sales average $18 million per unit) and ten to fifteen per year thereafter. The Atlanta-based chain expects to expand from its current base in the Southeast (primarily Georgia and Florida) through the Southwest (Arizona). "Our long-term strategy has always been to build a national chain," confides Marcus, "and our biggest investment, outside of inventory, has been in our people. Right now, about the only restraint we face is our ability to recruit and train new staff fast enough." (*Inc.*, May 1984.)

CREATIVE STRATEGY 5

HIGH-PROFILE CHIEF EXECUTIVE

Have a Committed Boss

ISSUES AND IDEAS

Problems

Chicago Electrical Supply, Inc., was a privately held company with high net worth but low profitability. The founder had become seriously ill and none of his children desired to run the company. Because of the current economy, and the fact that most of the firm's net worth was tied up in somewhat questionable inventory, any quick sale would not realize anywhere near even the book value of the company. The business (1983 volume was $25 million) was too small to support the salary requirements of an outstanding outside chief executive. How to get at least accounting value for the company?

Health World was a regional chain of twelve physical fitness studios with traditional exercise machines and free weights catering to "pumping iron" types. Its three partners were all longtime body-builders and the business was successful, though never steady and never sure. The partners made good money and, true to the philosophy of the industry, began enjoying it. The health studio business is high intensity, people oriented, and very much based on constant cash flow (i.e., signing up new members). When growth slowed (with the partners away), losses mounted fast (due to high fixed costs). Two of the partners did not want to go back to work.

Advanced Data Systems (ADS) had one of the best track records for designing, installing, and managing large-scale data processing operations in a large Eastern metropolitan area. Sales revenues topped $15 million—substantial for a regional systems house. As a by-product of their customized software programs, several innovative software products emerged. A few were absolutely state of the art for efficiency and cost as well as effectiveness and features. None, however, was successful—ADS just could not market products.

Solutions

Chicago Electrical Supply, Inc., *can* attract an outstanding outside chief executive—but only by offering a substantial piece of the action. Equity talks when salary cannot. The founder should recapitalize the company by putting the entire net worth into a preferred stock and giving the new CEO between 20 and 30 percent of the common (leaving 20–30 percent for other senior managers). In this way the CEO must work to pay off the full value of the preferred before any value is realized in the company. The founder's family gets the benefits of both the full current valuation, and a healthy slice of the future appreciation. The new CEO gets a tremendous opportunity to build his own business and personal capital—as well as to attract a first-rate management team. Getting the right top guy is vital.

Health World should recognize the new generation of health and fitness. The American people are health conscious and the fitness industry is booming. The senior partner recommended bringing in their most dynamic club manager, and though he was only 26 years old, making him a full partner and chief executive. The move was risky but brilliant. The fellow was a dynamo—fiery, aggressive, compulsive. Almost overnight he turned the business around. Employees rallied behind his vision. He promised to make

Health World the largest fitness organization in their region. He repositioned the clubs to take advantage of social and family interests. Sports were added, as well as dance, swimming, and aerobics. Within four years, he had thirty-five clubs.

Advanced Data Systems, on advice of an independent consultant, established a new subsidiary for marketing. This subsidiary would be managed with total independence from the parent organization. To run the new company, ADS used a recognized executive search firm to recruit the number two executive of the industry's leading software marketing company, a 38-year-old dynamo who would never become CEO since his current company was family controlled. The consultant advised ADS to build an iron wall between parent and subsidiary, with all business being conducted at arm's length. The new CEO must have the right to accept or reject any ADS product, and his own compensation package would be based 100 percent on his own performance, without any relationship to the overall company. In this way, ADS determined, their products would have best opportunity for market penetration.

CURRENT CASES

International Business Services (Washington, D.C.) designs and programs computer systems, primarily for the federal government (1982 revenue, $15 million; pretax profits, estimated to be near $1 million). It is one of the few computer-based companies owned by a black. Talk about knocking down barriers! The pitch he used to get his first government contract was a real curve ball. Pity the poor bureaucrat who, having rejected Marion ("Duke") Greene seven times before, couldn't say no again. "I don't want to marry your sister," began Greene. "I don't want to eat dinner at your house. I just want you to give my company some work, preferably in computer programming. But if nothing else is available, we will wash windows." (Now that's commitment!) He got a keypunching contract, and twelve years later, is still working with the government. Greene had trouble getting a line of credit in the 1970s and thus had to settle for clerical contracts rather than programming ones. "We would be doing $100 million in sales if I were white. . . .

But I'm not complaining. If I still lived in Georgia, I would probably be driving a truck." IBS has diversified into several areas of service. Its biggest job is helping the Department of Interior establish and manage a $200 million computer system to monitor royalties owed the government. Other projects include training of army instructors, producing hardware–software packages for law firms, and supplying statistical and accounting packages for public housing authorities. Greene would like to reduce his dependency on the federal government from 75 percent down to 50 percent. Defense contractors seem a good market possibility. "The key to our success," he notes, "is getting out there every day and knocking on doors trying to find places to send proposals." At the beginning, 80 percent of his employees were also black; now it's 35 percent. "I asked myself, 'Am I running a social program or am I running a business?'" Greene reflects. "Of course, I want to hire as many blacks as I can, but the nature of our work means that the number qualified to work for the firm is relatively small. And everybody wants to hire those who are qualified." (*Forbes*, July 18, 1984.)

Dysan Corporation (Santa Clara, California) manufactures and markets disks for computers (1983 revenues, $180 million; profits, $9 million—not including a $65 million pretax gain on sale of securities). The success of the company relates directly to the quality of its products (exemplified by the hard, solid feel of its disks for microcomputers—upon which, by the way, every bit of this book has been written). Then there's Dysan's founder, Norman Dion, an entrepreneur's entrepreneur who has invested $40 million of Dysan's public-generated cash into a dozen high-technology start-ups, of which five came from Dysan employees. Self-described as a gambler who likes to back new ideas before the venture capitalists would dare take a look, Dion normally scatters $500,000 as seed money—though two ventures have sucked up a massive $30 million. The benefits to the company? Dion is prepared for the question; he's answered it before. "I stop others from pirating my key people. I prevent my key people from spinning off and competing against me. I get R&D done outside my company. And I create a small company atmosphere that is more conducive to productivity than at a big company. And I'm making a lot of friends because they're all getting rich"—there are sixty Dion-made millionaires at last count. (The best story is Seagate Technology. Alan Shugart, Dion's old boss at Memorex and IBM, had an idea for 5¼ Winchester disk drives, which would use Dysan disks. Dion put in the first $500,000. In less than four years, Dysan had cashed in $55 million dollars and still held stock worth $100 million. Shugart? He did OK. From flat broke to $80 million.) Norman Dion, a good example of fulfillment driving commitment. (*Forbes*, September 12, 1983.)

JP Industries, Inc. (Ann Arbor, Michigan) is in the business of resuscitating marginal durable-goods manufacturers in metal and plastic industries (1983 revenues, $47.5 million; profits, $2.4 million). To call John Psarouthakis an "opportunist" would be high compliment indeed. This MIT engineer and space program alumnus has used his expertise to resurrect nine low-tech, industrial laggards located in the Midwest—small manufacturers of faucets, plumbing fixtures, strainers, drains, truck and tractor components, and cam shafts. Beginning with an "Acquisitions Wanted" ad in *The Wall Street Journal*, Psarouthakis' goal was to buy countercyclical companies at bargain prices. He narrowed product lines, shed excess inventory, consolidated marketing and administrative, and changed management. Eight of the nine were turned profitable—the ninth was sold off. "A lot of people are missing the boat in Michigan, chasing high tech, trying to duplicate [Boston's] Route 128 or [Northern California's] Silicon Valley," comments Psarouthakis. "They're missing the fact that there's a significant technology base here, not as glamorous, but one that can make money nonetheless." (*Inc.*, May 1984.)

Digital Switch Corporation (Dallas, Texas) designs and manufactures products for a segment of the large digital switching systems market for specialized carriers (1983 revenues, $127 million; profits, $25 million—up from $27 million in revenues and $6 million in profits in 1982, and no sales at all in 1981!). "I'm a real pusher," said James Donald, Digital Switch CEO, to the *New York Times*, "I always did want to build my own company." When he first came to Digital in 1981, he recalled, it "had no sales, no orders and no products." He moved the company to Dallas, taking only 6 of the original 30 employees with him. By the end of 1981, he had 60 employees—but still not a sale in the house. Today he has almost 1000 employees and a $358 million merger with Granger Associates to boot. This is the second time Donald took a company with product development but no sales and in a few years pushed it over the $100 million mark. (His first, Danray, Inc., was sold to Northern Telecom in 1978.) Who's next? We expect his phone is ringing.

Tyco Laboratories, Inc. (Exeter, New Hampshire) is a coherent conglomerate organized in three groups: packing and consumer materials, fire protection systems, and electrical and electronic components (1984 revenues, $650 million; profits, $30 million; 1974 revenues, $42 million). Tyco is the product of its longtime chief executive, Joseph Gaziano (recently deceased), who built the company from a small R&D house into a major enterprise through aggressiveness in acquisitions and dynamism in developing new ideas. His 1976 purchase of Grinnell (the largest manufacturer, designer, and installer of automatic sprinkler and fire protection systems in North America) energized Tyco's dramatic rise. Gaziano was known for his tremendous intensity and personal charisma.

Wang Laboratories, Inc. (Lowell, Massachusetts) a paragon mid-sized firm of the 1970s, has become a leader in computers and peripheral equipment designed for office automation, specifically word processing (1975 revenues, $76 million; profits, $3.3 million; 1983 revenues, $1538 million; profits, $152 million). The company is the personification of its founder and chief executive, An Wang, whose imagination and business brilliance built one of the premier companies in America. An Wang controls his company through his family's majority ownership of a special class of voting stock. This means that even though he owns well less than 50 percent of the equity or net worth of the company, he maintains a lock on two-thirds of the vote. A classic entrepreneur, Wang insisted on this control, unorthodox for a major corporation, before bringing his company public (and not qualifying for the New York Stock Exchange as a result). A question Wang likes to ask is, "How can the Company continue to grow rapidly and still maintain its innovative edge?" The answer, the company claims, is its people who produce a "practical approach to technological development . . . developing the first, best and easiest-to-use systems that solve real business problems." Wang states that their "entrepreneurial spirit" offers opportunity and rewards "to all who reach for them." Doors are open to new ideas, decisions are made quickly, and the excitement of challenge is maintained. Wang is a genuine leader of American industry, a proud mid-sized alumnus.

Decision Systems, Inc. (Mahwah, New Jersey) is a mini-conglomerate with operating segments in software systems and basic manufacturing (1984 revenues, $11 million; pretax profits, $537,000). An early company in computer software systems, DSI has taken advantage of, and has fallen victim to, opportunities for business advancement. DSI was founded by several computer programmers in 1960, and the company, though successful and outfront, never caught the crest of the computer wave. Sales remained moderate, profits not spectacular. Technical competence was outstanding, growing the business less so. (Customers include Grumman, the Long Island Rail Road and numerous medium-sized companies. Services range from turnkey systems and facilities management to systems consulting and contract programming.) Diversifying acquisitions brought in two manufacturing operations: adjustable steel shelving (primarily for law offices); and shock, vibration and noise reduction equipment (Korfund, an old line firm with a first-rate reputation). A foray into retail consumer electronics in 1982, an ill-conceived effort intended to support DSI's new computer games/education division (superb quality but weak marketing), generated large losses in 1983 and brought the company into a negative net worth position and near insolvency. Only through the extraordinary efforts of its indefatigable CEO, George Morgenstern, was the company able to survive. DSI has struggled for two years, and incredibly, without additional capital (which it still needs), has managed to effect a turnaround and generate consistent operating profits. Morgenstern is a computer systems/programming genius with an appetite for generating innovative solutions to complex problems and for making deals. He is also, not incidentally, an orthodox Jewish rabbi (who zealously and scrupulously separates his ecclesiastical and commercial worlds). A significant number of DSI employees in its computer software divisions are from the orthodox Jewish community; indeed many are Talmudic scholars who have found software programming a skill akin to their religious scholarship training. This source of manpower—DSI is the dominant computer programming firm in the orthodox Jewish community in the New York area—is an important resource. Building on this distinctive competency, Morgenstern began working in Israel in the early 1960s, donating his services for many years. (One of Israel's leading defense-related scientists commented that "Morgenstern was the first to teach us real-time programming. . . . the smartest damn rabbi I ever met.") In recent years, Morgenstern has built his subsidiary in Israel into a high tech computer systems house—one of the largest in the country and again staffed largely from the orthodox community. DSI's primary customer is Israel Aircraft Industries for whom DSI writes complex code for its most advanced aerospace and defense-related systems. The advantages of having software companies both in the United States and in Israel could become a strong comparative advantage and DSI is seeking mechanisms to exploit it. Strategic planning is a real issue. Working capital remains negative, and though improving steadily through operational profits, still a problem. Each operating division, while profitable, could be improved significantly by capital infusion. Yet, outside investment requires more equity than Morgenstern is willing to give up. Recently, a chief operating officer was brought aboard, freeing Morgenstern from incessant administration and enabling him to get back to his primary strength in developing software and structuring deals. He is determined to build on DSI distinctive competencies: Using his basic manufacturing divisions to generate profits and cash flow so that his software divisions in the United States and in Israel can grow by taking advantage of their unique positioning. (The author is a consultant to DSI and works with Morgenstern in strategic planning.)

CREAIIVE STRATEGY 6

EMPLOYEE OPPORTUNITY

Satisfy/Fulfill Personnel

ISSUES AND IDEAS

Problems

The Stark Dress Company, Inc., was a 40-year-old, well-established company with sales of $65 million per year and a stellar reputation. The founder was one of the most respected men in his industry, but having built the business was now devoting himself more to charitable endeavors. Though he maintained his titles, active management of the business was in the hands of two individuals, the vice-presidents for marketing and manufacturing. The two had dramatically different ideas for the future of the business: the marketing VP wanted to become more fashion oriented, offering enormous variety and constantly changing styles, patterns, and colors; the manufacturing VP wanted to expand his plant and make it state-of-the-art, and he needed long production runs of similar styles to justify his huge expenditures. For a time things ran well, with hot items and a good economy masking the strategic mismatch.

When both ended, the company plunged into heavy losses. The marketing VP said the requirements of manufacturing were killing his business; the manufacturing VP said the marketers were undermining him by placing orders too small and by changing them too frequently. Each VP thought the other should be replaced—or at least be reporting to him.

Tertia Tech Corporation was built on three technological strengths—telecommunications, signal processing, switching—the result of combining three small companies along Boston's Route 128. The company grew from under $1 million in sales in 1971 to over $90 million in 1980 strictly through internal growth. Tertia Tech was now organized into nine operating divisions (profit centers). In 1981 the company was rocked by two groups of young scientists splitting off to form their own companies, taking important personnel and R&D contracts with them. Tertia Tech's volume did not rise in 1981; it slipped 3 percent in 1982 and another 5 percent in 1983 following several more defections. A liberal stock option plan was less than effective since the most creative types cared only about their own areas, not the company as a whole.

The Dural Furniture Company was losing money. Sales had plummeted to $14 million from a high three years before of $26 million. Its manufacturing plant was operating below 30 percent of capacity and was in desperate need of repairs. The firm had a good reputation, but the recession and cheaper competitive products undermined business. The company had a core sales force that was excellent. They were loyal but worried about the future, even as signs of sales revival appeared on the horizon.

Darrow Chemical manufactured several commodity chemicals at three large plants in the Midwest. Sales volume was about $90 million, and profits were erratic. The company was earning well under industry standards and its general trend was down. Productivity was slipping. Labor costs were high and growing higher as a percentage of sales. Darrow had little in the way of R&D and competed largely on price within its general geographic region. It was considering investing in a still larger facility in the same area in order to keep pace with the economies of scale of its much bigger competitors.

Solutions

The Stark Dress Company, Inc., must make a critical decision. Marketing cannot be coerced into buying what it doesn't need, and manufacturing cannot be required to make what is inefficient. A coherent strategy must be chosen, and only one of the three choices can be adapted: (1) Marketing strategy, stress fashion and divest major plants; (2) manufacturing strategy, stress production and cut back fashion; and (3) decouple marketing and manufacturing, allowing each to develop its own business—without required intercompany transactions. Sustaining the current situation could ruin everything. Since the two vice-presidents were exceptionally able individuals, the third option is an interesting one. The two divisions should be set up as separate profit centers—totally independent—and each VP should be given profit participation in the one he runs.

Tertia Tech Corporation must give its key creative personnel entrepreneurial opportunity to continue growing. A radical approach is to spin off several of the divisions, giving top management 20 percent of the equity (keeping 80% for parent consolidation). Formulas can be established for either the parent to buy back the stock or to take the new company public so that the minority shareholders can realize value. A less radical approach is to establish significant profit-sharing incentives on a divisional basis. In either case absolute independence must be assured.

The Dural Furniture Company should become a variable-costs company. The manufacturing plants should be closed, and purchases made from low-cost producers. The company should stress its strong sales force. The company decided to pay an extra 1 percent commission (on top of the normal 6 percent) if a salesman would exceed a given target threshold. The salesmen were greatly excited, and in the first year five out of the eleven made it—and company sales climbed back to $22 million.

Darrow Chemical should consider restructuring its pay scale. Perhaps it should move its proposed plant to a new area of the country where it can institute innovation in employee compensation without union restrictions. A pay system based on productivity would generate maximum motivation. Give employees a chance to make more money than they would ordinarily, as long as labor dollars are pegged to product output and the minimums are sufficiently low.

CURRENT CASES

People Express (Newark, New Jersey) flies high-density routes at lowest fares, and is helping change the shape of the airline industry (1983 revenues, $292 million; profits, $10 million—one of the best margins in the business, though recently depressed). People has made Newark a major hub, running over 300 flights a day. There are few frills; baggage and meals are extra ($3 and $6 respectively) and all ticketing is done during flights. Passengers love it: Some flights are booked months in advance. The company's advertising boasts that "every employee is an owner"; indeed every employee must buy 100 shares of stock (financed through payroll deductions)—and many have built up sizable stakes worth $40,000 or more. President Donald Burr, considered one of the sharpest airline CEOs in the business, exults that his organization is filled with young people "having a blast." People Express has no unions, not even for pilots, and when work piles up, everybody—that means everybody including Burr—can be called upon, say, to load baggage. (The trail leads from employee fulfillment to company commitment to industry distinctiveness.) People's $159 single fare to London caused a storm, as did its $149/119 price to Los Angeles, as did its purchase of thirty-eight Boeing 727s at bargain-basement prices. The greatest testament to People's brash success has been that, according to Burr, "where other airlines have a choice, instead of putting planes against us, they are switching to where we are not strong." Yet, one might add.

W. L. Gore & Associates (Newark, Delaware—near Wilmington) developed and markets a Teflon fiber plastic insulation; the fiber is impervious to heat, cold, sunlight, and chemical degradation, and is used by 125 manufacturers around the world in products such as space suits for astronauts, high-quality outdoor items (tents, sleeping bags, gloves, boots, and the like), antipollution devices, electrical cables, and even synthetic vascular grafts (private company; 1983 revenues, about $170 million; profits, about $17 million; yearly growth rate averaging 30–40 percent). The story of this company is fascinating in many ways. Bill Gore's risk—leaving Du Pont to start a chancy business at age 45 with two kids in college—is inspiring. But how the company manages its 3000 employees, or more accurately, how the 3000 employees manage themselves, is remarkable. Talk about Japanese consensus, quality control circles, just-in-time inventory, and lifetime employment. Gore & Associates, the name mirroring the organization, goes beyond. First, everybody is an "associate"—there are no officers (other than the formality of what is legally required). Gore attributes his success to his associates ("the brightest, hardest-working people I have ever seen anywhere"), to the company's "lattice" organization, and, with characteristic honesty, to luck. Interested in the "nature of groups," Gore believes that organizations respond to a recognized authority or to individual commitment. "If you are going to have a lot of change in an organization, you better get a commitment. In the process, natural leaders will evolve." (For a discussion of the relationship between personal meaning and organizational mission, see Robert Lawrence Kuhn and George Thomas Geis, *The Firm Bond: Linking Meaning and Mission in Business and Religion*, New York: Praeger, 1984.) Gore's new associates are hired on recommendations from those already employed called "sponsors." This maintains the integrity of the group and secures the system. Sponsors help decide a newcomer's salary, and sponsors compete for bringing in the best employees. In Gore's opinion the system cannot work with groups larger than 200. When larger, he believes, individuals lose critical connections and interdependency dissolves. How to limit work forces to 200 when the company needs 3000? Simple, keep plants small—and have many of them (Gore has close to thirty). But surely some economies of scale are being lost? Perhaps, but according to Gore, productivity is double an average manufacturing force and creativity is triple. The company turns out innovations at a prodigious clip. (A classic example of personal fulfillment yielding company commitment, and from there on to distinctiveness, coherence, and most of the characteristics of top-performing mid-sized firms.) Lest other companies should try to copy his structure, Gore warns that you cannot transform an existing hierarchy into a lattice organization; you can only start it from scratch. (*Forbes*, May 9, 1984.)

Montgomery Securities (San Francisco, California) is a brokerage securities company dealing almost entirely with institutional investors. The company does about 1 percent of the transactions on the New York Stock Exchange. Though small compared to Goldman, Sachs' 5 percent or Merrill Lynch's 10 percent, Montgomery's volume has grown 60 percent since 1961. (A partnership, its revenues and profits have doubled in recent years, with top partners pulling in over $1 million and the average institutional salesman earning over $200,000.) How to play Wall Street from the Bay Area? Founding partner Tom Weisel keeps Montgomery focused; no general public appeals, no offices outside San Francisco. Targeting the major money managers, Montgomery gives them what they need: big block trading and, increasingly, venture-capital opportunities. How to play Wall Street when medium sized? Quality of performance generating quality of reputation. Called "idea oriented" and with a good track record, the company's success is derived from Weisel's intense desire to build a first-rate house. To do so he needed the best personnel; and in this business, to get the best, you must pay the best. Weisel offered partnerships, salaries, and bonuses with stratospheric Wall Street numbers attached to them; but he also offered something more—the chance to do something different, to build real substance anew. Thus Montgomery attracted a coterie of investment banking heavyweights and stock analyst superstars. Weisel gives the opportunity and gets the people. (Personal fulfillment yields company commitment. Also perceptiveness and progressiveness, as well as clarity and coherence, lead to strength in Montgomery's well-defined niche.) (*Forbes*, October 24, 1983.)

Kaypro Corporation (Solano Beach, California—near San Diego) designs, manufactures, and markets small-business computers and has become, to many people's surprise, America's fourth largest producer (1983 revenues, $75.3 million; profits, $12.9 million; the company's 17% after-tax return on sales is all the more impressive considering the low price of its computers). Marketing has been Kaypro's critical success strategy. The company treats its computers as a "commodity" and its employees as family. Marketing vice-president David Kay, the son of founder and CEO Andrew Kay, explains that Kaypro eschews the large distributors, representatives, and retail chains, opting instead for a distribution system of more than 1000 local dealers. These dealers are the core of the strategy, and they are backed by strong national advertising (e.g., humorous ads showing how competitors' $1500 computers really cost $6000), phone calls every week, visits every month, a telephone service hotline, and a rapid 48-hour shipping response time. Located north of San Diego, Kaypro's original facilities seem more like an arts and crafts camp than a manufacturing plant. No fancy offices or large production floors here. Small work rooms house tight teams of workers, who learn each aspect of the assembly process and are trusted to fill out their own time cards. (The new Solano Beach production plant was built based on employee recommendations.) Although the number of employees is approaching 1000, Andy or David still meets with each before he or she is hired; and once a month Andy, owning 66 percent of the equity, goes out on the shipping dock to update employees on company doings. However intense in business, he always has time for people. Andy loves his business, no doubting that. Personal fulfillment generates company commitment, producing in turn the clear distinctiveness causative of success. Kaypro, it is said, was the company that knocked Osborne out of the box, taking Adam's idea—transportable computer, bundled software included, low price—and beat him at his own game. This is a business, however, that is as turbulent as any in the history of business; technological competition is ferocious and to stumble once is to fall forever. (Kaypro is planning a series of innovative products, IBM-compatible and truly portable, to feed the world's addiction to personal computers. Yet recent problems portend a fitful future.) (*Inc.*, May 1984.)

Ametek, Inc., (New York City) is a diversified industrial manufacturer that produces both capital goods and components used in consumer products (1983 revenues, $448 million; profits, $38 million). The company makes thousands of products in four operating groups: Electromechanical (from the space shuttle's fuel handling system to unmanned undersea work vehicles); precision equipment (pressure and temperature measurement devices used in all industries); process equipment (heat transfer and winery equipment); and industrial materials (aluminum, plastic, and semiconductor). The company claims market leadership in several product classes: electric motors for office equipment, computers, and business machines; pressure gauges of all kinds; temperature measurement devices; vacuum appliance motors; and winery equipment. Ametek asserts that its success is derived from its "first-class management team" and decentralized structure. Senior managers are "asset managers," respecting profits but looking long term to maximize worth. Senior management works with a small staff of financial experts, leaving operations to the divisions. Management style is designed to need a "minimum of paperwork . . . with enough personal contact to be truly a 'no surprises' management." Ametek's CEO, Dr. John Lux, stated that "at each division, the general manager has absolute responsibility but Ametek also gives him the authority. He can operate on an hour-to-hour, day-to-day basis without ever contacting us." For problems, it's the phone or a quick trip by top executives to the trouble spot. "We very seldom ask a general manager to come to New York. He's on the firing line; he should be at the plant." Ametek is currently making a bid for technological leadership in solar energy. "All we want to be," said Dr. Lux, "is the General Motors of the solar energy industry."

Home Interiors & Gifts, Inc., (Denton, Texas—near Dallas) sells inexpensive decorative accessories through direct marketing at home parties; the critical element is the sales force, characterized by multilevel structure and evangelisticlike motivation (1983 revenues, about $400 million; profits, about $20 million). Mary C. Crowley, original founder and constant inspiration, is a born salesperson. She mixes scriptural wisdom, protestant ethic, communal self-help, and family values. It's a powerful brew—and some 40,000 managers and saleswomen have taken long drink. She links God's mission with personal mission and company mission. (In analyzing Home Interiors, one can follow the flow from fulfillment to commitment to distinctiveness to coherence.) The company fields some 550 products in its line—for example, brass leaf plaques ($5.95 for a set of three); flying-gull wall ornaments ($0.95 for two); gilt wall sconces, porcelain figurines, and other such stuff. It buys these items—none of which you'd call upscale—from twenty vendors and sells them at up to 100 percent markup. Where do those profits go? That's the fun part. Two-thirds of the gross margin goes to the saleswoman making the sale (she's called a "displayer"—all these kinds of organizations have their own slang); 10 percent to the various managers above her in the hierarchy. What's left (some 23%) goes to Home Interiors. All sales are for cash—no credit is given. This means little capital is needed, especially since manufacturing is done by others. No missing the corporate culture here. Displayers hear stories of Mary's sales prowess—how in the Depression she persuaded customers to buy four-cent spools of thread so they wouldn't have to wait for change; how she started Home Interiors on a borrowed $6000—and stories of Mary's munificence—how she paid Ethel Waters' hospital bills; how she gave her office staff a $200,000 shopping spree; how she "mothers" everybody within arm's reach. The IRS heard the stories too, and challenged her self-paid 1974 income of $1.6 million. The U.S. Tax Court, however, ruled against the Service, calling the money a legitimate business expense. Crowley, said the judge, had "a rare talent" for motivating women and "probably could not have been replaced." The keys to Home Interiors, of course, are the personal relationships, and those home parties where sales are based as much on companionship and values as on product and price. Women are given life meaning, though some high in the hierarchy can make real money. Displayers average about $3500 a year in commissions; managers getting a 2 percent override can make $12,000, and senior managers (with several hundred displayers under their wing) can top $100,000. Extra incentives—at all levels—give opportunity to build toward diamonds, minks, and vacations. (Compare Shaklee—Chapter 5—the "religion" is the same though the "doctrines" differ.) (*Forbes*, March 28, 1983.)

Knape & Vogt (Grand Rapids, Michigan) claims "excellent position in home decor products primarily for the do-it-yourself market. . . . We are the acknowledged leader in decorative wall shelving . . . to and through an estimated 35,000 retail outlets." (1984 revenues, $69 million; profits, $4.7 million—7.6% return on sales, 1976–1980). The company's "No. 1 policy" is "Quality at Competitive Prices." In addition to product development and retail relations, the firm is especially proud of its employees, who as the company likes to tell it (in the late seventies), "voted by a 4 to 1 margin to reject representation by the Teamsters' Union. We view these results as an overwhelming vote of confidence and we are grateful that all five plants remain non-union." Stability of employment is critical for the company, and it struggled with "no general layoffs" during the recent recession—a tough, though coherent strategy for a company dependent on the hard-hit building industry.

Sandy Howard Productions (Culver City, California) is a leading producer of low budget motion pictures. The company turns out some eight to twelve films per year with an average production cost below $4 million per picture. (A major studio would consume at least double the cash to put as much on the screen.) Subjects are normally action-drama oriented, with a fair share of violence and sex, for example, *Blind Rage*, *K. G. B.*, and *Opium Wars*. (Some might call the genre "exploitation"; yet the highly successful *Angel*, about a schoolgirl prostitute, carried social meaning and was not pornographic. Furthermore, quality of scripts, actors, directors, editing, and so on are unexpectedly high.) Financial efficiency is the touchstone for Sandy Howard who has produced some 40 motion pictures in his career including 23 with major studios. (He produced the acclaimed *A Man Called Horse* about American Indians.) Howard likes to "boast" about his losers, not a Hollywood characteristic, freely expounding on the costly lessons he learned very painfully and very well. (He lost significant money on the high budget *Meteor*—making mistakes, he says, he will never make again.) By keeping his budget tightly controlled and always below $4 million, and by pre-selling foreign distribution and other ancillary rights (such as cassette and cable), each Howard-produced movie is virtually guaranteed breakeven. Each movie is also tested in small markets, prior to running up any large-scale advertising and print costs. Whenever U.S. theatrical distribution strikes a hit, serious money can be made (even one per year works well with this formula). A key strategy is Howard's employees, their intensity and love of work. There is a reservoir in Los Angeles of brilliant, artistic people who live to make movies, and Howard has tapped into this stream. Their average age is under 30, and operational leverage is achieved by having almost everyone working on multiple pictures at the same time. (It seems incredible how few full-time people are producing so many pictures.) These are talented professionals and they bust gut at low rates. What they do for Howard, they could do nowhere else. Virtually all employees have positions they could never get at major studios, certainly not for many years. This is Howard's "secret weapon"—how he produces fine quality with bargain budgets; he spots good young talent and gives them broad early opportunity. These kids combine high energy with real flair. They are creative, resourceful, and relish their work. There is great *esprit de corps*.

CREATIVE STRATEGY 7

EFFICIENT INNOVATION

Optimize New Products, Services, Methods

ISSUES AND IDEAS

Problems

ABI Technologies was a manufacturer of microcomputer peripherals—modems, disk drives, hard disks, networking systems, en-
hancement boards, and the like. One of the rising stars of its
industry, ABI grew from $2 million in 1977 (electronic parts as-
sembly) to $70 million in 1983 by virtue of its state-of-the-art products
and image. But competition was enormous and the company's
early lead was vanishing. Technology and price were a two-front
war, with product half-lives measured in months. How could ABI
keep state-of-the-art with all its products in an industry invaded
by financial megaliths?

Trescott's was a well-known regional department store (annual
sales $175 million), catering to upper-middle clientele. Store sales
had been declining relative to competition, and margins had fallen.
Advertising as a percentage of sales was rising, almost uncon-

trollably, but it seemed that there was no other way to maintain sales.

Synergistic Systems was doing $80 million in a line of telecommunications products it had developed and held market lead. In order to maintain its position, the company had to allocate a huge amount of resources to R&D, 15 percent of sales or $12 million per year. Profits were completely absorbed in the effort, and the company was just breaking even. Yet to cut back any of R&D expenditures could eliminate vital technologies and skills needed for future product enhancements. It seemed impossible to sustain this level of activity in competition with the huge capital resources of its large competitors.

Electro Technologies, Inc., was a dichotomy. Sales were remaining flat at a mediocre $17 million, belying its superb R&D capability. The company had produced a series of innovative electronic products, but each had been less than a commercial success. The CEO spent 60 percent of his time in the laboratory, delegating marketing to a series of executive vice-presidents whom he replaced regularly.

Solutions

ABI Technologies could choose one of two alternatives. (Clearly it would be impossible to remain state-of-the-art in all its product categories). One approach is to focus on the product (or product family) in which the company has the best position, in terms of total market growth as well as firm market share. An alternative is to shift gears and stress "reliability" and low cost, not state-of-the-art. The general public is more concerned with their machines working and working well than with demanding the latest technology. Microcomputer performance is already beyond the needs of most users. Consumers require confidence and competitive cost. The latter would be a profound shift, from an R&D strategy to a manufacturing strategy—but it may produce more lasting stability.

Trescott's developed a direct-mail campaign, using targeted zip code areas to reach the upper income segment of its market—and cut general advertising back 70 percent. The program was so efficient they were able to decrease total marketing expenditures 30 percent while increasing penetration awareness 40 percent.

Synergistic Systems should maintain its R&D facilities at all costs. One approach is to contract out its R&D skills to other companies in order to maintain its capabilities. Joint ventures and royalty arrangements would be possible to construct—but the key point is to maintain the required level of activity.

Electro Technologies, Inc., should transform itself into an R&D contract house. The company should stress what it does best, and should take advantage of its CEO's proclivities. The company can look for joint ventures in marketing, licensing, royalties, and so on. (Note the differences between Electro Tech and Synergistic Systems. The recommended strategies are similar, but the driving motivations are different; the former is compelled to maintain a high level of R&D activity, the latter must stress the strength of its CEO and the competency of the company.)

CURRENT CASES

Genex Corporation (Rockford, Maryland), the fourth largest biotechnology company in the world, applies DNA recombinant techniques for developing and manufacturing nonpharmaceutical products (1983 revenues, $11 million; R&D phase loss, $5.4 million). Current products in the pipeline include a drain cleaner for janitorial services, a feedstock for farmers, an enzyme for making cheese, and the raw materials for an artificial sweetener. The latter is an amino acid being used by G.D. Searle & Company for making aspartame (brand name NutraSweet), the enormously successful, low-calorie sweetener taking over diet soft drinks and confections. Genex's strategy of avoiding the high-risk–high-return glamor of the drug world was deliberate, established from the outset as company mission. "To do the obvious, to develop pharmaceutical products," states CEO J. Leslie Glick, "would take lots of years and lots of bucks, and we would face serious problems with government approval, so the risk factor was enormous. Our route offered a lower total [R&D] cost and a faster timetable for bringing products to market." Genex is gearing up for big production of NutraSweet components for Searle, renovating a former Heublein Spirits bottling plant. While most of his revenues are now contract research (like all biotech companies), Glick expects revenues to jump to $30–$40 million by the end of 1984, with the drain cleaner hitting the market and the Searle contract coming on-line. (*Inc.*, May 1984.)

Matrix Corporation (Northvale, New Jersey) manufactures electronic film recorders used in 75 percent of all computer tomography (CAT) scanners produced today (1983 revenues, $54 million; profits, $5.3 million; return on equity has ranged from 19 to 28 percent). Matrix was founded in 1973 when two salesmen saw a need, and a market about to explode. They were working for a company that produced high-technology cameras for nuclear medicine, and a film recorder was a much-needed accessory. Sensitive to the coming revolution in medical imaging, they conceived products to support the new technologies (e.g., ultrasound). Matrix was profitable from the start, with pretax margins as high as 30 percent. (The company was organized as Subchapter S and when the principals took out all the profits—and paid taxes up to 70 percent—the company was unable to finance expansion and pay off suppliers. A forced merger brought in added management, and from a $2.5 negative net worth in 1978, Matrix now is very healthy.) What's most incredible is the modest level of R&D for a company at the leading edge of a high technology—only a miserly 3.5 percent of sales. How do they get away with it? "We get help with R&D from our suppliers, customers and film companies," says co-founder Ivan Volent. "This help has allowed us to introduce a whole stream of new products. In addition, we have strenuously avoided the not-invented-here syndrome prevalent in so many high-tech companies." Some needed technology has been bought, and at quite reasonable prices—for example, a company making high-performance videodisk recorders to store data for image making (thus reducing the amount of radiation exposure). "We have had no trouble competing with the larger companies," affirms President Jerry Bishop, "and we have been able to attract a cadre of talented and skilled people to the firm by making Matrix an attractive place to work." (*Forbes*, March 28, 1983.)

Trus Joist Corporation (Boise, Idaho) was formed to manufacture a unique type of structural component for the roofs and floors of stores, schools, and small office buildings (fiscal 1984 revenues, $96 million, profits, $6 million; earnings grew at more than 30 percent during the late 1970s). Today the company produces load-bearing construction components that are more cost effective than sawn wood products. The company weathered the recent recession and has recovered nicely. Trus Joist is "heavily oriented toward being a 'new products company,' "—this is its history and this is its future. Its R&D department is not large, but has "always initiated new product and manufacturing concepts considerably beyond the capability of the operational portion of the company to absorb." The commitment of the company to R&D is highlighted by the fact that it is directed personally by the cofounder of the company. "His inventive genius, combined with the talents of a dedicated group of professional engineers and technical specialists, has been responsible for the development of all the Company's products and much of its machinery. All products introduced commercially have been proprietary to one degree or another." (But the president comments, "Our marketing is what's most important in protecting our technical lead.")

PharmaControl Corporation (Englewood Cliffs, New Jersey) is a new pharmaceutical company specializing in unique drug delivery systems and improved drug formulations (fiscal 1983 revenues, $1 million; profits, $0.09 million). The company's business consists of four components: (1) it owns exclusive manufacturing and distribution rights to a patented soluble aspirin product; (2) it owns and operates a contract drug processing facility; (3) it conducts R&D projects in drug testing, formulating devices, and drug delivery systems; and (4) it operates a clinical testing facility. The innovative drug delivery systems are designed to lower dosages, reduce side effects, and increase patient compliance—for example, a trans-dermal tape that delivers medication through the skin and into the bloodstream at a controlled rate; a computer-controlled technology for monitoring a patient's response to a drug administered by intravenous infusion, adjusting the drug dosage according to need. PharmaControl, a pygmy in the drug industry, focuses on key areas of leading-edge research where it begins with comparative advantage; the company hopes to transform technological progressiveness into strong market position.

Micron Technology (Boise, Idaho) manufactures commodity memory chips, called by industry experts "the best combination of die size and cell capacity" (private company). In 1982 Micron shipped over 1 million chips from, of all places, Boise. Micron's 64K chips are about half the size of their Japanese competitors' (who have 70% of world markets), 40 percent smaller than Motorola's chip, and a third smaller than Texas Instrument's. Thus Micron should become the low-cost producer, because as chip size decreases, so do manufacturing costs—especially in volume production. Who put this winner together? The company is an unlikely pairing of financier J. R. Simplot, who started out raising pigs in the Depression and built a business empire, and chip designer Douglas Pitman, who dropped out of Idaho State after two years of difficulty with abstract math. Pitman is a true genius and exemplifies the special creativity needed for semiconductor leadership. After just a four-month course in circuit design, Pitman went to Mostek where he laid out the industry standards. Recognized as the top layout man in the business, Pitman believes that the best designs come from the mind of one individual, not the legions of degree-laden engineers amplified by computer-aided design systems. As for initial capital costs, Micron achieved its breakthroughs with less than $20 million, not the $50 million thought to be required to set up an adequate fabrication line—and well less than the $100 million anted up by its larger rivals in Japan and America. On the marketing side Micron confounded the conventional wisdom that a commodity memory chip cannot succeed without testing by the mainframe giants—the big boys don't bother with upstarts. So Micron simply made their chip more tolerant to uneven power sources and unsoldered sockets than any of its rivals. Thus Micron's baby became the chip of choice for microcomputers, and millions are being bought by the main manufacturers (including Apple and Commodore). Perceptiveness, progressiveness, and relevance yield success. (*Forbes*, March 14, 1983.)

Electro Rent Corporation (Santa Monica, California) rents sophisticated electronic equipment to aerospace, defense, and electronic companies (1983 revenues, $54.3 milllion; profits, $7.2 million; five-year average sales growth, 28 percent; five-year average return on equity, 20.6 percent). Talk about turning lemons into lemonade? Try this bit of prestidigitation. Electro Rent, quite successful, was suddenly dealing with a serious inventory problem. The issue was obsolescence. Customers didn't want to rent the older generation of electronic equipment after the newer ones had come out. What to do with all those now-archaic relics, many of which hadn't even been fully depreciated? Start a new business, that's what! "We went into the used equipment business, and created a market out of whole cloth," says Chairman Daniel Greenberg. "The equipment we rent is not like cars, which wear out in three to four years. What we do at the end of the three to four years—the average rental life—is recalibrate and refurbish the equipment. We need service centers as part of our rental business anyway. We often offer warranties (on used equipment) that equal those of the manufacturer." What price do these renewed machines go for? Up to 50 percent off from the then current list price. Many customers do not need state-of-the-art and prefer to save the money. Used equipment is now Electro Rent's fastest-growing segment, accounting for 25 percent of company sales. Innovation becomes alchemy as a serious liability is turned into a marvelous asset. (*Forbes*, November 7, 1983.)

HZI Research Center (Tarrytown, New York) uses the analysis of brain waves for the pre-clinical testing of new drugs (1983 revenues, about $1 million; nicely profitable even after funding high R&D). Customers are major pharmaceutical companies which contract with HZI to determine the psychotropic (mental and behavioral) effect of proposed new drugs. HZI's competitive advantage is its proprietary data base. A new product, felt to have substantial commercial potential, is a microcomputer system that analyzes brain wave patterns ("electroencephalography" or "EEG") for a non-specialist. HZI's founder is Dr. Turan Itil, an expert in the field, who has efficiently used his drug-testing organization (and cash flow) to design and build the new system. He claims that the machine is easy to use, and can quickly describe brain wave patterns and highlight any abnormality. Though the software programs can suggest possible problem areas or unusual EEG frequencies, they do not diagnose. It is expected that the computer will be both usable and affordable by psychiatrists and general practitioners, and it is hoped that EEG analysis will thereby become a regular part of office examinations.

CREATIVE STRATEGY 8

EXTERNAL PERCEPTION

Know the
Industrial/Market
Environment

ISSUES AND IDEAS

Problems

Bakers Emporium operated two dozen large hardware and household stores in the South. The stores were moderate in size and carried a large number of products. The company did little advertising, relying on customer loyalty and word-of-mouth. But then came serious competition. The advent of the very large retail operations (owned by giant public companies) was devastating. Bakers could not match price points on smaller items, nor did it have the distribution systems to maintain current stocks of so many things.

BioTech Diagnostics was one of dozens of biotechnology companies started in the early 1980s. The founding scientists were world-class, and the company had attracted an outstanding group of young Ph.D.s. BioTech had excellent working relationships with two nationally known teaching hospitals. The company raised $7 million in private placement capital and began research in several areas of low-cost, throw-away diagnostic tests and kits. The "burn rate" of cash expended, however, was surpassing budget—especially in relationship to projected income (which was lagging). Commercial products were still years away and the equity markets had dried up.

The Adler Music Corporation operated nine middle-to-upper end audio shops on the West Coast. For years the company stood for quality and customers paid full price for fine equipment. Then came the discounters, including the national mail-order houses, and business began falling off rapidly.

Sequoia International was a full-line paper manufacturer with several hundred kinds of products, from printing paper to business forms to low-grade industrial papers. Market share in each was low and margins were squeezed. (The company was competing across the board against all the billion-dollar producers.) Strategic confusion was typified by the shifting marketing budgets among product lines. (The company had expanded and contracted its product lines, not knowing what, where, or how to seek market-share strength.) Management confusion was indicated by the changing organizational structures. (The company had been set up first by geographic regions, then by product line, then by industry served.)

Solutions

Bakers Emporium must reposition its business or lose it. One approach is to concentrate on "big ticket" items, such as lawn-mowers and power tools, and leave the smaller stuff to others. The company cannot be located in the same centers as its larger competitors. Therefore a "low rent–high advertising" strategy might be in order. Customers are sometimes attracted by the "inconvenience" of making a special trip to an off-beat location if they believe that will get a real bargain there.

BioTech Diagnostics should seek associations with larger companies, national and international, desiring to expand into bio-technology. These firms, often in the chemical industry, are willing to pay very high prices for minority positions—in order to get a "window" on developing technologies. These associations often provide channels for marketing as well and can be a ready source of new capital, providing needs are legitimate.

The Adler Music Corporation cannot compete on price with the huge mass merchandisers. It must offer more value than just the product. Service, reliability, and customized home installations cannot be matched by the discounters. Also to be considered is enlarging the product mix to include video, especially as the technologies begin to merge. Personal computers, too, are a possibility—although this has become a specialized market itself.

Sequoia International must make a decision and stick to it. The vacillation is probably worse than making a suboptimal decision. Dominance in any one segment of the paper business is impossible to obtain considering the scope and size of competition. Rather, Sequoia should seek to supply top service to a selected list of customers, possibly in a specific geographic region or industry. The ability to deliver needed products on time to customers is critical. The major paper manufacturers can be, because of their size, rather smug order takers. There is room, therefore, for a real service-oriented company. Rather than spending money on advertising (where Sequoia would be hopelessly outgunned), it should put resources into people and product—to supply and service the needs and problems of targeted customers.

CURRENT CASES

Earle M. Jorgensen Company (Los Angeles, California) manufactures and markets diverse products of steel and aluminum; it stresses customer service and maintains for customer convenience large inventories—carbon, alloy, stainless, tool, and specialty steels as well as various kinds of aluminum (1983 revenues, $229 million; profits, $7 million—"the worst conditions in the metal industry in 35 years"; Jorgensen has maintained steady profitability in a difficult industry: 1981 revenues, $401 million; profits, $29 million; first half 1984: revenues, $148 million, up 31 percent; profits, $5.4 million, up 134 percent). In each company plant there hangs a sign that says "Only Customers Pay Wages." This is more than a motto, it's Jorgensen's motivating force. Customer service, the company asserts upfront in its annual report, is "not reactionary, but an affirmative, dynamic, and positive attitude." Even during the worst of the recession, Jorgensen kept inventory levels high to accommodate customers, continuing to upgrade and enlarge facilities. Inventory is stocked in bars, plates, sheets, strips, coils, tubes, and structured shapes. The company uses twenty-five plants and service centers for quick response to customer needs. Jorgensen Steel is family controlled (Earle M. is founder and chairman; John is president) and emphasizes motivated, fulfilled managers. The most visible aspect of company dedication to customer service is, according to official pronouncements, "the conduct and performance of Jorgensen salespeople. Each salesperson must possess the 'bedrock' values upon which the company was founded. These values are honesty, integrity, trustworthiness, hard work, and above all, knowledge of their products and the way customers do business. . . . Each sales trainee spends considerable time in various departments of the company. . . . Comprehensive classes in Metallurgy are a must. . . . Most important, they get to know and understand their customer's business, products, processes, and markets. The salesperson's total commitment is to see that the material ordered is delivered on time, and exactly according to specifications." Corporate commitment drives intense dedication to customer service, which generates sustained profitability.

Telophase (California) is the arch enemy of Hillenbrand's Batesville Casket Company (Chapter 7). Certainly not a rival in making burial caskets, Telophase is a cremation company (projected 1985 revenues, $12 million; 20 percent annual growth over the past twelve years). With eleven offices nationwide, Telophase—the name is the scientific term for the last stage in a cell's lifecycle—is the largest cremation company in the country, though tiny in comparison to the massive $6.4 billion funeral industry. Since the average funeral costs more than $3000, and since the average cremation rarely tops $500, Telophase founder Thomas Weber has spent a fortune on attorneys' fees. Why lawyers? In order to thwart the legal maneuvers, lobbied by the powerful funeral industry, to legislate or regulate him out of business. A recent problem has been more serious—a suit charging that certain crematoriums have been burning bodies en masse, so that relatives are not sure whose ashes they in fact receive back. Though Telophase was not named, Weber admits that "these suits are a blight on the industry." Yet cremations are a growth industry, having tripled to about 12 percent of all American deaths per year (about 240,000)—nearing 40 percent in trendy California. Clarity and coherence Telophase has, and distinctiveness certainly so. We'll see if they're enough. (*Forbes*, September 26, 1984.)

Gravity Guidance, Inc. (Pasadena, California) manufactures "gravity boots" for "inversion therapy"—hanging upside down to eliminate back pains (1982 revenues, $11.5 million; profits, almost $2 million; 1983 revenues, estimated at $20 million). Fad or fact? Doctors report "symptomatic relief" from sore backs, though no permanent cure. Invented by Dr. Robert Martin in 1965, sales inched from $35,000 in 1971 to an underwhelming $160,000 in 1979. Then came the stuff of which dreams are made. Out of nowhere, heart-throb Richard Gere was shown hanging upside down in the movie *American Gigolo*. His purpose? To prepare his slinky body for the performance requirements of wealthy Southern California matrons. Sales soared and Martin's son Bryce, no doubt dumbfounded at what was happening to dad's side business, came hurrying home from teaching international law in Europe. Bryce got to work immediately; he bought advertising in the sports section of the *Los Angeles Times*, and in magazines such as *Runners World* and *Tennis*. He got gravity boots placed alongside other exotica in snooty stores such as Abercrombie & Fitch, in sporting goods chains such as Herman's and Oshman's, and even in the mass merchandisers like J. C. Penney and K Mart—not to mention in almost 1000 independent retailers. Gravity boots retail at around $70 a pair; but, please, you can't use them without a doorway-mounted "inversion bar" for another $20–$25. For real aficionados, of course, only the "guider" will do—a stretcherlike contraption that goes for $200–$400. Gravity Guidance's capital costs are low and profits are high—the company merely assembles the pieces, subcontracting out all the parts. The younger Martin's new calling is to prove that inversion is "a form of keeping fit that will not come and go," and he is allocating big advertising bucks to the crusade. Whether or not his commitment is founded on the product or its revenues, this company is certainly both distinct and coherent, dominating its newly created niche. And whatever the ultimate outcome, credit the Martins with taking market advantage of a screenwriter's prop. (*Forbes*, September 26, 1983.)

Merry-Go-Round (Towson, Maryland) operates a chain of 224 retail clothing stores catering to 15- to 35-year-olds into the rock music scene (1983 revenues, $110 million—up 46 percent; profits, $6 million—up 71 percent; return on equity, averaging 24 percent). Stores, mainly in malls, are festooned with sharp shining decor (black walls, omnipresent chrome and mirrors) and asound with hard blaring rock (the latest hits). Merry-Go-Round began by selling jeans—harmless enough. Some years later, CEO Mike Sullivan, then an accountant and chief financial officer, seized the future after seeing the popularity of the movie *Saturday Night Fever*. "Every guy in America wanted a three-piece polyester suit," he recalls thinking. "They wanted to look like John Travolta and go to the discos. We sold tons of those suits." From then on, though he himself dresses conservatively, his company was into every clothing fad that came out. When it was jeans, he had every designer name. When Travolta went western in *Urban Cowboy*, Merry-Go-Round was loaded with leather, suede, and fringes. (Some tampering with the strategy convinced Sullivan of its merits. When the recession hit, Merry-Go-Round moved into cheaper clothing, worried that they would lose sales to discounters. Profits dropped three-quarters. "We found out that our customers weren't all that price conscious. They were more interested in fashion.") The newest influence on teen buying habits, both in styling and advertising, is MTV—and Merry-Go-Round is in the forefront of exploiting it. MTV, to the uninitiated, is Music Television, the 24-hour rock music channel on cable television featuring videotapes of leading rock groups singing and acting out their hit songs. The video productions are wild and innovative; they are often at the leading edge of television creativity (like it or not), and they exert strong influence on clothing styles. So through the medium of television, the great cultural equalizer (or sinker), young people from the suburbs and towns are as up to date as their city slicker peers. "Kids are looking at those videos and saying, 'Hey, that's how I want to look.' " And that's where Sullivan's buyers are looking; watching MTV is their most important window on the world. For example, when the lead singer of a popular group wore a Union Jack sweatshirt with cutoff sleeves, a Merry Go Round buyer put in a rush order for 600. The test sold out in a few days, at $15 a pop, signalling a frenzied craze spiralling to 40,000 over the next six months. Too cheap, that one? Try this one: A leather jacket with twenty-seven zippers and fine wire mesh on the shoulders worn by the white-hot Michael Jackson. The 100-order test sold out at $750! A less expensive version—at the bargain price of $350— brought much Christmas cheer. (Perceptiveness yields progressiveness, and progressiveness, distinctiveness, and relevance all yield dominance.) Wall Street, of course, is suspicious of businesses built on fads and crazes. Sullivan understands their attitude. "They look at this stuff and say, 'Nah, people don't wear that.' But somebody is buying it. There's cash in the bank [about $12 million, by the way], and we aren't making the numbers up." No denying the fad orientation. But how to attenuate the obvious risks? Merry-Go-Round stresses fast but careful market tests and inventory controls, using electronic registers to monitor results. The payoff is good. Merry-Go-Round stores average $260 per square foot, a cut above the average $180–$200 for average retailing. The conservative side of Sullivan is expressed by more than attire. All his profits aren't going back into the same shops; he is opening some classy men's stores, and, horrors and heresies, a chain of more conservative women's clothing—Ship 'N Shore. (*Forbes*, February 13, 1984.)

Continental Health Affiliates, Inc. (Englewood Cliffs, New Jersey) provides health care in the home, from nurses to sophisticated therapies such as dialysis and chemotherapy (1983 revenues, $14 million; profits, $1.5 million). With the increasing outcry over national medical costs, home care is already a $2.5 billion industry; it is considered the fastest-growing segment of America's enormous health-care industry. Gargantuan medical and hospital expenses are gobbling up an increasingly large proportion of the country's GNP. This trend simply cannot continue; fundamental change must occur—there is no rational alternative—and Continental Health's CEO, Jack Rosen, is setting up well ahead of the crest of the wave. He is both perceptive and committed; his belief in the importance of what he is doing is real. He asserts that patients generally prefer treatment at home when possible. "The biggest constraint we've faced," admits Rosen, "is winning acceptance by physicians and hospital administrators. Both groups traditionally earned their income within a hospital setting, and they are concerned with the loss of that income. But they'll have to learn to do their business in a nontraditional way." (*Inc.*, May 1984.)

Jeffrey Martin, Inc. (Union, New Jersey) markets old-time, brand-name consumer products with imaginative repacking and saturation media buys (1983 revenues, $66 million; profits, $8 million). These familiar health and beauty aids are almost like old friends, giving customers confidence mixed with nostalgia—in addition to product value. But make no mistake about Jeffrey Martin's approach—the company reestablishes its brands in the marketplace with modern, hard-ball advertising. Beginning with products such as COMPOZ Nighttime Sleep Ayd and TOPOL Smokers' Tooth Polish, Jeffrey Martin (derived from the first names of CEO *Martin* Himmel and his son *Jeffrey*, company vice-president) has added others. Some examples include Doans pills for backaches, AYDS Appetite-Suppressant Candies, and CUTICURA, a 100-year-old soap reintroduced as a product for "combination" dry and oily skin. (TOPOL, with a 3.7 percent share of the $950 million toothpaste market, is the big one, contributing more than 40 percent of company earnings.) Jeffrey Martin is fueled almost entirely on advertising energy. It doesn't manufacture any of its products; but wow, does it market them! You can feel the fire. The company is now the largest network radio advertiser in the country (spending $13.9 million through nine months in 1983); and the second largest transportation advertiser (over $6 million in 1983). (In the process its in-house agency has become one of the largest 100 ad agencies.) A full 50 percent of the company's gross margin income is spent on advertising, a good dose of which comes during off-peak radio time when air time is cheap and product receptivity is good—late-night talk shows are ideal for COMPOZ, though perhaps not for the talk show. (*Inc.*, May 1984.)

Seven Oaks International (Memphis, Tennessee) processes discount coupons for retailers (1983 revenues, $17.7 million; profits, $3.7 million—a fat 21 percent in after-tax profits that sure beats the hard-squeezed couple of points earned by their clients hawking food and household products). With some 4.5 percent of all discount coupons (like from Sunday papers) being redeemed at stores (compared to 2% a decade ago), there's an incredible amount of logistical work to be done. That's Seven Oaks' business—collecting coupons from retailers, reimbursing them for honoring coupons, and then turning in the coupons to the corporate issuers for cash. Seven Oaks earns a penny or two on each coupon. That means a lot of coupons—closing in on a billion a year—and that means a lot of business. The huge chains, like Safeway and Foodtown, use A. C. Nielsen to do their dirty work. But who's to take care of the independents? Nobody, and that's the niche that Seven Oaks created for itself. Sam Sarno, founder and chairman, was a grocer himself, struggling with those myriad pieces of paper when he realized that there was gold in those mischievous things. A market sense was the key here. "Nielsen didn't care about the small individuals, so the market was open. The timing was perfect. Couponing was starting to grow." It's big business, these coupons. About 2000 companies play the game, printing up 119 billion coupons in 1982 with a face value of $25 billion (more than the GNP of many countries). Seven Oaks makes its money in various ways. Example: Since the smaller independents are often strapped for cash, Seven Oaks can exchange the coupons for dollars more quickly, bumping their take for the trouble. If the grocer wants reimbursement of face value within 24 hours, Seven Oaks retains the grocer's fee of seven or eight cents per coupon paid by the manufacturer for the bother of handling. (Thus Seven Oaks acts like a virtual bank.) Who collects, sorts, counts, and does all the other things you have to do with those coupons? Cheap labor, that's who—and that's another secret of Seven Oaks' success. All coupons are processed in Juarez, Mexico, where 1300 workers earn about 85 cents an hour. Says Sarno, "We learned to do something that Nielsen wasn't able to do: how to handle small accounts very efficiently and make money doing it." Now Seven Oaks is second only to Nielsen in the business and, with their lower cost structure, is making noises about going after the leader's accounts. Not only are profits high in the industry; so are entry barriers. Not so much capital expenditures, but reputation and experience.

Fraud is a real problem, and issuers authorize retailers to deal only with the major clearinghouses. (*Forbes*, January 16, 1984.)

Shopwell, Inc. (New York City) owns and operates a chain of about eighty supermarkets in the New York region (1983 revenues, $512 million; profits, $1.8 million; earnings per share, deficit in 1974 and 1975, hit $2.18 in 1982) For years an also-ran among supermarkets in the highly competitive metropolitan area, Shopwell management perceived "a niche that was not being properly addressed," according to Glen Rosengarten, executive vice-president (father Martin is CEO, and the family owns 30% of the stock). "We saw that upscale marketing was not being done in New York [in supermarkets]," he recalls concluding, "and our stores were already located in some nice neighborhoods." The change began in 1979 when the Rosengartens (Glen's brother Jay is chief financial officer) commenced the transformation. Each remodeled store had a new character—and a new name, "The Food Emporium"—and by 1984 there were twenty of them. Foods normally found only in gourmet shops lined the supermarket shelves. Tanks of live fish were set up, and butchers were hired to cut meat on customer request. Shoppers could pick up French truffles, kiwi fruit, Belgian endive, five kinds of apples, and seventy-five varieties of mustard. Clerks had to wear ties and, importantly, know the differences among exotic cheeses. For these upscale stores to be successful on such a large scale (heretofore unknown in gourmet shopping), a higher degree of service was essential, as was a well-educated shopper. To accomplish the latter, each Emporium runs up to three demonstrations a week. Chefs explain new recipes and pass out samples. Pamphlets inform customers about Romanoff caviar (how to care for it), French croissants (history and composition), and Colombian coffee (how to choose the best kinds). The Rosengartens' market sense was correct; people were willing to pay more for better foods. Relevance as well as distinctiveness can dominate a niche. But the family had to learn as well. Glen and Jay had to begin thinking like specialty grocers, not like traditional, buy-it-by-the-bulk, cheaper-is-better supermarket executives. They also had to learn something else earlier. They had dropped a bundle trying to expand into Massachusetts and Vermont in the middle 1970s. "It taught us to build on our base as a regional chain," reflects Martin. (Compare Dr. Pepper, Chapter 10.) (*Forbes*, April 25, 1984.)

Endevco, Inc. (Dallas, Texas) the number one company in compound annual growth (1979–1983) on the *Inc.* 100, is a small, upstart, full-service natural-gas processor/transporter (1983 revenues, $92 million, profits, $1.6 million). Endevco does it all—handling everything from the wellheads to the wholesales, even exploration and development of reserves. But the company does it all with only fifty employees. "It's a marketing game now," states chief executive James Bryant. "Natural-gas marketing is the budding new development in this industry. Because of a temporary oversupply in delivery capacity, a lot of wells have cut way back on production. . . . What we do is go after industrial customers that have either been buying gas at spot prices or are considering switching to alternative fuels such as coal or fuel oil. Then we work our way back to the producers, often getting cheap gas released from existing contracts." To compete with energy behemoths, a prospect sounding suicidal to ordinary mortals, seems almost advantageous to the spunky Bryant. "You can't really blame the big companies because when they sold [the old gas] under contract, they thought prices and consumption would stay up. It hasn't, and that's stuck them with reserves that are pricing them right out of the market." Endevco's strategy has been to go after smaller accounts and take smaller margins, accounts and margins that The Majors could not afford to handle. The company markets off-price gas with relatively long contracts (up to five years) featuring "take or release" clauses that effectively open up the fixed-rate price schedule after a period of two years. The company protects itself on the production side as well, negotiating "marketing out" agreements that free it from having to accept expensive gas it cannot sell. J.R., move over. Who said you have to be big to make it in the oil business? (*Inc.*, May 1984.)

Deb Shops (Philadelphia, Pennsylvania) operates 121 retail stores catering to young women in the 13–21 age group (fiscal 1984 revenues, $96 million; profits, $7.5 million—after-tax margin of 7.8 percent is superb for the industry). The market is well defined— "older women" are those in their 20s and 30s—but the market is unforgiving. "If you do things right," says CEO Marvin Rounick simply, "you will make a lot of money, and if you do it wrong you won't have to worry. You will be out of business." Rounick took a hosiery and lingerie business (cofounded by his father) and built it into a thriving juniors business. The cause of his success? He gives the same weight to tight inventory and expense control as he does to merchandising. *Forbes* calls Deb Shops "one of the most profitable mid-sized retailers around," succeeding against competitors that are "big, tough and expert" (such as the junior divisions of Petrie Stores and Miller-Wohl; Lerner Stores and Charming Shoppes). Deb Shops are all located in malls, mostly in the East and Midwest, with more than one-fourth in Pennsylvania. Prosperous stores in prosperous regions? Not necessarily. Some of the best performers can be found in areas of depressed economies, and therein lies one secret of success. Deb stores offer "fashion at a price," sharp clothing costing well below designer extravagances. "Our customers are looking for value," remarks Rounick, "but they will not pay up to get designer labels." They would rather pay $20 to get a pair of jeans with fashion-cut styling than $40 for the same thing with the designer emblem. (Relevance, clarity, and coherence are the bedrock of critical success strategies.) Rounick insists on having fresh inventories at all times, and he will cut prices quickly to convert slow-moving items to cash. Customers like to come in and spot the bargains. "A blouse that is not attractive to many customers at $18 will find many more admirers at $15, and it will fly out of the store at $12," he reflects. "It's simply the question of finding the highest price at which that will happen." Financing is done through internally generated cash; long-term debt doesn't exist. (Some years ago, after a bank dropped the account, the company almost went under. "I vowed then to get the company in such a position that I didn't need banks.") (*Forbes*, October 24, 1983.)

CREATIVE STRATEGY 9

GROWTH–PROFITS TRADEOFF

Weigh Top Line
with Bottom Line

ISSUES AND IDEAS

Problems

Hospital Services, Inc., was a medium-sized operator of twenty-five nursing and acute-care hospitals in the Pacific Northwest. Sales volume was over $150 million and growth had been frantic—a tenfold increase in five years—largely through acquisitions. Hospitals and homes were located both in large and smaller cities and several emergency centers were being planned. The working strategy had been to keep pace with the industry giants, the $1–$3 billion health-care operators. The growth was being achieved, but profits remained razor thin. Furthermore, the balance sheet had been leveraged highly to make the cash acquisitions, and interest payments were soaking up whatever little profits were being projected.

Cowboy Bob's Family Restaurants combined sit-down variety with fast-food convenience. Incorporated in 1978, the nineteen locations had revenues of $47 million in 1983. The restaurants had a unique approach. The operations were like a franchise; individual entrepreneurs owned the shops and paid fees as a percentage of gross sales. But the parent company put up 80–90 percent of the capital required for fixed assets and working capital (giving the entrepreneurs options to buy back up to 50 percent at preset formulas). Cowboy Bob's profits were excellent, but cash flow had become a serious problem. Bank lines had been fully taken down and equity markets were currently closed.

Sterling Oil, an Oklahoma-based oil and gas exploration company, was playing in the major leagues—despite its relatively minor net worth of only $110 million and revenues of $135 million. Yet the company had put together a first-rate executive team, headed by a dynamic CEO with big-oil experience. Senior management had been attracted through a generous package of salaries and stock options. Yet profits remained weak and cash was tight. Executive overheads were well out of proportion to the size of the company. The board, however reluctantly, was considering executive cuts.

Solutions

Hospital Services, Inc., cannot compete with the giants and must not try. The company must stake out areas of special strength and limit growth to assure bottom-line profitability. Concentrating on smaller cities and towns is one approach. Stressing less glamorous areas such as nursing and rehabilitation homes is another. (The company could change its name, say to "Almost Home Care, Inc.").

Cowboy Bob's Family Restaurants must either give up its philosophy of partial ownership of locations or cut back growth. Since the former remains an important part of its long-term strategy, it was decided to hold back growth until cash flow catches up with profits.

Sterling Oil should not cut its executive team; they are the best part of the company, the strongest company competency and competitive strength. The key strategy here must be to expand. How? In a time of general weakness in oil and gas, many smaller companies are in serious trouble. These would be receptive to an acquisition with Sterling stock (as long as their debts would be assumed). Sterling could afford to pay slightly more than market value in order to amortize its superb executive team (eliminating overheads subsequently in the acquired companies). Trading off short-term profits (on an earnings per share basis) for long-term benefit is the clear indication.

CURRENT CASES

Tootsie Roll (Chicago, Illinois) manufactures and markets its well-known branded candy (1983 revenues, $80 million; profits, $5 million). Diversification to this fiercely independent confectionary has been largely limited to the lengths and sizes of its famous Tootsie Rolls, or in spurts of daring, to Tootsie Roll lollipops and Bonomo Turkish Taffy. A modern plant, paid for with operating funds, will add efficiencies. The company has $20 million in the bank and no long-term debt. Ellen and Melvin Gordon, as president and chairman, respectively (owning 47% of the stock), are quite content with their lot. (Ellen's father obtained control of the almost 90-year-old company a half century ago.) Though they are looking more seriously at acquisitions, the Gordons are in no hurry. "There aren't too many brand names like ours left," reflects Melvin. "The analysts tried to pressure us to buy something several years ago. 'Why don't you leverage the company?' they said. 'Look what everybody else is doing.' " (Analysts like leverage since it produces higher returns on equity and amplifies their idol-like earnings per share.) "Well," continues Melvin, "when interest rates went sky-high, the leveraged companies went into a lot of debt, and some didn't survive. We're glad we didn't yield. We feel we can make a fairly substantial acquisition now without getting heavily into debt. We don't believe in it." (*Forbes*, February 13, 1984.)

Tampax (Lake Success, New York) is a leader in the feminine hygiene industry, with a brand name that connotes quality and reliability, and market dominance that yields consistently high financial returns (1983 revenues, $346 million; profits, $51 million; five-year average after-tax return on sales, 16.7 percent; on equity, 26 percent). The industrywide scare regarding a tampon-related disease—toxic shock syndrome—affected Tampax only mildly, a remarkable tribute to its perceived trustworthiness. Tampax has been the leader in the internal protection market for forty years. Now after many years of limiting growth to its highly specific niche, the company has begun a cautious campaign of broadening its base of commercial activities. The introduction of "Maxithins" into the external pad category was the first step in the diversification program. It has become the fastest growing brand in the fastest growing segment of the sanitary protection market. "American women of all ages trust the Tampax name," asserts the company, "purchasing more than 800 million units of our new Maxithins brand since its [recent] introduction." (The company is changing its name to "Tambrands," reflecting its diverse interests.) Two criteria control the company's new business activities: "1) We will enter or acquire only those businesses we know how to manage; 2) We will not undertake a new business activity unless and until we have capable people available to manage that activity well. It's important that we not overreach our management depth, experience or skills." Amen.

Bandag (Muscatine, Iowa) is in the tire business; it is a perennially profitable medium-size company (1983 revenues, $304 million; profits, $39 million) in an industry where the bottom lines of multi-billion-dollar giants (Firestone, Uniroyal, General, etc.) have taken a roller-coaster ride. The key to Bandag's success is its positioning. The company does not make original tires and therefore does not compete head-on with its massive rivals. Bandag is in the *retreading* business. It reports "significant gains . . . though the country has been plagued with economic difficulties." Company direction is discussed in the CEO's 1983 letter to stockholders. Focus and coherence are highlighted; comparative advantage is stressed. "Bandag began as a retreading company and then branched out into a multidivisional structure. But it's becoming apparent that the headlong rush to diversification, which was characteristic of the seventies, is no longer appropriate for the intermediate term. Our future is inexorably tied to the retreading business; and as a matter of fact, Bandag's future has never been more exciting and promising." As more radial tires come onto the market, the company claims competitive advantage: "no one can retread them better than Bandag dealers." (Dealer service and support are critical: "When our dealers prosper, we prosper and vice versa.") The company's strong financial position reflects good cash flow and minimum debt. Goals are to achieve real growth of 3 percent higher than inflationary growth, and to average 28 percent return on average net assets. Bandag is altering its expense structure to be consistent with its "leaner, trimmer, and more sharply focused" approach. As part of a general program of overhead expense control, Bandag has eliminated some corporate positions (which were created originally to support a broadly diversified, multidivisional corporation). The CEO is blunt: "Our philosophy has changed, as our prior diversification program has not met with the degree of success which we feel meets our long-term financial goals. Bandag's future growth will not depend on acquisitions of unrelated, cyclical, vulnerable, low-margin, difficult-to-manage businesses. It will depend on effectively managing the business we know best—retreading."

Plantronics (San Jose, California) manufactures advanced telecommunications and factory automation equipment (1983 revenues, $114 million; profits, $8.3 million; average ten-year return on sales over 10 percent). Growth has been steady, though not explosive, reflecting itself in the excellent margins. Primary products include lightweight telephone headsets and infrared-based speakerphones (which overcome the "bottom-of-the-well" echo of conventional speakerphones in telephone conferences); computer-controlled in-circuit test equipment; and interface products. The company's products and systems, based on similar technologies and market needs, are used by the Bell operating companies, independent telephone companies, and other common carriers. The company calls "improving productivity" in office and factory the focal point of its corporate strategy. It places "high emphasis on individual initiative" in line operations. Plantronics considers itself an "entrepreneurial company."

General Housewares Corporation (Stamford, Connecticut) manufactures and markets cookware such as skillets and giftware such as candles (1983 revenues, $87 million; profits, $4.6 million). The interesting story here is the company's diametric difference in performance during the recent two recessions, 1982 versus 1974.

In the earlier year, loaded with a mess of diverse inventory and high debt (both the result of numerous acquisitions), GHC lost $7 million on about $50 million in sales. This time around, with only $74 million in sales (eight inflationary years later, they are in fact a smaller company), GHC earned $3.7 million. The lesson is clear. GHC traded off growth for profits; that's why it's here today— and flourishing. After surviving the middle seventies, though just barely, GHC shed various parts of the company (such as steel kitchen furniture) and resuscitated the balance sheet. Then they got to work—putting capital into efficient production facilities for the products that remained, and developing an upscale line of skillets and bakeware with higher margins. (An example is the "Magnalite Professional" line—adorned with a satiny-grey "professional" look, the result of a $350,000 electrolytic bath, it has grown at 50 percent over the past two years. A whole series of "designer" and artistic products is being introduced.) Though GHC has yet to make a successful acquisition, it is again on search. This time, however, it promises to stick closer to home. We hope so. (*Forbes*, April 11, 1984.)

Caressa, Inc. (Miami, Florida) manufactures and markets women's shoes costing $54 and up (1983 revenues, $61 million; profits, $8 million; 1982 return on equity, 29.7 percent; high liquidity, debt free). It has a respectable 5 percent share of what is a fragmented upscale market. Family controlled, Caressa has been successful with everything other than new venture expansions—yet they seem to keep coming. Repeated "synergistic" acquisitions have spilled red ink. An attempt to manufacture in Hungary to reduce labor costs reduced profits instead—Hungary had no leather and no easy way of bringing any in. Why does Caressa keep trying? Supposedly they worry about standing still—somebody said it was like death. (What's so wrong with standing still and making money?) Also, pricey shoes comprise only 5 percent of the overall women's shoe market. So Caressa is setting sights on larger markets—on shoes in the $38–$54 range, targeted for younger career women and comprising 26 percent of the market. (The company would like to take 5 percent of the $1 billion annual sales in this segment.) Where to make the new line? With $11 million in free cash, wherever they want. This time they chose Brazil—with lots of good reasons, except a good track record. Marketing is said to be Caressa's weakness, something management is determined to strengthen. Relationships with key accounts are being nurtured; consumer advertising is being planned. Yet the fundamental question remains, that growth–profits tradeoff. (*Forbes*, March 28, 1984.)

Standard Candy Company (Nashville, Tennessee) manufactures and markets a chocolate-caramel-peanut-marshmallow candy bar named "Goo Goo Cluster" (1983 revenues, $7 million; profits, private company). After taking over the Nashville-based firm in 1982, young entrepreneur Jimmy Spradley has tripled production to 150,000 bars a day. With family money invested in a company losing money, he concentrated on marketing, coming up with constant promotions, enticing brokers with incentives (e.g., bonus trips), and appealing to retailers with substantial discounts. Getting into Wal-Marts was an important hurdle, and Spradley made the leap by combining appeals to Southern chauvinism with good price breaks. After some testing, Goo Goos are now in all 680 Wal-Mart stores. A sharp deal with Delta Airlines offers travelers 200,000 Goo Goos every month with in-flight meals, garnering tremendous exposure. Marshall Fields in Chicago and the Kroeger supermarket chain have also begun carrying the bar. Spradley has started putting together a professional team, stealing two key marketing men from industry giants, Hershey and Mars. A rating service reports that Goo Goos have jumped from number 139 to number 79 in national rankings of America's favorite candy bars—quite an accomplishment in a highly competitive market where consumer preferences have long histories going back to childhood and are hard to disgorge. The youngster's not infallible, of course. Impatient for further growth, Spradley doubled usual discounts for five weeks. Sales skyrocketed but profits plunged. "I've learned there's more to my company's health than fast growth." Stories of the famous and the powerful ordering special shipments of Goo Goos—from Hollywood celebrities to Washington lawmakers—increase the candy bar's mystique. Flush with strong success in the South, Spradley wants to go national, yet he has only limited market tests and minimal ad budgets. He plans to consolidate current areas, then spread sales coverage in overlapping circles. (A University of Chicago MBA, Spradley might ponder the lessons of Dr. Pepper, and what can happen when a successful regional firm goes after the giants—M&M/Mars and Hershey each do over $1 billion; Snickers alone tops $300 million.) Spradley is indomitable: "I mean, let's face it: 'Goo Goos' is a dumb sounding name, but it sells the candy. No one ever forgets it." (*Inc.*, May 1984.)

Versa Technologies, Inc. (Racine, Wisconsin) produces two basic product lines: molded and extruded silicone rubber components and fluid-power products (fiscal 1984 revenues, $30 million; profits, $2.7 million; six-year return on sales, 8.8 percent). The company has a strong balance sheet, indicative that it could be growing faster. Yet Versa/Tek has opted for a strong bottom line in the tradeoff. The company strategy? Listen to Versa/Tek's CEO: "The company's strategy is to concentrate on market niches where customer needs for technological and engineering expertise, product quality, and superior service will command an above average return. . . . For many years we have been using the phrase 'niche management' to describe the way Versa/Tek is structured. Quite simply, this term means we are seeking niches where we can bring to the marketplace a technological expertise that will solve customers' problems so effectively that product quality becomes a more important consideration than price. This concept is our standard for new business, growth, and acquisitions. Customer service is stressed through a manufacturing strategy of smaller, geographically dispersed plants with compatible fabrication capabilities." Silicon products are sold to manufacturers of health-care and pharmaceutical products, business and data processing equipment, automotive components, and electronic apparatus. Fluid-power products include specially designed hydraulic cylinders, pressure boosters, valves, and other devices sold to manufacturers of machine tools, food handling, and industrial robots (e.g., Unimation, a world leader in robotics). In a recent restructure, a medical division was formed to concentrate on the high-growth health care market. Emphasis was shifted from organization by product produced to organization by market served. Versa/Tek's annual report shows flair and aggressiveness. Pride and excitement characterize the CEO's letter to stockholders. Quotes on the 1981 and 1983 covers reflect basic philosophy: "No institution which does not continually test its ideals, techniques and measure of accomplishment can claim real vitality" (Milton); "When it comes to technological innovation, how can muscle-bound Goliaths compete with quick moving little Davids" (Dr. Dwight Baumann). Versa/Tek markets to many *Fortune* 500 companies, a fact it flaunts with pride. A new area being explored is the imprinted all-silicon rubber "touchpads," used to environmentally seal the control keys on electronic devices. The company is candid in reporting that its fluid-power division did not meet sales and profit goals. Although company customers were affected by the recession, "the number of new customers and business created by our niche approach to the marketplace has enabled us to continue building the business." The company has a good cash position and low debt. Versa/Tek has the resources to capitalize on opportunities to grow. "We have an active acquisition search program but companies meeting our criteria are hard to find."

CREATIVE STRATEGY 10

FLEXIBILITY/OPPORTUNISM

Change Direction
and Move Quickly

ISSUES AND IDEAS

Problems

Rothson's Discount Marts were free-standing units selling soft goods—women's clothing, textiles, curtains, linens, and so on. The Marts competed largely on price, and made opportunistic buys of end-of-season merchandise from manufacturers. Rothson's had undergone rapid expansion in the last two years, expanding from fifteen stores in the Northeast to sixty-five stores across the country. To maximize efficiency, the units were all stocked the same—but profits started to slip. This was perplexing since with the increased size, management had expected greater profits from economies of scale in purchasing, distribution, and administration.

Top Shape, Inc. was a privately held manufacturing firm doing $6 million per year in specialty exercise equipment. Other than a few giants (such as Nautilus), the industry was fragmented. It was also highly competitive. Top Shape's profits were weak since almost all excess gross margin had to be put back into marketing. High advertising expenditures backed up a force of regional sales reps who did not work full-time for the company. It was thought that Top Shape was too small to support its own sales force. Yet other lines were swaying the reps, and they pushed whichever products were easiest to move at the moment. Switching rep firms did not improve the situation.

The Rawlings Steel Corporation lost over $250 million over the past four years and had filed Chapter 11 bankruptcy. Its antiquated steel mills were closed with no hope of reopening. The company had large land holdings that were supposedly worth over $150 million, although carried on the balance sheet for their historical low cost. The creditors wanted to liquidate the land and the company, getting 35, maybe 40, cents for each dollar of debt.

Neel and Klein was a Midwest real estate developer that had become expert in establishing "strip center" malls dedicated to the off-price boom. These malls were located in lower-rent areas; often they were in old factories, which they had remodeled to be clean and open but with no frills. The formula was successful and the company was besieged by offers to develop many such shopping centers. N & K's financial position, however, could not sustain the increased leverage, and the company had to turn down some lucrative opportunities.

Solutions

Rothson's Discount Marts had lost its initial flexibility to serve market needs. It was most profitable when working in a focused geographic area with well-defined tastes and where its name was well-established. Moving into other areas, especially so rapidly, attenuated rather than enhanced competitive position. Rothson's should attempt to regain flexibility by breaking units into regional centers, each a profit center, each managed by local merchandisers in tune with local needs. Store managers should be given profit participation in their stores, regional managers in their region.

Top Shape, Inc. must support its own sales force, and it must increase its company sales in order to justify the additional expense. How to increase sales without large R&D expenditures and significant risk? Top Shape decided to license overseas products for the American market, especially home exercise systems and concepts from Japan and Scandinavia. Top Shape determined to handle only high-quality products that would sustain its increasing reputation for quality.

The Rawlings Steel Corporation might find a better solution, giving all parties more value—but not immediately. By losing $250 million, Rawlings now has a huge net operating loss (NOL) carryforward that would shelter future earnings. But the company needs profitable operations in order to take advantage of the NOL. If Rawlings could sell its properties and use the $150 million to buy profitable businesses, it should be able to generate some $30–$45 million per year in pretax income—which would be sheltered by the NOL. The creditors should consider taking notes for their debt, plus getting a healthy portion of the stock—perhaps as much as 50–80 percent (depending on negotiations and the structure of the debt). With any reasonable success, the creditors will do far better, and the company will be reborn. (Penn Central, with billions in tax losses, used this approach to transform itself from a bankrupt railroad to a profitable conglomerate.)

Neel and Klein should devise innovative financing mechanisms to enable them to exploit the off-price boom and their own expertise before significant competitors can establish a strong position. Joint ventures could be structured with insurance companies, for example, giving away a good piece of the equity (up to 50 percent), in exchange for long-term financing at favorable interest rates. The same deal could also be offered to private individuals with the attendant tax benefits.

CURRENT CASES

Omark Industries (Portland, Oregon) manufactures specialized products that serve the timber industry; it is the world's leading producer of cutting chain for chain saws (the company's original business); it also manufactures a wide range of goods sold to firewood cutters, gun sportsmen, home do-it-yourself enthusiasts, carpenters, gardeners, and industry (fiscal 1983 revenues, $257 million; profits, $6.8 million—strong recovery begun in fiscal 1984; revenues and profits substantially higher; return on sales 1979–1981, 9.4 percent; earnings per share grew from $0.81 in 1976 to $3.57 in 1980). Omark has recently undergone a thorough self-appraisal. As a result, it is changing its management systems in order "to succeed in the competitive markets of tomorrow." The company must become "flexible and responsive," adapting to "changing markets, changing demand and changing values." Omark articulates "three thrusts of our change: the total involvement of our people, ZIPS (our new approach to manufacturing excellence we call our Zero Inventory Production System), and Total Quality Control." The companywide reduction of inventory by 23 percent in 1983 is a barometer of the early success of ZIPS; it is an "all-out war on the problems that have made high inventories necessary"— inefficiencies, waste, bottlenecks. High inventories, the company proclaims, hinder the early identification of defects in manufacturing. Omark holds ZIPS conferences, exchanging information and giving awards. (Omark proudly describes some detailed results: One pilot project reduced large-size drill inventory 92 percent with a productivity increase of 30 percent; lead times dropped from three weeks to three days, while scrap and rework were reduced about 20 percent. A change in manufacturing log loaders, from functionally oriented departments to product-oriented machine layout, reduced parts travel from 2000 feet to 18 inches, slashed work-in-process from sixty pieces to one, and cut lead time from thirty days to a few minutes.) Whereas some companies offer a short statement of overall philosophy (most give nothing at all), Omark presents two full pages worth (the product, we are told, of much intracompany discussion, debate, and argument). Highlights follow: *Preamble* (attractive return for investors; rewarding employment for people; quality products for customers). *People* (most important long-term asset; "Individual respect, mutual trust and a spirit of cooperation are a way of life at Omark"). *Customers* (fill needs with high-quality products at reasonable price). *Profit* (ensure healthy survival; satisfactory return; provide funds for future growth). *Growth* (necessary to provide the environment for employees to achieve personal advancement; made possible by creativity, dedication, and productivity). *Management* (participative management recognizing the importance and potential of each individual; managers must be visible, involved, and good communicators; management must assure consistency between short-range actions and long-term goals). *Business Risk* (necessary to achieve "excellence of performance"; blend internal development and other opportunities; a balanced portfolio of growth and mature businesses; national and international; early warning systems). *Manufacturing* (high quality as measured by functional efficiency; integrity to specifications and freedom from defects; operate with minimum inventories; emphasize flexibility; minimize fluctuations in work force; limit plant size to achieve proper balance between economies of scale and the ability to treat people as individuals). *Suppliers* (high standard of ethical conduct; build long-term relationships). *Citizenship* (to manage company affairs with integrity and excellence; to be an asset to our communities; to be a responsible and stable employer; to encourage employees to participate in government, service, and education organizations). While much here can be dismissed by the cynical as mere platitudes and generalities, the process itself, perhaps more than the content, develops a company more aware of itself and its position in the world.

Ultrasystems, Inc. (Irvine, California) concentrates on defense contracting, alternative energy projects (such as wood-burning electric generating plants), and heavy construction and engineering (1983 revenues, $46 million; profits, $2.1 million). Defense contracting (such as military communications software), now that makes sense. But wood power? Rather flakey, wouldn't you say? Well, take a gander at the customers: Pacific Gas & Electric, the nation's largest utility, and Procter & Gamble, the nation's leading marketing company. Rather blue-chip. Ultrasystems targets its wood-burning areas with careful economic analysis. Electricity costs have to be high and wood abundant (e.g., California, Montana, Alaska, Hawaii, Florida). The company chooses spots near power lines, water, and woods—locations where everybody wins, especially the local forest owners and woodcutters. Ultrasystems owes its success, says *Forbes*, to "raw aggressiveness and opportunism." Government programs are exploited for all they are worth—the 10 percent investment tax credit and the 10 percent energy tax credit can knock $4 million off the cost of a $20 million wood-burning plant. Depreciation deductions will consume $20 million in five years, effectively eliminating another $10 million in taxes for high-income investors. This means that tax incentives alone guarantee recoupment of two-thirds of the initial investment (face value, though, not present value). Not bad. Ultrasystems has also taken advantage of federal legislation that requires utilities to buy more power from outsiders rather than building their own new plants—thus reducing public upfront costs and spreading payments over many years. Ultrasystems' backlog more than doubled in a year (to $63 million), while the construction and engineering giants have seen their backlog shrink. Style more than substance is critical, believes CEO Philip Stevens, an alumnus of tough east Los Angeles (and UCLA engineering). Most good companies have the requisite technology; it's the package it comes in that counts. "We know how to respond to government requests," says Stevens, who once managed the billion-dollar Minuteman III program for TRW. The evidence backs his boast: Ultrasystems is buttressed by many government·contracts and loan guarantees. Although the company does respond to requests by customers much like any normal engineering and construction company, they go further. What they like to do, what they do very well, is to *invent* innovative projects: They bear the upfront feasibility risks, find potential customers, and convince them of their need. Ultrasystems then goes out and raises the financing, being sure to retain an equity interest in the project. "We are creating our own environment," affirms Stevens. By taking equity, Ultrasystems circumvents competitive bidding. With smaller overheads and strong experience, they are able to outmaneuver giant competitors such as Fluor Corporation and Bechtel Group, both of whom are sniffing after these markets (with the slowdown in Mideast construction). Ultrasystems is undertaking a host of unusual projects: a $35 million barley-to-alcohol conversion plant in North Dakota; a proposed $65 million fructose plant powered by geothermal energy (financed by Department of Energy guarantees and limited-partnership capital). The latter is another example of Ultrasystem's sharp, studied perceptiveness. Note the following advantages: an additional 15 percent geothermal power tax credit; continued government support for sugar prices (keeping fructose economically viable); Coke and Pepsi are using up to 80 percent fructose in their soft drinks. But with the price of fructose rising, there are risks. Ultrasystems, for its aggressiveness in operations, is downright conservative on its balance sheet. Borrowings are done through the outside ventures. Nice if you can swing it. (*Forbes*, October 24, 1983.)

Fort Howard Paper Company (Green Bay, Wisconsin) is one of the most consistently profitable firms in the paper industry, though small relative to the giants (1983 revenues, following a major acquisition, $786 million; profits, $107 million; five-year average return on equity was 24 percent; 1978 revenues, $296 million; the company has regularly achieved 17 percent returns on sales—both substantially better than the well-known giants; returns for the forest products industry as a whole average about 12.5 percent on equity and barely over 3 percent on sales). How does Fort Howard pull off such outstanding and consistent performance? First of all, the company concentrates on a narrow range of industrial tissue products (such as napkins, towels, doilies, and toilet and facial tissue— all sold to industrial and commercial users like hotels, motels, restaurant chains, schools, hospitals, and small and large companies). This type of segmented marketing concentrates forces in one arena and avoids the high cost and fierce competition (and high risks) of consumer product development and mass media advertising (consumer brands account for only 13 percent of sales). The unique commitment of Fort Howard's founder is still reflected in the efficiency of production as well as in the coherence of product. Not wanting to be squeezed by pulp suppliers charging high prices, the founder decided to use less costly, recycled middle-grade wastepaper instead of virgin wood—and thus the company escaped the instability of the paper industry over the years. This policy also generates cost advantages over competitors, most of whom have not followed Fort Howard's raw material innovation. (Maybe it's because they own so many trees?) Fort Howard's current management continues the tradition, stressing production efficiency "second to none" and complete internal self-sufficiency for maintenance and repair through "the finest machine shop capability north of Milwaukee." A stickler for efficiency, Fort Howard CEO Paul Schierl states that "the only thing worse than getting a shipment late, is getting a shipment early." The bulk of sales are made through some 2500 independent distributors who are motivated by Fort Howard's comprehensive products line and rapid response time. These distributors carry competing lines, and loyalty, you can be sure, is strictly to their own bottom line. So even though Fort Howard fields about 200 salespeople who call on large institutional customers, when a sale is made the distributor gets the credit. (Now that makes for real loyalty.) Asserting that their biggest asset is their employees, Fort Howard has outstanding benefits including a "goodwill bonus" (16–18 percent in recent years on top of salaries that are already competitive), and an employee stock ownership plan. Change, however, has come upon this paragon of mid-sized virtue, and sadly, the appellation will no longer apply. Fort Howard has acquired Maryland Cup Corporation, a company larger ($656 million in revenues) and less profitable (no surprise). Why is Schierl diluting margins? He hints that growth in the institutional paper-products market has slowed. Maryland Cup, he believes, focuses on the faster-growing fast-food market, and its plastic products (such as disposable tablewear) are growing faster than paper products. We worry, but wish him well (*Forbes*, October 10, 1983.)

Action Industries, Inc. (Chesnick, Pennsylvania) designs promotional ads and provides wholesale merchandise for retailers who want to move stuff fast (1983 revenues, $100 million; profits, $5 million). This is a case of a company finally realizing where it's good and where it's not. (Many companies, unfortunately, never come to this.) Action began as a lukewarm chain of thirty-two hardware and houseware stores in the Pittsburgh area. "Some years we made a little money," recalls Chairman Amos Comay. "Others we lost a little." Consistent profitability was always sought and never found. Only during the stores promotions—called "Dollar Days"—did the chain do well. (The low prices motivated customers to buy needed but not critical items.) Other chains soon asked Action to handle their promotions as well. In 1981 Comay concluded that he was in the wrong business, that he was better at promotion than retailing. (Clarity and coherence, remember, lead to dominance.) "We bit the bullet and started liquidating the stores." After thirty years, it was no easy decision for the 68-year-old Comay. Lucky he makes the hard ones. In fiscal 1983 Action handled a staggering 13,557 promotions. And "handle" means do it all. Action does all the work for the retailer. And who are some of these retailers asking Action to do their work? Your local mom-and-pop corner store? Try K Mart and Sears, which combined provide 25 percent of Action's revenues. Don't think promotions mean simplicity. Action is not rooted in seat-of-pants hunches. These boys use computer analysis of past promotions to select future merchandise. Sure the customer comes walking in for a low-margin glass jar, but the retailer wants her walking out with a high-margin microwave oven. Looking into the future, Action just purchased part of a company designing programs for personal computers. "We believe that many of the mass marketers' customers will be using personal computers within five years," says Sholom Comay, Action's senior vice-president and general counsel (and, not coincidentally, Amos' son). "I believe that they will be looking for software at attractive prices." (*Forbes*, February 13, 1984.)

Preway (Wisconsin Rapids, Wisconsin) caught the increase in energy prices and consumer awareness in the late 1970s perfectly with their fireplace product line (1979 revenues, $57.5 million; profits, $6.6 million). With the corporate slogan "A Nice Warm Feeling," Preway was the number one manufacturer of fireplaces in a fuel-conscious world. The company perceived the environment well when it moved from space heaters, a declining market, into wood-burning fireplaces. Energy efficiency was stressed: Preway fireplaces radiated more heat into the room than up the chimney. The company had 90 percent of the market for mobile homes. Changing demand, however, encouraged by the relaxation of the energy crisis, reduced Preway's revenues to $32 million in 1981 (though maintaining a respectable $2.2 million in profits). Additional products coming on the market—such as unvented gas heaters with oxygen depletion sensor control—brought 1983 revenues up to $40 million with profits of $1.9 million. Preway is using its distinctive competencies to exploit a clear niche in the market, and however volatile the niche, the company remains flexible enough to move with the times, being profitable at different levels of volume.

M.D.C. Corporation (Denver, Colorado) is a real estate developer and builder (1983 revenues, $167 million; profits, $11.9 million—up 100 percent and 92 percent respectively; five-year return on equity, 20.8%). Why did M.D.C. continue to make money during the years when high interest rates choked off new housing starts and most developers lost money? "We respond to change very rapidly," states Michael Feiner, M.D.C.'s president. "So even though housing starts in the Denver area fell last year [1982] to around 13,000 compared with a high of 42,000 in 1972, we did well because we noticed there were two areas that were relatively unaffected— the starter-home market and semi-customer-built homes in the $150,000-to-$250,000 range bought by executives transferred into the area. So that is what we concentrated on. We stayed out of the middle of the market, where historically the greatest number of sales take place." Retrenchment of competitors, especially larger ones who lack the ability to shift gears quickly, was fertile soil in which to grow. "When things are going well, you can't expand into another guy's market," Feiner continues. "He'll cut your pants off. But we figured that we could take advantage of the fact that 25 percent of our competition withdrew in 1981 and 1982. We sold $10 million of debentures and we then had enough capital to tie up land for 10,000 units. As things have gotten better, we are selling some of that land to other builders at a significant profit." (Flexibility leads to distinctiveness, and perceptiveness leads to progressiveness.) (*Forbes*, November 7, 1983.)

North Fork Bank & Trust Company (Hamptons, New York), a minuscule Long Island/New York-based bank ($260 million in total assets, about 1/500 of Citibank), is one of the few banks on *Forbes'* 1983 list of the best small public companies in the country. What kind of results have they shown? Assets have tripled in the last five years. The return on assets was 1.7 percent; on equity it was 21 percent—each twice the industry average for banks of this size. North Fork President John Kansa, a former schoolteacher, took over the languishing institution about eight years ago and decided that banks should be run like businesses. So he fired the seat-warmers and hired professionals whose careers and paychecks were coupled closely to North Fork's performance. Nothing like managerial commitment to get a company moving. With deregulation came the ability to pay higher interests. Deposits leaped 83 percent from 1982 to 1983—but interest paid on those deposits rose a dizzying 245 percent. "Now that we can pay all this interest," Kansa wonders, "how the hell are we going to make the spread?"

The answer, he feels, must be innovation: "Equity participation in real estate ventures, access to the general insurance business, including underwriting and discount brokerage, and real interstate banking." (The man sounds like Citibank's Walter Wriston.) Though the number of banks on Long Island has shrunk from thirty-one in 1963 to eleven in 1984, North Fork's niche is fortuitous geography; it is located in one of the country's hottest real estate markets, the Hamptons, way out near the eastern tip of Long Island, where many affluent New Yorkers keep second homes. Mortgage customers (25 percent of loans) warm a banker's heart. "The prime quality real estate out here attracts a prime quality buyer," says Kansa (and you can feel the warmth radiate). "It's nothing to us to see a loan applicant who makes $600,000 or $700,000 a year. That's routine." Most new loans are made with variable interest rates, avoiding the problem of locking in a low-rate loan if deposit interest soars (as it did several years ago). As compensation, the bank takes a slightly lower interest rate. "We're saying, 'You take the risk, we'll take a smaller margin.' " This is Kansa's philosophy. He notes that "next time there's a recession I'd assume more borrowers than banks will go broke because they'll be faced with 22 percent carrying charges on projects that make sense only at 14 or 15 percent." The deregulation sword that Kansa seeks, however, has more than one edge. Larger banks will be freed to attack new markets, and the ones they'll go after, you can be sure, are the lucrative ones. Kansa is planning some moves of his own—more branches, acquisitions in New York, and suburban Connecticut and New Jersey. Risky for tykes. More immediate is the opening of small loan offices; with only 350 square feet they can compete against larger rivals (such as Chemical). "With all the new areas people are talking about," states Kansa, "making loans is still our fundamental business. We don't want to take our eye off the ball." (*Forbes*, February 27, 1984.)

Byers Communications Systems, Inc. (Atlanta, Georgia) designs, installs, manages, and maintains a wide range of communication systems for cable television companies, common carriers (MCI, Bell Operating Companies, AT&T), and private networks such as universities and corporations (1983 revenues, $15.6 million; profits, $1 million). "Our project management skills are easily transferred from one area to another," boasts CEO Morgan Payne, "and that gives us terrific flexibility." These areas include coaxial cable, fiber-optic lines, satellite earth stations, microwave transmitters, and cellular radio operations. Byers operates in thirty states, taking advantage of the tremendous expansion in private communications networks triggered by the AT&T breakup. Asked about the retrenchment in cable television caused by huge installation costs and pressured profit margins, Payne explains that "we're involved only in the nonconverter part of the system, where service and maintenance contracts are still very much in demand." Some clever financial moves have positioned the company well. A reverse merger with Redfern Food Corporation netted $5 million in capital (after selling off the food operations) without incurring the $1 million costs of a normal public offering. A proposed $40 million stock acquisition of Cellwave Technologies, a manufacturer of fiber-optic and copper cables, would augment the company's service capabilities and strengthen its industry position. (*Inc.*, May 1984.)

APPENDIX I

MATCHED-PAIR ANALYSIS

Primary Results

The presentation of results from the matched-pair analysis of 167 pairs of mid-sized firms follows. Firms were "matched" by gross sales revenues and product-market/industry, and were differentiated by the rate of return on assets: the two-year average of the rate of earnings before interest and taxes to total assets (for the 1977 and 1978 fiscal years).

Each data point is the empirical resultant of a specific comparison for the same variable between the two firms of every matched pair.

+ means that the *more* profitable of the two mid-sized firms evinced a higher value

− means that the *less* profitable of the two mid-sized firms evinced a higher value

0 means either that the two firms were judged equal or that the variable was not applicable or the data were not available.

All the calculations of the quantitative variables and the coding of all the qualitative variables were done by five graduate students in management (M.S. and Ph.D. candidates) at MIT's Sloan School of Management. In general, the correlation between qualitative judgments among the various research assistants was about 65–75 percent, well above chance for a $+/-/0$ choice.

Although the dependent variable (earnings before interest and taxes to total assets) was calculated for a two-year average (1978 + 1977), most of the other variables were calculated for one year—a decision made primarily to save time. For conceptual reasons, several of the variables were calculated for the previous year (1977): variables 4, 5, 6, 7, 8, 9, 10, 24, 25, 26. Other variables were calculated for the current year (1978): variables 2, 3, 11, 12, 13, 14, 15, 16, 17, 18, 19, 20, 21, 22, 23. Variable 1 is the average of 1978 and 1977; and variables 27, 28, 29, 30, 31, and 32 through 100 (the qualitative variables) are self-explanatory. For statistical analyses of those data see Robert Lawrence Kuhn, *Mid-Sized Firms: Success Strategy and Methodology, op. cit.*

Variable	+	−	0
1. Which firm had the higher ratio of after-tax profits to equity?	164	2	1
2. Which firm had the higher ratio of after-tax profits to total sales revenues?	154	10	3
3. Which firm had the higher ratio of sales to assets?	85	76	6
4. Which firm had the higher ratio of total debt to total assets?	41	121	5
5. Which firm had the higher ratio of current assets to current liabilities?	101	64	2
6. Which firm had the higher ratio of net plant and equipment to total assets?	88	77	2
7. Which firm had the higher ratio of inventory to assets?	76	90	1
8. Which firm had the higher ratio of net plant and equipment to gross plant and equipment?	104	61	2

Variable	+	−	0
9. Which firm had the higher ratio of gross plant and equipment to sales revenues?	69	96	2
10. Which firm had the higher ratio of capital expenditures to sales revenues?	94	69	4
11. Which firm had the higher ratio of finished goods to total inventory?	50	58	59
12. Which firm had the higher ratio of sales revenues to total inventory?	102	64	1
13. Which firm had the higher ratio of sales revenues to net working capital?	83	83	1
14. Which firm had the higher ratio of accounts receivables to sales revenues?	72	93	2
15. Which firm had the higher ratio of its largest business segment to total revenues?	84	46	37
16. Which firm had the higher ratio of assets to employees?	63	41	63
17. Which firm had the higher ratio of sales to employees?	64	42	61
18. Which firm had the larger board of directors?	71	60	36
19. Which firm had the higher percentage of outside directors to total directors?	73	74	20
20. Which firm had the larger number of corporate officers?	63	70	34
21. Which firm had the older CEO (age)?	31	36	100
22. Which firm had the older mean age of corporate officers?	36	28	103
23. Which firm had the higher standard deviation of officers' ages?	28	36	103
24. Which firm had the higher ratio of R&D expense to sales?	27	22	118
25. Which firm had the higher ratio of advertising expense to sales?	17	10	140
26. Which firm had the higher ratio of maintenance and repair to sales?	30	33	104

(Table continues on p. 442)

Variable	+	−	0
27. Which firm had the higher ratio of total sales in 1978 + 1977 to total sales in 1976 + 1975?	132	31	4
28. Which firm had the higher ratio of after-tax profits in 1978 + 1977 to after-tax profits in 1976 + 1975?	121	46	0
29. Which firm had the higher five-year mean return on sales: after-tax profits to revenues?	149	17	1
30. Which firm had the higher standard deviation for the above calculated five-year mean return on sales?	73	85	9
31. Which firm had the higher coefficient of variation for five-year return on sales (i.e., the standard deviation normalized for size by dividing by the revenues)?	40	122	5
32. In which annual report is the CEO's picture more prominent?	77	34	56
33. Which CEO gives the visual impression of being the best leader?	76	31	60
34. In which annual report is the CEO's personal profile more prominent?	79	24	64
35. In which annual report is the personal profile of corporate executives more prominent?	59	27	81
36. In which annual report is the profile of the board of directors more prominent?	49	23	95
37. In which annual report is the profile of company employees more prominent?	45	33	89
38. Which annual report is more oriented toward stockholders?	48	17	102
39. Which annual report evinces a greater orientation to customers?	83	21	63
40. Which annual report shows a greater sense of social responsibility?	22	15	130

Variable	+	−	0
41. Which annual report shows a greater orientation toward selling and marketing?	80	27	60
42. Which annual report shows a greater orientation toward sales revenues growth?	77	10	80
43. Which annual report shows a greater orientation toward profits?	56	25	86
44. Which annual report shows a greater orientation toward financial structure?	59	40	78
45. Which annual report shows a greater orientation toward the company's products?	88	20	59
46. Which annual report indicates a greater importance for new products?	80	27	60
47. Which annual report shows a greater orientation toward innovation?	72	23	72
48. Which annual report shows a greater concern with production/manufacturing?	60	28	79
49. Which firm has more centralized plants and facilities?	37	28	102
50. Which annual report indicates a greater importance of state-of-the-art technology?	43	28	96
51. Which firm seems to have more vertical integration backward?	27	7	133
52. Which firm seems to have more vertical integration forward?	22	19	126
53. Which annual report (or 10-K) indicates a greater focus/relatedness for the entire business?	105	17	45
54. Which firm seems to rely more on industrial customers?	19	28	120
55. In which annual report does the firm stress greater product quality?	68	19	80
56. Which firm seems to engage in more customized production to customer specifications?	24	33	110

(Table continues on p. 444)

Variable	+	−	0
57. Which firm seems to have a greater market segmentation by product uniqueness?	65	13	89
58. Which firm seems to have a greater market segmentation by geographic specificity?	20	8	139
59. Which firm seems to have a greater market segmentation by customer/industry specificity?	49	19	99
60. Which firm seems more dependent on large customers?	22	24	121
61. Which firm exhibits a clear, prominent corporate slogan or subtitle (often on the annual report cover)?	23	11	133
62. Which firm has a brief specific business summary (often at the front of the annual report)?	59	17	91
63. Which firm presents a better detailed business description throughout the annual report?	49	31	87
64. Which firm seems to have a greater interest in/concern for issues of industrial economics (for example, market share)?	45	18	104
65. Which firm seems to sense greater competitiveness in its markets?	39	17	111
66. Which firm has (or claims to have) dominance (large market share) within its own corporate "niche"?	98	7	62
67. Which firm evinces greater clarity in goals/objectives/strategies?	97	30	40
68. Which firm evinces greater coherence in goals/objectives/strategies?	103	17	47
69. Which firm seems to have a better sense of its industry/market environment?	54	12	101
70. Which firm seems to better appreciate its own strengths and/or weaknesses?	78	24	65

Variable	+	−	0
71. Which firm seems to have a long-term/time corporate planning horizon?	69	23	75
72. Which firm seems to exhibit a more aggressive/bullish risk-seeking approach?	74	21	72
73. Which annual report evinces the greater corporate enthusiasm/excitement?	63	28	76
74. Which annual report evinces the greater corporate commitment/dedication?	95	20	52
75. Which firm seems to portray a greater degree of corporate uniqueness/distinctiveness?	86	13	68
76. Which firm is more dependent upon the use of brand names?	55	24	88
77. Which firm seems to use more advertising/promotion in business?	45	12	110
78. Which firm seems more dependent on patents/trade secrets/licenses in business?	29	28	110
79. Which firm is more family-controlled?	54	19	94
80. In which firm do the active executives hold more company stock?	43	15	109
81. In which CEO letter (in annual report) is more enthusiasm/excitement shown?	91	22	54
82. In which CEO letter (in annual report) is more commitment/dedication shown?	79	24	64
83. In which firm is the degree of unionization higher?	14	14	139
84. In which firm do employee relations seem better?	33	19	115
85. In which firm do international sales seem more important to overall sales?	55	36	76
86. In which firm is raw materials availability more important?	22	17	128
87. In which firm does seasonality seem to play a more important role?	8	7	152

(Table continues on p. 446)

Variable	+	−	0
88. In which firm are there more legal proceedings/involvements (10-K)?	37	47	83
89. Which firm evinces more divestments/dislocations?	20	43	104
90. In which firm are more corporate reorganizations mentioned?	31	47	89
91. In which firm are any shifts in corporate strategy more apparent?	13	38	116
92. Which annual report appears more expensive (or of better quality)?	80	36	51
93. Which annual report is judged to be more creative?	68	28	71
94. Which annual report projects a higher degree of promotional intensity?	75	38	54
95. Which annual report presents more nonrequired financial data?	41	20	106
96. Did one firm send its 10-K form when its matched firm did not?	33	17	117
97. Which firm sent more past annual reports in response to request?	54	26	87
98. Which firm sent additional materials (for example, a personal letter) along with the annual reports?	46	10	111
99. Did one firm substitute its 10-K form for the current year's annual report?	0	9	158
100. Which firm had the fewer number of four-digit SIC code numbers (see Table 9.6.)?	89	46	32

APPENDIX II

MATCHED-PAIR ANALYSIS

Aggregate Index Variables
and Success/Error Rates
for Classifying Better-Performing
Mid-Sized Firms

Aggregate Index Variables/Primary Variables[a]	Percent Success Rate[b]	Percent Error Rate[b]
Commitment	42/81	17/14
6: Net P & E/assets	53	46
16: Assets/number of employees	38	25
32: CEO picture presence	46	20
34: CEO profile	47	14
36: Board of directors' profile	29	14
71: Long-term planning horizon	41	14
72: Aggressive-bullish attitudes	44	13

(*Table continues on p. 448*)

Aggregate Index Variables/Primary Variables[a]	Percent Success Rate[b]	Percent Error Rate[b]
Commitment (*continued*)		
74: Corporate commitment	57	12
79: Family control	32	11
80: Active execs holding stock	26	9
82: CEO commitment	47	14
Fulfillment	36/64	19/25
20: Number of officers [reverse]	42	38
35: Executive profile	35	16
37: Employee orientation	27	20
73: Corporate enthusiasm	38	17
81: CEO enthusiasm	54	13
84: Employee relations	20	11
Distinctiveness	34/75	11/15
57: Segment/product uniqueness	39	8
58: Segment/geography	12	5
59: Segment/customer-industry	29	11
75: Corporate uniqueness	51	8
76: Brand name use	33	14
93: Creativity of annual report	41	17
Flexibility	41/67	28/15
4: Total debt/total assets [reverse]	72	25
7: Inventory/assets [reverse]	54	46
9: Gross P & E/sales [reverse]	57	41
14: Accounts receivables/sales [reverse]	56	43
44: Financial structure orientation	35	24
60: Large customers [reverse]	14	13
83: Unionization level [reverse]	8	8
85: International business	33	22
Coherence	43/81	15/11
15: Largest business segment/sales	50	28
51: Vertical integration backward	16	4

Aggregate Index Variables/Primary Variables[a]	Percent Success Rate[b]	Percent Error Rate[b]
Coherence (continued)		
52: Vertical integration forward	13	11
53: Focus/relatedness of businesses	63	10
68: Coherence of goals/strategies	62	10
100: Fewer number of four-digit SIC codes	53	28
Clarity	35/64	14/18
61: Corporate slogan/subtitle	16	7
62: Business summary	35	10
63: Detailed business descriptions	29	19
67: Clarity of goals/strategies	58	18
Progressiveness	43/78	20/14
8: Net P & E/gross P & E	62	37
10: Capital expenditures/sales	56	41
24: R & D expenditures/sales	16	13
27: Sales 1978 + 1977/sales 1976 + 1975	79	19
28: Profits 1978 + 1977/profits 1976 + 1975	72	28
46: New product importance	48	16
47: Innovation orientation	43	14
50: State-of-the-art technology	26	17
78: Patents/trade secrets importance	17	17
92: Annual report quality	48	22
99: 10-K substituted for annual report [reverse]	5	0
Perceptiveness	29/67	15/22
19: Outside directors/total directors	44	44
40: Social responsibility	13	9
64: Industrial economics orientation	27	11
65: Market competitiveness sensed	23	10
69: Industry/market appreciation	32	7
70: Firm strengths/weaknesses sensed	47	14
88: Legal involvements [reverse]	28	22
96: 10-K sent upon request	20	10
98: Additional note/letter sent	28	6

(Table continues on p. 450)

Aggregate Index Variables/Primary Variables[a]	Percent Success Rate[b]	Percent Error Rate[b]
Dominance	51/72	9/14
41: Selling/marketing orientation	48	16
42: Sales growth orientation	46	6
66: Large market share in own niche	59	4
Relevance (perceived need)	39/69	12/22
25: Advertising/sales	10	6
39: Customer orientation	50	13
45: Product orientation	53	12
55: Product quality stressed	47	11
77: Advertising/promotion importance	27	7
94: Annual report promotion intensity	45	23
Consistency	34/67	18/21
30: Profits standard deviation [reverse]	51	44
31: Coefficient of variation (of 30) [reverse]	73	24
38: Stockholder orientation	29	10
56: Customized production [reverse]	20	14
89: Divestments [reverse]	26	12
90: Corporate reorganizations [reverse]	28	19
91: Strategy shifts [reverse]	23	8
95: Nonrequired financial data	25	12
Efficiency	51/85	21/7
2: Profits/sales	92	1
3: Sales/assets	54	46
12: Sales/inventory	61	38
17: Sales/employees	38	25
26: Maintenance and repair/sales [reverse]	20	18
29: Five-year return on sales	89	10
43: Profit orientation	34	15

Aggregate Index Variables/Primary Variables[a]	Percent Success Rate[b]	Percent Error Rate[b]
Efficiency (*continued*)		
48: Manufacturing orientation	36	17
97: Past annual reports sent upon request	32	16

[a] The number preceding each primary variable refers to its position in Appendix I. There the reader can find a full explanation.

[b] Success and error rates describe how successful and unsuccessful each primary variable was in classifying or discriminating the better-performing mid-sized firm. We list two averages for each index variable: the first is a simple average of the success and error rates of the primary variables; the second is determined by taking the algebraic sum of each primary variable in the classification procedure as described in the text.

NOTES

PREFACE

[1] The contribution of small and medium-sized business to the creation of new jobs in the United States is critical. A 1979 study by David Birch at MIT argued that the level of such contribution was 82 percent. Using the same statistics, the Washington-based Brookings Institution came up with 40 percent. No matter. The number, to be sure, is a significant one. A simplistic comparison of the *Fortune* 500 between 1973 and 1983 is instructive. There was a net *loss* of 314,659 jobs. During this same period more than 20,000,000 new jobs were added to the economy (*Inc.*, April 1984). What can we conclude? First of all, since the sales and assets of these 500 largest manufacturing companies were growing both in absolute terms and relative to smaller firms, it means that these large companies had become more productive, that is, substantially increasing their dollar output per employee (even adjusting for inflation). This is surely good. Next, we should recognize the shift toward more service-oriented business not included in the *Fortune* 500. The overriding point, though, is clear. Much if not most of the new jobs in the American economy are coming from small and medium-sized firms. Here resides the driving energy of the economy.

[2] I had another concern. I saw a growing gulf between two approaches to business research: the qualitative or "clinical" method of investigating a few companies in great depth through personal observation and individual interview, and the quantitative or data base method of studying many companies in less depth through hypothesis testing and numerical analysis. Each alone was incomplete, the former lacking confidence, the latter relevance. I sought to harmonize the two methods. Nothing, I felt, short of complementarity and mutual reinforcement

could explain successful strategy and policy in complex business organizations. We need both qualitative insight and quantitative rigor.

[3] My research monograph *Mid-Sized Firms: Success Strategies and Methodology* (New York: Praeger, 1982) was, I believe, the first academic book published on the subject. It articulated qualitative and quantitative analyses of strategic management across a large data base of more than 350 medium-sized companies. The current interest in medium-sized firms is gratifying.

CHAPTER 1

[1] How were the Creative Strategies developed? We interplayed two contrasting methods—an impressionistic, intuitive sweep of corporate cases (qualitative); and a deterministic, rigorous analysis of industry data (quantitative). From the former we *induced* concepts; from the latter we *deduced* them. We always tested what we found. Each Creative Strategy was shaken out independently and run off against others. Explanatory strength and predictive power were key criteria. How would each Creative Strategy do in explaining or predicting company success? We tried, as best the experimental design would allow, to keep the two methodologies from contaminating each other. We wanted to compare the "pure" results of the two independent approaches. Though it was hard to eliminate all forms of cross influence, the results of the contrasting techniques were nicely coherent. Similar Creative Strategies emerged from each methodology.

[2] Market share is a measure of one company's percentage of the business in a given industry or a given segment of an industry; a market share of 25 percent, for example, means that the company sells one-quarter of the total products sold. Market share is normally counted in dollar revenues, though units sales can be used. The common difficulty in assessing market share is to determine the scope of the market, that is, which products are included and which are excluded.

[3] Concentration ratio is a measure of how much of an industry's business is controlled by a specific number of companies. The ratio describes how tightly or widely the industry is dominated by leading firms. The normal number of firms considered is from three to eight, with four being common. Thus an industry with a concentration ratio of 90 percent means that the four top firms account for nine-tenths of industry shipping (e.g., domestic automobiles).

[4] Growth patterns and trends measure the dynamic changes over time (as opposed to the static condition at the moment). Trending, at its best, should be as much an art as a science, embedding intuitive sense of reason as well mathematical projections of numbers.

[5] Powers of suppliers and customers sense the relative strengths in bargaining power of the firms from which one buys and the firms to which one sells. The strength/bargaining power relationships between suppliers and buyers is balanced on many factors, including relative firm sizes, industry concentration ratios,

relative importance of sales relationships, threats of forward and backward integration, and so on. See *Competitive Strategy* by Michael E. Porter (New York: The Free Press, 1980).

[6] Threats of new entrants and substitute products sense the relative likelihood of new companies entering the market and future products usurping current products. New firms coming into the market are encouraged by high industry profits and low cost of entry (low "entry barriers"). Substitute products can be as simple as saccharin for sugar and aspartame for saccharin or as complex as teleconferencing for airline tickets. See *Competitive Strategy* by Michael E. Porter.

[7] The story of Premier Industries is derived from an article in the August 22, 1983, issue of *Fortune*, "Making a Mint in Nuts and Bolts," by Susan Fraker. (Only the executive quotes are taken directly from the article, and Premier's 1983 annual report is the source of some of the material.)

[8] The story of Tandon Corporation is derived from an article in the November 7, 1983, issue of *Forbes*, "The Hard Driver Atop the Disk-Drive Heap," by Kathleen K. Wiegner. *Forbes* selected Tandon as its "Up & Comer of the Year" (1983)—thus touting it as one of the best small publicly held companies in America (though it's hardly small any more).

[9] See note 4, Chapter 2.

CHAPTER 2

[1] The Scripto account is derived from the Harvard Business School case "Scripto, Inc." (copyright © 1974 by the President and Fellows of Harvard College) in *Business Policy: Text and Cases* by C. Roland Christensen, Kenneth R. Andrews and Joseph L. Bower (Homewood, Ill.: Richard D. Irwin), fourth edition, 1978. Though the case concludes with the early seventies, the trend was similar into the eighties. In the first three months of fiscal 1983, Scripto lost $661,000 on revenues of $13 million. In June 1983 Scripto was acquired by Allegany International.

[2] R. G. Hammermesh, M. J. Anderson, Jr., and J. E. Harris, "Strategies for Low Market Share Businesses," *Harvard Business Review*, May–June 1978.

[3] The following reports are derived from "The Myth of Market Share" by William Baldwin in the March 14, 1983 issue of *Forbes*.

[4] The experience curve concept, popularized by the Boston Consulting Group, states that unit labor costs decline (say 10–25 percent) every time cumulative production output doubles. Bruce Henderson, founder of BCG, attributed this decline in cost with each doubling of experience to a combination effect of learning, specialization, increased scale of operations, and greater intensity of capital investment. This relationship between the decline in unit costs and cumulative volume produced was considered predictable enough to be plotted—and BCG labeled the resulting graphic representation "the experience curve." The expression

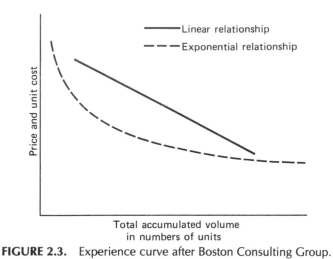

FIGURE 2.3.   Experience curve after Boston Consulting Group.

"riding down the experience curve" refers to the reduction in unit cost as total production experience increases (see Figure 2.3).

CHAPTER 3

[1] The reader should be advised that the author is a personal friend of Charles Hurwitz, and at the time of writing is contemplating possible ventures in high technology and in Israel involving Mr. Hurwitz, Dr. Kozmetsky, and Mr. Levin (the latter two are mentioned subsequently in the chapter). Dr. Kozmetsky is also a personal friend and intellectual mentor. The issue of conflict, for someone with both commercial and literary interests in business, is a troublesome one. Though my writing rewards have been more psychic than pecuniary, this in no way diminishes the strict responsibilities of the profession. Yet to expurgate all traces of conflict would strip the manuscript of personality, spirit, and individual insight. Better, I finally decided, is to tell good stories and make full disclosures.

[2] See "A Dialogue Between Barry Munitz and Robert Kuhn: A Comparison of University Management with Corporate Management." *Educational Record*, spring, 1984.

[3] Most categories, however familiar, are artificial constructs, the splitting of reality into synthetic divisions amenable to understanding. Nonetheless, the process is a necessary one as human minds attempt to understand the complexities of the environment.

[4] Of the 334 companies in my primary research sample of mid-sized manufacturing firms (based on 1977 and 1978 data), 78 percent had between $25 and $250 million in total assets and 87 percent between $25 and $450 million. With respect to total

revenues, 63 percent generated between $50 and $250 million and 91 percent between $25 and $450 million. The general range of employee numbers was broader, with 49 percent of the sample falling between 1000 and 4000, and 78 percent between 500 and 6000.

[5] The report on International Clinical Laboratories is derived from an article in the October 10, 1983 issue of *Forbes*, "Know Thy Business," by Geoffrey Smith.

[6] See Creative Strategy number five, "High Profile Chief Executive," in Part II.

CHAPTER 4

[1] The following story is derived from an article in *Forbes* magazine, August 1, 1983.

[2] Will Pannill was the fellow, and he was quite something. He was working in a North Carolina cotton-spinning mill when he caught the vision. So he took himself up to Utica, got a job as a janitor in one of the North's largest underwear factories, and took copious notes. (One of the earliest industrial spies, and surely one of the best.) He then returned to the South and established a series of knitting shops. He founded Pannill Knitting himself, helped a friend set up one of the predecessors of Bassett-Walker, and split off part of Pannill Knitting to establish Tutex in 1937.

[3] What we would find, using the model to be developed in Chapter 10, is that "clarity" and "coherence" lead to "dominance," and "dominance" and "efficiency" lead to "consistency"—all elements of that model. [Note: In early October 1984, Bassett-Walker announced that it would be acquired by VF Corporation, the large apparel manufacturer of Lee jeans.]

[4] Sources for the data: U.S. Internal Revenue Service, *Statistics of Income, Corporation Tax Returns, annual*. My research data base covered a healthy sample of the total mid-sized manufacturing corporations. In 1976, 1714 companies had assets between $25 and $250 million, and 3995 between $10 and $250 million (these are only *manufacturing*, remember). Of the 334 mid-sized manufacturing firms I studied in 1978, 259 had assets between $25 and $250 million. This means that my sample included about 15 percent of the total number of U.S. manufacturing firms within this range (and about 7 percent of the firms between $10 and $250 million). This high sample size supports the reliability of the study. (R. L. Kuhn, *Mid-Sized Firms: Success Strategies and Methodology*, op. cit.)

[5] The actual impact of these trends is not as dramatic since none of the numbers has been normalized for inflation. Consequently, though the slopes of the trends would remain in the same direction, they would all be, in operational reality, significantly flatter.

[6] F. M. Scherer has analyzed the profit performance of various asset size manufacturing corporations during different periods of the business cycle. (See *Industrial*

Market Structure and Economic Performance, Chicago: Rand McNally, 1980, pp. 92–93.) He begins by stressing the pitfalls and caveats facing the researcher, such as the tendency for owner-managers of small businesses "to pay themselves salaries including a generous dose of what would otherwise be called profit . . . to avoid double taxation. . . . As a result, small firms' reported profits may be biased downward." For larger firms profits may be equally distorted (but in the opposite direction) by "variations in accounting conventions governing depreciation, the valuation of assets acquired through merger, and the like." (Note that since the owner-managers of small businesses are likely to take funds out of the business, that would tend to keep capitalization low and return on capital high—as shown in the return on equity figures.)

Scherer states that "the comparative profitability of small versus large corporations appears to vary with the business cycle, with smaller enterprises doing relatively well in boom periods and poorly in recessions. This presumably reflects larger firms' greater monopoly power, their use of accounting discretion to smooth reported earnings, and/or their stronger tendency to accumulate organizational slack in prosperous times and reduce it in downturns."

Figure 4.7 plots Scherer's data relating average after-tax returns on stockholders' equity for manufacturing corporations in various asset size classes from 1963 to 1977. Scherer segregates the raw data (derived from the FTC's *Quarterly Financial Report*) into four time intervals corresponding to different positions in the business cycle, ". . . the nearly normal 1963–64 period, the Vietnam War boom of 1966–69, the generally sluggish 1969–71 period, and the unprecedented 1975–77 years of unusually high unemployment accompanied by inflation. . . . The differential (between smaller and larger firms) is most prominent during the normal 1963–65 period and the 1969–71 recession; it is least pronounced during the late 1960s boom and, contrary to historical precedent, the mid-1970s."

[7] See F. M. Scherer, *ibid.*

[8] T. R. Saving, "Estimation of Optimum Size of Plant by the Survivor Technique," *Quarterly Journal of Economics* 75 (November 1961): 569–607.

[9] Alan L. Feld contends that major provisions of the Tax Code, designed to encourage capital investment, "although neutral on their face, appear in fact to benefit big corporations" (work prepared for the Bureau of Competition and Office of Policy Planning of the Federal Trade Commission, 1979).

Figure 4.9 shows that large companies claim proportionally more in depreciation deductions (in relation to their net income) than do medium-sized companies. This means that large firms derive more tax benefit from depreciation than their proportionate due. It is interesting that at the other end of the scale, that is, for companies with less than $5 million in gross assets, the ratio increases: smaller firms also beat mid-sized firms in depreciation deduction per dollar of net income. Thus a pattern not unlike previous ones emerges. The mid-sized firm gets the short end of the stick. It is almost as if, to follow Feld's argument, government policy is punitive toward companies in the middle. (Figure 4.10 demonstrates that large corporations as a class claim more investment tax credit per dollar of

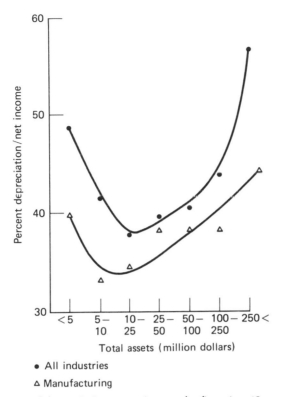

FIGURE 4.9. Ratio of depreciation to net income by firm size. (*Source:* Feld, 1979.)

net income than do small and medium-sized companies.) Feld comments that "rapid depreciation and the investment tax credit are supported on the ground that they encourage capital investment, which is said to be desirable for the economy. But they appear to confer their benefits disproportionally by size."

[10] See Eric Flamholtz' work for an introduction to human resource accounting. *Human Resource Accounting* (Encino, CA: Dickenson, 1974).

[11] See John M. Blair, *Economic Concentration: Structure, Behavior and Public Policy* (New York: Harcourt Brace Jovanovich, 1972). Blair prepared scatter diagrams for each of the thirty industries, with the size of each company (in terms of total assets) being expressed as a percentage of the size of the industry's largest company. The profit rate used was the after-tax rate of return on stockholders' equity. He then drew regression lines to discern the profit–size relationship. Some of the data were taken from the Federal Trade Commission's report, *Rates of Return for Selected Manufacturing Industries.* (Blair's data, however, do not convey confidence:

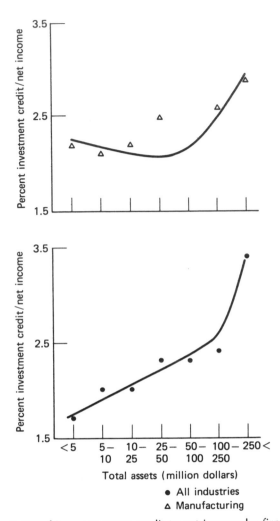

FIGURE 4.10. Ratio of investment tax credit to net income by firm size. (*Source:* Feld, 1979.)

The number of data points in each industry is small, there is wide variation in profit rate, and the leading firm has strong dominance.)

A 1969 study by M. Marcus ("Profitability and Size of Firm," *Review of Economics and Statistics*, February 1969, 104–107) found what can only be described as an erratic relationship between size and profits within industries; the relationship was positive in 35 industries, negative in 9, and not significant in the majority (74 of his 118 industries).

[12] See Michael Porter, "The Structure Within Industries and Companies' Performance," *Review of Economics and Statistics*, 1978, 214–227. Porter defines "leaders" operationally, as the composite of the largest firms that account for approximately 30 percent of the industry's sales revenues. The correlation between rates of return of leaders and followers within the same industry was "strikingly low" (0.14), negating the "shared asset theory" of traditional industrial organization thinking which predicts that the market power of an industry (as expressed through concentration ratios, entry barriers, etc.) should be equally distributed over all firms within the industry irrespective of firm size. Porter interprets the data in light of his concept of "strategic groups" within industries, clusters of companies that have the same market mobility.

[13] Do these data contradict the traditional wisdom that profitability is directly related to market share? Hard to tell. Certainly within these gross definitions of share and combining all industries, the data are not coherent—giving hope for mid-sized firms. (The argument can be made, of course, that gross revenues within industries are a poor surrogate for market share, and that if one could really determine a firm's operational market, then the share–profits relationship would hold. This may well be valid, but we begin to turn in circles since effective strategies for mid-sized firms often involve segmentation of all kinds; segmentation by product, by geography, by customer, by industry, etc.) .

[14] Certainly there is great year-to-year variation in the data. A few firms that lost 20–50 percent of their equity would bias the sample; similarly, the same firms could show huge increases in subsequent years since the denominator would be so low. Nonetheless, the finding that the variance among medium-sized firms' rates of return exceeds the variance among large-sized firms' rates of return confirms the work of other investigators: M. Hall and L. Weiss, "Firm Size and Profitability," *Review of Economics and Statistics*, August 1967, 319–331; M. Neumann, I. Bobel, and A. Haid, "Profitability, Risk and Market Structure," *Journal of Industrial Economics*, March 1979, 227–242; J. Samuels and D. Smyth, "Profits, Variability of Profits and Firm Size," *Economica*, May 1968, 127–140. Scherer (*op. cit.* 1980) reports that the variance of profits within the *same* company over time is higher in smaller companies than in larger companies (asset size, standard deviation: $10 million, .068; $100 million, .041; $1 billion, .014.)

CHAPTER 5

[1] William Shepherd, *The Economics of Industrial Organization* (Englewood Cliffs, NJ: Prentice-Hall, 1979).

[2] Harvey Leibenstein, "Allocative Efficiency vs. X-Efficiency." *American Economic Review*, June 1966, 392–415.

[3] F. M. Scherer, "Industrial Structure, Scale Economies, and Worker Alienation," in *Essays on Industrial Organization in Honor of Joe Bain*, edited by Robert T. Masson and P. David Qualls (Cambridge, MA: Ballinger, 1976), pp. 199–207.

[4] John Blair, *op. cit.*

[5] William Shepherd, *op. cit.*

[6] See F. M. Scherer, *Industrial Market Structure and Economic Performance* (Chicago: Rand McNally, 1971), pp. 377–378. "Very high concentration has a favorable effect (on innovation) *only in rare cases,* and more often it is apt to retard progress by restricting the number of independent sources of initiative and by dampening firms' incentive to gain market position through accelerated research and development. Likewise, it is vital that barriers to new entry be kept at modest levels, and that established industry members be exposed continually to the threat of entry by technically audacious newcomers."

[7] In the spirit of "full disclosure" the reader is advised that the author is on the Board of Eagle Clothes, structured the acquisition of April-Marcus (with attorney Walter Feldesman), is paid by the company, and is one of its largest stockholders. One continues to debate the wisdom of mixing personal business and professional writing; one frets about conflict of interest, whether real or apparent. In the end I thought this story to be a good one, and that, to a writer, is the ultimate touchstone.

(Note: Eagle's earnings declined sharply in fiscal 1984, to about $3 million before taxes and extraordinary items, off 40 percent from fiscal 1983; revenues were up about 8 percent, to $104 million, the smallest growth in recent history. Reasons appear to be a combination of flattening industry growth, increased competition, and some organizational slack. The latter, at least, is being addressed.)

[8] Corporate structure as a key determinant of business success first emerged in the landmark work of Alfred D. Chandler, Jr., *Strategy and Structure: Chapters in the History of American Industrial Enterprise* (Cambridge, MA: MIT Press, 1962), p. 385. His exhaustive study of Du Pont, General Motors, Standard Oil (New Jersey—now Exxon), and Sears, Roebuck and Company identified four distinct phases of corporate growth: "the initial expansion and accumulation of resources; the rationalization of the use of resources; the expansion into new markets and lines to help assure the continuing full use of resources; and finally the development of a new structure to make possible continuing effective mobilization of resources to meet both changing short-term market demands and long-term market trends."

[9] See John Welsh, "Entrepreneurial Characteristics: The Driving Force," in *Corporate Creativity: Robust Companies and the Entrepreneurial Spirit*, edited by Raymond Smilor and Robert L. Kuhn (New York: Praeger, 1984).

[10] C. Roland Christensen, Kenneth R. Andrews, and Joseph L. Bower, *Business Policy: Text and Cases*, 4th ed. (Homewood, IL: Richard D. Irwin, 1978).

[11] The relationship between individual meaning and organizational mission, epitomized at Shaklee's, is discussed at length in *The Firm Bond: Linking Meaning and Mission in Business and Religion* by Robert Lawrence Kuhn and George Thomas Geis (New York: Praeger, 1984). What is learned about commitment in religious organizations is applied to commitment in business organizations. Shaklee's organizational structure comes close to bridging the two.

[12] See *Corporate Creativity: Robust Companies and the Entrepreneurial Spirit*, edited by Raymond Smilor and Robert Kuhn, *op. cit.*

CHAPTER 6

[1] "Content analysis" is a technical methodology of social science research. Its objective is to ascertain the meaning, purpose, direction, intent, or effect of any type of communication message such as newspapers, magazines, electronic media, political speeches. Corporate annual reports fall into this class of information and are amenable to content analysis. The approach involves a standardized method of picking out, describing, studying, and evaluating the denotations and connotations of the content—the details, nuances, and implications of recurrent themes; the thrusts and directions of ideas being promulgated.

[2] R. B. Duncan, "Qualitative Research Methods in Strategic Management," in *Strategic Management*, edited by D. Schendel and C. Hofer (Boston: Little, Brown, 1979).

[3] Max Weber, *Economy and Society*, edited by G. Roth and C. Wittich (New York: Bedminster Press, 1968).

[4] Robert Bogdan and Steven Taylor, *Introduction to Qualitative Research Methods* (New York: Wiley, 1975).

[6] John Loftland, *Analyzing Social Life* (Belmont, CA: Wadsworth Publishing, 1971).

[6] Charles Hofer, "Toward a Contingency Theory of Business Strategy," *Academy of Management Journal*, December 1975.

[7] Reporting results from PIMS ("Profit Impact of Market Strategy"), a data base model built from analyzing over 2000 strategic business units from some 200 companies. See S. Schoeffler, "Capital Intense Technology vs. ROI: A Strategic Assessment," *Management Review*, September 1978. Also: Derek Abell and John Hammond, *Strategic Market Planning* (Englewood Cliffs, N.J.: Prentice-Hall, 1979).

[8] R. L. Katz, *Cases and Concepts in Corporate Strategy* (Englewood Cliffs, N.J.: Prentice-Hall, 1970).

[9] Are Katz's "small companies" similar to our "mid-sized firms?" The answer is probably "yes," since mid-sized companies are certainly smaller than large companies. Yet there may be higher-order contingencies lurking here, which could differentiate "small" and "mid-sized" firms in different situations (e.g., different industries). We also should keep in mind the evidence that shows diverse profit performance between small and medium-sized companies, and the consequent charge that mid-sized firms are not able to effect the economies of scale of the giants or be as versatile as the gnats.

[10] R. F. Abbanat, "Strategies of Size," Ph.D. dissertation, Harvard University.

[11] H. Woodward, "Management Strategies for Small Companies," *Harvard Business Review*, January–February 1976. (Note: The companies that comprised this sample, from in situ observation and/or active consulting, were probably smaller than our mid-sized class.)

[12] R. Hammermesh, M. Anderson, and J. Harris, "Strategies for Low Market Share Businesses," *Harvard Business Review*, May–June 1978.

[13] M. Porter and Z. Zannetos, "Administrative Regulation vs. Market Regulation in the Diversified Firm," *MIT Working Paper*, April 1978.

[14] John Welsh and Jerry White, "A Small Business Is Not a Little Big Business," *Harvard Business Review*, July–August 1981.

[15] Seventeen two-digit Standard Industrial Code (SIC) industries; thirty-four three-digit SIC industries.

[16] Return on equity (ROE) was determined by dividing after-tax earnings by the year-end book value of stockholders' total equity. Although the ROE was taken for only one year, 1978, each firm was analyzed over a five-year period, and was included only if its profit performance over the entire five years was unambiguously superior. 1978 was chosen as a generally representative year, relatively free from recession.

[17] The ROE for the largest companies in each industry was taken from *Forbes' 32nd Annual Report on American Industry*, January 7, 1980. The *Forbes* group consists of the 1035 largest American companies; it is their ROE, arrayed by primary industry, that becomes the standard of comparison.

[18] Warp knitting is a process in which synthetic yarn is placed on a warp beam, then knitted into unfinished fabrics on a knitting machine. These so-called "gray goods" are then dyed and/or scoured, and finally finished through embossing, printing, laminating, or napping, depending on ultimate product.

[19] One must always recognize the basic uncertainty in analyzing with quantitative numbers what must initially be encoded by qualitative judgment.

[20] Each company was classified into an average of 5.45 strategic categories (Outside-In).

[21] Robert Lawrence Kuhn and George Thomas Geis, *The Firm Bond: Linking Meaning and Mission in Business and Religion*, (New York: Praeger, 1984). The authors investigate commitment in terms of a commitment model, built inductively in the first part of the book and applied deductively in the second part. Religious organizations are the "special lens" with which commitment is viewed. The key elements of commitment are discerned under the "magnifying glass" of religious fervor, and then applied to institutions and companies of common kind. Personal, Organizational, and Experiential Factors are inputs to the model which yields Commitment Strength and Mission Contribution as its output. The model is used in numerous personal studies to improve relationships between individuals and institutions by bringing the benefits of commitment to both sides of the firm bond.

[22] These strategic categories, and the firms and numbers allocated to each, must still be considered for what they are—not as rigorously derived quantities but as intuitively ascribed qualities. We must wait for an analysis of the controlled match-pair data base of Chapter 9 before coming to firm conclusions.

CHAPTER 7

[1] Peter Drucker, *The Practice of Management* (New York: Harper & Row, 1954).

[2] Alfred Chandler, *op. cit.*

[3] H. Igor Ansoff, *Business Strategy* (Middlesex, England: Penguin Books, 1969).

[4] H. Igor Ansoff, "The Changing Shape of the Strategic Problem," in *Strategic Management*, edited by D. Schendel and C. Hofer (Boston: Little, Brown, 1979).

[5] Herbert Simon, Richard Cyert, and James March have pioneered new mechanisms of thinking about the theory and practice of management. Concepts propounded include the limits of rationality, the process of problem-driven search, the formulation of expectations, and the execution of managerial choice. Each articulates real-world relevance with sophisticated constructs. See Herbert Simon, *Administrative Behavior* (New York: The Free Press, 1976); Richard Cyert and James March, *A Behavioral Theory of the Firm* (Englewood Cliffs, NJ: Prentice-Hall, 1963).

[6] Operating profit is taken before corporate overhead, interest, and taxes.

[7] For a more complete discussion of strategic management see the following: Dan Schendel and Charles Hofer, editors, *Strategic Management* (Boston: Little, Brown, 1979); Kenneth R. Andrews, *The Concept of Corporate Strategy* (Homewood, IL: Richard D. Irwin, 1980); Arthur Thompson, Jr., and A. J. Strickland III, *Strategy Formulation and Implementation* (Plano, TX: Business Publications, 1983); Charles Hofer and Dan Schendel, *Strategy Formulation: Analytical Concepts* (St. Paul: West Publishing, 1978); Jay Galbraith and Daniel Nathanson, *Strategy Implementation: The Role of Structure and Process* (St. Paul: West Publishing, 1978); Max Richards, *Organizational Goal Structures* (St. Paul: West Publishing, 1978); Ian MacMillan, *Strategy Formulation: Political Concepts* (St. Paul: West Publishing, 1978); William Newman and James Logan, *Strategy, Policy, and Central Management* (Cincinnati: South-Western Publishing, 1983).

[8] For an interesting discussion of how goals are formulated in real organizations— the "power configurations" of "internal" and "external coalitions"—see Henry Mintzberg, "Organizational Power and Goals: A Skeletal Theory," in *Strategic Management*, Dan Schendel and Charles Hofer, editors (Boston: Little, Brown, 1979).

[9] John French, Jr., and Bertram Raven, "The Bases of Social Power," in Dorwin Cartwright, editor, *Studies in Social Power* (Ann Arbor, MI: Institute for Social Research, 1959).

[10] See Graham Allison, *Essence of Decision* (Boston: Little, Brown, 1971).

[11] See Robert Lawrence Kuhn, *Commercializing Defense-Related Technology* (New York: Praeger, 1984).

[12] See Michael Porter, *Competitive Analysis* (New York: The Free Press, 1980).

[13] Howard H. Stevenson, "Defining Corporate Strengths and Weaknesses," *Sloan Management Review*, Spring 1976. "An individual's cognitive perceptions of the strengths and weaknesses of his organization were strongly influenced by factors associated with the individual and not only by the organization's attributes. Position in the organization, perceived role, and type of responsibility so strongly influenced the assessment that the objective reality of the situation tended to be overwhelmed." (The problem is not unlike the Heisenberg Uncertainty Principle in physics which states that the precise measurement of one variable produces uncertainty in the measurement of another related variable.)

[14] Richard Rumelt, "Strategy Evaluation," in Dan Schendel and Charles Hofer, editors, *Strategic Management* (Boston: Little, Brown, 1979).

[15] Seymour Tilles, "How to Evaluate Corporate Strategy," *Harvard Business Review*, July–August 1963.

[16] Charles Hofer, "Toward a Contingency Theory of Business Strategy," *Academy of Management Journal*, December 1975.

[17] Sidney Schoeffler, Robert Buzzell, and Donald Heany, "Impact of Strategic Planning on Profit Performance," *Harvard Business Review*, March–April 1974.

[18] Michael Porter, *Competitive Strategy*, op. cit. "The Structure Within Industries and Companies' Performance," *Review of Economics and Statistics*, LXI, May 1979.

[19] Boston Consulting Group Staff, *Perspectives on Experience* (Boston: Boston Consulting Group, 1968). See footnote 4, Chapter 2.

[20] Alfred Chandler, *Strategy and Structure*. op. cit.

[21] Rudolf Knoepfel, "Practitioners' Views: Policy and Planning Research," in Schendel and Hofer (editors), *Strategic Management*, op. cit.

[22] Russell L. Ackoff, *The Art of Problem Solving* (New York: Wiley, 1978).

CHAPTER 8

[1] Governor Mark White has taken personal interest in developing high technology in Texas, recognizing the historic shift from energy to knowledge as the future foundation of the state's economic prosperity. Governor White was the central figure behind Austin's winning bid for the computer industry's new research consortium, Microelectronics and Computer Technology Corporation ("MCC"), headed by Adm. Bobby R. Inman (ret.). The Governor is also catalyzing economic cooperation and technology transfer between Texas and Israel. Texas was the only American state to send an official delegation to the widely acclaimed Jerusalem

Economic Conference in May 1984–which symbolized Israel's emergence as a world power in high tech. (The Texas delegation included attorney Wales Madden, Jr.; Texas A & M's Dr. Arthur Porter; and the Director of the Governor's Office for Economic Development, Harden Wiedemann.) Discussions are being held to implement joint ventures between corresponding universities and corporations in Texas and Israel at the leading edge of high tech from computer science and electronics to biotechnology and agribusiness.

[2] The *Handbook for Creative and Innovative Managers*, Robert Lawrence Kuhn (editor-in-chief), will be published by McGraw-Hill in 1986. Creative and innovative management is discussed in terms of fundamental concepts, functional areas, and industrial environments. It is a new field of business management, an exciting one rich with relevance.

[3] For every rule, there is an exception. In certain areas of the economy, especially in high-risk advanced technology, individual companies cannot afford to invest and America cannot afford to abdicate. Supercomputers, for one, have huge development costs and uncertain commercial revenues. Yet the United States must not lose world leadership, certainly not by default. Here is fertile substrate for an Industrial Policy.

[4] R. L. Kuhn, *Commercializing Defense-Related Technology*, op cit.

[5] See A. Charnes and W. W. Cooper, *Creative and Innovative Management: Essays in Honor of George Kozmetsky*, (Boston: Ballinger, 1984).

CHAPTER 9

[1] The author is senior editor of *Texas Business* magazine. He is also strategic advisor to its president and publisher. Writing for the publication, however, is an avocation, contributing less than 5 percent of annual wages. Jack Martin is a close, longtime friend.

[2] K. J. Hatten, "Quantitative Research Methods in Strategic Management," in *Strategic Management*, edited by D. Schendel and C. Hofer (Boston: Little, Brown, 1979).

[3] W. Glueck and R. Willis, "Documentary Sources and Strategic Management," *Academy of Management Review* 4:95–102 (1979). The authors suggest that the lack of content analysis in management research relates to the fact that "most strategic management analysts have training in the social and applied social sciences rather than in history" and therefore are reluctant to use documentary sources.

[4] Thus a contrast can be drawn with the Hammermesh et al. paper (1978) which sought effective strategies for low-market-share companies by investigating three such firms. The investigation was conducted well and some interesting strategies emerged; but the number of companies was still only three, and thus confidence in the conclusions would have to be guarded (especially if one of the three companies slips in performance—as has Burroughs).

[5] Several studies have used large-scale samples. The most well known is the PIMS project conducted by the Strategic Planning Institute and composed of some 2000 strategic business units in some 200 companies. Other examples include an analysis of 358 cases from *Fortune* (W. Glueck, L. Jauch, and R. Osborne, "Success in Large Business Organizations: The Environment-Strategy Connection," *Academy of Management Proceedings*, 1977); a study on the relationships among strategy, structure, and performance in 200 of the Fortune 500 companies (R. Rumelt, *Strategy, Structure, and Economic Performance*, Boston: Harvard Business School Division of Research 1974); and E. H. Bowman's studies in the food processing industry ("Strategy and the Weather," *Sloan Management Review*, Winter 1976), in data processing ("Strategy, Annual Reports, and Alchemy," *California Management Review*, Spring 1978), on corporate social responsibility ("A Strategic Posture Toward Corporate Social Responsibility," with M. Haire, *California Management Review*, Winter 1975), and on the relationship between risk and return where some 1600 companies were studied ("A Risk/Return Paradox for Strategic Management," *Sloan Management Review*, Spring 1980).

[6] E. H. Bowman, 1978, *op cit.* Since a content analysis of annual reports forms the foundation for the quantitative studies of this chapter, we spend some effort explaining the two validity tests. The first involves a matched-pair analysis among fourteen firms independently chosen as outstanding in their corporate social responsibility activities (by the editor of *Business and Society*) and fourteen other firms from the same industry, of approximately the same size, randomly selected where alternatives were available. A line-by-line count of social responsibility discussion was made for each annual report and a percentage calculated in reference to the total lines of prose in the reports for each company. Bowman states that "the test hypothesis of course was that the outstandingly responsible companies discussed issues of corporate social responsibility more in their annual reports on a line-by-line coding basis than did the neutrally chosen matched-pair companies. They did indeed." The independently chosen companies evinced a 4.80 percent discussion (social responsibility lines as a percentage of total annual report lines), while the matched-pair companies showed only 1.74 percent, a statistically significant difference with a confidence level of 0.017.

Bowman's second and completely different test of the annual report's reliability as a measuring probe or litmus test of company policies and practices was in the area of international activities of firms in the food-processing industry (using an entirely different set of annual reports). Again a line-by-line coding of the annual reports was conducted to determine the percentage of the total annual report discussion devoted to international activity. An independent assessment of the companies' international activity was acquired from *Standard & Poor's*, giving the percentage of each company's business generated by international activities. For the critical comparison, to quote Bowman (1978), "the rank order of the company international percentage on both lists [that is, annual report percentage and *Standard & Poor's* percentage of international business] could be compared. This comparison of the two lists, both ranked from high to low in activity rate, offers an additional test of annual report line-by-line coding." (The level of significance on the Spearman Rank Order Test was 0.001.) Thus the two tests, each independently verified by an outside source, and each attaining statistical significance, suggest that annual report discussions—and, by extension, graphics as well—are a reasonable surrogate for real activity.

[7] The five years were used to corroborate consistency, although only two years were used for the correlations with annual report content analysis. The two years chosen—1977 and 1978—were deemed "average" in terms of the business cycle. For a detailed description of the methodology see R. L. Kuhn, *Mid-Sized Firms: Success Strategies and Methodology, op. cit.*

[8] We used the ratio of earnings before interest and taxes to total assets as a measure of the *operational* efficiency of the business. The more traditional net profits as a percentage of equity embeds the financial structure and leverage of the companies. We were more interested in actual business management of the organizations, with financial structure (i.e., degree of leverage) factored out.

[9] Many of the ratios could be interpreted in opposing ways, and one must guard against choosing *ex post* (i.e., after the fact) the explanation that "works" (or fits the theory). For example, the ratio of finished goods to total inventory can be "understood" to mean that the better-performing mid-sized firm was either more "flexible" (if the ratio was low) or was more effectively able to respond to "customer needs" for its products (if the ratio was high).

[10] It would have been psychologically impossible for the author to code in an unbiased manner. Thus, five MIT graduate students were employed to do the actual content analysis of the source documents. Time limits were imposed and standardized. In most cases the quantitative and qualitative analyses were done by different people, and in no case were the financial calculations made first. To check consistency, several matched pairs were scored by more than one person. In these cases there was 65–75 percent agreement on the qualitative data. For the tedious task of transferring the raw data to summary sheets for all ninety-nine variables for each of the 167 matched pairs—for copying all those thousands of minuscule pluses, minuses, and zeros—the author gratefully acknowledges the help of his three children, Aaron, Adam, and Daniella.

[11] The variables are presented in order of statistical significance as determined by the binomial test.

$$z = \frac{X - .5 - Np}{Npq}$$

where X = the number of observed "hits"
N = the total number of trials
p = the probability of +, which = .5
q = the probability of −, which = .5

The higher the z score, the greater one's confidence in rejecting the null hypothesis that the observed results might have been the product of random fluctuations/

chance. *All* the variables presented in Tables 9.4 and 9.5 can reject the null hypothesis at a significance of .05 or greater. This means that the odds are at least 20 to 1 that no specific relationship between variables and their ability to predict better-performing mid-sized firms from this data base is due to chance. The median confidence level is better than .001 if the 0s are not considered, and better than .01 if the 0s are allocated evenly to both pluses and minuses.

[12] Perhaps through naiveté, perhaps through too readily equating the low-market-share literature with the mid-sized firms, we hardly considered "dominance," at least not at first. In fact, it was almost a contradiction in original boundary conditions for selecting our mid-sized firm universe. We had defined the mid-sized firm as not even being among the industry leaders in size; and yet, after including the "dominance" question almost as a curiosity, we found the stunning results that in a full 59 percent of the matched pairs, product dominance could discriminate effectively between the better-performing and the poorer-performing of the firms. (The error rate, i.e., when the variable would select the wrong company, was exceptionally low, 4 percent.)

[13] Corporate coherence is explored through an independent methodology in Table 9.7. The numerical count of Standard Industrial Codes (SIC) is a simple test. Using Standard & Poor's *Register of Corporations, Directors, and Executives 1980* as the sole source, we compared the number of two-, three-, and four-digit SIC codes listed for each of the two firms within each of the 167 matched pairs. A plus (+) was scored if the better-performing firm had a fewer number of assigned SIC codes, and a minus (−) was scored if the better-performing firm had a larger number—a zero (0) was scored if the two were equal. The comparisons were made separately for the two-, three-, and four-digit codes. It is apparent from the data that better-performing mid-sized firms had, on average, *fewer* numbers of SIC codes, indicating fewer primary business activities. This means that those similar-sized companies that were more successful in profit performance were also more focused and coherent. (The sloppy nature of most SIC designations would affect all firms equally and not alter the direction of the results in a large sample.) The significance of the data (better than .01), when combined with the success and error rate of prediction, confirms the importance of coherence as a primary success strategy for mid-sized firms. (Though powerful, the demonstration is still one of correlation, not causation. It may well be that firms doing poorly will diversify and firms doing well will not. This is logical, and there is some supporting evidence for this. For example, in metals the better-performing firms have more SIC numbers, reflecting their diversification.) Table 9.6 distills the essence of four tests of company coherence, verifying it as a mid-sized success strategy.

[14] Every index variable is significant at the .001 level or better. For the seventy-two matched-pair sample in six industries, we had 625 correct classifications ("hits") and 141 incorrect classifications ("misses"). For technical details of this analysis, including some tests of and problems in the experimental design, see R. L. Kuhn *Mid-Sized Firms: Success Strategies and Methodology, op. cit.*

[15] Ultimately, the real worth of the index variables for strategic management analysis must relate to the fundamental structure of each index varaiable itself. Does each of the primary variables contribute to the inherent meaning of the index variable within which it is contained? Do the essences of the elements enrich the substances of the compounds? The degree to which this question can be answered in the affirmative is the degree to which our conceptual strategic model can be validated (see Appendix II).

[16] This realization is not a late one. Indeed it was in anticipation of this very phenomenon that we made the initial decision to generate such a large sample of over 150 matched pairs. We desired to create a data base sufficiently broad and well structured to allow effective *inter*industry analysis and comparisons.

[17] If we combine the industries in which more of the better-performing firms had a lower ratio, the results are 28 pluses and 44 minuses, yielding a confidence level of .08 in the *reverse* direction from the overall average. (The industries in which more of the better-performing firms have lower sales–assets ratios seem to be capital-intense, although the selection process was hardly unbiased.)

[18] Although numbers are small within each industry and one must not be swayed by what could be mere random fluctuations, significance builds when the same industries run counter to the aggregate trend for all three inventory-related ratios. (These industries seem to be capital-intense and/or science-based: computers, electronics, auto/aerospace, instruments/controls, chemicals, and cosmetics/drugs.)

CHAPTER 10

[1] With twelve strategic categories, the possible permutations, combinations, and clever spatial arrangements are astronomical. No attempt will (can) be made to eliminate rigorously all (or any) other alternative models. No statement will assert this model to be in any way sacrosanct.

[2] Graham T. Allison, *Essence of Decision: Explaining the Cuban Missile Crisis* (Boston: Little, Brown, 1971).

[3] Relative strengths of association among strategic categories are determined by numerical tests. In order to discover the correlations between each of the strategic pathways, 3×3 contingency grids were established ($+/-/0$ for one variable versus $+/-/0$ for the other). To construct these thirteen contingency grids, it was necessary to choose an appropriate primary component to represent each higher-order strategic category. For most of these categories the choice was straightforward: commitment, distinctiveness, coherence, clarity, and dominance— each has a direct primary variable that explicitly expresses the precise concept. For fulfillment, the primary variable chosen was CEO enthusiasm; for flexibility, the debt–asset ratio (reversed); for progressiveness, three primary variables were evaluated (sales $1978 + 1977/1976 + 1975$, new products, and innovation orientation); for perceptiveness, the firm's appreciation of its own strengths and weaknesses;

for relevance, both product orientation and customer orientation; for consistency, the coefficient of variation on the average five-year return on sales; for efficiency, the average five-year return on sales.

Chi-square tests are the traditional method for determining the goodness of fit of "observed" frequencies in a sample to the "expected" or theoretically random frequencies. Such tests involve the construction of contingency tables. The simplicity of the chi-square test should not undermine its power.

Contingency grids were formulated for each of the thirteen strategic pairs. The expected values of each grid were calculated by determining the weighted average for each of the nine cells. The observed values were obtained by tabulating the raw data directly from each of the 167 matched-pair primary results. Following are one complete example, several highlights from others, and some discussion of all.

The relationship between clarity and coherence is made striking by the dramatic differences between the expected values (for each of the nine cells in a 3 × 3 contingency grid) and the observed values (see Figure 10.4). The expected values— the lower grid—were determined by calculating the weighted averages. Coherence had 103 pluses, or 62 percent of the total 167 possible; clarity had 97 pluses or 58 percent. Thus, the expected value of the +/+ cell would be 62 percent times

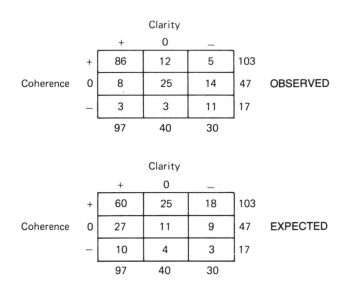

Note: Compare observed with expected: Note shift toward a direct relationship between the variables, toward +/+ (60 to 86) and −/− (3 to 11), and away from +/− (10 to 3) and −/+ (18 to 5). Even 0/0 increases (12 to 25). Chi-square significance is far greater than 0.001.

FIGURE 10.4. Testing the model: Relationship between clarity and coherence.

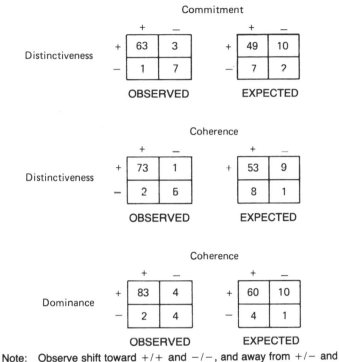

FIGURE 10.5. Testing the model: Relationship between commitment–distinctiveness, distinctiveness–coherence, and coherence–dominance.

58 percent times 167 (.62 × .58 × 167), or 60. The actual observed value is 86. The same calculations applied to every cell in every grid.

Although the chi-square significance is extraordinary (about 10^{-8}), a simple observation of the relevant cells is perhaps more meaningful. The expected value for +/+ was 60, while the actual value was 86. The same direct, positive relationship holds for the −/− cell: 3 were expected and 11 were observed. In other words, the two strategic categories—clarity and coherence—were moving in concert with each other far beyond the random expectation. Conversely, the indirect, negative relationships decline: The total number of +/− and −/+ was expected to be 10 and 18, respectively, while the actual was 3 and 5.

Figure 10.5 presents the important cells for commitment–distinctiveness, distinctiveness–coherence, and coherence–dominance. Note in each case the strong shift toward the direct, positive relationships $(+/+, \ -/-)$ and away from the inverse, negative relationships $(+/-, \ -/+)$ when the actual observed results are compared with the theoretical expected results. Commitment–distinctiveness, for example, shows 63 and 7 for $+/+$ and $-/-$, where only 49 and 2 were expected; and only 1 and 3 for $+/-$ and $-/+$ where 7 and 10 were expected. The same phenomenon can be seen in distinctiveness–coherence and coherence–dominance in the same figure.

Table 10.5 presents the chi-square evaluations for each of the thirteen strategic category pathways. All pairs attain significance, though the differences among them are large. (We should not attach undue importance to the significance levels since so much depends on the exact choice of primary variables, perceptions of the question to the different coders, and so on. In addition, there is probably some positional biasing going on here. If two primary variables were set closely together on the questionnaire, this could cause some artificial amplification. This was especially true of clarity–coherence, where even the phraseology of the two questions was similar.)

What seems most significant, in both the practical and statistical sense, is that two of the top three strategic category pairs relate to dominance: coherence–dominance and distinctiveness–dominance. (These associations seem logical; for a mid-sized firm to achieve dominance, no matter how tightly defined the market, it will most likely be coherent and distinctive.)

TABLE 10.5 Relationship between the Strategic Categories: Chi-Square Evaluations

Strategic Category Pair	Significance
Clarity–coherence	10^{-8}
Coherence–dominance	10^{-8}
Distinctiveness–dominance	10^{-8}
Distinctiveness–coherence	10^{-6}
Fulfillment–commitment	10^{-6}
Efficiency–consistency	10^{-4}
Commitment–distinctiveness	.001
Progressiveness–dominance	.015
Perceptiveness–progressiveness	.02
Dominance–consistency	.07
Flexibility–distinctiveness	.08
Relevance–dominance	.12
Coherence–progressiveness	.2

Note: Each strategic category is represented in the chi-square evaluations (of the 3 × 3 contingency grids) by the "best" primary variable, "best" in both the cognitive and statistical senses.

For a complete presentation of the data, plus more discussion on difficulties with the methodology, see R. L. Kuhn, *Mid-Sized Firms: Success Strategies and Methodology*, op. cit.

[4] Sections of the Dr. Pepper story are derived in part from the Harvard Business School case "The Dr. Pepper Company" (copyright © by the President and Fellows of Harvard College) in C. Roland Christensen, Norman A. Berg, and Malcolm S. Salter, *Policy Formulation and Administration.*, 8th ed. (Homewood, Illinois: Richard D. Irwin, 1980).

[5] How to overpay and get rich? Simple. Mix financial leverage with managerial ownership. It's called a *leveraged buyout*, and what it does is cure the healthy.

Take a sound company. Make it sick. Sell it. Make it better. Sell it again. Who wins? Old investors? New investors? Management? Employees? Society? Sometimes everyone; sometimes no one.

How can a few ordinary mortals offer $1.6 billion for Metromedia, Inc., the broadcasting chain, or $648 million for Dr. Pepper, in the latest and greatest examples of a growing rage?

The trick is called a "leveraged buyout" (LBO), and it looks like it's done with mirrors. Recall William Simon's $50+ million bonanza in a period so short he might have been caught for ordinary income, not capital gains. Simon simply bought Gibson Greeting Cards from a tired RCA and then sold part of it back to a ravenous public. His timing was good, but his structure was better. What did the former Secretary of the Treasury put up? Only a few hundred thou, which, if you look closely, was hardly put up at all. (Would that he had performed such miracles with the national debt.)

How do LBOs work? First, investors chip in preciously little cash. This equity is then "leveraged," 10, 20, even 50 times with debt. All senior funding—and this is the essential part—is secured by the acquired firm's own assets; lending limits, for example, might be 80 percent of receivables, 50 percent of inventories, 25 percent of plant and equipment. The financial institution gets a premium for its risk, thank you, usually 2–6 percent over prime. Often there needs to be a middle layer of subordinated debt—taken back by the seller or bought by a third party.

The touchstone of LBOs is cash flow. Almost nothing else matters. Profit and loss statements, surprisingly, are almost irrelevant. All that counts is whether, when, and with what safety, you can meet interest demands in the near term and pay back principal in the long term. (Payments can be staged, with endless variation, to match capabilities.) A nice feature in calculating cash flow is tax payments, or, more accurately, the lack thereof. Paying an inflated price thus presents no problem. The acquirer merely writes up company assets, generating higher writeoffs for depreciation—in addition to already hefty interest deductions.

You only have to watch the windows. Downdrafts in this business cause quick pneumonia. Sensitivity analysis is critical. "What if" games are not games. You had better be awfully sure you can weather any storm. Default sits right over the horizon, especially those first years. A slight change in market, pricing, margins, overheads, and especially interest rates, and in blow the banks with liens in one hand and auction blocks in the other. (Or do they? When you owe small money, you have a creditor; when you owe big money, you have a partner.)

Thus Dr. Pepper's strategy inverts. Remember why they *originally* retained investment bankers? A big brother was needed to battle the megaliths of soda pop, Coke and Pepsi. Having gone from strong regional (Waco drinks more Dr. Pepper than Detroit) to weak national (few primary bottlers), they had to be more competitive. Advertising and shelf space demand huge expenditures, and marketing muscle favors the mammoths. Suddenly, instead of a corporate giant, an LBO emerges. But does anybody ask how a debt-laden Dr. Pepper can be more competitive?

It's a pretty package for the fabled few of LBO stardom. But what about us normals? We make it happen. We pay the tab. Our tax dollars are subsidizing investors as they roll over companies and pile up profits. But where's society's return? Productivity? (How enhanced?) New jobs? (How created?) In fact, terribly weakened balance sheets can stifle productivity and put jobs in jeopardy. Capital purchases become less likely and firing employees more likely. A general downer, these LBOs?

Wait. There's another side here. More subtle, but just as real. Check the record. LBOs work. Few fail; most succeed; many prosper. The evidence suggests more vitality than torpidity. Why? Certainly not the added financial burden. The answer lies elsewhere.

In most LBOs senior management takes a part—as is the case with Dr. Pepper. The best LBO-makers insist on it. Not known for generosity, they seek only to assure success. Savvy investors never deal unless those who run target companies get a good piece of equity, at least 20 percent (often more), and put up hard cash to buy it.

The critical transition, then, occurs inside the head of these executives. Previously employees, they are suddenly owners. Professional managers change mystically into personal entrepreneurs. Participation and commitment reach in and touch the essence of motivation. It is a remarkable transformation. To be president of a conglomerate division managing public money is one thing; to be president of an independent company embedding personal wealth is quite another. Take the decision-making process. Which will it be, fellows, a new corporate aircraft or an upgraded manufacturing system? Think of the enhanced effort and reduced costs. When management is galvanized, the company is rejuvenated.

What's in it for small investors? Watch for companies ripening as LBO candidates. Some critical signs: high assets relative to price; low price/earning ratios; good cash flow; stable earnings. LBOs of public companies always jack the stock.

What's in it for Wall Street? An appetite is growing; the little guy wants in. Don't be surprised to see public funds dedicated to LBOs. (But don't forget fund administration.)

What's in it for managers? With a good company and an entrepreneurial spirit, talk to the LBO folks. They're a hungry bunch. Companies start deals, remember, not cash. Of the latter they have plenty; it's the former they need. You sit in the driver's seat; there are lots of them, but only one of you.

Finally, what's in it for society? Though at first glance LBOs seem detrimental to productivity and jobs, at second glance they may be quite beneficial, increasing productivity and creating jobs. LBOs energize executives and refresh companies; they are anonymous contributors to the "Entrepreneuring of America." Let's hope it works for Dr. Pepper.

[6] The difference between our results and those of the general management literature is even more pronounced because we had an *a priori* positive bias toward the published conclusions. We had expected to confirm efficiency, flexibility, opportunism, and the like as being crucial for the success of mid-sized firms. Our expectations went unfulfilled; our *a priori* assumptions proved erroneous.

Why the discrepancy? There are three nonexclusive possible explanations: the first attacks our methodology; the second attacks others' methodology; the third, presented in the text, attacks neither and approaches a resolution of the paradox.

We are somewhat vulnerable to the charge of "methodological bias" since our data are derived from company-prepared annual reports, documents not known for either objectivity or understatement. For example, it could be argued that successful mid-sized firms want to act like large-sized firms, so they talk about "growth and dominance," what they really enjoy, not "flexibility and efficiency," what they really do.

Our defense is threefold. The first line defends the annual report as at least a standardized document, prepared for specific reasons and with known motivations. It reiterates Bowman's (1978) validity tests (Chapter 9).

The second line of defense, articulating well with the first though stronger, states that the matched-pair technique attenuates annual report hyperbole, and the large sample size generates data that are statistically significant and pragmatically meaningful. (Indeed, such a large number of matched-pairs could have been constructed only by using standard reports as substrate for investigation.)

The substantial structure of this data base can critique the methodologies of those who claim different results. Our conclusions are based on empirical data; theirs often on ephemeral theory. (Theorists assume that "common knowledge" should validate their proffered points.)

Reinforcing the real-world sense of our study is its numerical magnitude, the raw, absolute size of the sample. It is not unimportant that 334 mid-sized manufacturing firms were a respectable percentage of the total number of mid-sized manufacturing firms in the United States in 1978.

The third possible explanation, we surmise, has the most merit. It states that our results and conventional wisdom do not contradict; rather they are answering different questions (see the text).

[7] The advancement of scientific research is dependent on the progressive articulation of empirical data and theoretical constructs, mediated by organizing hypotheses tested by experimental design. The procedure of building on the published

results of the past, repeating or negating the data and confirming or denying the conclusions, is the fundamental core of modern knowledge production. This has been especially true in the natural sciences where the reproducibility of results is directly derivative from the tight control of environmental conditions and relevant parameters. In the social sciences in general, and with complex human systems in particular, such controls become more difficult to enforce, often exceedingly so. This puts all the more pressure on the careful researcher to specify with precision the methodology of his study and to relate rigorously his data and conclusions to the previous work of others.

Nowhere is concern for proper procedure more important than in strategic management research, where environmental conditions are extraordinarily difficult to control and relevant parameters almost impossible to hold constant. In our research we have striven to provide, even at the cost of belaboring procedure, a detailed sense of the methodologies used and thought processes applied. We have also presented much of the raw data for independent reader analysis. Much raw data have been the subject of footnotes. For a complete treatment of the methodology and the data, see R. L. Kuhn, *Mid-Sized Firms: Success Strategies and Methodology, op. cit.*

[8] S. Liao, "The Effect of the Size of Firms on Managerial Attitude," *California Management Review*, Winter 1975. We do not take Liao's results as necessarily confirming our own regarding strong growth orientation. His data are an amalgam, coming from all kinds of medium-sized companies, better and poorer performing firms mixed together in some unknown fashion. (Controlling for profit was not part of his study.) As a methodological note, it may well be that the design bias of *which* CEO/firm responded to his survey skewed Liao's sample in the direction of better performers, thereby generating more confidence that his results (stressing firm growth and entity orientation) may in fact confirm our similar conclusions for successful mid-sized firms. Our data on company response to requests for Form 10-Ks and back annual reports suggest strongly that more profitable firms respond better to such requests. Liao reports that his 186 responses were from a total number of 400 initial requests.

[9] D. Mueller, "A Life Cycle Theory of the Firm." *Journal of Industrial Economics*, July 1972.

[10] T. Cohn and R. Lindberg, *How Management is Different in Small Companies* (New York: American Management Association, 1972).

[11] R. Rumelt, *Strategy, Structure, and Economic Performance* (Boston: Harvard Business School Division of Research, 1974). Of his nine categories of corporate diversification strategy, the two "constrained" categories (dominant constrained and related constrained)—where "constrained" was defined as diversification built on some particular strength, skill, or resource associated with the original activity—were almost always superior in profit performance.

[12] The area of innovation has been a controversial one for researchers and policymakers concerned with size of companies. In his 1972 book, *Economic Concentration: Structure, Behavior and Public Policy* (New York: Harcourt Brace Jovanovich),

John Blair hardly disguises his predilection by titling his chapter on innovation, "The Creative Backwardness of Bigness." He writes that "aside from some notable exceptions, particularly in the field of chemicals, the contribution of large corporations to technical progress has fallen far short of what would have been expected in view of their resources, their facilities, and their shares of market . . . [and] by the typically lengthy interval between the making of an invention and its introduction as an innovation."

Scherer (1980) reports the results of several studies and concludes: "What we find . . . is a kind of threshold effect. A little bit of bigness—up to sales of $250 to $400 million at 1978 price levels—is good for invention and innovation. But beyond the threshold further bigness adds little or nothing, and it carries the danger of diminishing the effectiveness of inventive and innovative performance." [*Industrial Market Structure and Economic Performance* (Chicago: Rand McNally), pp. 92–93.]

Though both Blair and Scherer, as industrial economists, are more concerned with the public policy implications of innovation in mid-sized firms (which is what Scherer's "threshold effect" in fact defines), we can turn the concept around and state that since larger-sized firms lag mid-sized firms in industry innovation, this would be a natural area for the latter to exploit their advantage. (Our data confirm that better/top-performing mid-sized firms are more likely to be oriented toward new products and innovation.)

The Soviet economist Y. Kvasha (1967) has propounded the pragmatic benefits of small and medium-sized enterprises, even though this opinion contradicts the reigning sociopolitical philosophy where establishing the "world's largest factory" in every industry is a source of national pride (however inefficient they are). After having demonstrated that the size of the average Soviet "enterprise" exceeds that of all other industrial countries, Kvasha states: "It is a mistake to assume that small enterprises are an unavoidable evil or alien appendages of the socialist economy. Such an appraisal of small or medium-sized enterprises would in practice degenerate into megalomania, which would lead to extremely unfavorable consequences for the development of the national economy and the progress of technology. Moreover, small and medium enterprises, with their simpler equipment and organization, with the shorter periods required for their construction and their smaller fixed assets, play an indispensable role in the national economy." (Y. Kvasha, "Concentration of Production and Small Scale Industry," *Voprosy Ekonomiki*, May 1967, pp. 26–31. Translated in *Hearings on Economic Concentrations*, United States Congress Pt. 7A, pp. 4358–4362.)

Whereas in a socialist economy the question for mid-sized enterprises is one of efficiency of production, in a market economy the question is one of sales of products. In this regard one of our most important findings was that the better-performing mid-sized firms are "distinctive," defining their products/markets so tightly that they even become dominant within them. This confirms the work of Abbanat ("Strategies of Size," Ph.D. dissertation, Harvard University, 1967), who concluded that successful smaller-sized companies do not compete directly with their larger competitors. Rather, they probe "for soft spots and gaps in the market—the neglected or untried products."

[13] R. G. Hammermesh, M. J. Anderson, Jr., and J. E. Harris, "Strategies for Low Market Share Businesses," *Harvard Business Review*, May–June 1978.

[14] Various publications and brochures, *PIMS: The Profit Impact of Market Strategy*, The Strategic Planning Institute, Cambridge, MA.

[15] We had intended otherwise. We had expected (desired?) to demonstrate that the existence of top-performing mid-sized firms—companies that consistently outperformed the leaders in their respective industries—would refute the dogma that profitability is always a prime function of market share. Mid-sized firms *qua* mid-sized firms, we had assumed, would automatically be low-market-share firms. Thus, if we could give evidence for the relative and continued success of substantial numbers of such mid-sized firms, then our point would be established.

This was not to be. We certainly found many companies that could be considered mid-sized with a three- or four-digit SIC classification and that returned very high profits. That confirmed our hypothesis. But then came the analysis of these companies, and the stunning impact of *dominance*.

These corporate claims of product leadership and market control were vigorous, persistent, and widespread among the sample. There could be no doubt. Either all these firms were guilty of some collusive, prevaricated plot, or our hypothesis that top-performing mid-sized companies would refute PIMS was dashed (with Occam's razor cutting away the first alternative).

[16] Several other PIMS results are corroborated in our study: businesses selling and stressing high-quality products and services are generally more profitable than those with lower-quality offerings; relatedness among businesses—shared production facilities, common customers, shared marketing programs—improve profitability among otherwise similar companies; and firms with a high degree of investment intensity are often less profitable than those with lower investment–sales ratios (S. Schoeffler, "Capital Intensive Technology vs. ROI," *Management Review*, September 1978). (This last finding is supported, though weakly, by the inverse relationship between the fixed capital intensity ratio—gross plant and equipment divided by gross sales—and the better-performing mid-sized firms in our sample.)

[17] P. Drucker, *Management: Tasks, Responsibilities, Practices* (New York: Harper & Row, 1973).

[18] What emerges is strategic management sitting at the interface of industrial economics, business policy, organizational development, and all the functional disciplines of corporate life. The fundamental framework is the mapping of organizational strengths and weaknesses onto environmental opportunities and threats in order to develop business strategies that will achieve corporate goals. This paradigm becomes modified, fine-tuned, by the critical contingencies of business reality, company size within company industry being not the least of them.

[19] For some of the issues involved (from an American perspective) see *Commercializing Defense-Related Technology*, Robert Lawrence Kuhn (New York: Praeger, 1984). The theme developed is that *comprehensive* national security in the contem-

porary world embeds economic as well as military factors. The future of the United States depends on our ability to apply the scientific and technological advances achieved through defense-related research and development to the generation of competitively superior products and services. In an attempt to bridge this gap, the book brings together leaders from industry, academia, and government. Civilian industry can take substantial advantage of the technological breakthroughs of military and aerospace R&D programs, and policies should be developed to transfer such information to the private sector. There is compelling need for business, universities, and government to work together to optimize this vital national resource. Private-sector strategies are not always straightforward, and different companies are often involved in the R&D and commercializing processes. (Interestingly enough, though the companies doing the military R&D are often large, the companies doing the civilian commercialization are often mid-sized.) Commercializing defense-related technology adds a novel element to the biblical vision of beating "swords into ploughshares and spears into pruning hooks."

[20] The capabilities available to Galram for application to civilian markets are illustrated by the broad range of technologies Rafael uses to produce a weapons system. For example, a guided missile requires optics; sensors (radar, infrared, television); signal processing; actuators (hydraulic, pneumatic, electric); control engineering; inertial guidance (accelerometers, gyroscopes); air measuring devices (for speed and pressure); computers (with real-time programming); power supplies (pneumatic, hydraulic, electrical, and electronic); warheads (metal forming for controlled fragmentation, and explosive-forming for shaped charges); propellants and rocket motors; mechanics (fine mechanics, structures, composite materials, packaging, heat transfer); and simulators. Other technological disciplines used in weapons development include lasers; communications (voice, data, and pictures including image processing); antennas and propagation; electromagnetic compatibility; reliability engineering; quality assurance; nondestructive testing; environmental testing; field testing; operations research; manufacturing engineering; automatic test equipment; microelectronics (sensors, microwave circuits, hybrid circuits); vacuum technology; glue technology and adhesives; and computerized analysis and design.

[21] At the time of writing the author was advising both the Government of Israel and potential American investors regarding Galram—a conflict of its own which both sides seemed willing to accept.

[22] Strategic management research is a dynamic business. Change is the rule, not the exception. Studies conclude, and data shift. This is unavoidable. To seek constancy would delay publication forever. Between the time of the original data base study of 334 mid-sized firms (1979) and the publication of this volume, changes have occurred. Most of our better-performing mid-sized firms have remained such, but some have not. Amdahl and Toro, for instance, suffered reverses, the former due to IBM's pricing practices, the latter due to weather disruptions. (Though Amdahl leaped ahead in 1983, and is no longer mid-sized,

our computer companies experienced the most violent disruptions, with more better performers hitting the skids as technological warping ran rampant.) Kennametal, as an example of several perennial better performers, was hit hard by the recession and showed a large loss in 1982, though recovering thereafter. The majority of our top-performing firms, however, are remaining consistent with that classification. Several other firms have disappeared through acquisition, a fact confirming their microeconomic character as a top performer, but at odds with our macroeconomic motivation for the study. Lawry's (branded food products, condiments), Binney & Smith (crayons), and Waters Associates (scientific instruments, chromatography) are examples; the latter, interesting enough, was acquired by another of our original mid-sized firms, Millipore, which showed ambitions of becoming a large-sized firm. Ten and twenty years from now a retrospective study of the 167 matched pairs, tracing and comparing the dynamic movements of the 334 companies, will be both fascinating and nostalgic.

[23] To achieve this potential of uniting the theoretical with the pragmatic, the conceptual with the tangible, we must maximize the resources of strategic and creative management. Alternative methodologies and approaches must be employed synergistically, noncompetitively, and interactively in order to analyze and improve the exceedingly complex interactions of human beings operating business enterprises. Qualitative and quantitative techniques each have their particular area of primacy (and attendant areas of deficiency), and often it is not so much the decision of which approach to use, but how to use both most efficiently within the same study. The iterative interplay between the perceptive judgments of case/company-oriented qualitative studies and the structured rigor of numerically/statistically oriented quantitative studies can only result in better overall work, which means closer proximations to the ideal. It is hoped that this present volume, in addition to offering descriptions and prescriptions for mid-sized firms, has contributed to the efficacy of multimethodological design for strategic and creative management.

INDEX

DATE DUE
